Philadelphia Revelations:

Twenty Tours of the Delaware Valley

George Ross Fisher, III

www.philadelphia-reflections.com

Library of Congress Control Number: 2020913577

ISBN 978-1-932109-54-2

Fisher, George Ross, III
Philadelphia Revelations: Twenty Tours of the Delaware Valley

Cover by Karin Fisher
Maps by Toria Affrunti
Editorial assistance by Evelyn Heinrich, Margaret Fisher

Printed in the United States of America

Ross & Perry Publishing

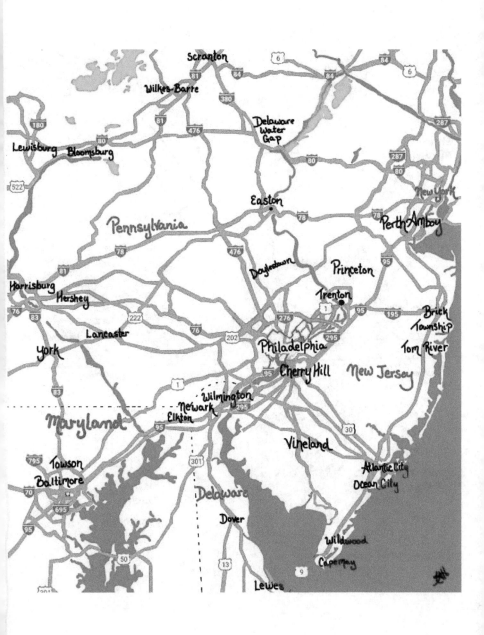

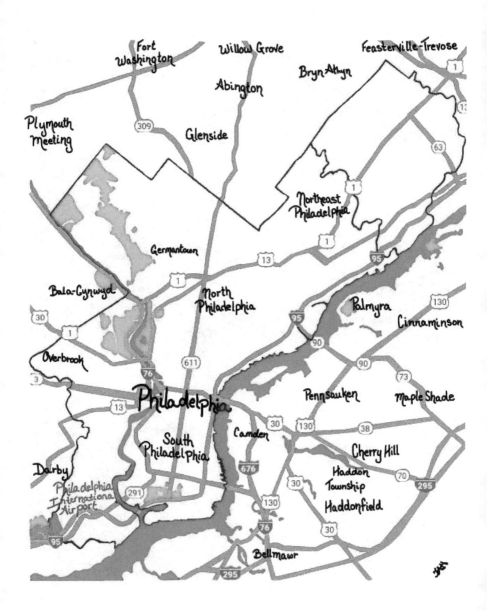

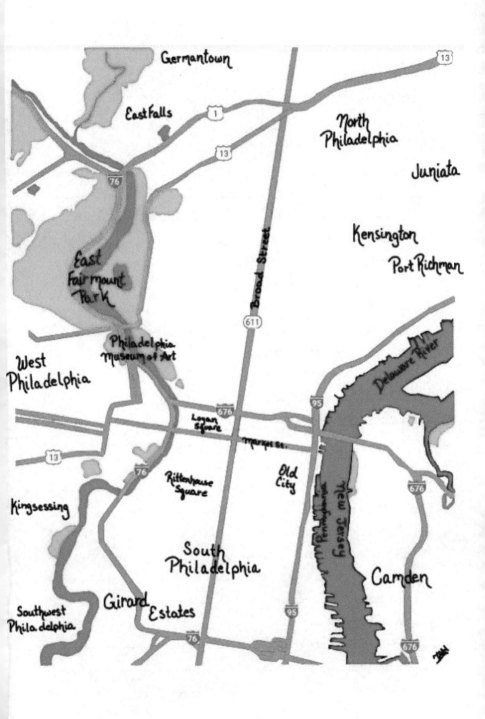

Contents

Introduction

My own history

I had other loves later, but I used to say that Pennsylvania Hospital was my first and only love - such a refreshing change from medical school in New York. One day, after a couple years in New York, I was pushing my way through a revolving door one and found myself pushing ahead of a little old lady. That was the moment I knew that New York was not the place for me, despite having been drawn into the Fifth Avenue crowd. I moved to Philadelphia to start a two-year rotating internship on July 1, 1948 at Pennsylvania Hospital, the oldest (and for many years the only) hospital in the country, and home to the first internship. Everyone was doing their best, working for nothing and doing it willingly at this "hospital for the sick poor, and if there is room, for those who can pay," as Benjamin Franklin wrote in the founding documents.

The dominant atmosphere of the hospital was Quaker, even though it was not a Quaker institution. The Quakers had abandoned their Holy Experiment after Pennsylvania settlers were massacred (as a result of their own foolishness) by the original occupants, and conscience would not permit the Friends to send soldiers to protect them. Nevertheless, when I arrived in Philadelphia, public life may have been dominated by Episcopalians and others, but when it came right down to it, Quakers were behind it all - making the decisions, putting up the money - usually not running for office, but seeing to it that the right institutions were created. The U.S. Constitution itself was based on William Penn's 1676 *Concessions and Agreements*, which included many of the principals we live by today, including trial by jury.

Internship and residency in the 1940's literally meant residing in the hospital, where laundry service was provided but you had to buy your own uniform. The salary was exactly zero for those first two years, as it was for the year of residency that followed at Jefferson Hospital. After a two-year detour to the National Institute of Health in Bethesda, I returned to Pennsylvania Hospital for one more year of residency, which paid a token $30 per month, and finally to an actual paying job for several years as Chief Resident. While continuing to teach and consult in various hospitals, I hung up my shingle at 8th and Spruce and practiced Endocrinology and Internal Medicine until I retired at age 80 in 2005. The appearance of four children had prompted a move to Haddonfield and a commute into center city that was soon shortened by the High Speed Line, but I returned to apartment living near Washington Square in 2017.

Introduction

As one of a small number of Endocrinologists in Philadelphia, one who had trained in prominent institutions, and a physician who never rejected a single patient, my practice gradually came to include the whole spectrum of society, from the homeless to those who lived on wealth that had been created generations before. When people first meet, they ask who you are or where you are from, but after a while they don't ask anymore: you have become part of the scene. That acceptance gave me a window onto Philadelphia society and connections to those who knew the inside scoop. Prostitutes, bank presidents, car thieves, anyone with endocrine problems - all told their stories to their doctor over the course of long relationships. Thus progressed my tutorial in Philadelphia history and culture, acquired in random bits and pieces over seventy-plus years, supplemented by books and by lectures that I attended at various Philadelphia social clubs, and summarized in several thousand blogs on my website "Philadelphia Reflections." This tour book uses several hundred of those blogs to give the reader a taste of Philadelphia life as it has been experienced over the last four centuries, interpreted by one who appreciates the grand and the foolish sides of human nature.

My father died at age 59, and every day has been a gift since I passed that age. As I got older and older, my friends started to die off, and I saw that if I did not write it down, there would be no one left to do it: an insider's tour of Philadelphia, which to a certain extent is a tour of American history, from one who has watched much of that history unroll on top of the many layers of buildings and events that came before.

Life expectancy has been extended by thirty years since I started medical school. The articles that make up this book were written during that period of extra time that I was granted. Part of what I had in mind was modelling a way to make a career out of the last third of life. Because they were written over such a long period of time, you may notice that the chapters contain some discrepancies that reflect the evolution of my own perspective. At age 95, I don't have time to research laboriously every point. On the other hand, I supply the trail that may help the reader discover the facts that underlie the stories.

Every building, street and farm in the Philadelphia area has a story, and in most cases multiple stories. As you pass by, you may wonder - or not. The goal of this tour book is to prompt you to wonder. What did this land look like before the European arrival? What role did this building play in the Revolutionary War? Why is it called the Skating Club and Humane Society? This tour book will give you a small taste of what there is to discover in the greater Philadelphia area.

Introduction

For twenty five years, Philadelphia was the nation's capital. It is where the Articles of Confederation were written and failed, where the Constitution was written and succeeded, where numerous industries started, thrived and finally left. Through all of this, the city has continued to be a wonderful place to explore. Philadelphians are happy with what they've got and with what they used to have, serene about the future. To a certain extent, this book is an answer to the book *Puritan Boston and Quaker Philadelphia*, which concluded that Boston is better. Not so - it just has worse weather!

A quick summary of Philadelphia History
At the time of the American Revolution, Philadelphia was the second largest English speaking city in the world and yet only boasted a population of under forty thousand, really a small town, where people would go fishing on Walnut Street and where Pennsylvania Hospital at 8th and Spruce was considered "way out in the country." Known as the red city because of the red brick that was mandated after the original houses were destroyed in a fire, its fortunes rose when it was made the capital of the new nation. The First National Bank was established in 1791, and Chestnut Street became the banking center of the country until Martin Van Buren sent it to Wall Street. The insurance industry sprouted here after Benjamin Franklin created fire insurance, and life insurance was founded as a Presbyterian minister fund. Philadelphia history is full of "firsts" like these.

After the national capital was relocated, Philadelphia continued on as a center of industry, with enormous wealth provided to the city by Stephen Girard in his will. As a result of Abraham Lincoln returning a political favor, the whole area became the arsenal of the north during the Civil War, home to the naval yard in Camden, the naval academy (now in Annapolis) in South Philadelphia, the Frankford arsenal, the 7,000 bed Philadelphia General Hospital and uniform factories at the foot of what is now the Benjamin Franklin Bridge. Philadelphia was the hub of north-south transportation, as the railways terminated in south Jersey before picking up again in Philadelphia, forcing passengers to transfer across the river, often spending the night. Pennsylvania oil was brought in by railway and refined into kerosene to be distributed around the country, and later into gasoline to fuel the auto industry, which flourished in this area as well. By 1900, Philadelphia claimed to be the richest city in the world.

By thirty years later, industrial Philadelphia had lost its upward momentum and started on its downward trajectory. Theories about what happened abound. The Civil War and Fred Taylor's invention of factory efficiency brought over-expansion of the steel and auto industries. The flu epidemic took an enormous toll during the First World War. The opening of the Benjamin Franklin Bridge in 1926 allowed through

Introduction

traffic to pass right by Philadelphia. Family businesses were superseded by stockholder corporations centered in New York. The shuttering of numerous enormous factories left Philadelphia with a central historic core surrounded by miles of empty and deteriorating houses.

More blows followed as the decades progressed. Transportation systems had created a national economy that provided other options for businesses. The movie industry started to migrate away after a fire destroyed the Fox film storage facility in 1937. The Penn Central railroad was sold off piece by piece. Stetson Hats took a blow when men stopped wearing hats. After Clark Gable took off his shirt in *It Happened One Night*, the undershirt industry dwindled. Wanamaker's and Strawbridge & Clothier department stores closed their doors. The computer industry was lost to Philadelphia as a result of a lawsuit. DuPont Chemical and Rohm and Haas were sold away. Campbell Soup, the only Fortune 500 company left in Camden, moved to California to be closer to the tomatoes. The insurance industry relocated to better tax havens.

The collapse of all these industries did generate the germ of revival, because Philadelphia became much cheaper than New York and is now attracting transplants, both of people and of businesses. Music, restaurants and theater are flourishing. "Meds and Eds" (medical schools, medical research and colleges) are booming, thanks largely to government money. Eighty percent of pharmaceutical companies are located within a hundred miles of Philadelphia; this is the place to be if you are a chemist. Numerous small firms have sprung up in industrial parks in New Jersey. Tourism is a major and growing employer, unfortunately joined now by gambling casinos with the concern that it might turn Philadelphia into an Atlantic City.

When I was a rotating intern in the 1940s, there were 250 farms within the borders of Philadelphia, converted after the war by developers into houses which deteriorated but which are now reviving in patches. The "Chinese Wall" - the raised railroad that had cut the city in half - was torn down in 1950, opening up valuable land to development. From long-standing tradition, no building in Philadelphia had been built higher than Billy Penn's hat on City Hall. In 1984, a developer flaunted that tradition, and Philadelphia went from a ten story to a sixty-story city. People who had moved to the suburbs for their children's schools are moving back for apartment living. Society Hill houses that sold for $1500 when I was a medical resident are now selling for three million. Gentrification spread from the Delaware to around 10th Street and continues to expand. Growth of the University of Pennsylvania has spurred the same phenomenon in West Philadelphia. The railroad land along the east bank of the Schuylkill was turned into apartments and a beautiful waterfront walk. The rivers have gone from toxic to clean, and the air is no longer redolent with

Introduction

the odor of distilleries and refineries. On balance, things are moving ahead, though some areas are still in retreat. Large swathes of land in Philadelphia and Camden remain impoverished, with some signs of revival but not yet certainty.

Bullseye Sociology

Philadelphia is turning inside out. It used to be a commercial, financial and business center, surrounded by beautiful suburbs. It is now turning into a marvelous urban residential area, surrounded by a ring of commerce based on the ring of interstate highways. Commuters leaving the city in the morning outnumber the commuters coming in, and traffic jams are worse in the outer ring.

More precisely, the metropolitan area is a series of concentric rings. The bull's eye is Center City, with urban residences, cultural venues, entertainment. Immediately surrounding the bullseye is a post-industrial ring that has recently been undergoing a renaissance. Surrounding that are the suburbs, and beyond them are the new malls and industrial parks. Further out is exurbia, where Philadelphia's "equestrian class" is mixed with what is left of the farmlands, rapidly being invaded by McMansions intended for employees of the commercial ring. Some people live their whole lives in just one ring.

Somewhere near Washington's old encampment at Valley Forge, there is an invisible line. The people who live inside that line, live in Philadelphia. But just one house further out, on the other side of the invisible line, orientation is toward central Pennsylvania. The people outside the ring mean "Pottstown" when they say they are going to town; if they say they are going to The City they mean "Reading". Going to Philadelphia is for them like going to Paris; they did it once.

There are other invisible lines. At the edge of the central city bullseye, there is gentrification; yuppie families are renovating the 19th Century mansions their grandparents abandoned for the suburbs, displacing working-class families who lived for a generation or two in decaying grandeur. The local bars are inhabited by one class, the neighboring restaurants are where the newcomers hang out. Beer in one, wine in the other, and sour looks when members of the wrong class blunder in. In London, England, you see the same thing, except it is usually a single building with two entrances.

Introduction

There is another border region out further, where upwardly mobile minority groups are pushing out toward the suburbs. Curiously, working-class Philadelphia always tended to live in "neighborhoods", and their out-migration has more commonly leap-frogged to "Jersey", their places being increasingly taken by Asian immigrants.

To view the maps and tour stops on your mobile device, go to

www.philadelphia-reflections.com

l Old City

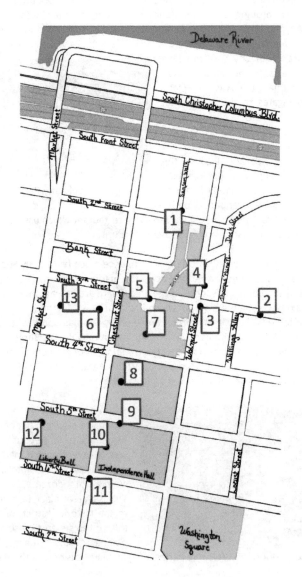

1 The Tour Starts Here

Welcome Park   129 Samson Walk   Philadelphia, PA
39.9474 -75.1441

The site of William Penn's home is now called the Welcome Park at South 2nd Street. (The ship which brought Governor Penn to his land holdings was called the Welcome.) Anyone who can prove descent from those who were on the ship is eligible to be a member of the Welcome Society. Welcome Park is across 2nd Street

from a restoration of City Tavern, which only serves meals (in authentic period dress) but at one time was the place where the delegates to the Continental Congress and the Constitutional Convention stayed overnight. And of course, did lots of negotiation at night over a cold beer. It's also next to the famous Old Original Bookbinder's restaurant which unfortunately is out of business but now has reopened under

Welcome Park

new management as The Old Bar. It's a very large restaurant which used to be able to obtain four-pound lobsters and bake them for tourists.

A hundred feet away is a quiet upscale Sheraton, once much favored by Society Hill residents. Over a footbridge is a Hyatt, next to the marina on the river, and favored as a hangout by the younger "sports" in the area. There are at least three charming bed-and-breakfasts along the block, of which the favorite is a 12-room hotel directly facing on Welcome Park. It is the former home of Dr. Thomas Bond, who founded the Pennsylvania Hospital with Ben Franklin's help. Not only did Dr. Bond found the Nation's first hospital, but he also started the tradition among American physicians of not charging for their services to the poor. Without that sort of leadership, the hospitals could never have survived their early years.

Thomas Bond House by Welcome Park

So, here is where to begin your tour if you are from out of town. A big garage to store your car, right next to several choices of quiet but moderately priced hotels, and a couple of dozen restaurants. This is a great place to branch out to the historic district, or Society Hill, or the seaport museums and marinas. And maybe some gambling casinos, although it is hard to imagine much tolerance between that group and the history lovers. By the way, Philadelphia hotels are like hotels everywhere else in one respect. If you forget to make a reservation in advance, just breezing in looking for a room for tonight, you must expect to find the price is nearly doubled.

2 Powel House, Huzzah!

The Powel House   244 South 3rd Street   Philadelphia, PA
39.9458 -75.1467

On 3rd Street in Philadelphia's Society Hill stands the finest surviving Georgian House of what Washington and Madison called the Republican Court. Many traditions of American high society were formed in the second-floor dining room of this house. But Washington hated all political parties, which then had a different meaning. If George Washington were alive we wouldn't have such a thing as political parties, at all. The term "Republican Court" had nothing to do with R's and D's. It was the Mayor's home.

The town had forty thousand souls, fourteen wheeled vehicles, and a Quaker pacifist majority. President Washington lived a few doors away, but the streets were unpaved. The court was a scheme cooked up by Washington and Madison to enlist support from the new government's important ladies. The best these males could imagine was a modified version of a European royal court, to fuse thirteen colonies into a cohesive nation. The most remarkable thing about it was its frank imitation of such royal courts, something only the Father of His Country could pull off in former colonies which had just fought an eight-year war to be rid of the monarchy. It is a great testimony to the faith of Americans in George Washington. But it also testifies to the power of enthusiastic women.

Chief among the leaders in this court was Elizabeth Powel, along with her niece living around the corner on Spruce Street, Anne Willing Bingham. Before Stephen Girard came along, her 28 year old husband was the richest man in America. Members of the early Congress were largely the same men as the founding fathers of the Constitutional Convention, hand-picked by Washington and Madison to persuade the legislatures of their former colonial states to give up new-state sovereignty for a unified nation. The difference was that now they brought their wives to live in Philadelphia during sessions of Congress. Those women wanted to know each other and wanted to have something exciting to do together in the largest city in the new nation. Their husbands knew how useful it was to be socially acquainted, so everybody liked the idea of suddenly becoming nationally connected. The initial idea proved unworkable. Martha Washington was supposed to become Lady Washington, reigning over weekly receptions.

But Martha, unfortunately, wasn't up to the task, and Anne Bingham whose rich husband had taken her on lengthy tours of European royal courts, moved right in

Republican Court

and took charge of this project. Besides her cousin Elizabeth Powel, notable members of this social whirl were the two daughters of Chief Justice Benjamin Chew, Alexander Hamilton's wife, and various members of the Shippen and Willing families. Members of the family of Charles Carroll of Carrolton, Maryland, Cadwaladers of various sorts, and a number of other names famous from then until even today joined their affiliations with ladies from other states through parties and even some weddings. Their prominence attracted social climbers. John Adams was particularly awestruck by the poise and beauty of Anne Bingham, although Abigail Adams may not have been quite so infatuated. It was a dizzy whirl, with dinner parties the central activity just as they are in Philadelphia even today. Country bumpkins had to learn how to dress, to talk and eat with the right spoon keeping their elbows off the table. Those who could tactfully show them what was what were friends for life. Centuries later, Emily Post made a fortune writing books about such rules.

In those days, they even had their war cry, which was to raise a glass and shout back "Huzzah" in response to the proposer of a toast, who had raised his glass starting the war cry. It wasn't "Skol" or "Cheers" or "Here, here," if you knew what was what. It was "Huzzah". Most fashionable dinners had at least twenty courses, but the ladies didn't eat them. It was a whispered instruction among the ladies that they should eat before the dinner, so they could gracefully decline to gobble up goodies, and spend their time in gay conversation or waiting to be asked to dance. Drinking and eating, especially drinking, was for the men at the party, although naturally the many courses of the banquet were put in front of the ladies to be airily ignored. When George Washington was present, as he often was, or even La Rochfoucault himself, it was important to remember every spoken word.

And, you know, it worked. When these important people went back home, they took the customs of the Republican Court with them. The American diplomatic corps found the equivalent of minor-league training for their efforts on behalf of the country abroad. Politics was easier if you personally knew your adversaries as well as your allies. The persistence of the same family names in the Social Register, the lists of The Four Hundred and other compilations of high society show that Anne

Bingham and Elizabeth Powel did indeed know what they were doing, and for that matter, so did George Washington.

If anyone else had been at the top of this heap, Thomas Jefferson stood ready to attack with all his might. But he and even Patrick Henry, who abhorred hierarchy, didn't dare attack Washington. The aristocrats of Old Europe probably did sneer at this amateur effort, and in some circles still, do. But the inability of absolutely any other group of nations, whether European, Asian or South American, to unite peacefully is a thumb in the eye of anyone who mocks George Washington's little Philadelphia creation. And to think it all began right here, right here in the Powel House, right here in the dining room on the second floor. For that, folks, one thunderous "Huzzah!"

At the foot of the stairs in Powel House, you will find on the newel post the Quaker builder's button, which he took off his own coat. There is a strong tradition in Philadelphia that these strange buttons are Amity Buttons, nailed there by the builder when the new owner had fully settled his construction debt, symbolizing the amity between a willing buyer and a willing seller.

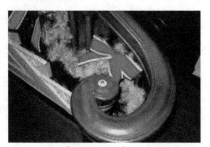

Powel House Amity Button

3 Fort Wilson: Philadelphia 1779

Fort Wilson   3rd and Walnut Street   Philadelphia, PA
39.947 -75.1465

-OCTOBER 4, 1779. The British had conquered then abandoned Philadelphia; order was still only partially restored. Joseph Reed was President of the Continental

Congress, inflation ("Not worth a Continental") was rampant, and food shortages were at near-famine levels because of self-defeating price controls. In a world turned upside down, Charles Willson Peale the painter was a leader of a radical group of admirers of Rousseau the French anarchist, called the Constitutionalist Party, leaning in the bloody direction actually followed by the French Revolution in 1789. Peale was quick

Fort Wilson (since torn down)

to admit he had no clue what to do with his leadership position and soon resigned it in favor of painting portraits of the wealthy. Others had deserted the occupied city, and many had not yet returned. The Quakers of the city hunkered down, more or less adhering to earlier instruction from the London Yearly Meeting to stay away from any politics involving war taxes. About two hundred militia roamed the city streets making trouble for anyone they could plausibly blame for the breakdown of civil order. Philadelphia was as close to anarchy as it would ever become; the focus of anger was against the pacifist Quakers, the rich merchants, and James Wilson the lawyer. Wilson had enraged the radicals by defending Tories in court, much as John Adams got in trouble for defending British troops involved in the Boston Massacre; Ben Franklin advised Wilson to leave town. It is still possible to walk the full extent of the battle of Fort Wilson in a few minutes, and the tourist bureau has marked it out.

Begin with the Quaker Meeting at Fourth and Arch. A few wandering militiamen caught Jonathan Drinker, Thomas Story, Buckridge Sims, and Matthew Johns emerging from the Quaker church, and rounded them up as prisoners. The Quakers were marched down the street for uncertain purposes when the militia encountered a group of prominent merchants emerging from the City Tavern. Unlike the meek Quakers, Robert Morris and John Cadwalader the leader of the City Troop ordered the militia to release the prisoners, behave themselves, and disperse; Timothy Matlack shouted orders. It was exactly the wrong stance to take, and about thirty prominent citizens were soon driven to retreat to the large brick house of James Wilson, at the corner of Third and Walnut, known forever afterward as Fort Wilson. Doors were barred, windows manned, and Fort Wilson was soon surrounded by an armed, shouting, mob.

James Wilson

Lieutenant Robert Campbell leaned out a third story window and was soon dropped dead by a lucky bullet. It remains in dispute whether or not he fired first. Crowbars were sought, the back door forced open, but the angry attackers scattered after fusillades from inside.

Down the street came President Reed (President of Pennsylvania) on horseback, ordering the militia to disperse, with Timothy Matlack at his side; both men were well-known radicals, here switching sides to maintain law and order. The City Troop arrived, an order was given the cavalry to Assault Every Armed Man. The radicals were finally dispersed by this makeshift cavalry charge, cutting and slashing its way through the dazed militia. When it was over, five defenders were dead and about twenty wounded. Among the militia, the casualties were heavier but inaccurately reported. Robert Morris took James Wilson in hand and retreated to his mansion at

Lemon Hill; later Wilson was the founder of America's first law school. Among other defenders huddled in Fort Wilson were some of the future framers of the Constitution from Pennsylvania: General Thomas Mifflin, Wilson, Morris, George Clymer. Equally important was the deep impression left on radical leaders like Reed and Matlack, and Henry Laurens, who could see how close the whole war effort was to dissolution, for lack of firm control. Inflation continued but the center-productive price control system was abandoned and never revived; the Patriots had a bad scare, and the heedless radicals forced to confront the potentially disastrous consequences of their own amateur performance when entrusted with the power and responsibility they had just been demanding.

It was one of those rare moments in a nation's history when the way suddenly opens to previously unthinkable actions. The Battle of Fort Wilson was the only Revolutionary War battle fought within Philadelphia city limits: a revolution within a revolution, every participant a Rebel patriot. Reed and Matlack were the two most visibly appalled by the whole uproar, forced by circumstances to attack the forces of their own political persuasion. But it seems very certain that Robert Morris and the other prosperous idealists were also left with an indelible conviction that even a confederation must maintain central command and discipline with an iron will, or all might be lost. A knowledgeable French observer estimated that Robert Morris then owned assets worth eight million dollars, an almost unimaginable sum for the time. But he would lose every penny if effective political control could not be restored. At the time of the Constitutional Convention, Morris then knew what was needed to work things in his favor. Fort Wilson made Federalists of people who experienced what an unruly mob can do.

4 Alexander Hamilton, Celebrity
Alexander Hamilton's Philadelphia home   226 Walnut Street   Philadelphia PA 39.9469 -75.146

It comes as a surprise that most of the serious, important things Alexander Hamilton did for his country were done in Philadelphia, while he lived at 79 South 3rd Street. That surprises because much of his more colorful behavior took place elsewhere. He was born on a fly-speck Caribbean island, the "bastard brat of a Scots peddler" in John Adams' exaggerated view, was orphaned and had to support himself after age 13. The orphan then fought his way to Kings College (now Columbia University) in

New York in spite of hoping to go to Princeton and has been celebrated ever since by Columbia University as a son of New York. He did found the Bank of New York, and he did marry the daughter of a New York patron, and he was the head of the New York political delegation.

As you can see in the statuary collection at the Constitution Center, he was a funny-looking little elf with a long pointed nose, frequently calling attention to himself with hyperkinetic behavior. Even as the legitimate father of eight children, Hamilton had some overly close associations with other men's wives, probably including his wife's sister. Nevertheless, he earned the affection of the stiff and solemn General Washington, probably through a gift of gab and skill getting things done, while outwardly acting as a court jester in a difficult dangerous guerilla war. There is a famous story of his shaking loose from the headquarters staff and fighting in the line at Yorktown, where he insolently stood on the parapet before the British enemy troops, performing the manual of arms. Instead of using him for target practice, the British troops applauded his audacity. Harboring no such illusions, Aaron Burr later killed him in a duel as everyone knows; it was not his first such challenge.

But in the clutch, General Washington learned he could always trust Hamilton, who wrote many of his letters for him and acted as his reliable spymaster. When the first President faced signing or not signing the fateful bill to create the National Bank, a perplexed Washington had to choose between the violent opposition of Thomas Jefferson and James Madison, or the bewildering complexity of Alexander Hamilton's reasoning in arcane economics. On the one hand, there was a simple principle that owing money was seemingly always evil; on the other was the undeniable truth that for every debit created, you create a balancing credit somewhere. Washington ultimately chose to go with Hamilton, whose reasonings he likely didn't understand very well. If you doubt the difficulty,

Alexander Hamilton

try reading Hamilton's Report on the Bank, written to persuade the nation and its first President of the soundness of his ideas. And then consider the violence of even present-day arguments about such "supply-side" economics.

All of these momentous events happened in Philadelphia at places now easily visited in a morning's stroll. But Hamilton's image as a Philadelphian, doing great things in and for Philadelphia, was forever tarnished at one single dinner he hosted. Jefferson and Madison, his political opponents but his guests, were persuaded to provide Virginia's votes for the federal takeover of state Revolutionary War debts, in return for offering New York's votes for moving the nation's capital to the banks of the Potomac. True, Pennsylvania allowed itself to be pacified with having the capital remain here for ten years while the southern swamps were being drained. But it was Hamilton who cooked up this deal and sold it to the other vote swappers.

Philadelphia felt it was entitled to the capital without needing to ask, felt that Hamilton was deliberately under-counting Pennsylvania's war debts, and this city has never appreciated the insolent idea that its entitlements were forever in the hands of wine-swilling hustlers. As the economic consequences of this backroom deal became evident during the 19th Century, it was increasingly unlikely that Philadelphia would lionize the memory of the man responsible for it. Let New York claim him if it likes that sort of thing. When Albert Gallatin, who was more or less a Pennsylvania home town boy, attacked Hamilton as a person, as a banker, and as a Federalist -- he had a fairly easy time persuading Philadelphians that this needle-nosed philanderer was an embarrassment best forgotten.

5 Stephen Girard 1750-1831

First National Bank of Philadelphia   128 South 3rd Street   Philadelphia PA 39.948 -75.1463

Girard was born in Bordeaux, France and never went to school. By the age of 23, he had become a sea captain, like his father and grandfather. By the age of 27, he owned his own ship and was thus launched on a successful career in a very dangerous occupation. Depending on the destination and weather during that era, up to forty percent of sailors were lost at sea on long voyages. From the point of view of the passengers and shippers, when you were selecting a captain you wanted one who had returned unharmed from many voyages. It was irrelevant whether he had been lucky, or diligent, or had learned a lot from his relatives in the trade.

Stephen Girard did start with a handicap, being born blind in one eye. It may have been a personality disorder which drove him to precise, minute instructions to his subordinates in excruciating detail; he might now be called a "control freak" and be disliked for it. For example, he kept a handwritten copy of all letters he wrote, and at his death, there were 14,000 of them, sorted and filed. His wife went insane, and after spending years at the Pennsylvania Hospital, was buried on the grounds. If this is the price of being rich, some might consider remaining poor. During his working years in Philadelphia, he would normally get to the counting-house at 5 AM, go to his bank at noon, and go to work on his 600-acre farm in South Philadelphia after 5 PM. He said he liked farm work the best. The image left behind by this role model, then, was workaholic. Nevertheless, if you wanted to become the richest man in America, here was the pattern to follow. Girard probably came as close as any rich man in history, to "taking it with him" when he died. His innately compulsive personality, combined with the sure knowledge that his relatives and others would probably try to break his will for their own benefit, led to the construction of a last will and testament that withstood a century of court challenges. It launched remarkable philanthropy for thousands of orphans and organized the whole Delaware Valley into an industrial machine unlike anything else in the country. Although he left the largest estate in the nation's history, that estate continued to accumulate money from his minute instructions to executors, eventually enlarging

Stephen Girard

his vast fortune fifty-fold, a century after his death. In retrospect, Philadelphia might well have slowly declined into obscurity after the nation's capital moved to Washington in 1800. Instead, the coal, canal, railroad and industrial empire of the Philadelphia region became the "arsenal of the North" during the Civil War and the main wealth generator of the Gilded Age which followed.

Girard's business career can be somewhat oversimplified as consisting of shipping at the base of his early good fortune, followed by banking during the era when banking was poorly understood and usually ineptly managed. He ended his career with an eager and successful embrace of the emerging Industrial Revolution. Throughout all of this, he characteristically took great risks for great profits, through recognizing what others were too timid to accept fully. On many occasions, his risky ventures resulted in very large losses, made acceptable by other risky ventures proving unexpectedly successful. An example would be Girard's Bank. When the Federal Government first started and then abandoned the First National Bank, Girard bought up the remnants and made a great private success of banking, where he had little previous experience. He saw the potential of the canals, and later the railroads when others were content to be farmers or country gentlemen. When he was 79 years old, he purchased vast tracts of wilderness containing some outcroppings of coal, because he could foresee a great industrial future for the region. No pain, no gain.

Another way of looking at Girard was as the most prominent French-American citizen of his time. He arrived in Philadelphia at about the same time Benjamin Franklin stepped off another boat, returning from abusive treatment by British officials which finally flipped him for American independence. Franklin recognized that independence from England meant an alliance with France, or else it meant defeat. It is possible to view the American Revolution as an episode of France searching for an American foothold after its expulsion fifteen years earlier in the French and Indian War; trouble between Britain and its colonies might re-open opportunities for France. Girard was extremely friendly with Thomas Jefferson, the most Francophile of founders and early American presidents. When the War of 1812 with Great Britain threatened disaster for the new American state, Girard staked $8 million dollars, his whole fortune, on financing that war. During the entire period from 1776 to the Louisiana Purchase, America was wavering between its gratitude to France and underlying loyalty to the English-speaking community. During that long formative period, Girard the very rich Frenchman was hovering in the background, probably influencing American foreign policy more than is known, even today. But the France that Girard stood for was neither aristocratic of the Lafayette variety nor intellectual of the Robespierre sort. It was France of the French peasant, crabbed, acquisitive, and morose, forever responding to a "hidden hand" of his own self-interest in a way that paradoxically benefited his whole community, and thus would have hugely amused the Scotsman Adam Smith. There is a marker on a building now commemorating his house, which is now gone.

6 Carpenters' Hall

Carpenters' Hall   320 Chestnut Street   Philadelphia, PA
39.9481 -75.1472

The relationship between France and the rebellious colonies was a complicated one, with intrigue and mistrust at every turn. One interesting episode had to do with Franklin's library on the second floor. The French ministry had sent over a spy, to size up the colonists before the French risked too much on them. So, the spy was led up to the library and allowed to overhear some bellicose conversations going on downstairs -- thoroughly stage-managed for the benefit of the "hidden" French visitor. The Carpenters Company was a guild of what we would now call builders and architects, and architects continue to use it. The first floor usually displays a few Windsor chairs dating to the Continental Congress, covered with a rich black patina that really lets you know what a patina was. Upstairs, the staff quarters are now, well, a little on the elegant side so you can't visit. The guild was formed in 1724, and fifty years later had just completed its building, in time for its historic role in 1774.

With the whole continent available for building, it is still not entirely clear why Colonial Philadelphia crowded itself into half a square mile, with crowded little row houses on crowded little alleys. But that's the way it was, now visible in the location of Carpenters' Hall down a little cobbled alley, in the center of a block. Elfreth's Alley gives you the same feeling, and perhaps Camac, Mole, and Latimer Streets. Carpenters' is a lovely little place, with lots of

Continental Congress

interesting features, but the main interest lies in what took place there. For that, you have to read a few books.

7 Museum of Chemical Heritage

The Chemical Heritage   315 Chestnut Street   Philadelphia, PA 39.949 -75.1466

Eighty percent of the medical drug industry is located within a hundred miles of Philadelphia, and the whole chemical industry has had its center here for two centuries. The chemical industry is the region's largest manufacturer, now that locomotives and beer brewing have come and gone, but its profile remains low. In fact, chemists personally have a low profile too and harbor a smoldering annoyance about it. No one was more determined to change that nerdy image than Arnold Thackray, the now retired President of the Chemical Heritage Foundation. He's not only a big idea man but bubbles with energy and persuasiveness. That largely accounts for the fact that CHF has the second-largest endowment among public institutions in Philadelphia, the best library of chemical history in the world, and a growing reputation for fine art concentrated in the field. That's not enough for him, so it came about that a new museum was envisioned, funded and created. But not built; building it was assigned to Miriam Schaefer, a famous go-getter who had the unusual qualification of being squeamish about chemistry. It was her assigned task to find a way to make chemistry exciting to people who were not instinctively excited by it, just exactly because she was the world's authority on that point of view. What was vital was that she was the sort of person who can't resist a challenge, and was capable of thinking, well, big.

Chemical Heritage Museum

With the unlimited backing of Arnold and his board and their almost unlimited financial support, Miriam set about soliciting big ideas from uninhibited people all over the world, and some of their suggestions were even a little too wild to be acceptable. But since the whole idea was to awaken the enthusiasm of anybody, however sullen, who happens to shuffle through the museum, many outlandish suggestions were forced through the filter of a skeptical, conservative, Philadelphia establishment. The result is a series of pleasant surprises, ranging from fine art with a focus on alchemists trying to make gold out of lead, to astonishing computerized graphic displays of the elements of the periodic table fifty feet high, to depictions of Joseph Priestley known as the father of chemistry, a personal friend of Benjamin Franklin, the founder of the Unitarian Church, and a resident of Philadelphia. There's Arnold Beckman's original Beckman spectrophotometer which made hundreds of millions of dollars, was a major factor in the Twentieth century blossoming of biochemistry, and is here shown to be a clever elaboration of a simple idea. Meanwhile, the museum is housed in a massive old bank building, with it is interior reamed out and replaced with as much transparent glass as could support the weight. Inga Saffron the architectural critic, more than foamed over with praise in her review of just the structure itself. Don't neglect to notice the stunning portrait of Gay-Lussac, the man who discovered that water is H2O. The pigments of his portrait were mixed with beeswax, and with clever lighting have an astonishing luminosity.

The museum is part of a conference center, which should attract audiences of chemists for decades. But that's not entirely the whole idea. The underlying vision is to convince those skeptical, non-chemical bozos that not only are chemists rather richer than the rest of us, and smarter, but clever and fascinating, too. Go visit this museum, before everyone else does.

8 Our Federal Reserve: Biddle's Bank

Biddle's Bank   420 Chestnut Street   Philadelphia, PA
39.9486 -75.1484

Nicholas Biddle

In 1823, the Biddles were prosperous, having made money in real estate (a Biddle ancestor had been a member of the Proprietors), and influential, having been Free Quakers who sided with the Revolution. So, Nicholas Biddle became the president of the Second Bank at 4th and Chestnut. Like all banks, he was given the ability to create money by taking deposits and loaning them out. Since in this process, two people (the depositor and the borrower) think they have the same money, there is effectively twice as much of it -- unless both actually demand it at the same time. If a bank has Federal revenues on deposit, as Biddle did, it is fairly easy for a politically active banker to predict whether that large depositor is likely to withdraw it. Political deposits seemingly make a bank stronger and safer, unless the banker has a fight with a politician. That's banking, but Biddle also became a central banker. Biddle had ideas, derived in part from Alexander Hamilton.

In those days, banks issued their own paper currency, or banknotes, representing the gold in their vaults or the real estate on which they held mortgages. There was a risk in one bank accepting banknotes from another bank that might go bust before you changed their notes into gold. The further away the issuing bank was, the riskier it was to rely on it. So, it was important to be a friendly sort of banker, who knew a lot of other bankers who would accept your money or who were known to be trustworthy. Nicholas Biddle himself was well known to be pretty rich, and utterly trustworthy. He had a good instinct for how much to charge or discount the banknotes from other banks, or even other states. It was quite profitable to do this, but it became even more profitable when people began to use Biddle's own banknotes because they were safe. By setting a fair standard, he could control the exchange rate -- and hence the lending limits -- of banks that dealt with him. Sometimes a distant bank would get into cash shortages, and Biddle would help them out; if the other bank had a bad reputation, he might not.

In this way, the Second Bank was a reserve bank for other banks, with its banknote currency coming close to being the currency for the whole country. Soon, within a few blocks of Biddle's Bank, there were dozens of other banks, making up the financial capital of the country. Although it was a little obscure, and even Biddle may not have completely realized what he was doing, in effect his system automatically

Second Bank of The United States

adjusts the amount of currency in circulation to the size of the economy. If the correspondent banks prospered, they issued more currency, and if there was a recession, the country had deflation. The volatility of this system was related to the volatility of a pioneer economy, so Biddle made lots of enemies whenever he guessed about the direction of the economy. It wasn't a perfect system, but at least he kept politicians from inflating the currency to get re-elected, and hence annoyed politicians by constraining them. During the great western land rush of those days, all banks were under pressure to issue more loans than was wise, and politicians were under pressure to make them do so. The worst enemy Biddle made was Martin Van Buren of New York. Van Buren was a consummate politician, one of whose many goals was to move the financial capital of the country from Chestnut Street--to Wall Street.

9 American Philosophical Society

Philosophical Hall   104 5th Street   Philadelphia, PA   39.9486 -75.1494

All of the red brick buildings on Independence Square look as though they were part of Independence Hall, but there is one exception. The building facing Fifth Street is Philosophical Hall, one of the four buildings of the American Philosophical Society. Right now, Philosophical Hall is used as a museum. It could be called the first museum in America, but not the oldest, because it had interruptions and different proprietorships. Charles Wilson Peale started his museum of curiosities there and then moved it to the second floor of Independence Hall, where he painted the famous portrait of himself holding up the curtain. In recent years, Philosophical Hall has again become a museum, holding treasures and curiosities   belonging to the Philosophical Society itself. The docent is pleased to alternate between calling it America's new oldest museum, and America's oldest new museum.

Charles Wilson Peale
The Artist in His Museum 1822

Patents were established by the Constitution when it was a piece of parchment lying on a table fifty feet away from here, and the early patent office required the submission of a working model of every application for patent. After a while, that got to be a lot of working models lying around, and many of the more interesting ones are on display in the museum. Like the model of Fitch's first steamboat or the gadget Jefferson used, to make simultaneous copies of documents he was writing. That's right near the Gilbert Stuart copy of Washington's portrait, and von Neumann's first algorithm to be stored in his stored-program machine, or computer, and Neil Armstrong's speech on the moon, concerning one step for mankind and all. It's a splendid museum, full of the real stuff, in a handsome Georgian building with sparkling immaculate marble staircases.

In the Eighteenth Century, Natural Philosophy was what we now call science. That's why PhDs get a degree of Doctor of Philosophy when they study chemistry and physics. The idea for forming a scientific society in America apparently originated with John Bartram. As so often happens, the originator couldn't quite get it established and had to call on Ben Franklin, that impresario of publicity, to get it off the ground. To be fair about it, Franklin was probably the more distinguished scientist of the two. To be even more fair about it, the organization struggled a bit until Thomas Jefferson (that's the one who was President of the United States) gave it a real publicity shove. During the depths of the 1930s depression, one of the members left it several million dollars with the stipulation that the investments should focus on common stock. Since buying stock in 1935 was widely regarded as about the stupidest thing an investor could do, this little episode reinforced a strong impression that membership in the APS is given to people who are very smart, not merely famous. The four buildings, the many fellowships, and the big endowment were largely made possible by this contraries investment decision.

John Fitch received a US Patent for the Steamboat August 26, 1791

There are eight hundred members, of whom 93 have won Nobel Prizes. Over the years, 260 members have been awarded Nobel Prizes, but you must remember that the organization existed for 150 years before there was such a prize. Several U.S. Supreme Court justices are members and lots and lots of people who are famous. The docent comments that they look pretty much like everyone else. There's a rumor that Bill Gates turned down the offer of membership, so now we will just see. He's young enough to have several decades' opportunity to reconsider an offer, although the APS might just be old enough to lack interest in any second chances.

10 Independence Hall

Independence National Historical Park   520 Chestnut Street   Philadelphia, PA 39.9489 -75.15

What Happened in Philadelphia on July 4, 1776?

The American colonies were growing too big, too fast, and the British Empire had too many international distractions, to have smooth relationships across three thousand miles of ocean, using uncertain communications available in the late Eighteenth century. Friction and misunderstanding were inevitable without far more statesmanship than either side thought was necessary. So, when the Continental Congress dispatched George Washington to Boston with troops to defend rebellious Massachusetts at Lexington, Concord, and Bunker Hill, it was hard for the British to believe the colonists were merely helping out one of their distressed neighbors. It seemed in London that the thirteen colonies had united, formed not only an army but a government, and gone to war. In December 1775 England passed the Prohibitory Act, essentially declaring war, and organized a huge invasion fleet to put down the rebellion. It now seems hard to understand the first notice the Americans had of this huge over-reaction was a private letter to Robert Morris from one of his agents in March 1776; no warnings, no negotiations, no attempt to investigate problems and correct them. The British just sent a fleet to settle this problem, whatever it was. It's all very well to say the Americans should have known they were playing with fire. They didn't see it that way; they were being self-reliant, responding to attack.

In June 1776 British patrol frigates were skirmishing in the Delaware River; late in the month, British troops landed on Staten Island. The American reaction to all this was a muddle of confusion. A few were delighted, most of the rest were amazed or appalled. Although the deeper strategic origins of the American Revolution are subtle, complex, and controversial, there is far less muddle about what happened on July 2, 1776, publicly proclaimed two days later. Adopting a resolution written by Richard Henry Lee of Virginia, the Thirteen Colonies stated they had now clarified their goals in the controversy with the British monarchy. For a year before that, the Continental Congress had been corresponding with each other and meeting in Carpenters' Hall with the goal of achieving representation in the British parliament - "No taxation without representation". The model for most of them was based on the Whig agitation for Ireland -- for a local parliament within a larger commonwealth. But the passing of the British Navy in Halifax, Nova Scotia, and then the actual appearance of seven hundred British warships in American waters showed that not only was Parliamentary representation out of the question, but King George III was going to play rough with upstarts. The new goal was no longer just representation, it was independence. If we were going to resist a military occupation at the risk of being hanged as traitors, we might as well do it for something substantial.

Spirit of '76

The meeting had a number of Scotch-Irish Princeton graduates, whose basic loyalty to England had long been divided. Pacifist Pennsylvania, chief among the wavering hold-outs, was mostly won over by its own Benjamin Franklin, who was optimistic the French would help us. Even so, both Robert Morris and John Dickinson refused to sign the Declaration; Franklin persuaded both to abstain by absence, which created a majority of the Pennsylvania delegation in favor. That's a pretty slim majority for a crucial decision. Franklin was soon dispatched back to Paris to make an alliance; Washington was dispatched to hold off that British army in the meantime. Jefferson was designated to write a proclamation, which even after editing is still pretty unreadable beyond the first couple of sentences. Meeting adjourned. This brief account may not qualify as a serious examination of the causes of the American Revolution, but it comes close to the way it seemed to the colonist in the street.

The rebels then spent eight years convincing the British they were serious and have been independent ever since. But, just a minute, here. Reflect on the fact that fighting had been going on for a year in Massachusetts, and that Lord Howe's fleet had set sail a month before the Declaration, actually landing on Staten Island at just about the same time as the Fourth of July. Add the fact that only John Hancock actually signed the document on July 4th, and some of the signers even waited until September. You can sort of see why John Adams never got over the idea that Thomas Jefferson had a big nerve implying the whole Revolution was his idea. What's more, loud talk from New England still made the rest of the country nervous. Philadelphia may have been the cradle of Independence, but that was not because it was a colony hot for war, dragging others along with it. Rather, it was the largest city in the colonies, centrally located. It had a strong pacifist tradition, and it had the most to lose from a pillaging enemy war machine. When Independence was finally declared the goal, many of Philadelphia's leading citizens moved to Canada. New England had started hostilities and was about to be subdued by overwhelming force. The Canadians were not going to come to their aid, because they were French, and Catholic, and enough said.

Colonist's Complaint

What New England and the Scotch-Irish needed were WASP allies, stretching for two thousand miles to the South. By far the largest colony was Virginia, which included what is now Kentucky and West Virginia; it even had some legal claims for vastly larger territory. Virginia was incensed about its powerlessness against British mercantilism, especially the tobacco trade. The rest of the English colonies had plenty of assorted grievances against George III, and almost all of them could see that America was rapidly outgrowing dependency on the British homeland, without a sign that Parliament was ever going to surrender home rule to them. It was perhaps unfortunate that New Englanders were so impulsive, but it looked as though a military confrontation with the Crown was inevitably coming. Without support, New England was likely to be torched, as Rome once subdued Carthage.

The last hope for an alternative of flattery and diplomacy, for guile and subtlety, had stepped off the boat a year earlier. Benjamin Franklin, our fabulous man in London, arrived with the news he had finally had it "up to here" with the British ministry. The story goes that he held an undying grudge against the King because of the public dressing down he had received in January 1774 by Wedderburn on the King's behalf. Franklin was a man who quietly made things happen, carefully selecting his arguments from amongst many he had in mind. One might wonder, though, whether it was less revenge and revolutionary zeal that inspired him to support the concept of independence as it was a desire to avoid the hanging offense of rebelling against the crown. Might Franklin have been thinking of the 1648 Treaty of Westphalia, which made disputes between sovereigns (and by extension, between sovereign nations) a simple matter of treaty negotiation, as opposed to cries of "No taxation without representation," in which the supplicants remained subjects at risk of capital punishment?

George Washington Demands a Better Constitution

George Washington was a far more complex person than most people suppose, and he wanted it that way. He was born to be a tall imposing athlete, eventually a bold and dashing soldier. On top of that framework, he carefully constructed a public image of himself as aloof, selfless, inflexibly committed to keeping his word. Parson Weems the biographer may have overdone the image a little, but Washington gave Weems plenty to work with and undoubtedly would have enjoyed overhearing the stories of the cherry tree and tossing the coin across an impossibly wide Potomac. Washington had a bad temper and could remember a grievance for life. He married up, to the richest woman in Virginia.

Growing up along the wide Potomac River, Washington early conceived a life-long ambition to convert the Potomac into America's main highway to the Mississippi. He did indeed live to watch the nation's new capital start to move into the Potomac swamps across from his Mount Vernon mansion, in a city named for him. For now, retiring from military command with great fanfare and farewells after the Revolution, he returned to private life on this Virginia farm. He made an important political mistake along this path, by vowing in public never to return to public life.

During the years after the Revolution but before the new Constitution, his attention quickly returned to building canals along the Potomac River, deepening it for transportation, and connecting its headwaters over a portage in Pennsylvania to the headwaters of the Monongahela River -- hence to the Ohio, then the Mississippi, or up the Allegheny River to the Great Lakes. Washington more or less gave up this Potomac ambition for a loftier one. During the Revolution, he had suffered the most infuriating abuse of himself and his soldiers from the state legislatures. Their urgent demands for victories were seldom matched with resources. The Continental Congress representing those state governments in a weak confederation that could not feed and pay its own troops seemed little better. He could be a mean man to cross, but perhaps with General Cromwell in mind, Washington possessed the firmest and most sincere belief in the proper subservience of military to civilian control. These conflicting feelings resulted in earnest obedience to a group of politicians he surely distrusted. This could not be described as hypocrisy; he respected their rank even though he suffered from their behavior. When Congress paid the troops in worthless currency which they promised to redeem after the war, it became clear that either lack of moral fiber or their system of governance led the states and the Congress in the direction of dishonoring their debt to the soldiers. This was a dreadful system, which led to death and suffering among the loyal troops, forcing the General into the humiliating position of assuring the troops Congress would stand by them, while he privately doubted any chance of it.

Washington did not easily forgive or forget. Here was a paltry outcome for eight years of war and suffering; this system of organized dishonor must be improved. He went about achieving his goal in a way that would not occur to most people. He chose a young ambitious agent, James Madison, who had caught his attention in the Virginia legislature, in the Continental Congress, and in the negotiations with Maryland over the development of the Potomac. Washington schemed with the young man for weeks on end about ways and means, opportunities, dangers, and potential enemies. Perhaps he failed to notice some ways where he and Madison fundamentally differed. Madison himself might not have recognized that his years at Princeton in the Quaker state of New Jersey had exposed him to novel ideas like separation of church and state, which were instantly appealing to the two Virginia Episcopalian religious doubters. Many people he admired, Patrick Henry, in particular, wanted the government to be as weak and ineffective as possible. Unfortunately, when Madison's turn later came for assuming the Presidency, he went along with reliance on diplomacy and persuasion until it almost cost America the War of 1812. Acting as Washington's agent in 1788, Madison was assigned to win over the Virginia legislature, make alliances with other states in Congress, identify friends and enemies, make deals. He performed as brilliantly as he would at the Constitutional Convention, so the basic conflict between the soldier President and his politician assistant was glossed over. As long as the original relationship held together, Washington felt it was useful to remain above and aloof, publicly wavering whether this was all a good idea, but fiercely determined to have a nation he could be proud of. There was to be a Constitutional Convention in Philadelphia, but while Washington was invited, he let it be known he was uncertain whether he should accept the invitation. What he really meant was he would preserve his political credibility for a different approach if this one failed. Considered from Madison's viewpoint however, this clearly meant Washington would dump him if things went badly. Meanwhile, the unknown young Madison on several occasions came to

Mount Vernon for three days at a time to talk strategy and give the famous General all the scoop.

Today, we would describe Madison as a nerd. Gouverneur Morris never thought much of him. Washington needed him, but there is no evidence he thought of him other than as a glorified butler. Little Madison was awkward among the ladies, a problem inconceivable to either Washington or Morris. But that little mind was surely working, all the time. Madison was in fact a brilliant politician, a dissembler in a different way, but a severe contrast with his mentor. To begin with, he was a scholar. Both as an undergraduate at Princeton and a graduate student working directly with the great Witherspoon himself, Madison was deeply learned in the history of classical republics. He spent an extra year at Princeton, just to be able to study ancient Hebrew with Witherspoon. But he was innately skilled in the darker arts of politics. When votes were needed, he had a way of persuading three or four other members to vote for a measure, while Madison himself would then vote against it to preserve influence with opponents for later skirmishes.

In fact, as matters later turned out, it becomes a little uncertain just how convinced Madison was that Washington's strong central government was a totally good idea. Before and after 1787 Madison expressed a conviction that real sovereignty originated in the states, just as the Articles declared. That was a little too fancy for practical men of affairs, who were uncomfortable to discover how literal Madison was after his break with the Federalists. Twenty years younger than the General. he prospered in the image of being personally close to the titan, and he certainly enjoyed the game of politics. The new Constitution was going to be an improvement over the Articles of Confederation, but Madison did not burn for long with indignation about injustice to the troops, or with disdain for nasty little politicians in the state legislatures. These were problems to be solved, not offenses to be punished. The new Constitution was a project where he could advance his career, skillfully demonstrating his prowess at negotiation and manipulation. This is not to say he did not believe in his project, but rather to suspect that he was a blank slate on which he allowed Washington to write, and later allowed others to overwrite. He was eventually to modify his opinions as a result of new associations and partners, and since he succeeded Jefferson as President, it was personally useful to adjust his viewpoints to his timing.

What would never change was that he was an artful politician, while Washington hated, absolutely hated, partisan politics. This is not just an emotional division between two particular Virginia plantation owners, but an enduring thread running through all elective politics. Washington set the style for generations of citizen leaders in America. In his mind, a person of honor distinguishes himself in some way before he enters public office, so on the basis of that honorable image, presents himself to voters for public office, and naturally is elected to represent their interests. He is expected to compromise where compromise is honorable and publicly acknowledged, in order to achieve one desirable outcome in concert with other outcomes, in some ways inconsistent but still honorable in combination. He reliably will not vote for either issues or candidates in return for some personal consideration other than the worth of the issue or the candidate, with the possible exception of yielding to the clear preferences of his local district. Such a person is not a member of a political organization very long before he encounters another group of colleagues -- who regularly swap votes for personal advantage, join a group who agree to vote as a unit no matter what the merits, and recognize the frequent necessity to talk one way while secretly voting another. The first sort of politician is usually an amateur, the second type is typically a professional politician. Although it seems a violation of ethics and common public welfare, the fact is the professional vote-swapper almost always beats the sappy amateur. The response during the Eighteenth Century was for idealists to condemn and attempt to abolish partisanship and political parties. The American Constitution does not make provision for political parties and other forms of vote-swapping or even anticipate their emergence. Although Madison ignited the process in the United States, Jefferson really organized it; every recent politician except Adlai Stevenson has openly participated in a version of it.

That the Constitution has still not been amended to provide for parties seems to reflect a persisting nostalgic hope that somehow we can return to Washington's stance. Washington's conception of open representative politics was not entirely perfect, either. In order to maintain an image of impartiality, Washington and his imitators isolated themselves in a cloak, holding back their true opinions in a sphinx-like way that hampered negotiation. Unwillingness to be seen swapping votes can lead to an unwillingness to compromise, and in the final analysis, the difference is one of degree. However, the overriding issue is that each representative or Senator is equal to every other one. When vote-swapping gets started, it leads to placing power over supposed equals in the hands of the more powerful manipulators, masquerading as political leaders. Ultimately, it leads to the adoption of house rules on the very first day of a session which force lesser members to surrender their votes to a speaker or minority leader or committee chairman, when the theory is that there is no such thing as a lesser member. The claim of a party-line politician is that he obeys the will of the party caucus; the reality is usually that he obeys the will of some tough, self-advancing party leader. The final reality is that most legislatures must now deal with thousands of bills per session, leading to the necessity of appointing someone to set priorities, which in turn leads to the power of party leaders over their grudging servants. These various subversions of the equal rights of elected representatives can lead to such discrediting of the system that honorable people may refuse to stand for office, leaving foxes in charge of the hen house. Benjamin Franklin, who was to play an invisibly controlling role in the impending Constitutional Convention, had his own way of coping with the political environment. "Never ask, never refuse, never resign."

Signers and Non-Signers of the Constitution

Old City

John Dickinson was active in designing both the Declaration of Independence and the Constitution, but he signed neither one. His position on the Declaration was that England had behaved in an offensive way; but the situation was getting better and it was still possible to patch things up, even with a British fleet in New York harbor displaying hostile intent. His later position on the Constitution is less clear. Dickinson asked George Read to sign his name because he was sick. Whether this was a real illness or a diplomatic illness is not readily known.

Three active delegates made no bones about their opposition to the final product: Edmond Randolph and George Mason of Virginia were not mollified by private assurances that a Bill of Rights was necessary but could be added later. They refused to sign a constitution that did not currently include this most passionate of their demands. There is little doubt of their sincerity, but any politician today would recognize they also needed to protect their flank from Patrick Henry who stayed at home denouncing the whole enterprise. Henry was a powerful speaker, representing the Scotch-Irish Virginia Piedmont area. In Scotland, Ireland, and America, that group had been abused by English kings three times and wanted iron-clad protection against backsliding to English rule or English government models.

Signers of the Constitution

It's quite possible that Virginia's George Wythe and James McClurg left the convention early in order to avoid the local political consequences of signing the document, or the equally uncomfortable stance of opposing George Washington. The sentiments of Virginia can be surmised when of the seven delegates sent by Virginia, only John Blair joined the two instigators, George Washington and James Madison in announcing their approval. A majority of the Virginia delegation was thus held back on ratification until only one last vote was needed for enactment. Without George Washington, there can be little doubt the whole effort would have failed. Indeed, a case could be made that the location of the District of Columbia and the election of Virginians as four of the first five presidents also has the appearance of trying to persuade the six hundred pound Virginia gorilla to play nice.

Elbridge Gerry of Massachusetts similarly refused to sign any constitution which did not include a Bill of Rights. However, Gerry undermined his stance on principle by inventing the technique of packing his opposition into one voting district (by shifting its borders) so his own party could win narrow majorities in several other districts. This sleazy manipulation of loopholes in the system has become known as Gerrymandering and raises a question, perhaps unfairly, of where Gerry actually stood on every other issue in the Constitutional Convention. By contrast, it is impossible to imagine George Washington doing such a thing, and quite possible to imagine he would never again speak to someone who did. In addition to the three delegates who stayed to the end but refused to sign, an additional four left early to demonstrate their protest.

We are left less clear about the opinions of seven more who simply left the convention early. The same uncertainty extends to the eighteen delegates who were invited to attend but either refused or regretted their inability to attend. These men were originally selected because of their local eminence, so some of them may have been unable to spend several months in a city that took days to reach on horseback. On the other hand, we certainly know where Patrick Henry stood, and a large number of other abstentions from certain states suggests more than personal inconvenience was involved. After all, Rhode Island refused even to nominate anyone to the Delegation. In this last case, a political issue was highlighted. The Articles of Confederation which were being replaced not only required unanimous consent to change them, but they affirmed the Articles to be permanent. Under ordinary contract law, that would be dispositive. But George Washington was hell-bent on replacing the Articles of Confederation, so what they said would then no longer matter.

There remains a need for someone, perhaps in a doctoral thesis, to examine the voluminous correspondence and recollections of the large group of non-signers to assess the true nature of their failure to attend or sign. There was plenty of room for honest disagreement, personal business back at home, illness, or feelings of inadequacy. On the other hand, plenty of other subsequent politicians have exhibited an unwillingness to offend anyone, a hope to seek advantage from both sides, or a habitual tendency of waiting to see who would win before stating an opinion. Politics would be better without such personal inadequacies, but politics would not be politics without them. In fairness to their quandaries, the voting on the Constitution was by states, requiring nine to adopt it. If the vote of their state was a foregone conclusion, some delegates probably had a right to go home and let it happen in their absence.

In the case of Alexander Hamilton, here stood the sole New York delegate in attendance at the final signing. Since he had been agitating for this sort of reform for seven years before Madison and Washington convinced each other, it seems possible that others withdrew to let him have the limelight. There is little doubt the single remaining responsibility of the signers was to go home and "deliver" their state for ratification, and Hamilton went at that with a vengeance. Although the moment of final signing appears on portraits and in sculpture, it was only the beginning of the battle for adoption, not the final victory. Indeed the Constitution as we now perceive it did not take more or less final form until the early government shaped its operation in actual practice. Most of that shaping process also took place in Philadelphia, during the first ten years while the seat of government was still located there. In particular, many if not most of the elected members of the First Congress had been members of the Constitutional Convention, returning to Philadelphia to finish the job by writing the Bill of Rights.

11 Elias Durand

Site of Durand Pharmacy   6th and Chestnut Streets   Philadelphia, PA
39.9492 -75.150

Philadelphia has a long and bumpy history with the French, more or less paralleling the British wars with them. But when the guillotine threatened aristocratic necks,

Philadelphia offered a sanctuary of new world enthusiasm and sophistication. A few years after the terror, during the reign of Napoleon Bonaparte, Americans scorned his monomaniacal approach to government, returning to the British disdainful view of Frenchmen. In another era, Philadelphia would change its view, displaying a prominent collection of sculptures by the famous French artist, Rodin. And in a more recent political climate, the French and their socialist leanings were akin to the devil incarnate. It cannot be denied, however, the French had a major influence on the Philadelphia society and culture. Elias Durand, a former member of the Academy of Natural Sciences whose portrait hangs in the Library Reading room, was a French refugee whose love of Botany greatly expanded American understanding and knowledge of

Elias Durand

plant life in North America. Somehow, that seems appropriate for an educated Frenchman. But his achievements in commerce were at least as important to his adopted city as his intellectual ones.

The youngest of fourteen children, Durand was born in Mayenne, France in 1794. A passionate chemistry student, he studied pharmaceuticals in school where he was also introduced to the subjects of natural history, mineralogy, geology, and entomology. His rich education in both Mayenne and Paris expanded his interest in chemistry to include the interplay between the hard sciences and the natural world. In 1813, after studying in Paris, Durand joined Napoleon's army, where he served as a medic and "Pharmacien," overseeing the opening of hospitals and the care of wounded soldiers. Even while serving in one of France's most historic wars, Durand remained passionate about the world of plants, by some accounts even collecting plants during the notoriously bloody Battle of Leipzig.

When Napoleon's luck turned bad, Durand focused his attention back on chemistry. In 1814 he left the army and moved to Nantes, where he worked briefly as an apothecary, as well as a lecturer on Medicinal plants in the regional Academy. Durand would remain a teacher throughout his life, instilling those around him with a fascination and passion for the Natural Sciences. Always a patriotic Frenchman, however, Durand rejoined Napoleon's forces during the general's final hurrah, the "100 days."

Former pharmacy at 6th and Chestnut

After Napoleon sustained his ultimate defeat at the battle of Waterloo, Durand retired from military duties and focused once again on the study of pharmaceuticals. His earlier connections to Napoleon, however, led to some uncomfortable clampdowns on the young man's freedom; Durand left the country in disgust in 1816 at being forced to report himself to the police every morning. He sailed to New York in pursuit of a life free from politics and dedicated to his passions of botany and chemistry.

Durand was quickly welcomed into the homes of other French ex-patriots living in Boston and soon met ambitious and science-oriented men who encouraged the young chemist to stay in the country. Hearing there might be work with Dr. Gerard Troost, the first president of the Academy of Natural Sciences, Durand traveled by foot to the mid-Atlantic region. This adventure brought him into contact with local Native Americans, whom he found friendly, as well as local native colonists, whom he found less so.

After a long and arduous journey down the East Coast, Durand finally arrived in Baltimore, only to learn that Troost was not in need of an employee. He was, however, desperate for a companion, and after spending several weeks in Troost's company, Durand left to find work in Baltimore with increased enthusiasm for Botany and in particular native species of North America.

In Baltimore, Durand found work with Mr. Ducatel as a pharmacist and apothecary. He quickly settled into the business, gaining experience in the field and eventually marrying Mr. Ducatel's daughter. But after five years in Baltimore, both his wife and his father-in-law had passed away, Durand left Baltimore to search for new opportunities.

He found them in Philadelphia. Perhaps because of the city's burgeoning field of Natural History or its emerging reputation as a medical town, Durand became committed to forging a career in Philadelphia. With the hope of opening a pharmacy in the finely decorated "European Style," Durand returned to France in 1825 to collect materials for this undertaking. Upon his arrival back to town, he set up a shop at 6th and Chestnut streets. His store quickly became world renowned for its unique and finely produced medicinal pharmaceuticals, unique in its access to both the old world and new world innovations. Philadelphia proved to be a good move for the young Frenchman; in the next few years, he married Marie Antoinette Berauld, a refugee from the St. Domingo Insurrection, and achieved election to the Philadelphia College of Pharmacy.

After his wife died in 1851, Durand gave up business to pursue the study of Botany. He was elected to the Academy of Natural Sciences in 1852, and during his membership published numerous articles and books on the botanical findings of expeditions to the American West and the Arctic. Durand also contributed to the study of Botany through the publication of several biographies about the lives of botanists Thomas Nuttall and Andre Michaux, the famous arborist. Durand's deep and lifelong appreciation for the study of Botany helped bolster the Academy's resources during his membership.

As Durand grew older, his French roots called him back to the homeland. In 1860 he returned to France, and finding the collection of North American specimens lacking in the Jardin des Plantes de Paris, determined to expand the collection himself. He returned to Philadelphia and spent the remainder of his life developing his collection of North American specimens with the help of his son. Eight years later, in 1868, Durand shipped his collection of 10,000 species herbarium to Paris where it was arranged in a special gallery named after him, the Herbier Durand. Much of Durand's remaining collection, however, was left to the Academy after his death. After this long, varied and successful career in the world of Natural Science, Elias Durand died in his home on 9th and Broad Streets in 1873 at the age of 80. He had contributed greatly to the fields of Botany and helped to establish Philadelphia's respected reputation in the world of medicine. Although a Frenchman at heart, Durand remains a feather in Philadelphia's cap and an important face at the Academy of Natural Sciences.

12 American Succession

The President's House   524 Market   Philadelphia, PA
39.9502 -75.1494

It may seem a startling focus for a famous war hero, but one of the most important precedents George Washington wanted to establish as America's first president, was

Old City

that he was determined not to die while in office. His original intention was to serve only one four-year term as president, only accepting a second term with considerable concern that it would increase his chances of dying in office. His reasons are perhaps not totally clear since he repeatedly stated his concern that he had promised the American public that he would retire from public office when he resigned his commission as General and was determined to seem a man of his word. While this sounds a little off-key to modern ears, it must be remembered his resignation as General had caused an international stir, even prompting King George III to exclaim that this must be the greatest man who ever lived. Washington may have sincerely thought he was following the pattern of Cincinnatus, the Roman citizen-soldier who declined further public life in order to return to his farm. But in retrospect we can see that for a thousand years before Washington's military resignation it was essentially unheard of for a leader with major power to be removed by any means except death.

Regardless of where he might have got the idea, Washington was consciously trying to establish a tradition of public service by those who were natural leaders, dutifully responding to the need of the nation, and stepping down when the service was completed. It was an important day for him and for the nation when he stood before John Adams in 1796, honorably and humbly turning over supreme power to a successor who had been chosen, by others, in a lawful way. Peaceful succession is part of the original intent of the founders of the Constitution if anything is. Some have written that Washington was not our first president, but our eleventh if one counts those elected the presiding officers of the Continental Congress, under the Articles of Confederation. But none of them could be said to be the head of state, and absolutely none of them could be confident the public would re-elect them indefinitely. Washington was not so much aiming for a two-term limit as he was setting a pattern for returning the choice to the people after a stated term, and deploring anyone who sought unlimited power for its own sake. The office should seek the man, not the man seek the office, and even if the public got carried away by adulation, the man should in good time step aside.

For over a century the two-term tradition was later unchallenged until Franklin Roosevelt succumbed to exactly the temptations that Washington foresaw. We have seldom amended the Constitution, but after Roosevelt, it was soon amended to emphasize what so many had previously considered it unnecessary to state. The idea of a fixed term of office has had an unexpected calming effect on partisanship in America. In parliamentary systems like the British, a prime minister answers weekly questions from his opposition, with a full realization that he can be dismissed from office at any moment he angers a majority into a vote of no-confidence. Under the American Constitution, a recent election mandate eats into the stated time in office, making it progressively less rewarding to evict the officer for the residual time before another election does it automatically. America does indeed have an impeachment process, but in fact, it has been rarely employed. In America, if someone is elected for a specific term, it is almost certain he will serve out the full term. There are times when partisanship seems unlimited, but in fact, we probably have less of it than if we encouraged partisan outcry to go on to evicting an incumbent from office.

Washington was not so successful in promoting another component of his ideal statesman. In his view, a district would naturally select the most prominent citizen available to represent the district, since that person would do it more ably than anyone else and give up the office when duty was completed; that was behind the stated ideal of republican government. Madison was for a time persuaded that such choices should be filtered a second time, with the House of Representatives electing Senators from its midst, but that failed to win approval. In the Eighteenth Century, the concept of professional bureaucrats and professional politicians had not yet taken hold. In its place was the fear of "ambitious" leaders, who would be held in check by a tradition of underpaying elected representatives, or even of gentlemen of means who would refuse to accept any pay for doing their duty. It proved unanswerable when ambitious men assailed this republican concept by protesting the establishment of aristocracies, oligarchies, and the failure of the upper class to understand the needs and anxieties of the common man. This viewpoint eventually replaced the "natural" local leaders with those who had experienced life in a log cabin or endured the purifying experiences of other hardships. The original idea of the founders was to elect leaders who could not be bought; ambitious men could be bought. When political parties made their appearance, a new thought appeared; perhaps ambitious men could be controlled.

As the practical realities of politics in action began to surface, members of elected bodies with varying degrees of ambition and altruism sought refuge from pressures being applied to them. After all, one of the undeniable implications of the Constitution was that every single member of an elected body had just as much power and rights as every other one. Out of this tension emerged the seniority system, another unwritten rule with the power of reality forging it into an implicit rule. In time, everyone would achieve seniority at the same point in his career, and hence the procedural powers necessary to running the place could be assigned with lessened fear of improper pressure. Newcomers regularly complain about the seniority system but eventually yield to it as the least bad accommodation to necessity. But even minor imperfections will be exploited if a system endures long enough. In this case, political parties in the home states are persuaded that the fruits of seniority might be disproportionately available to them if they elect young candidates and keep them in office indefinitely. Eventually, such stalwarts can rise to positions that allow them to reward the home district. This has the interesting consequence of creating political families, whose senior representative acquires the power to select his son or grandson to take his place in the rising chain of command. That's not as bad as an inherited aristocracy, perhaps, but it has several similarities.

13 Franklin Court

Franklin Court Museum   322 Market Street   Philadelphia PA
39.9498 -75.1465

When Judge Edwin O. Lewis was seized with the idea of making a national monument out of Colonial Philadelphia, he wanted it big. Forty or so years later, it's big all right, but not big enough to encompass the whole of America's most historic square mile. Government ownership in the form of a cross now extends five blocks north from Washington Square to Franklin Square, and four blocks East from Sixth to Second Streets. Restoration and historic display have spread considerably beyond that cross, however, and the Park Service has created ingenious walkways within the working city in the neighborhood. If you thread your way through these

Franklin Court Museum

walkways, you can stroll for miles within the world of William Penn and Benjamin Franklin. One such unexpected walkway is now called Franklin Court, which essentially cuts from Market to Chestnut Streets, within the block bounded by 3rd and 4th Streets. Hidden in the center is the reconstructed ghost of Franklin's quite large house, sitting in an interior courtyard bounded by a colonial post office and a newspaper office once operated by Franklin's grandson. And along the side of the walkway near Chestnut Street is a fascinating museum of Franklin's personal life, built by no less than Frank Venturi, and operated by Park Rangers in the polished but low-key manner for which the U.S. Park Service is famous.

For some reason, this jewel of a museum has not received the high-powered publicity it deserves. It's off the main Park premises, as we mentioned, and some of the problems have to be attributed to Venturi. As you walk through, you don't expect a huge museum to be there, and it can look pretty inconspicuous as you walk past because it is mostly underground. Take my word for it, it's worth a visit. There are long descending ramps inside the doors, which can be pretty daunting if you are elderly and tired. But, also inconspicuous, there's an elevator if you look around for it. Venturi didn't seem to like windows very much, which is a problem for some people.

There's a movie theater inside there, playing a long list of fascinating documentaries. There's an ingenious automated display of statuettes that utilize spotlights and revolving stages to present Franklin in Parliament, resisting the Stamp Act, Franklin being his charming self before the French monarchs, and the frail dying Franklin getting the Constitutional Convention to approve the document. There are also a variety of ingenious inventions of Franklin's on display in the original, including bifocal glasses, the first storage battery, a simplified clock, several library devices, the Franklin stove, and so on. In some ways, the highlight is the Armonica. Everyone knows Ben Franklin spent a lot of time holding a wine glass. Evidently, he noticed a musical note emerges if you run your finger around the open mouth of the drinking glass, and systematically studied how the tone can be varied by varying the level of liquid in the glass. The same variation in the emitted tone relates to variations in the thickness of the glass. So, he set up a series of different sized glasses impaled on a horizontal broomstick, enough to cover three octaves, rotated

Ben Franklin's Glass Armonica

the broomstick with a treadle like those used for spinning wheels -- and made music. The tone has a haunting penetration to it, which induced both Beethoven and Mozart to write special compositions for the armonica, and the Eighteenth Century went wild with enthusiasm. Unfortunately, a number of young ladies who played the armonica went mad. We now recognize that since the finest crystal glass was used, with very high lead content, the mad ladies were suffering from lead poisoning after repeatedly wetting their fingers on their tongues. As a matter of fact, port wine at that time was stored in lead-lined casks, resulting in the same unfortunate consequences, which included stirring up attacks of gout. Franklin himself was a famous sufferer from gout, which was more likely related to the port wine than playing the armonica, in his particular case.

Anyway, the reputation for inducing madness added to the spooky sort of sound the instrument made, attracting the attention of a mountebank named Franz Anton Mesmer, who falsely claimed to be the father of hypnotism. Mesmer enhanced the society of his stage performances by hypnotizing subjects while an assistant played the armonica, meanwhile relating all sorts of wild tales about animal magnetism. This was pretty sensational at the time until a young man in an audience suddenly died. It is now speculated that the victim probably had an epileptic seizure, but the news of this public fatal event pretty well finished Mesmer as an evangelist and the armonica as a musical instrument.

Old City

Benjamin Franklin, Prophet

Judged by his public and private writings, Franklin was a deist. That is, he believed God sort of wound up the Universe like a clock, then let it run by itself. Furthermore, the Constitution which he had a hand in writing, pretty clearly maintains a wide separation between church and state. Nevertheless, historians by the droves have identified a uniquely American culture, apparently based on some fiercely held convictions. We might just as well say America has a secular religion with prophets, and Benjamin Franklin was an early prophet. His enduring message for all time was: *Honesty is the best policy.*

By this he did not mean, as lawyers do, strict word precision, or as our military academies add, resolute avoidance of half-truths and double-talk. Ol' Ben never admitted who the mother of his illegitimate son was, and positively chortled at hoodwinking the Pennsylvania Assembly into matching private contributions for the nation's first hospital, which he secretly knew he already had in hand. Late in life, he set enduring standards for the American diplomatic service, which some have defined as a profession dedicated to lying for your Country. Not only was Franklin rather sly, he gleefully projected the image of slyness. In

Benjamin Franklin

recent years, some historians have proposed his adventures with many women were just acting out a playful pose. Frankly, this suggestion is hard to accept.

Poor Richard Almanack

The author of *Poor Richard's Almanack*, aged 26 at the first edition, was a young man totally consumed with advancing himself in the world; at that stage, he defined himself as a businessman. Like J. Pierpont Morgan, who could thunder "I will never do business with a man I don't trust", Franklin had one set of principles for business and another for love. Or, if you please, one set for men, and another for women, who were thought to play by their own set of rules. Historians have struggled with this paradox or hypocrisy, but it would have seemed strange even to comment on it in Franklin's era, and a conflict is not suggested in eighty volumes of his life writings. Lord Byron, another famous philanderer of the day, stated the matter delicately as "Man's love is to man's life a thing apart; 'tis a woman's whole existence." And that was just the way it was, in their view.

Franklin, who as an escaped apprentice might well have been punished like a felon in Boston, came to the big town to make his fortune, and found himself in a culture of Quakers. Boston Puritans might well have punished him severely, or at least stood by approvingly while his brother beat the daylights out of him. The Dutch in New York were well known as rough customers; just to the south in Delaware, the inhabitants were to maintain a whipping post for two hundred more years. But in Philadelphia, non-violence was eventually carried to the extreme of confining miscreants to solitude until they spontaneously perceived it really was better to

behave. Poor Richard's little motto about the best policy was in fact just the Golden Rule, applied to business. Even today, anyone starting a business soon finds a discouraging number of people ready to cheat the businessman; it was even truer in colonial America. Somehow, if you enter the business world, it is to be assumed you are ready to defend yourself. Competitors have little respect if you fail to conduct business warily; even less if you complain and whimper.

Little Benny Franklin, fresh off the boat from Boston, watched with amazement as Quaker merchants and vendors conducted trade on the assumption the counterparty was honest, refused to bargain an openly set price, and avoided violence when cheated. At the same time, Franklin could not fail to notice that Philadelphia was prospering much more rapidly than Boston. After a business trip to England, he could see that London worked at the same disadvantage as Boston. Honesty, it would appear, makes you rich; cheating may sometimes work, but fairness gets you ahead more steadily.

In later years, Franklin shared rooms with John Adams, who became positively livid at the suggestion a person should be honest for any other motive than to be taken into Heaven. It was degrading, even dishonest, to be honest in order to get rich. There is no evidence that Franklin's reaction to this sermon was anything but contempt for the other man's intelligence. Although probably not directly related to this exchange, Franklin's assessment of Adams was "always an honest man, often a wise one, but sometimes and in some things, absolutely out of his senses." Ben Franklin was born in Puritan Boston, fled from it as soon as he could, and thereafter seldom regarded Puritans as having two feet on the ground. It thus emerges that Benjamin Franklin who was certainly no pacifist, greatly admired Quakers. On the one hand, in desperation he organized Pennsylvania's first militia when in 1730 the Quaker Pennsylvania government refused to act against French and Spanish marauders in Delaware Bay, and took the lead again in assisting the British during the French and Indian War while Quakers resigned from government rather than defend the state. He even volunteered to go to London to lobby against the Penn family. None the less, Franklin was completely converted to Quaker principles of doing business, perceiving a deep underlying truth to them. Honesty, as suggested by the Golden Rule, or fair trade as they say in commerce, is the key to prosperity. Honesty is not just good advice for a young man, it is a principle which brings prosperity to a whole nation, while readily suggesting a clear simple explanation of why it should. Don't you want to be rich? Plenty of other people want to be rich.

Unfortunately, many kings, barons, confidence men, bullies, cheaters, and tough guys have also become rich. Generations of immigrants have come to our shores with the idea that life is a zero-sum game. The way to get money is to take it from someone else. The way to lose money is to give a sucker an even break. But gradually, one generation after another learns the truth, as enunciated by Poor Richard, that everybody is better off if almost everybody tries to be honest.

Benjamin Franklin and Daylight Savings
Ben Franklin's father was a candle maker working out of his home. Little Benjamin was thus in a position to watch the rise and fall of candle sales with each passing season; it must have been a central fact of that household's economy. Many years later when he was Ambassador to France, the suggestion of Daylight Savings Time was likely less a demonstration of his ingenuity than a testimony to his powers of observation and reflection. It's a striking thought, even quite a revolutionary one. Until you remember that Franklin, more than any one person, also discovered electricity.

II North of Market

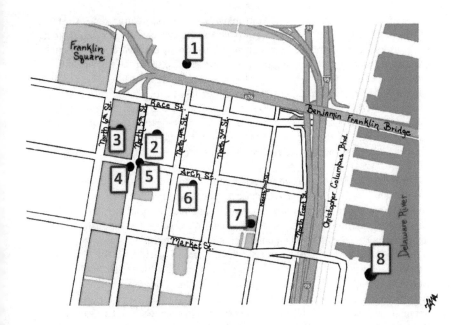

In their 1956 book "Philadelphia Scrapple", Harold Donaldson Eberlein and Mrs. Henry Cadwalader give an interesting description of the evolution of the term "North of Market". In the early days of the city, almost all of the town was South of Market Street. In fact, an early 18th Century visitor once wrote that he always brought a fowling-piece when he visited Philadelphia because the duck hunting was so good at the pond located at what is now 5th and Market.

When the Quaker meeting house was built at 4th and Arch Streets, many of the more important Quaker families thought it was important to build their houses nearby. In that way, Arch Street developed the reputation of being a Quaker Street. So the original meaning of the "North of Market" term was the Quaker ghetto. Quaker families continued to spread West along Arch Street or nearby, and this accounts for the location of the Friends Center and related local activities at 15th and Cherry. When the Free Quakers were evicted from the meeting at 4th and Arch because of their activities during the Revolution, they built their own meeting at -- 5th and Arch.

During the Civil War, a number of people made fortunes that socially upscale people over in the Rittenhouse Square area considered disreputable, so elaborate but ostracized mansions marched due North up Broad Street, where they can still be observed as stranded whales, leaders without followers. The show houses of manufacturers of shoddy war goods soon gave the meaning of parvenu to the term North of Market.

And then the Pennsylvania Railroad ran an elevated brick structure from 30th Street to City Hall Plaza, the so-called Chinese Wall. For nearly a century this ugly looming structure on Pennsylvania Boulevard, now John Kennedy Boulevard, with its smoky engines above, and dark dripping tunnels at street level, sliced the town in half and made it very unattractive to build or to live North of Market. The Spring Garden area had some pretty large and expensive houses, but it was cut off by the railroad trestle and has only recently started to revive. It helped a lot to tear down the Chinese Wall, but that was fifty years ago, and the area has taken a long time to recover from the earlier diversion of social flow to the South of it. And, psychologically, North of Market will take even longer to recover from the implication of -- industrial slum.

Meanwhile, of course, Asian immigration settled along Arch Street at 9th to 12th Streets, and we now have our Chinatown there, complete with street signs in oriental lettering. In effect, we have a real Chinese Wall, a social one. Just what will happen to this group is unclear, since it is readily observable that they like to cluster together, unlike the East Indian immigrants, who head for the suburbs as fast as they can. Since the Chinese colony is physically blocked on all sides by the Vine Street Expressway, the Convention Center, and the Ben Franklin Bridge, it is hard to know where they will flow if the group gets much larger. The depressed Vine Street crosstown expressway makes a definitive border for downtown, and the contrast between the two sides of this expressway is striking. On one side is Camelot, and on the other side, almost nothing is being built. The future of North of Market, at the moment, is a little unclear.

1 The Revolutionary Origins of the Methodist Church

Saint George's United Methodist Church   235 North Fourth Street   Philadelphia, PA 39.9555 -75.1464

St. George's Church is the oldest Methodist Church in continuous use in the United States, its view unfortunately obscured by the approaches to the Ben Franklin Bridge.

There were no signers of the Declaration of Independence who were official Methodists, for the simple reason the Methodist Church was not created until 1784 when John Wesley secretly ordained its first ministers. However, there is room to believe the movements eventually creating the Methodist Church played a central role in American agitation for independence. The origins are a little confusing. John and Charles Wesley were both priests in the Church of England, and John famously declared, "I will live and die an Anglican." While at Oxford, they founded a bible and ethical study society which came to be called the Holy Club, and because of systematic thoroughness were familiarly known as Methodists. A systematic study

of the Bible in small class groups was a central feature. There was no dissatisfaction with, or rebellion from, the Church of England. Missionary zeal was a second early feature of the group, and some early missionaries like Bishop Francis Asbury were especially active in the American colonies. When Asbury came to America there were 1200 adherents of the general concepts, and when he

Saint George's Methodist Church

died there were a quarter of a million formal members of the church. This rapid growth soon became its main problem, because the Anglican Church simply could not supply enough priests, and so the local congregations demanded the right to ordain their own ministers. Wesley agreed but did it secretly. America was a long way from England, and the idea of a local church, independent of England, soon made its appearance, particularly as local practices began to diverge from the Anglican ones.

Missionary zeal soon evolved into more exhortation evangelism. In the Pennsylvania Quaker country, restlessness with Quaker silence produced a reaction of joyous outcry during religious meetings, creating the description "shouting Methodists". Hymn singing was important as a result of Charles Wesley's influence, and many Methodist hymns have been adopted by other Protestant denominations. Drunkenness was a major problem in the colonies, and anti-drunkenness or temperance was the main feature of Methodist attention. A century later, Methodist ministers were to found the Salvation Army, which embodies many of the principles of evangelical, hymn singing anti-drunkenness crusading.

From its earliest days, Methodism welcomed blacks into membership, although a segregationist strain to it ultimately caused trouble. A central figure in the configuration of the early Methodist Church was John Newton, the captain of a slave ship. After nearly perishing in a storm, Newton attributed his rescue to God's intervention, writing the famous hymn, Amazing Grace. He spent the rest of his life in evangelical activities, with particular emphasis on black people.

Although his American visit preceded the formation of the Church, George Whitefield the evangelical preacher played a major role in preparing the Colonial Philadelphia populace for the concepts of Methodism. He attracted great crowds to his sermons, and Benjamin Franklin describes in his autobiography the great impact Whitefield had on him. Now, as it happened, the German Reform church had started but was unable to complete a church building at 235 North 4th Street, which was sold at auction to members of the local Methodist Society. This church building, started in 1763, purchased in 1767, and completed in 1769, can fairly claim to be the oldest Methodist Church building in continuous service in the world, although the dates of these things are pretty confusing for a church officially created in 1784.

John Wesley

Just to make things more difficult to understand, Barratt's Chapel, ten miles south of Dover, Delaware, was completed in 1784 on land donated in 1780. If you say it slowly, you can see that it is possible to describe Barratt's Chapel as the oldest house of worship built by and for Methodists. John Wesley's chapel, on City Road, London, is however still the mother church, so to speak. St. George's Church in Philadelphia is notable for ordaining the first black minister, Richard Allen, who had been born a slave of Benjamin Chew (the Chief Justice, whose house was Cliveden, the scene of the Battle of Germantown). Allen was obviously a remarkable person, who bought his own freedom by working as a shoemaker, and who later drove wagons from Rehoboth, Delaware to Valley Forge during the Revolution. (Allen had actually been sold by Chew to Stockley Sturgis, a Delaware plantation owner, who is the one who remorsefully sold him his freedom). Allen often preached five times a day, built up a huge following in the black community, and broke off to form the African Methodist Episcopal Church. The first Church was Bethel, replaced several times at 6th Lombard Streets, but there are now many others across the country.

Benjamin Franklin Bridge

Visitors from New Jersey, crossing the Benjamin Franklin Bridge, will be able to see the top half of St. George's Church as they descend into Philadelphia. At Christmastime, the windows are lit with real candles, and the interior is a beautifully simple white room. It now has less than a hundred members but houses the genealogy and other church records for a wide area and is very popular with people doing research. The bishop's chair dates from Bishop Asbury. Barratt's Chapel is smaller and simpler, but the highway makes a wide swing around it and its burial ground, so it remains a prominent feature of the area around Frederica. It takes several minutes to drive around it, even at high speed, on the way to the Delaware beaches. Wesley College is not far away.

2 The Mint

Philadelphia U.S. Mint   151 N Independence Mall E   Philadelphia, PA 39.9534 -75.1476

Judge Edwin O. Lewis finally got his way, the Pennsylvania State Government acquired four blocks of Chestnut Street stretching to the East of Independence Hall, and the Federal Government acquired four blocks stretching to the North. Judge Lewis was determined that a real revival of historic Philadelphia required the clearance of a lot of lands. Those who heard him describe it will remember the emphasis, "It must be BIG if it is to serve its purpose."

The open land is rapidly filling in, but for a time the movers and shaker of this town had to scratch a little to find something to put there. That's fundamentally why the historic district has a Mint, a Federal Reserve, a Court Houses, a Jail, and a big Federal Building to house various local offices of the landlord, the federal government. It's where you go to visit your congressman, or to renew your passport, or to argue with the Internal Revenue Service. If you have certain kinds of business, there's an office for the FBI and the U.S. Secret Service. The mission of the Secret Service is a little hard to explain with logic.

The Secret Service is a federal police organization, charged with protecting the President of the United States, and enforcing the laws against counterfeiting money. In unguarded moments, the Secret Service officers will tell you they only have one function: to guard three-dollar bills. The President only comes to town from time to time, but the mandate extends to the President's family, and to the extended family of official candidates for election to that office. So, there is always a certain amount of activity relating to running behind limousines with one hand on the fender, or poking around rooftops near the speaker's platform at Independence Hall, or talking apparently to a blank wall, using the microphones hidden in their ear canals. The rest of the time is taken up with counterfeiters, but even then the excitement is only occasional, depending on the business.

3 National Constitution Center

525 Arch St   Philadelphia, PA   39.9536 -75.1491

During a speech, Senator Arlen Specter "let it slip" that he had a lot to do with obtaining federal financing to establish the new Constitution Center on the north end of Independence Mall. Probably even more important, he intimated that his wife, Joan Specter, did a lot of domestic agitating to see that it happened. The earmarks were his, the fingerprints were hers.

Some have worried that the Supreme Court might be uneasy about a center telling the world what the Constitution is because the Justices see Constitutional interpretation as their unique function. The point that is sensitive is the emphasis on the words "We, the People", which could be seen as urging easy modification of the document by shouting demands or repetition of certitudes without passing due process in order to be considered. The second floor of this enormous new building is devoted to some very skillful exhibits relating to the history and significance of certain features of Constitutional history. The many auditoriums are the site of public lectures and programs, and there is a very interesting set of life-sized bronze figures of every member of the original Constitutional Convention. A striking feature of the display is to show how short and inconsequential Hamilton and Madison seemed to be in person, while Ben Franklin and Gouverneur Morris appear imposing and formidable in the flesh. These things matter in politics.

In 1789 the Constitutional Convention met in Independence Hall, and our national form of government was somewhat strengthened from the Articles of Confederation also written here. Benjamin Franklin had a hand in both documents, but the Articles of Confederation were mainly composed by John Dickinson, and the Constitution by Gouverneur Morris using James Madison's notes under the supervision of George Washington and Robert Morris. George Washington only wanted unification; Robert Morris persuaded him that taxes were needed to pay for it.

4 Free Quaker Meeting House

Free Quaker Meeting House of Philadelphia   500 Arch Street   Philadelphia, PA 39.9524 -75.1487

If Independence Hall, which after all is a block long, is overwhelmed by the new constructions, the Free Quaker Meeting is totally hidden. This perfectly charming Eighteenths Century Quaker meetinghouse is just across Fifth Street from Benjamin Franklin's Grave, and just across Arch Street from the Constitution Center, completely in its shadow. Charles E. Peterson designed the restoration of the building, which had been added to and detracted from, over the years, but you can be sure its interior is now both beautiful and authentic. Before you go in:

By General Subscription for the FREE QUAKERS.
Erected in the Year of OUR LORD 1783 and of the EMPIRE 8.

The Quakers who built this building seem to have thought they were part of a new empire, but that implies an emperor, and of course, one was never created. If you go into the Free Quaker building, it seems to be a single large room with an interior balcony, and a couple of small staircases in the back leading down to what would presumably be restrooms. As a matter of fact, the Park Service extended the basement to include a kitchen and dining room, and several offices for themselves which are a surprise if you are allowed to go down to see them.

History of the Free Quakers

Charlie Peterson wrote a book about the restoration, but the main book about the spiritual history of this group was written by Charles Wetherill. Quakers, as everyone ought to know, are pacifists. The American Revolution put a number of them in a quandary because they agreed that Great Britain was injuring their rights by denying them a representative in the Parliament which ruled them, but resorting to violence was another matter entirely. Eventually, a group did break away from the main Quaker church to fight for independence. They were promptly "read out of the meeting", the equivalent of being excommunicated, not allowed to worship in the regular meeting houses they had helped finance or to be buried in the church graveyards. Samuel Wetherill was one of the leaders of this group, just as his descendants are the most active today in the surviving historical society. Samuel created quite a furor, demanding to use the Orthodox meeting house and burial grounds. He

was, in his own view, just as much a Quaker as the others since no doctrine is absolutely fixed in that religion, and was freely entitled to speak his mind to persuade others of the rightness of his sincere positions. The main body of Quakers would have none of it, and the Free Quakers were firmly expelled, forced to hold a public subscription and build their own meeting house. Wetherill of course personally knew every one of the members who expelled him, and there may be some truth to his loud, pointed and unchallenged contention that the true division was not between pacifists and fighters, but between Tories and advocates of

Independence. Whatever the truth of these accusations, it does seem in retrospect that the split was fairly divided between wealthy established merchants, and small shopkeepers and artisans. Quite a few now-famous names appear on the rolls of the Free Quakers, like Timothy Matlack (the actual Scribe of the Declaration of Independence document), Biddles, Lippincott, John Bartram, Crispins, Kembles, Trippes, and Wetherills, some of whom had been disowned for other reasons besides their opinions on the war. When the meeting had dwindled down in 1830 to two lone parishioners, one was a Wetherill, and the other was Betsy Ross, herself.

5 Franklin's Funeral

Christ Church Burial Ground   50 N Independence Mall E   Philadelphia, PA
39.9524 -75.1482

Just across Fifth Street is the gravesite of Franklin and his wife in the Christ Church Episcopal graveyard. This is the site every wintry (April 21) morning when the organizations Franklin founded re-enact his funeral march, ending with a speech, a luncheon, and a celebration. It's as close as you might come to remembering Franklin's funeral at age 84, and being gently reminded simultaneously that Franklin was a deist, not a Quaker, not an Anglican. And you do sort of get the

Benjamin Franklin's Grave

idea that Franklin was possibly the most remarkable man who ever lived.

"Philadelphia's silver decade began with the death of Benjamin Franklin, at the age of eighty-four, in 1790. On April 21, some 20,000 people, nearly half the city, lined the route of Franklin's funeral procession from the State House to the Christ Church burying ground. The procession was led by the clergy of the city, and the coffin was carried by six pallbearers: General Thomas Mifflin, president of Pennsylvania; Thomas McKean, chief justice; Samuel Powell, mayor of Philadelphia; Thomas Willing, president of the Bank of North America; David Rittenhouse, professor of astronomy at the College of Philadelphia; and William Bingham, the richest man in America, member of the Pennsylvania Assembly, and soon to be appointed United States senator from the state.

There followed the family and close friends, members of the state Assembly, judges of the State Supreme Court, gentlemen of the bar, printers with their journeymen and apprentices, and members of the Philosophical Society and a host of other associations that Franklin had founded. Doctor Rush sent a lock of Franklin's hair to the Marquis de Lafayette, and when the news reached France, the National Assembly heard a eulogy on the "sage of two worlds" by Mirabeau and sent a letter of sympathy to its sister Republic."

--E. Digby Baltzell, Puritan Boston and Quaker Philadelphia

Those who have experience with arranging state funerals will notice the strong Pennsylvania character of the funeral, and the subdued prominence of national figures, especially those from Virginia, Massachusetts, and New York. Some historians have noticed this anomaly, even surmising that Washington and others were jealous of Franklin's fame. However, the capital was in New York City until August 12, 1790, and did not move to Philadelphia until December 6, 1790. Under the circumstances, it might have been difficult even to be certain the news of his death on April 17 had reached all the national leaders by April 21, let alone orchestrate arrangements of the funeral ceremonies around their uncertain presence at it. Furthermore, he had a long life, from rags to riches, through three wars, after many publications, organizations, discoveries and honors, and some heavy tribulations. But those who have themselves lived 84 years will recognize that it all passes rapidly, and seems like a short dream to the central figure.

6 Down to the Foot of Arch
Arch Street Meeting House   320 Arch Street   Philadelphia, PA
39.9518, -75.1461

Going down Arch Street from Fourth to Third, you can visit the orthodox pacifist Meeting House, its interior largely unpainted and grimly plain -- quite different from the effect of pristine simplicity of the Free Quakers. If you go inside the meetinghouse, a quiet and unprepossessing Quaker will be more than happy to give you a magnificently short and simple explanation of what Quakerism is all about. The cemetery at 4th and Arch set aside as early as 1684 as a burying yard, is known to contain at least 40,000 unmarked graves, many of them from the yellow fever epidemics of the late 18th Century. The meetinghouse was built right on top of them, a fact which may now offend some visitors. But it was in keeping with the ancient tradition of burying the dead in the consecrated ground of a churchyard, more or less as a sanitation measure. It is also in keeping with the tradition of early Quakers not to allow their pictures to be displayed, or even their names to be placed on tombstones.

Crossing Arch Street and heading east, you will pass the building once said to have been the house of Betsy Ross. When the Free Quaker meeting was "laid down", it naturally had to define a purpose for the funds and assets of the inactive church, and one purpose was to care for the poor. According to the records, the first recipient of such charity was Betsy Ross. Anyone who knows anything about Quakers would be pretty sure there was nothing irregular about this. Money designated for indigents would positively be used for indigents. So this little scrap of information is really just a sad little footnote to her personal history.

A lot of Philadelphians don't like Betsy Ross and won't say why. Maybe it shows I am not a true Philadelphian, because I don't know the secret. Maybe it traces to having several husbands of different religions, but you could say the same of lots of other colonial dames, notably Katy Greene. Possibly they don't like Betsy for being the last surviving Free Quaker, and giving herself the remainder of the assets, but she needed it and somebody had to get it. Maybe it was because she was a Quaker and Quakers have a tradition of taking your medicine in silence, regardless of short-term consequences.

In any event, Betsy was a heroine, a Quaker, and an Episcopalian, but she didn't quite pull it off. This is her part of town, her survival, and she did her best in trying times.

In passing down Arch Street, glance at the warehouses on the left, covering the site of what was once a major factory for shoes and uniforms for Union soldiers in the Civil War.

Elfreth's Alley

Behind the buildings on the north side of the street, as the ground slopes sharply toward the river, you can sense the rough, tough waterfront of the Eighteenth Century. Charles Dickens might have felt entirely at home in the Nineteenth Century. Elfreth's Alley runs for one block east and west between Second and Front (1st) Streets. Some of the history of this street is obscure, so some of it is probably synthetic because nothing particularly historic happened there to create detailed records. Elfreth's Alley claims to be the oldest street in America, a claim that can be substantiated back to 1702. The street is filled with little "workers houses", presenting a solid front of buildings on both sides of the cobblestoned street. Most of the houses could vaguely be called "father, son and holy ghost houses", looking as though they consisted of three rooms on top of each other, although in fact most of them are larger. A moment's consideration shows that the street consists of many double houses, with three doorways in front. Each house had a door to the interior, and most of them have a third door opening to a shared tunnel between the two houses, leading to the back yards. These tunnels were called "easements", a term that has migrated from its earlier usage. Although William Penn envisioned large single estates in his "Greene Country Towne", he sold considerable land to people who remained in England as absentee landlords, who soon found that many small houses produced more rent than one or two big ones. Their tiny size is also a reminder that placing taxes disproportionately on land will result in small residential plots, even though a whole continent of vacant land stretches to the Pacific. One of the houses on Elfreth's Alley acts as a museum, with tours; there is an active civic association, and once a year in June there is a street fair.

What we now call Arch Street in Philadelphia was originally named Mulberry Street. Just when that change officially occurred could be argued about, but it took its new name from the fact that a road was cut through the high river bank for easier access to riverside shipping, and an overhead arch connected the two cut ends of Front Street at the point of crossing. A model which is still on display in the Friends Meetinghouse at 4th and Arch depicts this arch in place in 1684. The model displays Thomas Holme, Penn's surveyor, and map-maker, pointing up at the arch. It is a matter of record that Thos. Holme owned the property at the corner of Front and Mulberry, so presumably, the red brick house stranded by the newly excavated street was Holme's. The model depicts that even in 1684, Arch Street led straight to the Schuylkill.

By the time of the Revolution, the Arch Street dock was the commercial heart of town, and the London Coffee House at Front and Market was the thriving center of international gossip. Tradition has it that it was Bradford, the owner of the London Coffee House, who first got the news of the Stamp Act, and started the agitation which famously resulted. The construction of the elevated "Chinese Wall" of the Pennsylvania Railroad along what is now John Kennedy Boulevard, sliced off the Northern side of town as a quiet fashionable place to live for nearly a century. And while the Benjamin Franklin Parkway was

The foot of Arch Street

intended to correct this situation, it actually finished "North of Market" as even inhabitable. Things are gradually improving, particularly with infusions of public money, but it takes a long time for such urban scars to heal.

7 Christ Church

Christ Church   20 N American Street,   Philadelphia PA   39.9527 -75.1422

The north side of Dock Creek (now, Dock Street) was lower than the Society Hill and somewhat swampy. The tendency to flood caused the north side to have smaller and less permanent buildings, and so it became the Colonial waterfront area remaining more commercial, and in parts, shabby, even during the 19th Century. Still further to the north, this was not the case, but the waterfront and food market patch more or less marooned Christ Church, now the single most graceful and elegant Colonial building still standing. This formerly commercial area is now called Old City, with many loft apartments mixed among surviving warehouse outlets, and of course the ethnic restaurants characteristic of such gentrified areas.

Because the land was swampy and the neighborhood congested, Christ Church soon outgrew its backyard burial ground and buried important people under slabs in the walkways and corridors. Visitors who did not come from that sort of religious background had to go several blocks westward to create a "new" burial ground. Most of the famous names from the Revolutionary era, like Benjamin Franklin and four other signers of the Declaration of Independence are found on the tombstones at Fifth and Arch, just across the street from the Free Quaker meeting house, and opposite the Philadelphia Mint.

Christ Church

8 Gazela Primeiro

**Gazela Primeiro   301 South Columbus Blvd   Philadelphia, PA
39.9493 -75.139**

The Portuguese sailing ship Gazela Primeiro is parked at the foot of Market Street, where it can be reached by going down 45 steps of a winding staircase. It would be well to remember that you will have to climb 45 steps to get home if you go that way, and so there are attractions to parking your car on the lot which is right next to the ship. No one seems to be sure why it is the Primeiro, but the best guess is that there were

The Gazela Primeiro

several issues of this model, and this was the first. If you overlook the history of the ship largely carrying a cargo of dead fish in its commercial days, it's a beautiful tall ship, with a cheerful helpful crew.

III Market Street

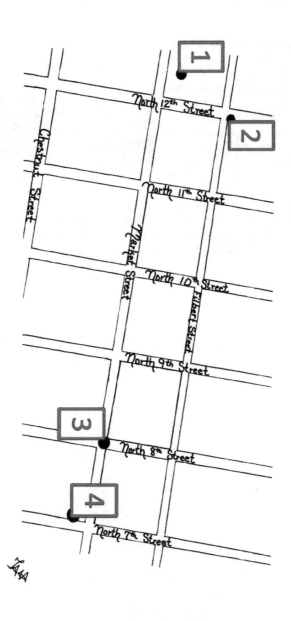

1 Market Street, East

PSFS Building   1200 Market Street   Philadelphia, PA   39.9523 -75.1604

The central keel of the city, Market Street, must be considered in three quite different sections, east and west of City Hall, and west of the Schuylkill River. The street was once called High Street, and the name was slow to change. It will be enough, for now, to consider only the oldest section of fourteen blocks from City Hall to the Delaware River, which is almost a lesson in archeology. Start at Victorian City Hall and face east to Penn's landing on the Delaware.

William Penn had laid out the city plan like a cross, with Market and Broad Streets intersecting at the green central park which now holds the massive building with his statue on top of the tower. It's doubtful that Penn intended his statue to be there, since the early Quakers were so scornful of vainglorious display that they prohibited the naming of streets after persons, declined to have their portraits painted, and the strictest ones would not even consent to their names on their tombstones. The cult of personality in dictatorships like the Soviet Union, Maoist China, and Baathist Iraq more recently illustrate the sort of thing they probably had in mind, and it wasn't just a quaint idea to discourage the portraits of leaders in public places.

2 The Reading Terminal Market

Reading Terminal   51 N 12th St   Philadelphia, PA   39.9530 -75.1595

Market Street has several unifying historical themes, but there is one notable feature that stands by itself. The PSFS building is now the site of a luxury hotel, but it once housed the Philadelphia Savings Fund Society, the oldest savings bank in the country, having been founded in 1816. Setting aside the place of this institution in American finance, and passing quickly by the deplorable end of it with swashbuckling corsairs in three-piece suits, the building itself remains so remarkable that the hotel still displays the PSFS sign on its top. The imagination of the architects was so advanced that a building constructed seventy-five years

The Reading Terminal Market

ago looks as though it might have been completed yesterday. The Smithsonian Institution conducts annual five-day tours of Chicago to look at a skyscraper architecture, but hardly anything on that tour compares with the PSFS building. From time to time, someone digs up old newspaper clippings from the 1930s to show how

Market Street

the PSFS was ridiculed for its odd-looking building, but anyhow this is certainly one example of how the avant-garde got it right.

At the far eastern end of Market Street - right in the middle of the street - once stood a head house, which in this case was called the market terminal building. In those days, street markets were mostly a line of sheds and carts down the middle of a wide street, but usually, there was a substantial masonry building at the head of the market, where money was counted and more easily guarded. An example of a restored head house can today be found at Second and Pine, although that market ("Newmarket") was less for groceries than for upscale shops. The market on Market Street started at the river and worked west with the advancing city limits, making it understandable that buildings which lined that broad avenue gradually converted to shops, and then stores. The grandest of the department stores on Market Street was, of course, John Wanamaker's, all the way at the City Hall end, built on the site of Pennsylvania Railroad's freight terminal (the passenger terminal was on the West side of City Hall). Well into the Twentieth Century, a dozen major department stores and hundreds of specialty stores lined the street. The pinnacle of this process was the corner of Eighth and Market, where four department stores stood, one on each corner, and underneath them three subway systems intersected. The Reading terminal market is Philadelphia's last remnant of this almost medieval shopping concept, although the Italian street markets of South Philadelphia display more authentic chaos. Street markets, followed by shops, overwhelmed by department stores, showed a regular succession up Market Street, and when commerce disappeared, it all turned into a wide avenue from City Hall to River, leaving few colonial traces.

The history of Market Street is the history of the Reading Terminal Market. Farmers and local artisans thronged to sell their wares in sheds put up in the middle of the wide street, traditionally called "shambles" after the similar areas in York, England. Gradually, elegant stores were built on the street, and upscale competitors began to be uncomfortable with the mess and disorder of the shambles down the center of the street. By 1859 the power structure had changed, and the upscale merchants on the sidewalks got a law passed, forbidding shambles. After the expected uproar, the farmers and other shambles merchants got organized, and built a Farmers Market on the north side of 12th and Market. Relative peace and commercial tranquility then prevailed until the Reading Railroad employed power politics and the right of eminent domain to displace the Farmer's Marketplace with a downtown railroad terminal that was an architectural marvel for its time, with the farmers moved to the rear in the Reading Terminal Market, opening in 1893. Bassett's, the ice cream maker, is the only merchant continuously in business there since it opened, but several other vendors are nearly as old. The farmers market persisted in that form for a century until the City built a convention center next door. As a result, the quaint old farmers market became a tourist attraction, with over 90,000 visitors a week. That's fine if you are selling sandwiches and souvenirs, but it crowds out meat and produce and thereby creates a problem. If the tourist attraction gets too popular, it drives out everything which made it a tourist attraction; so rules had to be made and enforced, limiting the number of restaurants, but encouraging Pennsylvania Dutch farmers. Competition and innovation are the lifeblood of commercial real estate, but they are always noisy processes. The history of the street is the history of clamor and jostling, eventually dying out to the point where everyone is regretful and nostalgic for a revival of clamor.

3 The Birthplace of Radio
8th and Market   39.9511 -75.1535

Public radio had its origin in Philadelphia, during the early 1920s. While it is true that KDKA in Pittsburgh can claim to be the oldest radio station around, there are those who say that radio as we now know it had its origins on the rooftops of four department stores clustered at Eighth and Market Streets, busily announcing what was on sale today, and helping draw teeming crowds to that center of dry goods merchandising that many of us are still alive to remember. Strawbridge and Clothier, Lits, and Gimbels were on three corners of the intersection, Snellenbergs was a block up Market, and John Wanamaker's big store was a couple of blocks still further west. In those early days, names like David Sarnoff and Arthur Atwater Kent were the equivalents of Bill Gates and Andy Grove today. Eighty years before the dot-com revolution, the public radio revolution made zillionaires of kids who had been working in cigar stores a year or two earlier, and not merely communication but world culture was forever changed. And in both cases, a sudden drop in the stock market wiped out a lot of them, although a few survived.

It seems you ought to know about "Absorption" which is some kind of electrical phenomenon whereby a lot of microwave and computer traffic wipes out the AM (as opposed to FM) signals in big cities. Because everyone knows that the political right-wing likes the red expanses of the map, while the left or liberal way of thinking is concentrated in cities, hence blue parts of the map, the overall effect is that AM radio is more a phenomenon of the exurbs, rural districts, and highways. And a further consequence is that call-in radio is heavily right-wing in its audience, hence programs, Rush Limbaugh and all that. Because of the innate remorselessness of paid political consultants, it doesn't take long for politicians to recognize that getting rid of absorption would make radio call-in shows more likely to reach urban liberals. We can't have that, or we must have that, depending on the bias of the observer, and hence a sort of radio signal called XM is something we predict will be made forbidden or made mandatory because it makes urban liberal talk radio possible again. The beauty of this cutthroat battle is that it is so obscure that the public won't notice its significance until it happens, and when it does there will be few fingerprints on it.

Commentators will rattle on about shifting tides of opinion when in fact some manipulation of the Federal Communications Act or the local broadcast licensing regulations by people who know very well what they are doing is what has gone on. Heh, heh.

To get back to Philadelphia, the dreary hulks which now stand where the department stores once stood are a reminder that shopping centers, or collections of strip malls, have killed the department store. Two phenomena are at work here. The brand name which gave credibility and comfort to the department stores' reputation is being replaced by national brand names with local franchises, and national advertising rather than regional. That might have been bearable if the department stores had not placed so much unwise reliance on the concept of the "full-service operation". If you try to sell everything in one-stop shopping, as for example selling pianos as well as perfume, some of the things you include are going to be losers. Consequently, the perfumes on which you made your profits will have to become more expensive to pay for the losses on pianos, and eventually, the perfume specialty stores will destroy your profit center, ruining the whole full-service business. This phenomenon, by the way, is beginning to eat away at the economics of hospitals as well.

4 From 9th to the Delaware

Declaration House   700 Market St   Philadelphia, PA   39.9507 -75.1522

At Ninth and Market Philadelphia had once built the White House or at least a mansion for the President of the United States. Secret deals between James Madison and Alexander Hamilton had agreed to move the nation's capital city to Virginia in return for nationalizing the states' Revolutionary War debts, although the circumstance which made it acceptable to the public had been the Yellow Fever epidemic. After that happened, no amount of logic or log-rolling was going to keep the government in this city. Philadelphia vainly built a very elaborate mansion for the President, but President Washington never occupied it, and it was converted to housing the University of Pennsylvania. That University eventually tore it down and replaced it with two somewhat more suitable buildings, meanwhile using the Walnut Street Theater and the Musical Fund Hall, at Ninth and Walnut and Ninth and Locust Streets respectively, for commencement exercises and the like. No one can be completely certain, but it is felt by many that 9th and Market was the general area where Benjamin Franklin had flown his famous kite. This definitely later was the site of Leary's second-hand bookstall, which had the remarkable history that it was once run by a former Philadelphia mayor. Ninth and Market Street is now the site of a Post Office on one corner and a vacant lot on the other. But let the imagination wander a little, and see Ben Franklin, The White House, the University of Pennsylvania, and a former mayor tending a bookstall. Some strange developments grow out of proximity.

There is a restoration of the house, the very house, where Thomas Jefferson wrote the Declaration of Independence at the corner of 7th and Market. Although hidden among the hulks of former department stores, some idea of the former elegance of the area is given by the description of the stir raised by that rich young Virginian arriving in Philadelphia for the Continental Congress with his fancy carriage, a team of horses, and several footmen. All of that colonial splendor has just about vanished in a sea of Victorian commercial architecture, which has in turn become merely a quaint relic. Over the front door of what was Lit's Department Store is still to be seen the mystifying motto, "Hats trimmed free of charge.", and today almost no one knows what that meant. The National Park Service brings colonial history crashing across Market Street, with tourists, a vista of Independence Hall, and lots of federal money. Dare we mention pork barrels?

Notice in particular the corner of Sixth and Market, where the real White House really stood. Robert Morris once had a mansion there, which Benedict Arnold occupied for a while after he was in charge of recovering Philadelphia from the British occupation, and subsequently, both Washington and then John Adams lived there, as Presidents. Unfortunately, a fire took it away around 1830, and the remains were covered with trashy commercial buildings for decades, until the Park Service built a big public restroom there, now torn down. President Washington brought nine black slaves with him, and a memorial now marks the site of their quarters and the house.

Several blocks further east, Market street comes to the brow of what was a cliff overlooking the Delaware, where the earliest settlers lived in temporary caves while they built houses. The trolley lines once made a loop at the bottom of the hill at the river. Prior to that time, horse trolleys had to stop at the top of the hill at Front Street because the hill was too steep for them. At the lower level on the waterfront, there was a terminus for the ferry from New Jersey, bringing commuters, shoppers and farm produce from the Garden State. In time, a subway was built down Market Street, taking a sharp turn at the brow of the hill and heading off toward Frankford and the far northeastern parts of the city. The conjunction of the trolleys, the subway, and the ferries brought throngs of shoppers, mixing with other crowds emerging from three subways at 8th Street, still others from two train stations at 13th Street, and trolleys or buses at every one of the fourteen cross streets. This fourteen block strip was surely a great place to sell dry goods. But today, with the ferry terminal gone and the trolleys vanished, it is mainly a question whether the foot of the hill at the Delaware River is destined to become a museum or an amusement park.

IV Center City

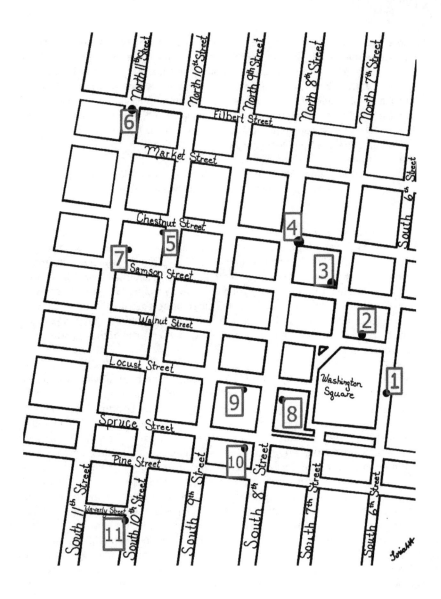

1 Mayors and Limos

Mayor Richardson Dilworth   **225 S 6th Street**   **Philadelphia, PA**
39.9467607 -75.1512669

A number of prominent figures participated in the downtown revival of Philadelphia after the Second World War, with a surprising amount of jealousy among them. Mayor Richardson Dilworth would have to be mentioned in any list of those leaders, but one who was more admired than loved. Aristocratic and flamboyant, he disdained the little hypocritical dissembling so characteristic of politicians. In fact, he didn't see himself as a politician at all, he was a leader. Once Dilworth became convinced that Society Hill's revival was not only desirable but feasible, he moved there. He purchased two houses next to the Athenaeum on Sixth Street, and in spite of the protest of preservationists that those two houses were particularly fine examples of Federalist style on Washington Square, he had them torn down. Furthermore, in spite of the outcries that the house he was building in their place was merely a pseudo-colonial gesture, he constructed a very expensive but extremely comfortable modern house. Those of us who were familiar with the neighborhood were impressed with the courage he displayed in doing this, because the area was just a little dangerous, and almost no one else lived there. You could buy dozens of twenty-room houses in the neighborhood for less than $2000 apiece, and it seemed foolhardy to make such a large personal investment in what might become a stranded gesture. This was described as flaunting his personal wealth because it was not just a fine house, it was possibly going to be a big loss.

Mayor Richardson Dilworth

Dilworth got away with it. He was seen as courageous, and a leader. Others started moving into the area, mostly rehabilitating old mansions. By the time the house was eventually sold by his estate, his conspicuous consumption turned out to be a profitable investment. Smart.

Dilworth had some practical problems. It wouldn't have been smart politics to have a long black limousine pick him up in the poor neighborhood. The only people who do that are undertakers and the Mafia. On the other hand, the driver of a limousine often doubles as a bodyguard, and a bodyguard wouldn't be a bad idea. Those of us who drove down 6th Street every morning at 8:30 gradually noticed what Dilworth did to solve the problem.

Washington Square

Every morning a Yellow Cab could be seen parked outside his door. It always had the same uniformed driver, and on closer inspection, the cab was the cleanest shiny late-model car, painted yellow. It was only six or seven steps from the door of the house to the door of the car, and he was off and gone in a moment.

Other mayors have had quite different styles. Frank Rizzo had his long black car and several like it parked on the sidewalk outside City Hall. His image was that of a poor boy from the neighborhoods who had made it to the top. No matter where he went, Rizzo was leading a parade. Ed Rendell, on the other hand, was playing the role of America's Mayor. His driver would blow the horn, put on the headlights during the day, roar through town, making screeching U-turns right and left. Several times a day he would put on this act, going two blocks from City Hall Annex to the Convention Center, to address an audience of visitors.

Well, mayors and bank presidents are supposed to have limousine service. Anyone else would have to ask whether it was worth all the trouble if instead, you could just catch a cab. Those long cars are surprisingly uncomfortable to ride because the roof is so low you have to crawl on hands and knees to get in a seat. Finding a place to park one of those monsters, or even a wide enough opening next to the curb to let out the back-seat occupant, can be a problem in the center of a city. Even with portable cellular phones, there is a delay after you call for the car when you are ready to leave your appointment. Those who have tried it find that hiring a driver almost always confronts you with a demand to circumvent taxes by paying the driver in unrecorded cash. In South America, where bodyguards are really necessary, the great majority of them flee in terror at the first sign of the underworld. Limos are a pain.

At least in Philadelphia, you can get a fairly clean, fairly new cab with a fairly knowledgeable driver, by simply holding up your hand at any center city street corner. During business hours at least, you can hail a cab in three minutes. That doesn't just happen that way, and the mayor has something to do with it. Cities usually have a Medallion system of cab licensing, and existing cab companies don't want any medallions issued to competitors. In politics, such a situation helps campaign funds considerably. The result is a shortage of cabs, surly drivers, and high prices. Boston is such a town. On the other hand, if medallions are easy to obtain, as they are in Washington DC, the cabs become numerous enough but are shabby dilapidated old vehicles, driven by recent immigrants who don't know the street names. In Philadelphia, we take our good fortune for granted, but we do owe a debt to the city government for managing the supply and demand situation to the point where it mostly would be foolish to have your own car and driver. In this town, every man a king.

As a matter of fact, in Boston, it got so bad that Ned Johnson, the richest man in town (he personally owns the Fidelity Mutual Fund Investment Family) got so enraged that he couldn't even get a cab, that he founded his own cab company. It's a very elegant one, although a little expensive. The Boston Coach Company supplies immaculate and impeccable service for a fee. At first, it was only available to Fidelity executives but now has spread out to anyone willing to pay for it, and flourishes in many cities, plus chartered airplanes if you don't like to wait in security lines at airports. You have to admire Johnson for his golden business touch, but in Philadelphia, we can just use cabs (or rideshare).

2 Curtis: Those 1905 Delivery Trucks

**The Curtis Publishing Company   170 S Independence Mall   Philadelphia, PA
39.9479 -75.1521**

The Curtis Publishing Company was symbolic of Philadelphia in a lot of ways, like the silhouette of Ben Franklin on its masthead, and the deliberately old-fashioned type font of the Post's title above the Norman Rockwell paintings on the cover. Since Curtis stopped publishing magazines, the sturdy old buildings have been converted to modern office space. If you stroll around today, you get a completely misleading impression of the headquarters. To some extent, the present lavish interiors are a response to the Tax Act of 1975, which specifies that the cost of a rehabilitation project must exceed the previous value of the building. And to some extent, the present luxury reflects the deluded ideas of architects and dreamers about the

The Saturday Evening Post

proper lifestyle for captains of industry. To view this rehab, you might suppose:

If you came to visit Curtis in Philadelphia, you would be invited to have lunch in the Down Town Club, and then enter the office complex proper through ornate bronze doors, going down spectacular gleaming interiors past a splendid indoor fountain at the foot of a magnificent huge marble staircase leading who knows where. There would be opulence on all sides, punctuated by an enormous glass mosaic constructed by Louis Comfort Tiffany on a design by Maxfield Parrish. Curtis must have had a wow first floor, designed to impress visitors, and every bit as successfully impressive as anything in New York or Washington DC. In case you didn't get the point, this looming structure did its looming right across the street from Independence Hall. That's the impression you would get today, without a uniformed guide to explain things to you. But as a matter of fact, those high, high ceilings were meant to enclose printing presses, which are notoriously noisy, smelly, and greasy. This was a place of business, a manufacturing plant, not a tourist attraction.

The real symbolism of no-nonsense Philadelphia manufacturing could be seen, every day on the streets. It was those funny old delivery trucks. Everyone in Philadelphia in the morning was familiar with these relics, great lumbering elephants traveling at about five miles an hour or less making grinding noises, slowing up traffic, looking terribly old fashioned. As a matter of fact, they were built in 1905 and were powered by electric batteries. Indestructible, requiring neither maintenance nor fuel except for recharging the batteries overnight. They did their job of transporting paper and magazine product back and forth from Washington Square to the printing plant at Sharon Hill, and their cast iron construction was such that there would probably never be an economic reason to replace them; funny looking, maybe, but they were money in the bank. Philadelphia loved them like a dotty old maiden aunt.

But just imagine the impression they gave the two-martini crowd when they came down from New York for a job interview or for business negotiations. The trucks symbolized the fuddy-duddy city with its fuddy-duddy magazine. Imagine working for a place that would tolerate those things, and what's even more unimaginable, the local yokels actually defended them. The word "cool" was invented to represent everything that these old trucks were not; didn't want to be. Just seeing one of them was enough to make you take your hard-leather heels back to Madison, and Lex, and The Village.

Even after first impressions faded, the true symbolism of those trucks was troublesome to glitterati. The impression the trucks gave to visiting readers of the *Post* was quite in keeping with the magazine's decades-long message of hard work, frugality, and no-nonsense pruning of expenses. A chance visitor to Independence Hall could plink the Liberty Bell and then wander over to that Taj Mahal on the West side of Sixth Street, quite likely thunderstruck by the interior. Out of town readers would, of course, have been even more dumbstruck to see the mansion that the Curtis family lived in on Rittenhouse Square and elsewhere, but all that was at a discreet distance. And then, one of those nice old trucks would come lumbering along. Now that's the spirit. That's the message of crafty old Ben Franklin. Who cares what people think about the outward show, especially those, ugh, people from New York.

Curtis: The Business Plan

Years ago, Cyrus Curtis maintained you could tell who read a magazine by simply looking at the ads. In his view, a magazine was a means for advertisers to reach selected customers; the text was just bait. Hearing this offensive view, I immediately picked up a high-brow glossy magazine, one with rather advanced literary pretensions, and flipped through its ads. They consisted entirely of ads for cigarettes and liquor. In a flash, I got an entirely new insight about that magazine, and maybe an important truth about high-brow readers.

Well before World War I, Cy Curtis had grasped the idea that the real revenue of magazines could be advertising revenue, and the secret of rich revenue was getting potential customers to read the thing. Giving it away free wasn't good enough, you even had to be willing to bribe people to read. The form of bribing people was to provide high-quality reading material at less than cost.

Curtis was a businessman, not an editor. His business plan was to hire good editors and then leave them alone. If circulation numbers increased, that must be a good editor. The *Post* would run eight or more long articles each week, and at least two serials. From the parochial point of view of the weekly magazine, a serial was a teaser, getting the reader interested and eagerly looking forward to the next installment and the next after that. Another way of looking at it, however, was as one very long piece, larger than a magazine article, but not as big as a book. Sometimes, an eight- or ten-piece serial was longer than a small book. This was a wonderful incubator for new authors, and for advance publicity for established authors planning a forthcoming book on the same topic. The big

Cyrus Curtis

magazines paid pretty well for articles, so writing for the Post was a good way for an author to support himself during the long famines between big books.

For many years, the *Post* by that definition had good editors. Its circulation rose into the millions, followed by advertising revenue in the hundreds of millions. It happens that the editorial mix which produced this result was a combination of first-rate fiction and interesting articles built around the theme of glamorous home improvements (for women) or how to make your way as a small business entrepreneur (for men readers). The Post was a how-to manual for a population moving off the farm, into the towns. If it were still published today, it would be called the Bible of the "red" states, the core of the Republican Party. That's what the picture of Ben Franklin on the masthead was meant to signify, not the rather tenuous connection with Franklin's printing press.

In retrospect after the glory days of the *Post* were over, there developed a general agreement that what killed the magazine was television. Free television; with huge expenditures on entertainment programs. Television is a way of funneling gobs of money from national commodity advertising into the pockets of the entertainment industry. In effect, show biz robbed publishing biz and Hollywood robbed the libraries and bookstores. New York and Hollywood robbed Philadelphia and Boston. And the brokers for this transaction were the advertising agencies of Madison Avenue.

That's how it may seem in retrospect, but at the time it was more personal. It seemed as though *Life* and *Look* beat the *Post*, when in fact they just lasted a couple of years longer. It looked as though single-subject magazines beat out general-topic magazines, but notice that *PC Magazine* rose to a thousand fat pages an issue in the 1980s and then fell to fifty skinny ones.

A particular source of bitterness lay in the fact that during the last ten years of its life, the circulation of the *Saturday Evening Post* actually doubled, far higher than it had ever been. If circulation was what advertisers wanted, where were they? The editors of the *Post* felt they had been betrayed by a conspiracy of a handful of two-martini advertising agents in New York, and it must be

Ben Franklin on the Cover

admitted there was a wide cultural divide between Sunset Boulevard and Walnut Street, between Greenwich Village and Bucks County. Between the flower children and the gardening clubs. And even, we have to say it, between the Ds and the Rs.

Working Girls Get the Faints

Curtis Publishing Company once covered a full city block of Philadelphia, from Sixth to Seventh Streets, Walnut to Chestnut. The northern half of this complex was the Public Ledger Building, once housing a failed diversification move into newspaper publishing, and later rented out as commercial office space after the newspaper died. On the top floor of the Ledger Building was the Down Town Club, quite a palatial meeting place for the whole publishing industry which stretched for blocks around. Both Curtis-owned buildings have the same architectural design and together make a massive looming presence next to Independence Hall on one street and Washington Square on the other. To build from Walnut to Chestnut means shutting off Sansom Street in the middle, and that permits the jewelry trade to nestle in a cul de sac on the West side of the publishing complex.

Curtis Building

So Curtis was once a little city within a city, and most of the rest of the town only saw its facade and the crowds of people coming and going through the entrances. To a neighborhood doctor on an emergency call, however, it was almost exclusively inhabited by young women. Kitty Foyles, you might say. I certainly formed that impression after having a medical office two blocks away, getting occasional calls.

So far as I can remember, Curtis had only one medical problem, repeated over and over. An anguished call would come that someone at Curtis was unconscious, come immediately, take the elevator to the third or fourth or fifth floor. At the elevator, the doctor would be met by a somewhat older woman, obviously the den mother of the working girls. Into the ladies' room, we would go, where a young woman was usually sitting on a couch looking sheepish, although occasionally she was still passed out. The key finding was a very slow pulse. She had fainted, she was better, and now what. It was Curtis's policy to send the fainters home after the faint, and I never could see any particular objection to that. For me, there were never any men to be seen, at Curtis. Surely there must have been dozens of writers and editors and advertising people, but somehow they would vanish when one of these fainting things happened. Curtis was nothing but Women when I was there, mostly watching me like a beach full of seagulls, watching a fisherman.

3 Jewelers Row

Safian and Rudolph Jewelers   701 Sansom Street   Philadelphia, PA
39.9488 -75.1527

Since the late nineteenth century, jewelers have clustered on Samson Street mostly between 7th and 8th Streets, and for a block or two in all directions. Sixty years before that, the area had been the site of the most elaborate mansion in America, commissioned by Robert Morris, the Financier of the American Revolution, and built by Charles L'Enfant, the architect of the District of Columbia. About 300 jewelry and jewelry-related businesses are now located in this district, and their outward appearance suggests progressively improving prosperity for them. Some of this reflects the fear of impending inflation (national budget deficits and all that), or a possible decline in the value of the dollar, which amounts to the same thing. During inflationary times, the value of commodities increases; gold and diamonds are the ultimate commodities. In fact, it is widely believed that the price of gold has little to do with jewelry or commodities, and is mainly dependent on the prevailing level of distrust of paper money. For their part, diamonds additionally suit themselves to be hidden in the heel of your shoe if things get tough enough.

Jewelers Row

However, J. E. Caldwell's moved out of the center of the city, and Bailey, Banks and Biddle were sold to people from Texas or somewhere. So the jewelry trade is not universally prosperous, just Samson Street, the Jewelers' Row. Why in the world would 150 little jeweler shops want to cluster together, where people mostly can't tell one from the other, and the products look pretty much alike to anybody who isn't in love and looking for an engagement ring? You would think a competitor next door on either side, and another competitor upstairs, and still others across the street would be something a shrewd merchant would flee, not seek out. Come to think of it, the same thing is true of Antique Row, or the fabric cluster, or a dozen similar clusters in New York City. In New York, it is possible to see a dozen shops next to each other, every one of them selling trombones.

Michael Porter of the Harvard Business School has offered an explanation of the economics of a business cluster as an "Innovation cluster". He feels clustering is one of the important ways businesses hold down costs and improve productivity, by innovating rather than merely stressing efficiency. The innovative, latest and greatest, of any product, commands the highest mark up among similar objects. If you position yourself as producing the latest and greatest, you are going to get a continuously higher markup. Clusters provide vigorous price competition, all right, and that automatically assures that true prices levels are likely to be trustworthy measures of value, even in a shabby little hole-in-the-wall. Making jewelry is not rocket science, but there's enough to it that it helps to be located in an area with an abundant supply of skilled and experienced employees. Philadelphia's diamond cluster is the oldest, and still the second largest, jewelry district in the country.

Having a lot of portable but largely unidentifiable merchandise concentrated in a few blocks creates a special need for police protection. These shops all have safes, and probably most of them have handguns, but there is a great deal of street traffic among shops, carrying valuable gems in their hip pockets. The City provides extra policing out of recognition of the risk, and the local merchants contribute to hiring extra private detectives to lounge around. When basement flooding at the local electric power substation recently caused a blackout, a lot of extra police were immediately dispatched to Jewelers' Row, just in case somebody got the idea that looting might be attractive. And then it is said, just rumored, that some of the merchants who have plenty of goods loaned to their neighbors on consignment employ private protection of an unlicensed sort, in case they have a problem getting their goods back.

It must be pretty boring to sit all day every day in a little shop that makes one or two sales a week, except at special holidays. One jeweler I know has a portable computer under the counter and spends a lot of time day-trading, which is buying stocks in the morning and selling them in the afternoon. Although competition in the district goes well beyond vigorous, there is an active fraternity of jewelers in the area, steering customers to each other when they don't have a requested item themselves, eating lunch at one of the local bistros, exchanging gossip of the trade, carefully observing the traffic up and down the sidewalks. And then, if there is no traffic they can always have their wives, daughters or neighbors sit on a high stool in front of the counter. Trying on jewelry.

4 Fanny Kemble

Pierce Butler Mansion   Eighth and Chestnut Streets   39.9494 -75.1538

Frances Anne Kemble, universally known as Fanny, was just about the most magnificent Philadelphia woman of the Nineteenth Century. She spent much of her time abroad and others claimed her, but she was ours. Coming from a famous English theater family, the niece of Mrs. Siddons and the daughter of the founder of Covent Gardens, she quickly rescued the failing family fortunes by becoming the most striking Shakespearean ingénue of the time. It took very little time for her to know Lord Byron, Thackeray, and various other luminaries of the literary and artistic world of Europe, along with Queen

Fanny Kemble (Sully)

Victoria. One might as well say she knew everybody unless one made the point that everyone knew her.

On a theatrical grand tour of America, she met and married the Philadelphian Pierce Butler, one of the richest bachelors in the nation, heir to huge estates in Georgia. She had plenty of other choices, including the most dashing and romantic devil of the century, Trelawney. That glamorous friend of Byron's had been the one to drag

Percy Shelley's body from the ocean and was surely the greatest heartthrob of the century.

Toward the end of her life, Fanny demonstrated the range of her appeal by totally subjugating the intellectual novelist Henry James, who was 34 years younger than she was. Her portraits by Sully now hang in the Pennsylvania Academy of the Fine Arts and in the Rosenbach Museum. Although Sully was said to have glamorized her a bit, her movie star qualities are evident. But appearance alone could not have mesmerized Henry James, known in literary circles as The Master. She was evidently one of those powerfully self-assured personalities encountered from time to time, who dominates every conversation, fills every room she enters, inspiring admiration rather than jealousy. As a youth, she was enchanting, as a mature woman, magnificent. Henry James described her as having "an incomparable abundance of being."

But this was not just another Cleopatra. Fanny Kemble had two personal achievements of enduring note. Because of health limitations, she went beyond being a Shakespearean actress to inventing a style of a public reading of Shakespeare, taking all the parts herself. She and Dr. Samuel Johnson were the two successive forces transforming Shakespeare's reputation from a quaint playwright of the past into a permanent towering figure of the English language.

Pierce Butler

Her other achievement destroyed her private life. As the wife of the owner of a thousand slaves, she led the attack on slavery before the Civil War. However, the publication of her journals was the last straw in a tumultuous marriage, and Pierce Butler divorced her, taking custody of their daughters, exiling her to England.

Fanny's daughter married Dr. Caspar Wistar, of Grumblethorpe and the grounds of present LaSalle College. Her grandson was Owen Wister, the college roommate of Teddy Roosevelt, later the author of The Virginian. Famous for the phrase "If you say that to me, smile", Owen Wister and his roommate created the fable of the romantic cowboy which still dominates movies and fiction, and, from time to time, the Presidency of the United States.

5 Ball Lightning, Regular Lightning and B. Franklin

Franklin and the Kite   **10th And Chestnut Street**   **Philadelphia, PA**
39.9499 -75.1571

Just about everybody knows that flying a kite in a lightning storm is too dangerous to consider, but hardly anyone appreciates the enormous scientific significance of what happened at 10th and Chestnut Street in 1752. Benjamin Franklin discovered electricity, essentially explained it, displayed its commercial value with lightning rods (but never patented or profited from them), and received the acclaim of the scientific community which would have won him a Nobel Prize if such a thing had existed then. It's true this didn't happen overnight; in many ways, he made the clinching demonstration on the shores of France. Something called the torpedo fish lives there, and Franklin gathered a group of friends holding hands in a circle, demonstrating the electric shock started with the fish and traveled around the circle. Out of this appreciative circle of scientists emerged his rightful reputation as a scientist of the first rank, soon to be the most famous American in the world.

But while millions of people had observed lightning flashes before Franklin connected one to a Leyden jar, those millions were merely content to go inside the house before it started to rain. Millions more still think of the whole episode as a quaintly stupid thing to do, without much scientific or practical value. Dangerous it was indeed, and it knocked young Franklin for a loop at another time and killed several other people who tried to repeat it. But to grasp the scientific feel of it, let's put yourself in Ben's shoes. Let's look at a probably related issue, called ball lightning.

Ball lightning is relatively uncommon, but some chronicler has calculated that about a half of one percent of the world's population has observed it. Counting from the beginning of history, that means a lot of ball lightning. Let's describe it here in the words of two Philadelphians who have actually seen it. One lady describes that she was in her kitchen on the Main Line during a thunderstorm when a big ball of light about the size of a basketball bounced through the door and sat on her stove for at least a full minute. It didn't give off much heat, didn't explode, and didn't smell bad. Although she was badly shaken emotionally, she doesn't remember anything much more. It just went away.

And another Philadelphian was on an airplane in a thunderstorm, back in the days when planes mostly flew below the clouds. A smaller blob of ball lightning appeared from nowhere and rolled down the aisle. Although no one kicked it or did anything else stupid, it created its sensation and then was gone.

A student of this matter says that although ball lightning is comparatively rare, it does occur often enough for extensive credible descriptions to exist. The size is most commonly between that of a pea and a sofa. It is not reported to give off much heat, usually but not invariably appears during a thunderstorm. Ball lightning appears to favor appearances over the ocean, and surfaced submarines seem over-represented among reporters of it. By report, the ball usually disappears with an explosion which does not sound like thunder but leaves behind a sulfurous odor. People who physically tangled with it, have been killed.

Ball Lightning

From the descriptions of crowds of people surrounding some of them, it seems unlikely these phenomena are merely visual hallucinations induced by lightning strikes, as has been suggested by some. And just what it would feel like to be that close to astronomical black holes, has not been reported by any survivors. Black holes are found scattered all over the universe, so there is no reason small ones couldn't appear on the Main Line, but it would seem likely they would be surrounded by a turbulent force field of some kind. Lots of other theories have been propounded, but haven't developed much scientific traction. In short, the state of ignorance about ball lightning today is about as total as about regular lightning bolts in the Eighteenth Century.

So, there you are, a mysterious natural phenomenon which everybody ignores, just waiting for some amateur to get curious enough to devise a simple experiment to explain it. The remarkable thing about the discovery of electricity was not that it was a problem crying out for a solution, or a dangerous dragon needing to be slain. It was just something that everybody noticed, and everyone ignored. What was remarkable about this episode was not the nature of the phenomenon, but the unusual nature of the curiosity of a local printer named Ben.

6 Chinese Canyons

Chinese Wall   11th and Filbert Street   Philadelphia PA   39.9527 -75.1579

Until well after the Second World War, the entire western side of city hall was facing the Pennsylvania Railroad. An enormous rambling smoke-stained Broad Street Station squatted right across the street, and westward behind it to 30th Station stretched -- the Chinese Wall. The railroad tracks were elevated forty feet above street level, resting on top of a very wide brick wall with openings at each cross street allowing traffic to go under the tracks. It was dark, dirty, gloomy and hard to ignore, and the tunnels at each cross street were even darker. They had a tendency to drip water on the sidewalks. Whether these tunnels were a place for crime to take place is not certain, but it looked as though that would be true since an army of panhandlers and stumble-bums reinforced the impression by keeping out of the rain under there.

Consequently, the two streets which paralleled the Chinese Wall (Market Street, West, and Pennsylvania Avenue) were lined with dubious structures housing questionable businesses. After the War, Broad Street Station was torn down, the Chinese Wall of train tracks was removed, and it suddenly became clear that City Hall was now approached by two wide boulevards stretching west, with the handsome classical 30th

Chinese Wall

Street Station framed in the center of one of them, renamed JFK BLVD. High rise buildings were built in large numbers along both sides of the two boulevards in what now are four parallel rows, twelve blocks long. Because these buildings were put up under the gentleman's agreement that City Hall would be the height limit, Philadelphia avoided the dark canyon effect so depressingly present in the Wall Street financial district of New York City. However, the two boulevards do not escape the Marilyn Monroe effect.

Named after a famous movie scene in which that actress had her skirts blown upward in public, the phenomenon usually has to be explained to newcomers. Winds blowing against the tall face of the buildings are blocked and scoot down to the sidewalk along the side of the buildings. When they reach the ground they have no direction to go but up again. Billowing skirts are in reality not particularly noticeable, but these two stretches of the street usually are windy, and in mid-winter, it is bitterly uncomfortable to walk there. Because rentals are high, these new high-rise buildings are too expensive for the small stores and merchants to set up their shops on the first floor, so almost no one is on the street except those in a hurry to get somewhere else. After five o'clock, these commercial centers are totally deserted and quite forbidding. One response has been to go underground.

The Market Street subway goes underground the whole length of Market West, paralleled by a "subway-surface line", which is to say, trolley cars. So it has seemed natural to tunnel pedestrian walkways along with the basement level of Market Street, and little shops have tended to find a place there, although when commuter traffic declines, they turn out the lights and pull down the steel shutters. It's a nice place to duck out of the rain (and wind), but Philadelphia isn't Montreal or Minneapolis, with tons of snow to drive people underground. Long before the 9/11 tragedy, Wall Street's financial district was deserted at night, too, so this is a generic problem of districts, waiting for somebody to suggest a solution. In a way, New York's Park Avenue suggests that when you are moving railroads underground in a city, apartment houses may make for a better new neighborhood than office buildings do.

But such reflections are part of what is called Philadelphia's inferiority complex. Let's face it, the renovation of the Market Street West project is a vast, vast improvement over the mess that was there for a century. It's a success, right?

7 Hospital Elevators

Thomas Jefferson Hospital   111 South 11th Street   Philadelphia, PA
39.9498 -75.1583

Elevators are a problem for any architect in any building because they are expensive in a number of ways. If the building is no more than four stories high, it can manage to have hydraulic elevators, quite sturdy and comparatively inexpensive, but agonizingly slow. Taller buildings need high-speed electric versions, but the elevator itself is not the most expensive part. More important is that every elevator bores a hole in every floor, more elevators bore more holes, and the usable floor space on each floor is reduced. Further, the mechanical stress is mostly on the doors on each floor, which open and close hundreds of times each day, rather than the lifting engine of the cab. Elevators that seem to be breaking down continually, are mostly in need of new doors. In building a hospital, the architect confers closely with the administrator until the place is built and then the architect leaves. The administrator may leave soon afterward, too, because the hospital personnel who use the new building soon discover that when pennies were pinched, the result was fewer elevators. There's no right answer to this problem; nobody is ever satisfied.

The surgeons long ago learned to cope with the problem by beginning their day before everyone else arrives. If the elevator comes immediately after being summoned and skips all intervening floors to the surgeon's destination, it can save at least a half-hour of his time to make rounds at 5 AM. Multiply that imposed delay on hundreds or thousands of hospital employees, and it is possible to conjecture that hospital employees generally only work a 7-hour day, and spend the 8th hour waiting for the elevator. Whatever the actual calculation, it is a cost seldom actually calculated into the equation of constraining the installation of elevators because of cost considerations. Unwelcome crowding is a social cost, too. Bereaved relatives coming down in the elevator must meet students of various disciplines going up the elevator holding coffee cups and chattering. And all ranks and conditions must crowd into the unyielding back of the elevator when the door opens to confront a hospital bed with an afflicted patient aboard, surrounded by a team of attendants in pajamas, holding up bottles and tubes. Attempts are usually made to assign separate elevators for patients and/or equipment, but the attendants soon find out about elevators that save time, flocking to them in spite of signs, threats, administrative letters of admonishment, and dreary staff meetings. It is easy to identify new staff; they are the people who take elevators down. Everyone else learns to go to the top floor and walk down the stairwells. Outta my way!

So, hospital elevators evoke recollections. Mine includes the many times I rode up beside a sullen teenager named Harry Gold, who was going to the chemistry department of the old Philadelphia General Hospital. If we ever exchanged a word I don't remember it, so I have to regret that I missed out on striking up an acquaintance with a real, convicted Soviet spy, the one who passed hydrogen bomb secrets to those Rosenbergs who went to the electric chair protesting their innocence. Something to tell my grandchildren I guess.

On another occasion, Dr. John Y. Templeton was standing impatiently for an elevator at Jefferson Hospital. John was a brilliant surgeon from Virginia, one of the inventors of the heart-lung machine, and also one of the quickest, most irreverent wits in Medicine. The door of the elevator opened, to reveal a completely crowded crowd of assorted folk, with a Doctor Zimskind standing in the front. Templeton's southern accent boomed out, "Going down?" "Going dow-un?" Lost in thought, Zimskind had trouble finding his voice and simply poked his index finger skyward two or three times. To which, Templeton shouted out, "The same to you, Dr. Zimskind. But are you going dow-un?"

And, much earlier when I was a resident wearing a long white coat, accompanied by a jolly sort named Carroll who wore the same, we got on an elevator which was empty except for a surgical resident wearing his particular uniform of a short white coat covering his green surgical pajamas. We had gossiped earlier about this surgeon, who had returned for training after some harrowing experiences in the Normandy beachhead. He was a mean, silent, sort, but Carroll was an irrepressible joker. "Well," sez Carroll, "I hear you carry a gun around with you. Do you carry it into the operating room?" To this, the surgical resident opened his jacket and, so help me, pulled out a pistol from his belt. "When I was in Germany," he murmured, "I killed lots of better men than you are." Under the circumstances, there was little more to be said, and we stopped breathing just to be sure. Those Jefferson elevators are awfully slow to reach the next floor.

And finally, there was Herman, who ran the hydraulic elevator in the original old building of the Pennsylvania Hospital. Herman the German we called him, although his accent was probably Central European. This elevator was an antique, with a big iron steering wheel that Herman turned to release the oil or water or whatever pumped the excruciatingly slow cage up two floors. There, for our contemplation, was America's first building of the first hospital, with the first operating room on the top floor. It has long been replaced with a fancy new self-service elevator. But so have the patients been replaced; one hundred sixty patient beds entirely replaced by administrators.

Eakins and Doctors

Thomas Eakins is known to have painted the portraits of eighteen Philadelphia physicians. Several of these portraits have been highly praised and richly appraised, seen in the art world as part of a larger depiction of Philadelphia itself in the days of its Nineteenth-century eminence. That's quite different from its colonial eminence, with George Washington, Ben Franklin, the Declaration and all that. And of course entirely different from its present overshadowed status, compared with that overpriced Disneyland eighty miles to the North. Eakins depicted the rowers on the Schuylkill, and the respectable folks of the professions, every scene reeking with Victorian reminders. It's a little hard to imagine any big-city mayor of the present century in that

The Gross Clinic

environment. Indeed, it is hard to imagine most contemporary Americans in a Victorian environment -- except in Philadelphia, Boston, and perhaps Baltimore. So, Mayor Street can be forgiven for not knowing exactly what stance to take and was not alone in that condition.

S. Weir Mitchell, for example, became known as the father of neurology as a result of his studies and descriptions of wartime nerve injuries. But the repair of injuries is a surgical art, and many novel procedures were invented and even perfected, many textbooks were written. Amphitheaters were constructed around the operating tables, for students and medical visitors to watch the famous masters at work.

In The Gross Clinic, we see the flamboyant surgeon in the pit of his amphitheater at Jefferson Hospital, in the background we see anesthesia being administered. Up until the invention of anesthesia, the most prized quality in a surgeon was speed. With whiskey for the patient and several attendants to hold him down, the surgeon had one or two minutes to do his job; no patient could stand much more than that. After the introduction of anesthesia, it might overwhelm newcomers to observe leisurely nonchalance, but in truth, the patient felt nothing, so the surgeon could safely pause and lecture to his nauseated admirers.

What made an operation dangerous was not its duration, but the subsequent complications of wound infection. By 1876, Eakins could have had no idea that Pasteur and Lister were going to address that issue in four or five years, making operations safe as well as painless. But his depiction of a surgeon with bloody bare hands, standing in Victorian formal street clothes, gives the most dramatic possible emphasis in the painting to the two most important scientific advances of the century. Modern medical students spend days or weeks learning the ceremonial of the five-minute scrubbing of hands with a stiff and somewhat painful brush, the elaborate robing of the high priest in a sterile gown by a nurse attendant, hands held high. The rubber gloves, the mystery of a face mask and cap. In some schools, the drill is to cover the hands of a neophyte with charcoal dust, blindfold him, and insist that he scrub off every speck of dirt that

Operating amphitheater

he cannot see before he is admitted to the operating theater for the first time. If he brushes some object in passing, he is banished to the scrub room to start over. So the Gross Clinic has an impact on everyone who sees the surgeon in street clothes, but it is trivial compared with the impact that painting has on every medical student who has been forced to learn the stern modern ritual. For at least fifty years, that painting hung on the wall facing the main entrance to the medical school, where every student had to pass it every day. To every graduate, the lack of clean surgical technique by the famous man was a wrenching sermon on every doctor's risk of trying his utmost to do his best but doing the wrong thing.

That painting, hanging quite high, was rather cleverly displayed to the public through a large window above the door. With clever lighting, every layman who walked along busy Walnut Street could see it, too, and it became a part of Philadelphia. That was a feature the medical community barely noticed, but it was probably the main reason for public uproar when a billionaire heiress offered the school $68 million to take the painting to Arkansas. The painting was not just an icon for the medical profession, it had become a central part of Philadelphia. Philadelphia wanted to keep that painting for a variety of reasons, and one of the main ones was probably a sense of shame that we were so poor we had to sell our family heirlooms to hill-billies.

The doctors didn't pay much attention to that. They were mad, plenty mad, that a Philadelphia board of trustees would appoint a president from elsewhere who would give any consideration at all to such an impertinent offer.

8 Cushman Club for Lonesome Actresses

Morris House Hotel   225 South 8th Street   Philadelphia, PA
39.9472 -75.1544

Lydia Ellicott Morris was married to another member of the Quaker colonial aristocracy, George Spencer Morris; both of them were active members of many organizations, including the Philadelphia Savings Fund Society, Friends Hospital, and several of the clubs on Camac Street. Their home for many years was located at 225 South Eighth Street. George Morris was a senior partner of Morris and Erskine, Architects. One day, Lydia was riding on a trolley car.

On the trolley, she overheard two young actresses fretting over the problem that traveling actresses were forced to live in hotels and boarding houses along with traveling salesmen. This circumstance forced them to experience much-unwanted attention and made being an actress a difficult occupation for respectable women. Lydia promptly got off the trolley and formed an organization raising funds to create in 1907 a boarding home to provide safe, respectable, inexpensive lodgings for actresses in traveling shows, playing in Philadelphia. It was named after Charlotte Cushman, the first internationally famous American actress, and located at 1010 Spruce Street. Charlotte Cushman had no connection with the club, but her fame can be appreciated from the fact that in 1874 after her final performance, 15,000 people were reported to have serenaded her outside of New York's Fifth Avenue Hotel. The Ninth Regimental Band played, while fireworks illuminated Madison Square. Ms. Cushman died in 1876.

Another major donor to the club was a Mr. Peterson, otherwise unidentified, who gave them $50,000. Further funds were raised at five annual teas. In 1925, Philadelphia was a major center for the film industry, and much of Charlotte

Charlotte Cushman

Cushman Club's early history relates to movie associations. Much of the early endowment was unfortunately lost in the 1929 stock market crash, however, and the club continued only a subdued presence for a number of years. By 1999, it was clear that the original purpose was not really needed, and the club was disbanded. Its possessions, including the last of several clubhouses, the collections, and a rather valuable library, were sold off, and most of its other belongings were donated to the Franklin Inn Club. The club began a new existence as the Charlotte Cushman Foundation, first endowing the Charlotte Cushman Board Room and Exhibit, at the University of the Arts, and then in 2001 began making grants to local nonprofit theatre groups. At present, the Foundation dispenses an income of about $45,000 yearly among 43 non-profit theatrical societies which continue in Philadelphia. Present dominant activity is to select the Leading Actress in a Play, as part of the annual Barrymore Awards. The rise of the club reflected the vibrant downtown social life of Philadelphia at a time when almost all Philadelphians were residents of the center city. And its decline parallels the loss of civic-minded center city residents following the spread of household automobiles and the continuing wreckage of traditional civic feelings following the 1929 crash.

9 Musical Fund Hall

Musical Fund Hall   808 Locust Street   Philadelphia, PA   39.9469 -75.1551

At the corner of 808 Locust stands a condominium building with a colorful history. It was originally the First Presbyterian Church, and then in 1820 the famous architect William Strickland converted it into the largest musical auditorium in the City. For several years, a group of music lovers had been meeting to discuss the problem of aging and retired musicians, most of them impoverished. The idea arose of giving several benefit performances each year to raise money for retired musicians, and the idea was enlarged to create a Musical Fund Society to put on regular concert series. Since it was by far the largest public auditorium, it also served for graduations, speeches, conventions.

It thus came about that in 1856 the Republican Party held its first national convention there, nominating for President John C. Fremont, the famous explorer of the West. The Republicans had two main components, the advocates of the abolition of slavery, and the residual of the Whig Party, which had come apart. The Whigs were mainly concerned with using government effort to promote the economy, building canals and roads, and similar ideas for public benefit. Abraham Lincoln had been a fervent Whig.

William Strickland

As a musical society, the Musical Fund was quite instrumental in persuading this Quaker City that music could be used for purposes other than religious incantations and frivolous entertainments. And it was useful in bringing the new instruments and musical concepts from Europe to the New World. Louis Madeira has written an interesting history of the early musical significance of the Musical Fund. When the Academy of Music opened in 1856, the old hall on Locust Street became a relic of the past. It had assets, however, and the organization continues to function as a granting agency for musical production and development in the Philadelphia area, even though it is itself no longer in the business of musical production.

And then the third strain of history in this old place is the development of Musical Unions. This is natural enough, in view of the original purpose of helping indigent musicians. But unfortunately, several competing unions appeared, most of them on Locust Street, and the dissention was bitter and continuing. In 1871 Philadelphia was the scene of the creation of the National Musical Association, and although the local 77 became a part of the national movement, it was stormy. Competitive musical unions had a history of calling the police to shut down speakeasies run as private clubs by their competitors. During the Depression of the 1930s, there were many accusations of Communist infiltration and counter-accusations that Joseph Petrillo, the national president, was a Nazi. An underlying theme among musicians was that foreign immigrants were willing to work for less than the standard

Musical Fund Hall

wage, and hence many of the coercive features of the union were aimed at forcing immigrant musicians to become members and to refuse to work for substandard pay.

Some idea of the bitterness in the situation can be gained from the strike against the Philadelphia Orchestra in 1956. Ten years later, only one in ten members of the union was employed.

10 The First and Oldest Hospital in America
Pennsylvania Hospital   800 Pine Street   Philadelphia, PA
39.9444 -75.1558

Pennsylvania Hospital

There is a painting of the region around 8th and Spruce Streets in the 1750s, depicting a pasture, with cows, and three or four buildings between 8th and 13th Streets. When the Pennsylvania Hospital moved there in 1755 from its temporary location in a house located a block from Independence Hall, there were complaints that it was now located so far out in the woods that it was difficult and dangerous to go there. Still another description of the area is evoked by the provision which the Penn family placed in the deed of gift of the land, strictly forbidding the use of the land as a tannery. Tanneries have always been notorious for giving off noxious odors, so most people wanted them to be somewhere else, anywhere else. In any event, the main activity of Penn's "green country town" at that time was concentrated closer to the Delaware River, and the nation's first hospital was definitely placed in the outskirts. Two blocks further West the almshouse was already in place, but not much else. We are told that Benjamin Franklin had flown his Famous Kite at 10th and Chestnut, using a barn there to store his materials. It might be recalled that the population of Philadelphia, although the second-largest English-speaking city in the world, was less than forty thousand inhabitants at the time of the Revolution, and in 1751 was even smaller.

In any event, the first and oldest hospital in America was built on 8th Street between Spruce and Pine, and the Eighteenth Century buildings on Pine Street still present a breathtaking view at any season, but particularly in May when the azaleas are in bloom, and fragrance from the flowering magnolias fills the evening atmosphere for blocks around. Although some people today mistake the Pennsylvania Hospital for a state hospital, it was founded in the reign of George II, decades before there was such a thing as the State of Pennsylvania. The Cornerstone was laid by Benjamin Franklin, with full Masonic rites. Most doctors regard a hospital as a mere workshop, but the affection with which many Pennsylvania physicians regarded their special hospital is indicated by the number who have requested that their ashes be buried in the garden.

For two hundred years, beginning with the first American resident physician Jacob Ehrenzeller, the interns and residents were paid no salary, so they had to live on the grounds. An Intern was just that, interned within the four walls for at least two years. Because the resident physicians had no money, they stayed in the hospital at night and on weekends, playing cards and swapping stories. The hospital was home for them, as it was for the student nurses, likewise unpaid but more strictly confined and supervised. This penury seemed acceptable because the patients were mostly charity ward patients, otherwise unable to pay for their own care. Ehrenzeller finished his medical apprenticeship and went to practice for many decades in the farm country of Chester County, but gradually upper-class Philadelphia moved from 4th Street westward to and beyond the hospital, and two of the richest men in American history, Morris and Biddle, had houses within a block of the hospital, although Morris never lived in his house, having more pressing matters in debtor's prison. Therefore, later resident physicians at the hospital had the potential of setting up a private practice in the area and becoming society doctors as well as academically prominent ones. Being a charity hospital in a rich neighborhood created the potential for volunteer work by the town aristocrats and large bequests for charity. The British housed their wounded in the hospital during the Revolutionary War and shot deserters against the red brick wall of the small cemetery to the north. A century later, there were a couple of dozen rooms for private patients in the hospital for the convenience of the doctors and the neighbors, but everyone else was a charity patient. And a century after that, the hospital still did not have an accounting department to collect bills and tended to regard people who asked for a bill as a nuisance.

Benjamin Franklin is regarded as the Founder of the hospital, and his autobiography famously describes how he fast-talked the legislature into matching the donations of the public, not mentioning to them that he had already collected enough promises to see the project through. This seems in character; Franklin's biographer Edmond Morgan summed up, "Franklin doesn't tell us everything, but what he does tell us, is straight." The idea for the hospital was that of Dr. Thomas Bond, whose house is now a bed and breakfast on Second Street, but it was characteristic of Franklin to be the secretary of the first board of managers of the hospital. In Quaker tradition, the clerk of a meeting is the person who really runs the show. It thus comes about that the minutes of the founding board were recorded in Franklin's own handwriting, among them the purpose of the institution, which is to care for the Sick Poor, and if there is room, for Those Who can pay. This tradition and this method of operation continued until the advent in 1965 of Medicare when charity care was displaced by concepts that the nation had decided were better. The Pennsylvania Hospital was not only the first hospital, but for many decades it was the only hospital in America. Its traditions, sometimes quaint and sometimes glorious, cast a long shadow on American medicine.

Lin

I find in retirement that most of my colleagues are now willing to tell stories of the "old days" which they were unwilling to tell at the time. One such story recently surfaced. It concerned Lindley Reagan. Lin was a member of an old Quaker family, surprising everybody during the Second World War by volunteering as a junior physician in the Navy. He was assigned to a marine regiment in the Pacific Theater and went through some of the most murderous fighting on Iwo Jima and Guadalcanal. Our grapevine reported that the enlisted Marines in his outfit absolutely worshipped him, and I easily believe there was a lot of quiet heroism behind that gossip. He told me he had decided to become an internist while in the Pacific, but somehow only a surgical residency was available when the War was over, so he took it. He was probably the best internist on the staff, and it showed in his conduct of surgery, where it sometimes matters more what you decide to cut than what you cut. He always looked exhausted, but never hesitated to drive himself another hour when the situation demanded it. One day, he had to

Lindley B. Reagan, MD
1918-1995

excuse himself from an operation, an almost unheard-of event, and testing his own urine, found it loaded with sugar. So, the soft-spoken Quaker internist who was primarily doing surgery had to add the burden of insulin injections to his load. If he ever complained about that or any other thing, no one could remember hearing it.

My old friend, like the rest of us, had to spend a year as a surgical intern during the two-year rotating internship; he hated surgery and didn't mind telling the world. At the moment in question, he was the assistant at some neck surgery, with Lin performing the actual surgery. He was told to take a long pair of scissors and cut off the excess strands of sutures after Lin tied the knots; that was known as trimming the ligatures. They were working deep in the crevices of the patient's neck. Lin held up the loose ends of the knot and ordered, "Cut". My friend inserted the long scissors into the hole and snipped -- accidentally cutting right through the jugular vein.

As would be expected, a fountain of blood came up out of the hole, and Lin stopped it by putting his thumb on the cut ends of the vein. "Well," said Lin, "I guess we'll have to fix that." And did.

With tears in his eyes, my octogenarian friend cried out to the startled clubroom. "God bless you. God bless you, Lin."

Perhaps the point isn't clear to those who didn't go through the process, so let's be more explicit. Both my friend and I worshipped Lin, as a person, a teacher, and a surgeon. He was the perfect agent for his patients, without the tiniest trace of conflict of interest, income-maximizing or whatnot. He was as technically skillful as it is useful to be, but he was the thinking man's surgeon as well as the utterly faithful servant of the best interests of the humblest patient. He was, in the opinion of his closest professional associates, the best surgeon in the world. In need of surgery ourselves, all of us would have flown the Atlantic to have him operate on us. For reasons of his own, he was to spend the forty years of his professional life in a small country town with a small hospital, scarcely a famous surgeon but a beloved one to his community. Over the past sixty years, I have had a number of opportunities to know many surgeons who would be in contention for the title of the best surgeon in the world. Some have written books, some have struggled successfully upward through vicious competition, some of them would be called "Rainmakers" if the research world followed the pattern of lawyers and architects. One or two have won Nobel Prizes for surgical innovations, but that's different from being the best surgeon around. The best surgeon in the world was Lin, faithfully plying his trade in a little town that could not possibly know how lucky they were.

Keeping Lunaticks off the Streets
One of the functions for America's first hospital was proposed by Benjamin Franklin and Thomas Bond to be the humane treatment of Lunaticks, who would otherwise

be wandering the streets of Philadelphia. Nearly three hundred years later, it is possible to look back on the topic and see an uncertain history.

Essentially, the pendulum swings between a humane goal of bringing these poor victims inside, out of the weather, on the one hand, and getting them out of those snake pits so they can enjoy the benefits of being part of the community, on the other. Every couple of decades, the disadvantages of one approach attract attention, and public opinion demands the opposite. Even the era of effective treatment, which began with Thorazine in 1960, has not relieved the central difficulty, because these people often or usually rebel and stop taking their pills; it is not clear that forcing them to take pills is any greater denial of liberty than forcing them to live in a small room. In 2006 and for the prior five years, a grizzly, disheveled old man who talks to himself pulled old cardboard around him and slept on the steam grate across the street from the Pennsylvania Hospital. Occasionally, someone summons a passing patrol car which sometimes does and sometimes does not, haul him away.

In March 1765, a remarkably neat and tidy sailor was admitted to the Hospital as insane, and was kept among the other insane patients in the basement rooms. He wandered out, however, and was chased around until he took refuge in the glass cupola that still adorns the roof of the East wing, facing Eighth Street. It was obvious that he would soon have to come down to eat, but the Quakers who ran the hospital at that time would have none of it; they didn't starve their patients. So a mattress was passed up to him, and regular meals. Nothing much could be done about the cold, which must have been pretty severe, but the patient was allowed to remain in the cupola until 1774 when he died. Nine years of room service in the cupola.

In 1790, the wife of Stephen Girard, the richest man in America, became insane and was admitted. The hospital felt she could go home in a couple of months, but her husband insisted that she stay. She died there, twenty-five years later. At today's rates, comparatively few people could afford that approach, even if the ethical issues could be settled. However, for over a century a great many people were essentially domiciled in the chronic psychiatric unit at Market and 44th Streets.

For fifty years after that, a subacute psychiatric unit was maintained at 49th and Market, but ultimately the Federal Government found a smokescreen of confusion, sufficient to hide the awkward political backlash. One by one, the huge human warehouses at Byberry, Philadelphia General Hospital, Bellevue in New York and similar places, went out of business. The public wouldn't stand for "snake pits", even Medicare couldn't afford to put millions of insane people into luxury hotels like 49th and Market. And even though there were a few hundred or even a few thousand families who could afford to pay for humane domiciliary care, they had to be sacrificed. A government medical system essentially runs as a political pork barrel, cannot afford to permit the continued existence of a visible rebuke by a two-class system.

So, now we're giving these people the benefit of integration into community life, right?
We're saving money, that's what we are really doing.

Dr. Cadwalader's Hat

The early Quakers disapproved of having their pictures painted, even refusing to have their names on their tombstones. Consequently, relatively few portraits of early Quakers can be found, and it might, therefore, seem surprising to see a picture of Dr. Thomas Cadwalader hanging on the wall at the Pennsylvania Hospital. A plaque relates that it was donated by a descendant in 1895. Another descendant recently explained that the branch of the family which continued to be Quaker spells the name, Cadwallader. Dr. Cadwalader of the painting, famous for presiding over Philadelphia's uproar about the Tea Act, was then selected to hear out the tea rioters because of his reputation for fairness and remains famous even today for his unvarying courtesy.

Dr. Thomas Cadwalader

In one of the editions of *Some Account of the Pennsylvania Hospital*, I believe the one by Morton, there is a story about him. It seems there was a sailor in a bar on Eighth Street, who announced to the assemblage that he was going to go out the swinging doors of the taproom and shoot the first man he met. So out he went, and

Pennsylvania Hospital

the first man he met was Dr. Cadwalader. The kindly old gentleman smiled, took off his hat, and said, "Good Morning, Sir". And so, as the story goes, the sailor proceeded to shoot the second man he met. A more precise rendition of this story comes down in the Cadwalader family that the event in the story really took place in Center Square, where City Hall now stands, but which in colonial times was a favored place for hunting. A man named

Brulumann was walking in the park with a gun, which Dr. Cadwalader took as a sign of a hunter. In fact, Brulumann was despondent and had decided to kill himself, but lacking the courage to do so, had decided to kill the next man he met and then be hanged for murder. Dr. Cadwalader's courteous greeting, doffing his hat and all, befuddled Brulumann who went into Center House Tavern and killed someone else; he was indeed hanged for the deed.

I was standing at the foot of the staircase of the Pennsylvania Hospital, chatting to a young woman who from her tailored suit was obviously an administrator. I pointed out the Amity Button, and told her its story (supposedly installed to symbolize that the builder had been paid, symbolizing amity between a willing buyer and a willing seller), along with the story of Jack Gallagher, whom I knew well, bouncing an empty beer keg all the way down to the Great Court from the top floor in the 1930s, which was then being used as housing for the resident physicians. Since the young woman administrator was obviously beginning to regard me like the Ancient Mariner, I thought one last story about courtesy was in order. So I told her about Dr. Cadwalader and the shooting.

"Well," she said, "The moral of that story obviously is that you should always wear a hat." There was no point in further conversation, so I left.

11 Henry George, Single Tax
Birthplace of Henry George   413 South 10th Street   Philadelphia, PA
39.9443 -75.1586

Philadelphia was the birthplace of Henry George at 413 South 10th Street between

Henry George

Pine and Lombard, in 1839. The house has been restored to its 1839 condition and serves as the Philadelphia extension of the Henry George School for Social Studies, where you can take a course or two on the economic theories of Henry George, especially the Single Tax. If you do so, you can join the rest of us in pondering whether Henry George was a genius or a nut; he certainly combined some elements of both. Leo Tolstoy no less felt there was a conspiracy to keep people from knowing about the theories of Henry George, saying, "People do not argue with the teaching of George, they simply do not know it." In 1879 Henry George published a book, "Progress and Poverty," which made him so famous he became a candidate for Mayor of New York City. Although he lost the election, he outpolled the third candidate, Theodore Roosevelt. The underlying thesis of his book would probably not find much approval among

contemporary economists, who would likely say he was fooled by a cyclic increase in the value of land as an asset class. What he said was there was a remorseless trend of land to increase in value, while the proportion of wealth represented by labor and capital steadily diminished. Nevertheless, it can still be argued that: proceeding from the wrong premise about the causes of poverty, he might have propounded an attractive cure -- the single tax. Henry George asserted that we should stop taxing buildings ("improvements") and place all municipal taxes on land.

There could be something to this. It is uncomfortably true that your taxes go up whenever you build a new building or substantially renovate an old one. The increased taxation of improvements is a disincentive to the building, renovating and improving a property. Placing taxes on the underlying land, by contrast, would create a positive incentive to build something and put the land to use.

Take a look at Arden, Delaware, which is a nearby town to try the Henry George approach. Arden is a little country suburb of Wilmington which became a summer art colony, with theater groups, especially favoring Shakespeare. Arden, which is Shakespeare-speak (in As You Like It) for the Ardennes Forest in France, applied the Henry George rules to tax the land, not the summer houses of the area. So, go take a look there at the result. More and more houses

Henry George House

crowded closer and closer together -- on the same land. There's plenty of open land over the next hill where Arden supporters could drive or even walk in ten minutes, so the Henry George system is quite effective all right. But the effect is not entirely what was intended.

V On and Off Broad Street

1 The Franklin Inn Club

205 S Camac St   Philadelphia, PA   39.9486 -75.1614

Camac Street is a little alley running parallel to 12th and 13th Streets, and in their day the little houses there have had some pretty colorful occupants. The three blocks between Walnut and Pine Streets became known as the street of clubs, although during Prohibition they had related activities, and before that housed other adventuresome occupations. In a sense, this section of Camac Street is in the heart of the theater district, with the Forrest and Walnut Theaters around the corner on Walnut Street, and several other theaters plus the Academy of Music nearby on Broad Street. On the corner of Camac and Locust was once the Princeton Club, now an elegant French Restaurant, and just across Locust Street from it was once the Celebrity Club. The Celebrity club was once owned by the famous dancer Lillian Reis, about whom much has been written in a circumspect tone because she once successfully sued the Saturday Evening Post for a million dollars for defaming her good name.

The Franklin Inn

Camac between Locust and Walnut is paved with wooden blocks instead of cobblestones because horses' hooves make less noise that way. The unpleasant fact of this usage is that horses tend to wet down the street, and in hot weather you know they have been there. Along this section of a narrow street, where you can hardly notice it until you are right in front, is the Franklin Inn. The famous architect William Washburn has inspected the basement and bearing walls, and reports that the present Inn building is really a collection of several -- no more than six -- buildings. Inside, it looks like an 18th Century coffee house; most members would be pleased to hear the remark that it looks like Dr. Samuel Johnson's famous conversational club in London. The walls are covered with pictures of famous former members, a great many of them cartoon caricatures by other members.

There are also hundreds or even thousands of books in glass bookcases. This is a literary society, over a century old, and its membership committee used to require a prospective member to offer one of his books for inspection, and now merely urges donations of books by the author-members. Since almost any Philadelphia writer of any stature was a member of this club, its library represents a collection of just about everything Philadelphia produced during the 20th Century. Ross & Perry, Publishers has brought out a book containing the entire catalog produced by David Holmes, bound in Ben Franklin's personal colors, which happen to be gold and maroon, just like the club tie.

The club was founded by S. Weir Mitchell, who lived and practiced medicine nearby. Mitchell had a famous feud with Jefferson Medical College two blocks away, and that probably accounts for his writing a rule that books on medical topics were not acceptable offerings from a prospective member of the club. So there.

The club has daily lunch, with an argument, at long tables, and weekly round table discussions with an invited speaker. Once a month there is an evening speaker at a club dinner, with the rule that the speaker must be a member of the club. Once a year, on Benjamin Franklin's birthday, the club holds an annual meeting and formal dinner. At that dinner, the custom has been for members to give toasts to three people, all doctors, including Dr. Franklin.

A Toast to Doctor Franklin
Benjamin Franklin's formal education ended with the second grade, but he must now be acknowledged as one of the most erudite men of his age. He liked to be called Doctor Franklin, although he had no medical training. He was given an honorary degree of Master of Arts by Harvard and Yale, and honorary doctorates by St. Andrew and Oxford. It is unfortunate that in our day, an honorary degree has degraded to something colleges give to wealthy alumni, or visiting politicians, or some celebrity who will fill the seats at an otherwise boring commencement ceremony. In Franklin's day, an honorary degree was awarded for significant achievements. It was far more prestigious than an earned degree, which merely signified adequate preparation for potential later achievement.

And then, there is another subtlety of academic jostling. Physicians generally want to be addressed as Doctor, as a way of emphasizing that theirs is the older of the two learned professions. A good many PhDs respond by rejecting the title, as a way of sniffing they have no need to be impostors. In England, moreover, surgeons deliberately renounce the title, for reasons they will have to explain themselves. Franklin turned this credential foolishness on its head. He invented the rubber catheter. He founded the first hospital in the country, the Pennsylvania Hospital, and he donated the books for it to create the first medical library in the country. Until the Civil war, that particular library was the largest medical library in America. Franklin wrote extensively about gout, the causes of lead poisoning and the origins of the common cold. It would be hard to find anyone with either an M.D. degree or a Ph.D. degree, then or now, who displayed such impressive scientific medical credentials, without earning -- any credentials at all.

2 Mary Cassatt

The Cassatt House   1320 Locust Street   Philadelphia, PA   39.9479 -75.1632

Mary Stevenson Cassatt (1844-1926) is variously proclaimed as the greatest woman artist ever, and America's greatest impressionist painter of either sex. She is thus, from a Philadelphia perspective, the greatest Philadelphia woman artist. Mary was, in truth, born in Pittsburgh and spent most of her artistic career in Paris, and relatively few of her numerous pictures are to be found in Philadelphia. But she spent four years training at the Pennsylvania Academy of Fine Arts, her family moved to Philadelphia, and what is most important of all, her brother Alexander was president of the Pennsylvania Railroad at a time when such a position was nearly the same as being King.

The most famous Philadelphia Cassatt

Almost all of her many paintings used members of her family as models, and almost invariably the paintings portray women or young girls. If there is a male in the picture (and there are a few), you have to recheck the label to be sure it is a Cassatt. This bias raises questions about her private life, which she would certainly have regarded as no one's business. She was the long-term competitor of a slightly less famous Philadelphian Paris artistic exile, Cecilia Beaux, and she was very active in the suffragist movement. On the other hand, she had a forty-year relationship with Degas, with whom she was professionally very close, as well as personally.

Mary Cassatt was a classmate at the Pennsylvania Academy of Thomas Eakins, but they did not get along. The master anatomist and the greatest woman impressionist were certainly hampered by professional disagreement; apparently, they both took it personally.

3 Logan, Franklin, Library

The Library Company of Philadelphia   1314 Locust Street   Philadelphia, PA 39.9478 -75.1631

James Logan was the Penn Proprietors' chief agent in the Colony. Logan has been described as a crusty old codger, living in his mansion called Stenton and scarcely venturing forth in public. He was known as a fair dealer with the Indians, which was an essential part of William Penn's strategy for selling real estate in a land of peace

James Logan

and prosperity. Unfortunately, Logan was behind the infamous Walking Purchase (see Stop 4 of the Delaware River North tour), which damaged his otherwise considerable reputation. Logan must have been a lonesome person in the frontier days of Philadelphia because he owned the largest private library in North America and was passionate about reading and scholarly matters. When he acquired what was the first edition of Newton's Principia, he read it promptly and wrote a one-page summary. Comparatively few people could do this even today. It's pretty tough reading, and those who have read it would seldom claim to have "devoured" it.

Except for young Ben Franklin, who never went past second grade in school. The two became fast friends, often engaging in such games as constructing "Magic Squares" of numbers that added up to the same total in various ways. For example, Franklin doodled off a square with the numbers 52,61,4,13,20,29,36,45 (totaling 260) on the top horizontal row, and every vertical row beneath them totaling 260, as for example 52,14,53,11,55,9,50,16, while every horizontal row also totaled 260 as

The Library Company of Philadelphia

well. The four corner numbers, with the 4 middle numbers, also total 260. Logan constructed his share of similar games, which it is difficult to imagine anyone else in the colonies doing at the time.

Logan and Franklin together conceived the idea of a subscription library, which in time became the Library Company of Philadelphia in 1731. The subscription required of a library member was intended to be forfeited if the borrower failed to return a book. Later on, the public was allowed to borrow books, but only on deposit of enough money to replace the book if unreturned. We are not told whose idea was behind these arrangements, but they certainly sound like Franklin at work. More than a century later, the Philadelphia Free Library was organized under more trusting rules for borrowing which became possible as books became less expensive.

Logan died in 1751, the year Franklin at the age of 42 decided to retire from business -- and devote the remaining 42 years of his life to scholarly and public affairs. He first joined the Assembly at that time, so he and Logan were not forced into direct contention over politics, although they had their differences. How much influence

Logan exerted over Franklin's plans and attitudes is not entirely clear; it must have been a great deal.

4 German Origins of the Philadelphia Orchestra
The Academy of Music   240 South Broad Street   Philadelphia, PA
39.9481 -75.1648

At Broad and Locust Streets stands the old lady, the Philadelphia Academy of Music. Now reverted to its original purpose of presenting grand opera, the 1857 acoustical mansion long housed the Philadelphia Orchestra. Electricity has replaced gaslight, and there are a few elevators to the upper balconies. But the Academy is a surviving example of a class of music halls which once dominated every large city in the Western world. Opera hasn't changed; why should the Academy?

A book called Philadelphia Scrapple, written by several anonymous Philadelphians gives a succinct description of the conception and design of the Academy building: "Joseph R. Ingersoll became chairman of a committee to secure subscriptions for a building fund. When what was thought to be an adequate fund had been raised, the committee for the building went to consult Napoleon Le Brun and his partner about plans.

"Mr. Le Brun asked the committee how much money they had to work with. In Mr. Le Brun's own words:

"'Upon their telling us, we said you cannot build a beautiful opera house inside and outside both for that amount, but you can build the interior thoroughly complete and build the outside perfectly plain and simple like a market house, and if you ever have the money later on you could easily face it with marble and make the exterior beautiful, too.
When the question was asked us, "If we do that how are we to know that the acoustics will be thoroughly good in every respect?", I replied that there was but one large theatre in the world at that time that was perfect acoustically, and that was La Scala at Milan, and that to be quite sure of the new Academy before we began to build, the Scala interior, stage, and auditorium should be duplicated.'

"To aid in securing acoustic perfection, over and above the meticulously studied proportions and dimensions, there is an intricately-devised system of inverted barrel-vaulting underneath the orchestra and, underneath the center of the parquet, a counter-vaulted sounding well, walled in with bricks, 12 feet deep and 20 feet in diameter."

The histories of the Academy of Music and the Philadelphia Orchestra are distinct but intertwined. At the moment, the Orchestra owns the Academy, but it was not always so. The Academy of Music of Philadelphia was built in 1857, but the Philadelphia Orchestra was not founded until 1900, just for instance.

It is undeniable however that Philadelphia orchestral music began its present direction with the German immigration wave of 1848, bringing with it the new musical concepts of Felix Mendelssohn. Except for the wedding march which has sent innumerable brides down the aisle, most people now have a little trouble naming a piece of music written by this composer, but in fact, he produced twenty to fifty pieces a year from 1820 to 1847. In terms

Academy of Music

of pure virtuosity, Mendelssohn was probably the most prolific and gifted composer after Mozart. His lack of really notable productions has sometimes been attributed to his wealthy childhood and too-easy success, but in his day he was nonetheless a musical revolutionary with an enormous following.

One of the orchestras in the Mendelssohn tradition was the Germania Orchestra which moved to Philadelphia but had trouble getting accepted, and disbanded. The members of the orchestra scattered and eventually reformed a Philadelphia Germania Orchestra, which largely took over the place and some of the members of the disbanded Musical Fund Orchestra, struggled for a few years, became part of Henry G. Thunder's Orchestra, which in turn was almost entirely taken over by Fritz Scheel's Philadelphia Orchestra. Even with this thoroughly local name, the Orchestra struggled for a few years, and would quite likely have dissolved into still other formulations, until the local Women's Committee took matters in hand. Leadership was provided by Fanny Wister, sister of Owen Wister the novelist, and granddaughter of Fanny Kemble. From that time on, particularly from the day of the hiring of Leopold Stokowski as a conductor, the Philadelphia Orchestra has pressed forward, and never looked back.

L. Stokowski and the Philadelphia Orchestra
Leopold Stokowski remains unchallenged as the greatest musical leader in Philadelphia's history. Serious musicians acknowledge his eminence in musicianship, while it must be admitted he enhanced his reputation with a great deal of showmanship. Showmanship makes Philadelphia grit its teeth.

Stokowski lived to be 95, so it is easy to forget the Philadelphia Orchestra was pretty insignificant when he arrived in 1912. Together with a great deal of money available from the Curtis family, he pretty much had a free hand in upgrading the players, one by one, making radical changes in the ingredients of his unique "Philadelphia Sound" by changing the proportionality of various instruments, modifying the physical variants of each instrument, rearranging the seating arrangements of the players on the stage, and responding to the acoustical properties of the Academy of Music. He conducted hundreds of personal recordings of classical pieces and introduced dozens of new modern composers

Leopold Stokowski

and soloists. He was a musician's musician, and partly because of his very long life he was able to change the nature of American classical music, putting Philadelphia at the very top of the heap.

He was also very quick to make use of new technology and new instrument variants. It was perhaps a bit of luck that RCA Victor was located just across the river in Camden, so the revenue from recordings was very substantial, right from the early years of this new form of entertainment. He appeared on the radio and later on television. His movie Fantasia was the first to make a smashing success of classical music. Behind the scenes, he took great care of arranging the instruments for recording sessions. Much of the vaunted acoustics of the Academy of Music was simply peculiarities of it, against which he made the musicians adapt their effort to create a characteristic sound which was partly due to the hall, and partly a conscious response to it. When the Orchestra took its many trips to other cities and nations, great care was taken to adjust the volume of component sounds to the size of the hall, emphasizing various instruments to exploit local peculiarities.

And finally, the exasperating part. He discarded the baton, directing with his bare hands. He discarded the score and directed it from memory. He arranged the lights to shine only on his head and hands. He had temper tantrums with questionable justification. His first wife was named Lucie Hickenlooper but she changed it to Olga Samaroff to seem more exotic and urged Leopold to affect a continental accent and emphasize his middle European ancestry, even though he had been born and educated in England. He had a famous affair with Greta Garbo; it probably did not need to be famous. He married two heiresses with great fanfare and notoriety. They said he was gorgeous. Just how much of all this was due to his innate egotism, and how much was the affectation of an impresario is left to one's imagination. It is not difficult to imagine friction between him and the members of his board of directors.

As time has gone on, the physical acoustics of the Academy of Music has changed. Carpets have been added, seatbacks replaced. When a new pipe organ was added, its weight required a second layer of flooring to hold it. Somehow, Stokowski's successors were unable to change the orchestra to compensate completely for these subtle modifications; perhaps they had a different emphasis. In 2001, the orchestra moved to its present home in the Kimmel Center.

Today, the players are far superior in quality because of fame and the Curtis Institute; except for personality and showmanship, most of them could qualify as soloists. Consequently, any new conductor is on trial with the players, and the players' glory in it a little. In a profession filled with neurotic insecurities, there isn't room for quite so many egotists. Everybody seems on the edge of asking whether they need the orchestra, or the orchestra needs them; at times of financial downturn, that extends to the board of directors as well, and even to the audience.

The Philadelphia Orchestra is far stronger than it used to be. It trails a century of triumphs, a pantheon of stars, and the remarkable strength of the Curtis Institute continually renewing its talent. But like so many institutions with a glorious history, it must be careful not to rest too confidently on its strengths.

5 Victorian Broad Street

Broad Street   **Philadelphia PA**   **39.9479 -75.1652**

Starting at the Delaware River and walking east-west on Spruce Street, it is possible to envision an architectural museum that begins in 1702 and ends at the Schuylkill River about two hundred years later. As Spruce Street crosses Broad (14th Street), it reaches the level of Victorian architecture, and for this discussion, we now face North on Broad Street and visit the string of solid masonry fortresses which exemplify Philadelphia at the height of the Industrial Revolution.

Broad Street

At Broad and Samson Streets stands the Union League
itself. Not the Union League Club, please, that's a name used in other cities; this is the home of the franchise, the Union League itself. Although it's a house, it is a very big brownstone house, attached to another building in the rear which must be ten times as large. When you are inside, you pass from the 1860 building to the 1902 building without noticing the change, but viewed from the outside, it is easy to overlook the connection.

Brownstone is soft and easily attacked by the weather, so the League requires a lot of maintenance. And gets it; the place is spick and span. If you appear there without a jacket or tie as someone's guest, they won't eject you, but they will wordlessly bring you a jacket and tie to wear, and most people don't have the brazenness to do it twice. Inside, the furnishings are comfortable but reflective of the Civil War origins of the club, with marble floors and walnut walls, stained glass windows and awesome rooms

Union League

dedicated to Lincoln and other Republican Presidents, plus Civil War Admirals and Generals. One of the dozen dining rooms is outfitted like a Victorian saloon, with portraits of semi-nude buxom ladies on the wall that once graced the walls of Edward Stotesbury and others, with needlepoint furniture on oriental rugs for the ladies to have afternoon tea. You can hold a wedding banquet in one room, and a cigar-smoking bachelor brawl in another, without one group likely to see the other.

At the head of Broad Street, dominating the view from the middle of the street is City Hall. When it construction started in 1871, it was to have been the tallest building in the world, but politics intervened, and when it was completed in 1901, the Eiffel Tower and the Washington Monuments were taller. It is almost impossible to guess how opulent and ornate City Hall once was, but a guided tour is provided, and with coaching, you can see the huge staircases, the arching ceilings, the palatial offices for the Mayor, City Council and the Supreme Court. You can take a 44-story elevator ride, but you can no longer go up to William Penn's hat. The views of the city are spectacular, showing off the rivers, the parkways, the clusters of skyscrapers, and the vistas of Broad Street, stretching north and south to form what is said to be the longest straight road in the country. A tour of City Hall, which most residents never bother to take,

Philadelphia City Hall

teaches an impressive lesson in the way the city residents once loved their town, contrasted with the shabby neglect and decay which now overtakes city politics. For years it was said that City Hall should be torn down and replaced with something functional. But anyone who tours the place today comes away appalled at such an idea. The demolition cost alone makes the project indefensible. No one can now guess whether the future holds a revival of reverence for this massive monument, or whether, like the statue of Ozymandias, it is destined to lose all significance except to point a moral or adorn a tale.

To go further north on Broad Street, you must go either east or west around City Hall. To the east is a department store striving to keep up the standards set at that location by John Wanamaker, who made famous the saying that the customer is always right. Or, going west around City Hall, you might tip your hat to the place where the old Pennsylvania Railroad had its Broad Street Station. It's hard to believe, but the trains from Washington and New York really did puff and jingle right up to fifty yards from the

Wanamaker's

Mayor's office. They came into Center City on an elevated track, creating a barrier long known as the Chinese Wall. After the tracks were removed, the urban land became the railroad's most valuable property and may eventually become the center of a city moving slowly westward.

On Broad Street, north of City Hall are two more notable Victorian buildings, and then we'll stop. On the East corner, at what is known as number one North Broad Street, is the Masonic Temple, looking like a Norman church or fortress, which is much the same thing. The Masons were here first. Their temple was moved here in

Masonic Temple

1873, some fifteen years before City Hall was completed. It is likely, however, that the plans were made after 1851 when City Hall was originally conceived, and the Masons were just more skillful in getting a building built, as you naturally might expect of them. And what a building. There are seven meeting rooms inside which would rival in size the auditorium of most good-sized churches. Cantilevered staircases astound the viewer, and there are acres of marble flooring and paneled walls, hung with portraits of former masons, like George Washington and Benjamin Franklin. Different components of the organization, like Knights Templar, can meet simultaneously, and the size of the rooms gives some idea of the size of the organization. In fact, it is only part of the Pennsylvania Chapter, since the Shriners are somewhere else. The Masons have always been bewildered by a Pope who once ordered his faithful to abstain from Freemasonry, a dispute possibly having to do with the Twelfth Century disputes of the Popes at Avignon and the confiscation of the Knights Templar, but it's hard for an outsider to judge. The Masons will invite you to join, but they won't tell you what they do until you join. If you don't know what an organization is all about until you join, it's an impediment to membership recruitment. Or perhaps it's the other way around. Perhaps it is a testimony to the large number and esteemed public reputation of its members that so many can be induced to join, purely out of respect for the people they know who are already members. In any event, Masons certainly can build impressive buildings. If you are one of the many people who have lived in Philadelphia for six decades without visiting the place, make a note to go there soon.

And then the final stop on the tour, the Pennsylvania Academy of Fine Arts. For the moment, never mind the towering reputation and history of this cradle of American Art, of Eakins and Rush and Peale. Just look at the looming red building designed by Frank Furness on Cherry Street, all massive and funny-looking and Egyptian or something. First of all, it would be wise to learn how to pronounce his name, which is more like Furnace than fur-Ness, since there are lots of descendants around who are in a position to snub you if you stumble. It's maybe a little hard to understand why a building has to be so massive to hold pictures at an exhibition, but perhaps the thought simply was to make it cheaper to leave it standing than to tear it down. The City moved away from the Academy of Fine Arts, and now it is moving back again, but the permanent collection never changes. Some say that modern exhibitions never change, either, but that's just post-modern slander. In time, the Academy will overcome.

6 Astral

Astral Artists   230 S Broad St.   Philadelphia, PA   39.9486 -75.1648
(Soon to be moving to 1500 Walnut Street)

Brotherly love assumes all kinds of unexpected shapes in this city, and one of them is Astral. Vera Wilson recognized a critical gap in the Philadelphia classical music world and quite successfully filled it. Our town attracts the world's outstanding classical music talent to its schools, especially the Curtis Institute. It also supports the great established performers in its concert halls and recording studios. But how does a young virtuoso get from here to there, from a conservatory to the concert stage? Quite often, they don't make it at all, because no one helps them.

Pretty much single-handedly, and single-mindedly, Mrs. Wilson established a non-profit organization to act as a bridge for young people with the talent and ambition to be classical musical soloists. What do such people need? Well, they need an incubator. They need membership in an organization that will provide them audiences, press notices, experience, a little emotional support, and some unobtrusive advice. And while Philadelphia is a world-renowned musical center, it could always use a few more concerts, a larger environment of musical enthusiasts, and a more enhanced reputation as the place to go if you plan to be a star.

Just about all these things are rapidly taking place. Astral has put on major concerts that would not have been put on, and every year puts on over two hundred local performances. Auditoriums that never thought of themselves as anything special are becoming the location of fine performances by performers who are clearly going somewhere. Musical affinity groups have formed around the idea of getting to know some virtuosos, helping some gangling kids, and even forming friendships with other local musical fans. Enthusiasm.

Vera Wilson

The formula involves a lot of hard work. Famous musicians have to be persuaded to contribute their time to auditioning prospective protégés. Concerts have to be planned, and auditoriums found to house them. Audiences have to be drummed up; pamphlets, advertising, and publicity have to be created. And paid for. Foundations have to be approached, grant applications have to be written, private donations solicited. Somewhere, $800,000 a year has to be raised to promote 25 rising stars. The whole thing would cost ten million a year if it were commercial.

Today, Astral has a roster of 28 musicians and 90 laureates, all of whom have remained in the music field. Some of its most prominent laureates include pianists Simone Dinnerstein, Natalie Zhu and Henry Kramer, violinists Soovin Kim, Benjamin Beilman and Judith Ingolfsson, soprano Angela Meade and bass Eric Owens, guitarist Jason Vieaux and harpist Bridget Kibbey.

Astral's recitals and chamber concerts take place at two principal venues, the American Philosophical Society, and the Church of the Holy Trinity. Astral's educational programs take place in Philadelphia's Public Schools and its community engagement programs are placed in senior and assisted living facilities for residents in the entire Philadelphia region.

Mrs. Wilson, who is not herself a musician, likes to describe herself as a groupie. It is a little hard to reconcile this elegant cultivated Argentine expatriate with the groupie concept. But maybe not. Perhaps we all have some enthusiastic groupie-ness talent in us.

7 Philadelphia in 1976: Legionnaire's Disease

The Bellevue Stratford Hotel   **Broad and Walnut Streets**   **Philadelphia. PA**
39.9491 -75.1647

John B. Kelly, the father of Grace, once the Mayor of the town, and a Democratic power baron, used to hold court at lunch every day in the main dining room of the Bellevue Stratford Hotel. The Republicans held a daily luncheon war dance at the Union League a couple of doors away, and you had to be careful where you ate lunch if you had political involvement. Although the ballroom of the Bellevue was the only suitable place for a debutante function or a really fancy banquet, there were many hostesses who were uneasy about going to the place which was the center of Democrat politics and felt they had to ask around before they announced a decision. No other city in America is remembered for an epidemic; Philadelphia is

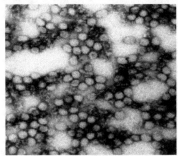

The Yellow Fever virus

remembered for two of them. The Yellow Fever epidemic, for one, that finished any Philadelphia's hopes for a re-run as the nation's capital. And Legionnaire's Disease, that ruined the 1976 bicentennial celebration. One is a virus disease spread by mosquitoes, the other a bacterial disease spread by water-cooled air conditioners. Neither epidemic was the worst in the world of its kind, neither disease is particularly characteristic of Philadelphia. Both of them particularly affected groups of people who were guests of the city at the time: French refugees from Haiti and attendees at an American Legion convention.

In 1976, dozens of conventions and national celebrations were scheduled to take place in Philadelphia as part of a hoped-for repeat of the hugely successful centennial of a century earlier. Suddenly, an epidemic of respiratory disease of unknown cause struck 231 people within a short time, and 34 of them died. Every known antibiotic was tried, mostly unsuccessfully, although erythromycin seemed to help somewhat. The victims were predominantly male, members of the American Legion of a certain age, somewhat inclined to drink excessively, and staying in the Bellevue Stratford Hotel, one of the last of the grand hotels. Within weeks, it was identified that a new bacterium was evidently the source of the disease, and it was named Legionella pneumophila. Pneumophila

The Bellevue

means "love of the lungs" just as Philadelphia means "city of brotherly love", but still that foreign name seemed to imply that someone was trying to hang it on us. Eventually, the epidemic went away, but so did all of those out-of-town visitors. The bicentennial was an entertainment flop and a financial disaster.

Since that time, we have learned a little. A blood test was devised, which detected signs of previous Legionella infection. One-third of the residents of Australia who were systematically tested were found to have evidence of previous Legionella infection. A far worse epidemic apparently occurred in the Netherlands, at the flower exhibition. Lots of smaller outbreaks in other cities were eventually recognized and reported. It becomes clear that Legionnaire's disease has been around for a very long time, but because the bacteria are "fastidious", growing poorly on the usual culture media, had been unrecognized. And, although the bacteria were fastidious, they were found in great abundance in the water-cooled air conditioning pipes of the Bellevue Stratford Hotel. Even though the air conditioning was promptly replaced, everybody avoided the hotel and it went bankrupt. When it reopened, 560 rooms had shrunk to 170, and it still struggled. Although there is little question that lots of other water-cooled air conditioning systems were quietly ripped out and replaced, all over the world, the image remains that it was the Bellevue, not its type of plumbing, that was a haunted house. There is even a website devoted to its hauntedness.

8 Philadelphia Drink

Union League of Philadelphia   140 South Broad Street   Philadelphia, PA 39.95 -75.1645

Pennsylvania was founded as a religious colony, but it should not be assumed that the early Quakers were all tea totalers. The drinking water was suspect in all parts of the world, especially in the swampy Delaware Bay area. A great many colonial houses had brew-houses nearby and made no bones about it. Prohibition traces its more recent origin to a counter-reaction to the craze for gin which swept the country in the early 19th Century, leading successively to the Salvation Army, which was a Methodist movement, and to the Volstead Act. When all that settled down, Pennsylvania was left with a system of State Stores, a monopoly of packaged liquor by civil servants. As usually happens with such government adventures, the State Store system led to higher prices and less choice, famously poor service, and usually rude salespeople. If you wanted to develop a private wine cellar, you were pretty much out of luck, and it usually was not successful to come home from a foreign trip and ask for something new you had encountered abroad.

It thus happens that Philadelphia has only three traditional alcoholic drinks, and all three are sort of fading out. Madeira used to be the big party drink. Probably because of the trade routes, but possibly because of preference for the taste as compared with port and sherry, many parties were held for the sole purpose of opening a new keg of Madeira, and many annual celebrations had Madeira toasts as the official tradition. S. Weir Mitchell enshrined that tradition in a story, "The Madeira Party", and F. William Sunderman, who died at the age of 104 in 2003, wrote a similar ode to the Madeira tradition. Occasionally a hostess will go to the trouble of assembling a modern Madeira party, but it takes some effort to do so. Being quaint is not the same as being traditional.

Delbay

The ingredients of Fish House Punch, on the other hand, are not difficult to obtain. A bowl of punch will do away with the need for a bartender and tends to assemble a jolly crowd around a table. The point was recently reaffirmed when the manager of the Union League converted one dining room to a luncheon buffet for regulars at the club tables. The idea was to allow businessmen in a hurry to get started with lunch without the delay of waitress service, but what quickly developed was that the buffet table became a greeting and gathering place, valuable in itself for enhancing the camaraderie of a club.

The Fish House referred to is now next to Andalusia at the junction of Philadelphia County and Bucks County, although originally on the Schuylkill, and is one of those really traditional clubs where the members do the cooking and serving. The origins of many things are symbolized by the Tally Ho bowl of the Fish House, derived from the pre-Revolutionary Gloucester (NJ) Hunt and given by the First City Troop in honor of the joint membership of Captain Morris in both organizations. If you don't happen to have a Tally-Ho bowl, any bowl will do.

The Union League has a similar drink, called the Union League Special*, which tastes much like a Whiskey Sour Punch, and is usually stored back of the bar in gallon jugs. Instead of a punch bowl, the Special is usually served in a tall glass. There is a general impression that the Special is stronger than the Fish House, but it is only a matter of personal opinion as to which tastes better.

* UNION LEAGUE APPETIZER (Individual 6oz. Cocktail)

1 oz. RYE 1/2 oz. MYERS JAMAICAN RUM 1/2 oz. TRIPLE SEC 1 oz. LEMON JUICE 1 oz. ORANGE JUICE 1/2 oz. SUGAR
(Shake Well With Cracked Ice and Strain)

GALLON RECIPE
1 BOT RYE 16 oz. MEYERS JAMAICAN RUM 16 oz. TRIPLE SEC 36 oz.
HALF LEMON & HALF WATER 26 oz. ORANGE JUICE 8 oz. SUGAR
(Stir with Block Ice or Cubes until Cold)

There used to be several fine breweries in Philadelphia but they went away because of globalization, unions, or local taxes, or something, and it is probably true that there is no distinctively Philadelphia beer or wine. At parties, a large number of people are often seen walking around with a glass of clear liquid with some ice cubes in it. An onlooker can't tell, and it is intended that onlookers can't tell, whether the glass contains plain water, or gin, or vodka. None of your business, right?

To return to the point that Quakers have not universally believed it is necessary to conform to a sour prohibitionist stance, there is a famous story of the Vaux family, whose country place used to be about where the Chestnut Hill Hospital now stands. Young Richard Vaux was attached to the American legation in London about the time of the inaugural of Queen Victoria and cut a rather fine figure. At the inaugural ball, he gaily danced with the new Queen, and word of it soon reached his mother in America. After summoning the young man to see her, she put down her sewing and came right to the point. "Richard," she said, "I do hope thee will not marry out of meeting."

9 Old Girard Trust Building

Old Girard Trust Building   10 Avenue of the Arts   Philadelphia, PA
39.9512 -75.164

Effingham Buckley Morris

The vibrant chatter of schoolchildren is familiar at the Academy of Natural Sciences; its museum is a standard stop for local school trips and family outings. Effingham Buckley Morris, the president of the Academy from 1928 until his death in 1937, is largely to thank for the museum's youthful spirit. A giant of the Philadelphia banking community, Morris used his success in business as well as his connections to other local institutions to advance the Academy's outreach. In 1936, after conducting a comprehensive survey of the Academy's work, Morris and his associates announced the Educational Development Program. One goal was to create a specific Education Department, dedicated to educating children from local private and public schools. As Morris put it on the day of the Program's public unveiling, "We want a museum where ideas are on display rather than things." The Academy has certainly succeeded over the years in fulfilling Morris' ambitions.

Morris had quite a knack for inspiring people and institutions to think big and move in new directions. He was often quoted as having a unique ability to "enlist the loyal co-operation of his colleagues," garnering followers and supporters wherever he went.

Old Morris Mansion

A member of the well-known Quaker "Morris" family of Philadelphia, Effingham Buckley came from a long tradition of civic engagement. Effingham was born in the old Morris mansion on Eighth Street, the son of Israel Wistar Morris and Annis Morris Buckley. After receiving his graduate degree in Law from Penn, Morris worked exclusively in that field for several years. During this period of American expansion and economic growth, Morris was heavily involved in the booming railroad business throughout Pennsylvania, helping to settle deals during its various organizational forms. Because of its many mergers and acquisitions, a successful railroad mainly embodies a successful lawyer. During the long period when railroads were at the heart of the Philadelphia economy, a majority of railroad presidents were lawyers.

Perhaps the crowning achievement of Morris' career, however, was his wildly successful Presidency at the Girard Trust Company. One of his first moves as President was to set the company's important presence in stone through the construction of the Pantheon-esque Girard Trust Company building on Chestnut and Broad streets. Attached to this building, and now home to the Ritz Carlton hotel. is a tall, impressive skyscraper that is also part of Morris' legacy. This white skyscraper had many

Girard Trust Building

critics during the days of its construction in 1888, but it was to become the first "office" building of its kind. Although the Witherspoon building at 13th and Chestnut makes the same sort of claim, the two Girard structures across the street still dominate the heart of the city today.

During his career, Morris managed to become involved with a host of financial institutions in Philadelphia: he was the director of the Philadelphia National Bank, the Fourth Street National Bank, the Commercial Trust Company and a manager of the Philadelphia Saving Fund Society. He also became the trustee of large estates, including those of Anthony J. Drexel, and William Bingham.

Effingham became a member of the Academy of Natural Sciences in 1896. He was later elected Chairman of the Finance Committee in 1905, then to the Board in 1925 where he was then elected president in 1928. Effingham approached his presidency with caution and modesty, aware of his limited knowledge in the scientific field and often enlisting the advice of his so-called "alter-ego," and the Academy's future president, Charles M. B. Cadwalader. Morris used his unique skills and local connections to help the Academy grow in new directions and expand its educational capacities.

Morris remained active until his death in 1937 and was, in no doubt, a dominant force in the development of Philadelphia and the improvement of its institutions. His portrait in the Academy of Natural Science's Library serves as a reminder of the Institution's deep and historical connections to the Philadelphia non-scientific community.

10 The Center of Town
Philadelphia City Hall   Broad and Market   Philadelphia PA   39.9528 -75.1635

It took two hundred years for the inhabited part of the city to reach the square which William Penn had envisioned for the center of his green country town, and by the time it did, the area around City Hall had come to resemble the town planning concepts ordinarily associated with the Scotch-Irish immigrants.

It sort of goes like this: the Scotch-Irish had been kicked out of Scotland, and they were soon kicked out of Ireland, so they were far less emotionally attached to their local soil than other European groups. So they were probably the first group to regard real estate as a commodity rather than a repository of wealth, or a religious shrine, as other groups often do. It soon became evident to them that the best real estate was usually found at the crossroads, and the more important the intersecting roads, the more valuable that real estate was going to be someday. Accordingly, early Scotch-Irish settlers roamed around their new country, looking for likely crossroads, and buying up the local property for speculation.

The pattern of the diamond appeared, with a town square placed at the crossroads, traffic diverted around the square, and commercial real estate established around the rim of the square which usually had a flagpole placed in the middle of the central park. New England had city centers and town commons, but the two were usually not the same thing. The diamond pattern is very characteristic of rural Pennsylvania, and up and down the Appalachian valleys where the Scotch Irish had spread. It is the pattern of Philadelphia City Hall Square, no matter whose idea it was originally. Let's face it. City Hall is at a crossroad of the two main traffic arteries, Broad and Market Streets, wide and straight. After a period functioning as the city water-works, the intersection has been occupied by City Hall for over a century. The tower of City Hall still dominates the landscape in all four directions for a considerable distance. It also stands at the foot of the diagonal Benjamin Franklin Parkway, so City Hall stands like a Parisian intersection rather than the Scotch Irish Diamond it once was. Nevertheless, when you look down the long canyon of each intersecting street, the tower in the middle of the street dominates the view.

Billy Penn's Hat
Philadelphia City Hall was intended to be the tallest building in the world, so there

Billy Penn's Hat

was no reason to suppose anything in Philadelphia would be taller. Gradually, taller buildings in other cities were built, but there grew up a gentleman's agreement that no skyscraper would be built in Philadelphia that was taller than William Penn's hat atop his statue on the tower of City Hall. Planning in the city was organized around this premise, which affects subways and other transportation issues in the city center. Because of assassination fears, a similar tradition in Washington DC was enacted into law, and it must be admitted that the flat skyline of that city looks a little dumb and boring. But Philadelphia neglected to pass a law, and so at the end of the Twentieth Century first one and then half a dozen skyscrapers were built that were twice the height of City Hall, immediately destroying the organizing visual center of the city. Pity.

But there are more serious issues involved. Aesthetics aside, who cares if someone bankrupts himself building an inappropriately tall building, with excessive elevator costs, problems with reinforced foundations, shortage of parking space, and the like? And the answer to that is the new tall building will bankrupt the older office buildings, not itself. Using offers of low, low rents to fill the new building, tenants will be drained from other spaces, and other areas of the city will deteriorate unless there happens to be a general shortage of office space in the region. Carried to an extreme, all of the center city business might be envisioned to reside in one thousand-story building, and the rest of the region would be a desert.

On and Off Broad Street

City Hall

The obvious response would be that no landlord wants to have competition, and new construction is the way a city renews itself, creatively destroying the old to make room for the new. You must not allow the vested landlords to capture the political process with agitation if not bribes. Push things too far in that direction, and you will find that political corruption has destroyed the fabric of the town more effectively than a couple of skyscrapers ever could. Market East has been devastated, it is true. But that's the price of conducting the commerce of the region on the basis of market economics instead of through bureaucracy which masks corrupt politics with high-flown language.

VI Rittenhouse Square

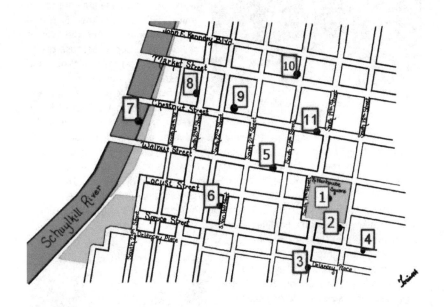

1 Rittenhouse Square Area
Rittenhouse Square   **Philadelphia, PA**   **39.9495 -75.1719**

The Rittenhouse Square "area" has far outgrown the square itself, and the term
when used by locals usually refers to the whole area of central Philadelphia West of
Broad Street to the Schuylkill, bounded roughly by Chestnut Street on the North, and
Pine Street on the South. Rittenhouse Square Park is in the center of this primarily
residential area and is now mostly ringed by apartment buildings. Rittenhouse Park
was once enclosed by a high cast-iron fence with sharp-pointed palings and gates
that could be locked at night, just like so many London Squares. The fence
disappeared around 1900.

Logan Square

Rittenhouse Square

Around 1840 the first house was built on the square, and then a fifty-year building boom (reflecting the burgeoning prosperity of the city) filled the fashionable area out to the limits defined by the Schuylkill bridges at South Street and Walnut or Chestnut Streets. Because of the advent of central heating and inexpensive window glass manufacture, the low ceilings and small windows to the East of Broad Street (promoted by the need for fireplace heat, plus laws taxing both windows and white paint) were replaced by tall ceilings and big windows without mullions. These townhouses were big, often with twenty or more rooms, and the occasional narrow streets filled with small houses were for servants, however gentrified they may have recently become. The center of fashion shifted over the years, and right now probably Delancey Street is the pinnacle, although it is patchy and arguable. After the 1929 crash (of the stock market), many fashionable Families had to abandon the unmaintainable big house and move into the little servant house in the neighboring alley in order to remain in the fashionable area. The Big house with its big taxes then became several apartments or a storefront with apartments above. Or it just deteriorated and then was torn down, unless some economic up swelling happened to rescue it again. The fact is that the number of big houses in the area exceeds the number of wealthy people who want to live in them, and the fashionable area has thus had to contract, but it has not disappeared, either.

Spruce Street

Within this district, churches abound at the northwest corner. Clubs are strung along the Eastern border, between the residences and the financial district along Broad Street. And the Southern border is where the doctors used to be. I had an office once at 19th and the Square, but the main concentration of doctors was on Spruce Street. If you have seen Harley Street in London, you will recognize the pattern. Originally, the doctor had his office on the ground floor and lived upstairs. The zoning regulations in both London and Philadelphia permitted professional use of the first floor only if the professional lived in the house. So, when the advent of automobiles induced most doctors to live in the suburbs, the office continued on the first floor of these houses, and the doctor's nurse lived upstairs, to satisfy the requirement of the zoning law. But that was just a transient phase; the advent of health insurance during World War II induced a more hospital-centered medical practice, and Spruce Street soon lost its medical flavor as doctors concentrated their offices around hospitals and their ample parking lots.

As traffic heading for the South Street bridge or the Walnut-Chestnut-Market bridges defines the limits of the district, the Rittenhouse Area has more or less contracted to the four blocks of East-West streets which terminate at the river, creating a more quiet and peaceful cul-de-sac.

Rensselaer

Some idea of the former grandeur of the area can be gained by looking at the former Van Rensselaer home at 18th and Walnut, which had a brief fling as a private club before it became a gift shop. Or the Wetherill Mansion further South on 18th Street which now houses the art alliance. Or the grey stone house a couple of doors to the West of it which was where Governor Earle lived and was the last single-family house on the square. One of the houses on DeLancey Street was featured in the movie "Trading Places" as Hollywood's idea of real opulence, and a great many other houses tell a famous story. The Rosenbach Museum is at Spruce Street, very well worth a visit, particularly on Bloomsday. And the Thaw House at 1710 Spruce tells a particularly lurid tale of murder in the Gilded Age.

2 Frank Furness - Rittenhouse Square

Joseph Roberts D.D.S   1804 Rittenhouse Square   Philadelphia, PA
39.9484 -75.1714

George Washington had two hundred slaves, Benjamin Chew had five hundred. It wasn't a lack of wealth that restrained the size and opulence of their mansions, particularly the ones in the center of town. The lack of central heating forced even the richest of them to keep the windows small, the fireplaces drafty and numerous, the ceilings low. Small windows in a big room make it a dark cave, even with a lot of candles; a low ceiling in a big room is oppressive. Sweeping staircases are grand, but a lot of heat goes up that opening; sweeping staircases are for Natchez and Atlanta perhaps, but up north around here they aren't terribly practical. Building a stone house near a quarry has always been practical, but if there is insufficient local stone, you need railroads to transport the rocks.

So to a certain extent, the advent of central heating, large plates of window glass, and transportation for heavy stone and girders amounted to emancipation from the cramped little houses of the Founding Fathers. Lead paint, now banned for its effect on premature babies, emancipated the color schemes of the Victorian house. Many of the war profiteers of the Civil War were indeed tasteless parvenu, but it is a narrow view of the Victorian middle class to assume that the overdone features of Victorian architecture can be mainly attributed to the personalities of the Robber Barons. This is not the first nor the only generation to believe that a big house is better than a small one. The architects were at work here, too. It was their job to learn about new building techniques and materials, and they were richly rewarded for showing the public what was newly possible. Frank Furness was as flamboyant as they come. He affected the manners of a genius, and his later decline in public esteem was not so much disillusion with him as with the cost of heating (later air-conditioning), cleaning, and maintenance which soon exceeded provable utility. The simultaneous arrival of the 1929 financial crash and inexpensive automobile commuting to the suburbs stranded square miles of these overbuilt structures. It was the custom to build a big house on Locust, Spruce or Pine Streets, with a small servant's house on the back alley. During the Depression of the 1930s, there were many families who sold the big house and moved into the small one. Real estate values declined faster than property taxes and maintenance costs; incomes declined even faster.

It thus comes about that large numbers of very large houses have been sold for very modest prices, and the urban pioneers have gentrified them. You can buy a lot of house for comparatively little if you are willing or able to restore the building. We thus come back to Frank Furness, who was the idolized architect of the Rittenhouse Square area, in addition to the massive banks and museums for which he is perhaps better known. Unfortunately, most of the Furness mansions on the square have been replaced by apartment buildings, but one outstanding example remains. It's sort of dwarfed by the neighboring high-rises, but it was originally the home of a railroad magnate, on Locust Street just west of the square, and it holds its own, defiantly. Inside, Furness made clever use of floor-to-ceiling mirrors to diffuse interior light and make the corridors seem wider. Although electric lighting made these windowless row houses bearable, modern lighting dispels what must have been originally a dark cave-like interior on several floors, held up by poured concrete. Furness liked to put in steel beams, heavy woodwork, and stonework, in the battleship school of architecture. If you were thinking of tearing down one of his buildings, you had to pause and consider the cost of demolition before you went ahead.

There are several others of his buildings around the corner as you head south on 18th Street to Delancey Place, one of them set back from the street with a garden in front.

Logan Square

That's what you expect in the suburbs, but the land is too expensive in center city for very many of them; this is the last one Furness built before rising real estate costs drove even him back to the row-house concept. On Delancey Street, there is a house which he improved upon by adding an 18-inch bay window in front. The uproar it caused among the neighbors is still remembered.

Frank Furness

A block away on the part of 19th Street facing down Delancey, Furness built another reddish brownstone house to glare back at the neighbors. The facings of the front suggest three-row houses, and it was indeed the home of a physician who had his offices on one side, entrance in the middle, and living room on the right. The resulting staircase in the middle is used to good effect by opening a balcony on the landing overlooking the parlor below. As befits the Furness style, the wall is thick, the wooden beams heavy. And, in a gesture to the lady of the house, the room adjoining the living parlor is a modern kitchen so the kids can play while mama cooks or guests can wander by as she gets dinner ready. Times have changed, the servant's quarters once were plain and undecorated. The lady of the house never set foot in the kitchen so she could care less what it looked like.

As a matter of fact, that's the remaining problem for these places, the rate-limiting factor as chemists say. Automatic washers, microwaves, electric sweepers, spray-on cleaning fluids and similar advances are the new industrial revolution which makes these hulking mansions almost practical. What's still lacking is the social structure of Upstairs and Downstairs, the servant community overseen by the lady of the house, who once was sort of the Mayor of a town. The lady of the house is now a partner in a big law firm, or similar.

Perhaps an accountant can for a fee be trusted with the finances; perhaps a butler can be found who can boss the staff. But the plain fact is these monster houses were built around the assumption that the lady of the house would run them, and the old style of manorial life cannot return unless the house is completely redesigned for it. Someday, perhaps a genius of the Frank Furness sort will make an appearance, change everything, and make everybody want to have it. But it is asking for something else when you insist on this happening in an old stone fortress that was designed to house a different style of life.

Frank Furness' name is often mispronounced, but his thumbprints are all over the architecture of 19th Century Philadelphia. Take a look at the Pennsylvania Academy of Fine Arts, Boathouse #13 of the Schuylkill Navy, the Fisher Building of the University of Pennsylvania, and many other surviving structures of the 600 buildings his firm built in 40 years. One of them is the Unitarian Church at 22nd and Chestnut, where his grandfather had been the fire-brand abolitionist minister.

The Civil War seems to have transformed Frank Furness in a number of ways. He had been sort of in the shadow of his older brother Horace, a big man on the campus of Princeton, later the founder of the Shakspere Society, and the *Variorum Shakespeare*. Frank was quiet, and good at drawing. However, at age 22 he was socially eligible to join Rush's Lancers, the 6th Pennsylvania Cavalry, which contained among other socialites the great-grandson of Robert Morris, and a member of the Biddle Family who put up the money to equip the troop with 7-shot repeating rifles.

Pennsylvania Academy of Fine Arts

Cavalry units like this were a vital weapon in the Civil War because they needed young well-equipped expert horsemen with a strong sense of group loyalty. Rifles were considered too expensive for infantry, who were equipped with muskets that took several minutes to reload, and were unwieldy because they were only accurate if they were very long. When bands of daredevils on horseback suddenly attacked with seven-shot repeating rifles, they could be devastating against massed infantry. A flavor of their bravado emerges from their rescue of General Custer's men from a tight spot, later known in the annals of the troop as "Custer's first last stand."

The Undine Barge Club Boathouse #13

There are two famous stories of the exploits of Frank Furness, first as a second Lieutenant and later as a Captain at Cold Harbor two years later. In the first episode, a wounded Confederate soldier lay on the no man's land of forces only a hundred yards apart. His screams were so heart-rending that Furness ran out to him and put a handkerchief tourniquet around his bleeding thigh. Because the fallen man was a Confederate soldier, the Confederates held their fire and later cheered the Union cavalryman for his kindness.

In the second episode, the cavalry had spread out too much, leaving some isolated parties trapped and out of ammunition. Furness lifted a hundred-pound box of ammunition to his head and ran through the gunfire with it to the trapped men. For this, he later received the Congressional Medal of Honor. Somehow all of the public attention he received in the war transformed Furness from a younger brother who was good at drawing into a dynamo of energy, much in the model of what law firms call a "rainmaker". He traveled to the Yellowstone area of Wyoming at least six times, bringing back various trophies. He was known to get people's attention by using his service revolver to take potshots at a stuffed moose head in his office.

His final publicity venture was to advertise, forty years later, in Southern newspapers for the whereabouts of the Confederate soldier whose life he had saved. Eventually, a man named Hodge who had later been a sheriff in Virginia, stepped forward to renew his blessings and thanks. Hodge was brought to Philadelphia for a celebrated 6th Cavalry reunion, and a picture of the two former enemies was spread in the newspapers. It was a little embarrassing that Furness and Hodge found they had

First Unitarian Church

very little to say to each other for a five-day visit, but Hodge eventually proved able to be one-up in the situation. He outlived Furness by five years.

Although the style of Furness confections seemed and seems a little strange to everyone except Victorian Philadelphians, he did leave a major stamp on American architecture. His most noted student was Louis B. Sullivan, who put an entirely different sort of stamp on Chicago. And Sullivan's best-known student was Frank Lloyd Wright who created a modernist image of architecture for the West. The buildings of these three don't look at all alike, but their rainmaker personalities are all essentially the same.

3 Mrs. Meade's House

Gordon Meade's house   333 S 19th St, Philadelphia
39.947 -75.1729

General George Gordon Meade, the hero of Gettysburg, lived in quite an elegant house during the six years (1866-72) he was a Commissioner of Fairmount Park. The house (at 19th and Delancey) has "MEADE" carved over the stately entrance facing 19th Street, and while the neighborhood has run down somewhat, it was obviously once an imposing mansion. The house belonged to Mrs. Meade. From that, you might suppose that the General had married a rich woman, but that would be wrong.

When General Lee was advancing on Gettysburg, it was widely supposed that his goal was to conquer Philadelphia, the Arsenal of the North. The town was in a panic, built some forts on the Schuylkill to defend itself, and later lionized the hometown hero who had saved them. Mrs. Meade was living at the time in a modest little place, and the town fathers took up a collection to buy General Meade a proper house.

A delegation of officials traveled down to Virginia to present him with their gift of gratitude, but Meade would have none of it. He was only doing his duty, and could not consider for a moment accepting major gifts for his soldiering. No, he was very sorry, he had to decline.

So the delegation came home, all a fluster. Someone then had the idea of offering the house to Mrs. Meade. And when they visited her, she promptly said "Sure."

**Union General
George Gordon Meade**

4 The Girl in the Red Velvet Swing
**Former Thaw Residence   1710 Spruce Street   Philadelphia PA
39.9476012 -75.1702073**

The brownstone house at 1710 Spruce Street is seemingly not remarkable, it's just an Edwardian house now converted to lawyers' offices on the first floor. But it's nevertheless a landmark, curiously linked to that 13-foot statue of Diana which dominates the top of the main interior staircase of the Philadelphia Museum of Art. Many Philadelphia gossips believe the model for the statue was Evelyn Nesbit, who lived in the brownstone on Spruce Street. But she was born in 1884, whereas Augustus Saint-Gaudens created the statue for the 1892 Columbian Exhibition. Since Evelyn was only eight years old at that time, however, it must have been some other woman who took off her clothes to pose for the sculpture; for us, it doesn't matter who she was. The statue was moved to the top of Madison Square Garden when that structure was

Statue of Diana

really still located on New York's Madison Square, but when the Garden was demolished in 1925,the Diana statue came to Philadelphia. Madison Square Garden itself has moved twice in the meantime and is mostly associated in the public mind with prize fights and political conventions. However, when the first Garden was built, it had theaters and roof-top restaurants, and its spectacular nature instantly made the architect, Stanford White, the most famous architect in New York, eventually maybe the most famous one in the world at the time.

Meanwhile, two residents of Pittsburgh independently came to New York where the action is, the iron and coal millionaire Harry K. Thaw, and an impoverished teenager named Evelyn Nesbit. Evelyn was accompanied by her mother who, recognizing the girl's extraordinary beauty, set about to steer her to fame and fortune. At the age of

Thaw

thirteen she was posing for artists, and in time became the favorite model for Charles Dana Gibson. Gibson created the "Gibson Girl", an idealized role model for millions of women who dressed the way she did, wore their hair the way she did, and behaved in the proper Edwardian style they imagined she did, too. It was in Gibson's studio that she encountered Stanford White. Evelyn had another life, however, as a "Florodora Girl", and one of her many stage-door Johnnies was Harry K. Thaw, the millionaire. That was no saint, having a reputation for using a dog whip on his numerous lady friends.

Evelyn was one of the principle entertainers in half a dozen hideaways that Stanford White is said to have established for naughty parties to amuse New York's fast set. Stanford White had been Evelyn's boyfriend before Thaw married her, and the two men cordially hated each other. One evening, some provocation made Thaw walk over to White's table in the rooftop restaurant of Madison Square Garden, and shoot him dead -- in front of hundreds of people. It's a curious sidelight that Stanford White was carrying a train reservation to Philadelphia, to discuss plans for the domed structure of the Girard Bank building. The notoriety of the murder trial was the sensation of the decade, with the prosecutor remarking that White deserved what he got, and Thaw's mother offering Evelyn a million dollars if she would give testimony supporting a plea of insanity. Everyone seems agreed that the money was never paid, although the jury was sure as impressed as the newspaper reporters with Evelyn's refusal on the witness stand to testify against her husband, quite

Evelyn Nesbit

evidently a sign of loyalty. Anyway, the jury let him off, and a famous cartoon depicted Stanford White in the pose of the statue of Diana.

Evelyn sort of dropped out of sight after the trial and the subsequent divorce, until TV interviews were conducted for the movie about the episode, "The Girl in the Red Velvet Swing". By 1957, Evelyn was decidedly less of a beauty. Meanwhile, Harry K. Thaw had continued to live in the brownstone house in Philadelphia, where once he got sick and called a friend of mine to be his doctor, and eventually another famous professor to be a consultant. When the butler answered the door, the consultant told the butler to tell his employer that he must insist on cash in advance, an action that thoroughly embarrassed my friend in view of the famous wealth of the client. But the consultant had rightly assessed the situation since later Thaw's lawyer called up and told the family doctor he was sorry but his client was not going to pay his bill since the medicine was stated in some botanical book to be a poison in excess quantity. In consternation, my friend called up the professor and asked what to do. "Chalk it up to experience," was the answer. "But what have I learned?" The consultant paused, and said, "Maybe you have learned to extend credit only to decent people."

5 Northwest Rittenhouse Square

John Wanamaker's Mansion   2032 Walnut St   Philadelphia, PA
39.9505 -75.1745

Market, Chestnut, and Walnut Streets go right across the Schuylkill on bridges. That fact was once their glory but now is the source of their problem. The first bridge to be built, at Market Street, was originally placed there in 1804. Placing your mansion on an important street makes you prominent, but if the street gets too busy, crowded and noisy you eventually wish you lived somewhere else. Air conditioning helps somewhat by allowing your windows to be closed all the time, but eventually

John Wanamaker's Mansion

the increasing commercial value of the location gives you unwelcome neighbors. So right now the last few blocks of Chestnut and Walnut before you reach the river are pretty run down. Students from the Universities on the far side of the river make for street activity at night, but most of them head for the Eastern edge of Rittenhouse Square, where droves of them sit at sidewalk tables on a summer evening. John Wanamaker had one of his many mansions just past the Square at 2032 Walnut, but it now is mostly an entrance to an apartment building towering above it.

What now distinguishes this most are the surviving churches.

Logan Square

The Unitarian Church at 22nd and Chestnut is one of Frank Furness' finest buildings, and next to it is a renovated former Church of the New Jerusalem (Swedenborgian Church), now used for an advertising agency. Frank Furness won the Medal of Honor during the Civil War before he thought much about architecture. Swedenborg, for his part, founded what is known as a thinking man's religion, since Emanuel Swedenborg (1688-1772) himself was a scientist of the first rank who might have won a Nobel Prize if there had been such a thing in his day. The Mother Church of this religion moved out to Bryn Athyn, abandoning the center city after what is reported to be a heated dispute. While the new cathedral is absolutely spectacular, the old one on Chestnut Street is still pretty fine, itself.

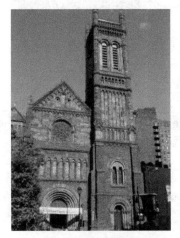

Holy Trinity Church

Across Chestnut Street is the Lutheran Church, which proves to be astonishingly large when you enter it, and it has great acoustical qualities related to the Moravian influences of the last century. Up at the northwest corner of Rittenhouse Square is Holy Trinity. Its minister, Phillips Brooks, wrote the words of the Christmas carol "O Little Town of Bethlehem", a poem of considerable merit and sophistication. In view of the far from peaceful scene of present-day Bethlehem, the message of the carol warrants recollection indeed. And, yes, the church is reddish-brown in color, as most Episcopalian churches seem to be.

There once was a time when Anthony Drexel walked down Walnut Street to work every day. One can easily imagine him tipping his hat to passers-by, striding along in front of formerly elegant mansions that line the street but are now too big to maintain. This area was a place of show houses, of downtown places to hold parties during the social season, from thence fleeing to a second house in the suburbs, or in Maine, or in Europe, during the summer. The Great Depression of the 1930s forced most of these people to choose between their various residences, and because of the advent of the automobile, they mostly chose the other places, abandoning these. It was the end of the Gilded Age.

6 The Savoy and the Orpheus

The Orpheus Club of Philadelphia   254 S Van Pelt St   Philadelphia, PA
39.9492 -75.1771

Much of the music in Philadelphia is world-class, produced by eminent professionals who command high salaries for their work. As a result of many years of striving, through unions and otherwise, it is getting a little difficult to afford all this talent and

excellence. That's one reason there is so much amateur musical effort, although it must be admitted that a city that appreciates music will almost surely generate a lot of amateur effort, just for the love of performing.

The Savoy Company, putting on Gilbert and Sullivan operettas, and the Orpheus Club, which is an all-male choral society, were founded in Philadelphia around 1875. Both groups have little trouble attracting membership, although the members of the Savoy generally only perform for four or five seasons and then become inactive members. Members of the Orpheus commonly remain active members for fifty years, so it's harder for a newcomer to find a vacancy.

The Kimmel Center

At one time, fifty or more years ago, both organizations had a reputation for hard drinking, but during those days of Prohibition, many clubs served that function. Nowadays, alcohol is not a necessity with either of them.

Many performers in the Philadelphia Orchestra donate their time for the Savoy, among whom William Kincaid the famous flutist was one of the most enthusiastic. Without this help, it's unlikely the organizations would survive. Certainly, it would be hard to distribute complimentary tickets to members of the clubs, while striving to keep membership high.

All of this is just one facet of the general dilemma that it is increasingly impossible to break even in the performing arts, by ticket sales alone. Many taxpayers are lukewarm about music and see no reason why they should support it with taxes. It's a delicate balancing act because philanthropists are easily infuriated by strikes, and politicians are seldom attracted by what may be called the finer things. When the economy turns sour, ticket-buyers flee.

7 Hidden River

The Dock at 24th and Walnut Street   **Philadelphia, PA**   **39.9519 -75.181**

In Dutch, Schuylkill means "hidden river", thus making it redundant to speak of the Schuylkill River. As soon as you become aware of this little factoid, you start to come across Philadelphians who do indeed speak of the Schuylkill in a way that acknowledges the origin of the term. To give it emphasis, it is common to speak of the "Skookle". The point comes up because cruises have started to leave from the dock at 24th and Walnut Streets, where it becomes quite noticeable that the Schuylkill really is rather hidden as it winds seven miles south to the airport, in contrast to the wide-open vista we all are accustomed to seeing from the Art Museum northwards.

The bluff at Gray's Ferry, where the University of Pennsylvania's new buildings now dominate the scene, was originally the beginning of dry land, or the end of the rather large swamp, through which the river winds its way essentially shaded by trees along the riverbank. Never mind the junkyards and auto parks you happen to know lurk behind the trees on the west side or the oil tanks which loom above the trees on the south bank. As evening closes in on the riverboat, the gaily lit towers of Center City are looming in the stern, but some

Schuylkill River

fishermen along the bank proudly hold up a respectable string of six or seven rather large catfish. If you are there in the evening, the river has the same feeling of wilderness that the Dutch traders would have experienced three hundred years earlier. No swans, however. There were many reports in the Seventeenth Century of large flocks of swans sailing around the entrance of the Schuylkill into the Delaware River. A noted local ornithologist on the recent cruise remarked that forty or fifty species of birds are found there. Even a flock of owls still live within the city limits. You don't see owls, even if you are an ornithologist; their presence is made known by taking recordings of the sounds of the night.

The geography of swampy South Philadelphia was created by the abrupt bend in the Delaware River at what is now thought of as the airport region. As the river flows at the bend, sediment is deposited in mudflats that once created Fort Mifflin of Revolutionary War fame, and later Hog Island of the Naval Yard, home of the hoagie. Swans are beautiful creatures, but they seem to like a lot of mud. The Lower Schuylkill is tidal, and the industrial waste of the region is cleaned out of the land by cutting drainage ditches laterally from the river, flooding the lowlands as the tide rises, and draining it again as the tide falls. This cleansing seems to be working, as judged by the return of spawning fish. And maybe mosquitos, as well, but it would seem rude to inquire.

Fort Mifflin

The Bartram family seems to have known how to make use of river bends and riverbanks, placing the stone barn and farmhouse higher up the bank, but below where the bluff of Gray's Ferry forces a bend in the Schuylkill, below which of course flatlands were created. It's a peaceful place, now made available for tours and excursions by placing a landing dock on metal pilings so that it can ride up and down with the tides. The great advantage is that riverboat landings are no longer restricted to two a day, at high tide, with limited time to visit before the tide falls again. Bartram recognized how popular strange plants from the New World would be in England, and his exotic plants were quite a commercial success. Nowadays the big sellers are Franklinia trees, available the first week in May. The last Franklinia (named of course for his friend Benjamin) ever found growing in the wild, was the one John Bartram found and nurtured. Every Franklinia is thus a descendant of this one. They look rather like dogwood but bloom in the early fall. If it suits the fancy, a dogwood next to a Korean dogwood which blooms in June, next to a Franklinia, can make a continuous display of bloom from May to October. And best of all, no one will appreciate it, unless they are in the know.

8 Tales of the Troop

First Troop Philadelphia City Cavalry   The Armory   22 South 23rd Street Philadelphia, PA   39.9532 -75.1782

In all its history, there have only been 2500 members of the First Troop, Philadelphia City Cavalry, but they have been a colorful lot, leaving lots of history in bits and pieces. The troop boasts that it has seen active duty in every armed conflict of America, and means to continue to fight as a unit of the Pennsylvania National Guard. However, we have lately had so many actions, the troop has had to split off units to be able to go to the Sinai Peninsula, Bosnia, Kosovo, Iraq, Afghanistan and whatever is going to come next. An eighteen-month tour of active duty takes a lot out of a citizen soldier's life, but no one is complaining, and there is no fall-off in volunteers.

Although most troopers are polite and taciturn, it is probably hard to remain unaffected by association with people like A.J. Drexel Biddle, a pioneer of the bayonet and hand-to-hand fighting, much sought after for training other units of the military. Or George C. Thomas, who was a golf course architect, but also a seaplane expert, responsible for the seaplane ramps next to the Corinthian Yacht Club along Delaware. Or Rodman Wannamaker, responsible for aeronautic development,

The Armory

also down in the marshes where the Schuylkill joins the Delaware. Robert Glendinning, who was notable for other adventures, was also an early pioneer in airplanes. As a matter of fact, Henry Watt had himself flown from Society Hill to Wall Street in a seaplane, when he was President of the New York Stock Exchange.

It's hard to believe, but a former trooper named Eadweard Muybridge distinguished himself in the art world, as a result of a bet with Leland Stopford, that a horse at a gallop reaches a point where all four feet are simultaneously off the ground. The consequence was a set of rapid-sequence photographs which are quite famous at the Pennsylvania Academy of Fine Arts. There are elephants, horses, people in various states of undress which remain as interesting artworks, as well as scientific evidence that horses' feet do indeed leave the ground. But in case anyone believes that Muybridge was some sort of sissy from the art world, there is the story that he caught his wife in an affair and shot the other man dead. As one might expect, the jury found him not guilty, on the grounds of justifiable homicide. With a name like Eadweard, it's probably necessary to demonstrate your manliness.

Robert Glendinning, class of 1888 at Penn, became Governor of the New York Stock Exchange and founded Chestnut Hill Hospital and the Philadelphia School for the Deaf. And Thomas Leiper makes a pretty good claim for starting the first railroad in America. It was only 2 miles long, in Swarthmore, and built because he was not permitted to extend his canal for the purpose of transporting stone from upstate quarries. The railroad developed into the Pennsylvania Railroad; Leiper's house, "Strathaven" is still an important Delaware County landmark.

And then, there's the story of the salute to the QE2. When the liner made a tour up the Delaware, a search was made for cannons to provide a proper salute, and the call came to the Troop. Well, they had a tank, and they could fit a simulator on the tank's gun. So, the tank rumbled down Broad Street to do its duty. South Philadelphia responded in character, too. Instead of stopping to admire the novelty of a moving tank, the drivers just honked their horns and drove around it.

9 Joseph Priestley, Shaker and Mover

First Unitarian Church of Philadelphia   2125 Chestnut Street   Philadelphia, PA 39.9526 -75.1764

Joseph Priestley, sometimes also spelled Priestly, is surely one of the more undeservedly neglected men of history. He has been called, with justice, the Father of the Science of Chemistry. He might also be called with equal justice, the father of the First Unitarian Church. The First Unitarian Church of Philadelphia is the first and oldest Unitarian church and was indeed started at the urging of Priestley, whose principal residence was in Northumberland PA, at the confluence of the West and North Branches of the Susquehanna. Priestley wrote a scholarly work on the teachings of Jesus, which so captivated Thomas Jefferson that Jefferson wrote him the outline of another book that needed writing. Apparently, Priestley didn't have time, so in 1803 Jefferson wrote it himself, in the four languages he was fluent in, English, French, Latin, and Greek. Although those were simpler times, there have been few if any others who have told a President of the United States that he was just too busy to respond to a presidential request, particularly when the President could then find he had time to do it himself.

Priestley's theological teachings were based on scientific reasoning. They were highly controversial views, to say the least. He rejected the concept of a Trinity (he was a Calvinist minister, mind you), the divinity of Christ, and the immortality of the soul. Essentially, he rejected the concept of an immortal soul on the reasoning that perceptions and thoughts were functions of material structures in the human brain (Edmund O. Wilson's idea of Consilience is largely similar), and therefore will not outlive the cerebral tissue which produced them. In 1791, mobs burned his house in Birmingham, England, his patronage was revoked, and he hastily emigrated to Philadelphia. It isn't hard to see why these ideas were particularly unpopular with the Anglican Church, which is probably the main reason England made him into a non-person, and his scientific ideas were denigrated as the product of other people.

Joseph Priestley

That's too bad, because he really was a scientist of immense importance. As a young man, he encountered Benjamin Franklin in England and was certainly a man after Franklin's heart. He noticed funny things about gases that rose from swamps and over mercury salts, and Franklin encouraged him to systematize and analyze his observations into theory. Although he called it anti-phlogiston, he had discovered oxygen. And then hydrogen, and nitrous oxide, and sulfur dioxide, and hydrochloric acid. Priestley really was the first organized and coherent scientific chemist, the Father of Chemistry. Franklin, Lavoisier, and Priestley became scientific friends, and enthusiastically exchanged ideas and observations, eventually leading to Lavoisier's fundamental principle: Matter is neither created nor destroyed, it only changes its form. In the end, it made no difference; Priestley had offended some pretty large religions, and nothing he did in chemistry was going to get much attention. Perceiving the value of the land at the confluence of rivers, he made his home for the last ten years of his life in Northumberland, now three hours' drive northwest, somehow managing to maintain an active scientific, political and theological influence worldwide. Visiting this rather sumptuous estate in a little river town is well worth a tourist visit. He died in 1804, just after his friend and kindred-religionist Thomas Jefferson became President of the United States.

Priestley's life can be summarized in one of his own most quoted remarks. "In completing one discovery we never fail to get an imperfect knowledge of others of which we could have no idea before, so that we cannot solve one doubt without creating several new ones."

10 Philadelphia Green

The Pennsylvania Horticultural Society   **100 N. 20th Street**   **Philadelphia, PA**
39.9539 -75.1734

The Philadelphia Flower Show is the best in the country. Getting crowds of visitors every March, it would get even more if the Convention Hall were bigger. Obviously, it is a financial success for its owner, the Pennsylvania Horticultural Society. What six or eight million dollars of profits go for is a city-wide outdoor beautification effort called Philadelphia Green. That, too, is the biggest, oldest and best effort of its kind in the country.

Pennsylvania Horticultural Society

About a hundred employees and four thousand enthusiastic volunteers spread out over the City, to make it look half-way decent. As the momentum grows, the political strength grows, too; and politicians notice that. The people who run this effort hit the school system pretty hard for volunteers, and the enthusiasm of inner-city kids for an activity not often seen in the asphalt jungle is very heartening. The

Horticultural Society also hits local businesses with appeals; if flower gardens aren't your thing, just give us the money and we'll do it for you.

Philadelphia Green has created four hundred community gardens and seventy neighborhood parks, planted 20,000 trees in 4 years, and vigorously pursued vacant land management. If the ground is hopelessly covered with concrete, they bore holes in it to drain off the water, and pour on enough dirt to get grass to grow. Among the many things which volunteers contribute, novel ideas rank high.

Someone approached the Wharton School, and it is asserted that unbeautified vacant lots are worth 18% less than average, while beautified ones are worth 30% more. Since only 10% of the City's many vacant lots have been cleaned up, there's lots of room for economic improvement in the future. But the improvement is already quite visible, isn't it?

11 Friends of Boyd

Boyd Theater (closed)   1908 Chestnut St.   Philadelphia PA 39.9518 -75.1724

The old Boyd Theatre was the last standing movie palace in central Philadelphia. It was built in 1928, just before the stock market crash, and closed in 2002. In fact, it changed its name to Sam Eric in its dying days, but the public remembers it as the Boyd, one of ten movie palaces in Center City. The definition of a "palace" is arbitrary but is generally taken to be a theater with more than a thousand seats, normally with hyperbolic architecture to fit its hyperbolic advertising. Scholars of the matter say the earliest movie houses were constructed in Egyptian style, soon evolving into French Art Deco. Ornate, whatever it's called.

The palace concept developed in the era of silent films, with subtitles. Anyone who has experimented with home movies knows that the silent film sort of lacks something, particularly between reels and at times of breakdown in the projection. That's why brass bands played on the sidewalk outside, pipe organs played during intermissions, and all manner of vaudeville appeared on stage. Sound movies, or talkies, were immediately much more popular when they appeared in 1927 and had less need of the window dressing from other distractions which had grown into a movie house tradition that was slow to die.

Boyd Theater

Logan Square

The movie studios owned the films and soon built theaters to display them. The movie business was quite profitable from the start, so studios had the necessary finance to spread a network of very large theaters across the country quickly. The ability to concentrate hyped-up advertising with immediate display of the product in large captive theaters tended to drive the model of the "palace", which was able to sustain higher ticket prices than trickling a larger number of film copies to myriads of small "mom and pop" local theaters. In very short order, going downtown to see movies became at one time the largest reason for suburbanites to go to the center of town on public transportation, fitting in nicely with the concentration of huge department stores, also located there. Restaurants, bars, bowling alleys, and shops grew up to address the crowds. Furthermore, the economic depression of the 1930s slowed down what was to become a relentless automobile-flight to the suburbs.

After the spread of free television at home in 1950, the downtown movie palaces were doomed. The legal profession helped, too. Small suburban theater operators eventually won an antitrust suit against what they described as monopoly power of

Sam Eric

studio-owned center city palaces, so a host of small sharks in the suburbs started to eat the whales downtown. Furthermore, the sound quality was easier to achieve in a smaller auditorium. To tell the truth, fire hazard was also lessened without the arc-lamps needed to project images across a long distance.

So, a new technology interacting with an old theatrical tradition quickly created the movie industry in its downtown movie palace form; more advancing technology quickly destroyed it, with a little help from economics and politics. Good luck to the friends of this historical epoch, who have a monumental task ahead to work up the public nostalgia and political strength required to overcome a huge economic obstacle of the "highest, best use of the land". After a long and unsuccessful struggle to have it restored, the Boyd was demolished in 2015. Department stores are gone, going in town to the movies is over. How else are you now going to get the couch potatoes to go downtown voluntarily, and often?

Just imagine ten palaces simultaneously filling up with several thousand suburbanites apiece, seven nights a week. Without those additional drawbacks on ample display in Atlantic City and Las Vegas, please.

VII Logan Square

1 Pennsylvania Academy of the Fine Arts

**Pennsylvania Academy-Fine Arts   128 North Broad Street   Philadelphia, PA
39.9555, -75.1630**

The Pennsylvania Academy of Fine Arts is notable for its place in Art history, for its faculty over the centuries, and for its influential student graduates. It is therefore not to slight the institution's remarkable place in the world of art if we pause to notice that the building itself, the place that houses all this, is itself an outstanding work of art. Whenever mention is made of Frank Furness, its colorful and influential architect, the first stop on the list is the building he built to house a school and display its glories. Perhaps the best way to illustrate the achievement is to compare it with the old Barnes Museum, which also was built to house a school. It also had an outstanding permanent collection, perhaps a greater one than PAFA. But the Barnes building scarcely gets a mention and was abandoned for the preferable location. The Furness building, however, is a massive pile of solid rock, immovable throughout massive changes in its neighborhood. To move that building out to the Parkway has never even been suggested. You can move if you like; we were here first.

The exhibition rooms are interesting, even clever, but the hand and mind of the architect are best seen in the school, the Academy. Seldom seen by the public, the entrance to the school is underneath the front staircase which sweeps the public visitors off to see the exhibition. Up to the stairs, admire the carved walls, the massive supports and the iron railings and out into  rooms with scarlet and gold walls, and a blue ceiling with stars. When it leaves, the public sweeps back down the inside stairs and out the tunnel-like entrance, then down the outside stairs. Where was the school? It's underneath the exhibition area, reached by a door under the stairs, unnoticed unless you ask for it. There you will find a darkened lecture hall and corridors lined with plaster casts for teaching purposes. But an artist's studio must have diffused northern light, and lots of it; the problem for the architect was to provide a huge slanted northern skylight over a basement. This trick was accomplished by pushing the walls of the first floor out to the street and installing a slanted skylight in the "ceiling" of the overhang. When the overall effect is that of a fortress meant to defend against a barbarian invader, built with massive walls and roof -- hiding a glass skylight is quite an achievement. Furness was a showman; it was not beyond him to place an architectural tour de force right in front of generations of students looking for something to portray.

Logan Square

PAFA Marker

We are told the building was five years in construction, designed and redesigned as it rose. The resulting effect is achieved by building around its interior as it evolves from bottom to top. Quite a difference from buildings laid out in advance, forcing the interior contents to conform to the initial design without regard to cramming down its contents. There is an overall design at work here; it's evocative of a Norman church with side extensions, but you have to look for that rather than having the architect thrust it in your face.

Cecilia Beaux (1855-1942) was certainly the most famous woman portraitist of her time. She had the misfortune of being a contemporary of Mary Cassatt, who enjoyed the reputation of the finest woman Impressionist at a time when the Art world disdained traditional painting techniques in an Impressionist stampede. So, although these two temperamental artists might never have been chums, much of their famous rivalry was probably invented for them by art world politicians.

In time, the assessment will emerge that these two well-born Philadelphia ladies were each the world's female leaders of two competing schools of art. Comparisons of the two will also have to be filtered through the fact that Cassatt was a rebel who spent most of her life in Paris, while Beaux was a prominent faculty member of the Pennsylvania Academy of Fine Arts for twenty years. Strikingly beautiful herself, she was gifted, elegant and fiercely ambitious.

Cecilia Beaux

Once Beaux had established a reputation as a portrait painter, she shrewdly began to select her subjects. She wanted famous men (Henry James, for example) and beautiful women subjects. She made the mistake of turning down her niece, Catherine Drinker Bowen because she didn't have the right kind of cheekbones. She learned, of course, that it's unwise to tell a famous author she is ugly.

Cecilia Beaux's mother died two weeks after she was born. Cecilia rejected many offers of marriage, was never brushed by scandal, devoted her life almost entirely to the pursuit of excellence as a portraitist of women and children. It does not take much of an amateur psychoanalyst to surmise she was dominated by fear of pregnancy, and possibly guilt about being the cause of her mother's death. But living

Henry James

in the Victorian era before Lister and Pasteur could finally make childbirth safe, her sort of life was not as unusual as it is today, except for her notable thirst for achievement. An aristocratic upbringing almost certainly contained a strong condemnation of boasting and self-promotion, with the result that she is sometimes referred to as a perfect model for the graduates of Bryn Mawr College, although she did not attend there. Placing its emphasis on success for women other than or in addition to marriage, the quietly determined graduates of that college make a goal of achievement, not fame. Beaux became the finest woman portraitist in America, possibly the finest portraitist anywhere, but it was a title she earned and deserved without theatrics or egotism. Lots of eligible men found this attractive, but she retreated for her own reasons in her own graceful way.

2 Quaker Gray Turns Quaker Green

American Friends Service Committee   1501 Cherry Street   Philadelphia, PA
39.955618, -75.164919

Miriam Fisher Schaefer, at one time the Chief Financial Officer of the American Friends Service Committee, had to cope with the economics of renovating the business headquarters complex for various central Quaker organizations. They're housed in a red-brick building complex, naturally, located on North 15th Street right next to the Municipal Services Building of the Philadelphia City Hall complex. The original building within the complex is the Race Street Meetinghouse, funds for which were originally raised by Lucretia Mott. The Quakers needed to expand and renovate their offices, a nine million dollar project. Miriam, a

American Friends Service Committee

CPA, calculated that the job could be made completely environment-friendly for an extra $3 million. The extra 25% construction cost explains why very few buildings are as energy-efficient as they easily could be. However, in the long run, a "green" building eventually proves to be considerably cheaper. Not only would a green Quaker headquarters be a highly visible "witness" to environmental improvement, but it would also pay for itself in reduced expenses after about eight years. That is, if the friends of the environment would provide $3 million in after-tax contributions, they would provide a highly visible example to the world, and reduce the running expenses of the Quaker center by a quarter of a million a year, indefinitely. Effectively, this is a charitable donation with a permanent tax-free investment return of 12%, quite nicely within the Quaker tradition of doing well while doing good.

Energy efficiency isn't one big thing, it is a lot of little things. If you dig a well deep enough, its water will have a temperature of 55 degrees, and only require heating up another 15 degrees to be comfortable in winter, or cooling down thirty degrees to be comfortable in the summer; that's described as a heat pump. Then, if you plant sedum, a hardy desert succulent plant, on the roof it will insulate the building, slow down rainwater runoff, and probably never have to be replaced. Rockefeller Center, you might be interested to learn, has a "green roof" of this sort, which has so far lasted seventy years without replacement. The Race Street Meetinghouse was built in 1854 and has so far had many roof replacements, each of which created a minor financial crisis when the need suddenly arose.

The ecology preservation movement is full of other great ideas for city buildings because buildings -- through their heating, ventilating and air conditioning -- contribute more carbon pollution to the atmosphere than cars do. For another example, fifty percent of the contents of landfills originate in dumpsters taking construction trash away from building sites. What mainly stands in the way of more recycling of such trash is the extra expense of sorting out the ingredients. Catching rainwater runoff allows its reuse in the toilets, eliminating the need to chlorinate it, meter it, and transport it from the rivers. You could save a lot of air conditioning cost by painting your roof white. At first, that would look funny. But do you suppose oddness would bother the Society of Friends for one instant? No, and you can expect them to make it popular, in time. People at first generally hate to look funny, but with the passage of time, they grow to like looking intelligent.

A lot of people want to save the planet. So do the Quakers, but they have come to the view that the public is more easily persuaded to save money.

Two things uniquely characterize the work of the Friends Service Committee (AFSC): it's often both dangerous and unpopular. That's not required for relief following Indonesian tidal waves perhaps, but the work that really needs someone to do it is often both dangerous and controversial.

The Service Committee was founded in 1917, mostly by Rufus Jones and Henry Cadbury, as a way of helping conscientious objectors to World War I. The Mennonites, the Brethren, and the Quakers were opposed to all wars, not just that particular one, but two of those religions are of German ancestry, and lacked the same credibility of the English-origin Quakers in a war with English allies against the

Huns, Boche, and Kaiser enemies. The early focus of the Committee was on the Field Service, or Ambulance Corps; which was plenty close to the action, and plenty dangerous. After the War, the defeated German population was starving, and the Quaker Herbert Hoover directed the relief effort with great credit to the Quaker name, and immense European gratitude.

After that, when German Jews were suffering persecution by the Hitler administration, the Quakers initially responded in a uniquely Quaker way. Rufus Jones and two other Quakers went to see Reinhard Heydrich, to tell him the world disapproved of his behavior. They fully realized they represented a pool of important world opinion, particularly within Germany, and it was time to speak truth to power. The Germans left the room to confer, and the three Quakers bowed their heads in silent prayer. Apparently, the room was tape-recorded, and when the German officials returned, they did promise some efforts to improve matters. As the situation for the Jews soon got much worse, many Quakers risked a great deal to shelter and rescue the persecuted exiles. Relief to the defeated German populace had to be repeated after that war, as well. Each effort built up more credibility to be able to switch sides for the next effort, and sincerity has seldom been seriously questioned.

The Japanese were also our hated enemies in World War II, and once more a long history helped the relief effort. Nearly 100,000 American citizens of Japanese origin were interned on the West Coast in 1941, often under deplorable conditions. Clarence Pickett was a director of AFSC at the time, and his sister had spent years in Japan as a missionary, so his remonstrations with the American government were prompt and credible. One of the more active workers was Esther Rhoads, the sister of the famous surgeon, who had spent time in Japan earlier. One of the ingenious efforts with the Nisei was to assist 4,000 of them to get into college and find them hostels and jobs while they were away at school. Many of these college students later became prominent in various ways, greatly assisting the post-war reconciliation between the two countries.

Two Quaker ladies at the AFSC made a totally unique contribution when a request was received to provide a suitable tutor for the Crown Prince, now Emperor. He didn't convert to Christianity, but he later married a Christian, and you can be sure he got a plenty good dose of Quakerism from Elizabeth Gray Vining. This tall, strikingly handsome Philadelphia woman had Bryn Mawr written all over her and turned heads whenever she entered a room. When she went back home, she was followed as a tutor for seven years by, guess who, Esther Rhoads who by then was the director of the Tokyo girls school.

And then the Service Committee did its work in Vietnam, in Iraq, in Zimbabwe, and Somalia on the unpopular side, in every case. There are stories of venturing into war zones with hundred-dollar bills scotch-taped to their torsos, where every fifty feet there was someone who would cut your throat for a dime. One worker in Laos entertained a group of us tourists with tales of living for weeks with nothing to eat but grasshoppers and cockroaches. Dangerous, unpopular, and uncomfortable. It sounds like a wonderful outlet for someone who is a perpetual rebel without a cause, but if you can find one of those at the Service Committee, you must have done a lot of looking.

The Service Committee, like the Quaker school system, is mostly run by non-Quaker staff. That means that neither of them exactly speaks for the religion itself. This little religious group is stretched thin to provide a vastly greater world influence than its numbers imply. Hidden in the secrets of the group is an enduring ability to attract sincere non-member adherents to their work. And a quiet watchfulness to avoid losing control to any wandering rebels without a cause.

Henry Cadbury Dresses Up For the King

There are a few old Quaker Clothes in the attics of their descendants, and on suitable occasions, an old broad-brimmed hat or two will appear at a Quaker gathering, for amusement. Quakers gave up the old style of "plain dress" when it became generally agreed that such an eccentric dress was not plain at all but rather drew attention to itself. On the other hand, there is a distinctly unfashionable quality to almost everything Quakers do wear. When silk and nylon stockings were fashionable for women, Quaker women often wore black stockings. When it became the style for women to sport black stockings, Quaker women usually wore flesh-colored nylons. Among men, thin metal-trimmed spectacles displayed the same counter-fashionable tendency. Nowadays, these little quirks are often public signals among strangers, a way of wig-wagging "I notice you are a Quaker, so am I" And of course, unfashionable clothes are cheaper, and that's always a good thing, even if you are a millionaire.

And so it happened in 1947 that the Quakers were awarded the Nobel Peace Prize, with information passed along that white tie and tails were the expected form of dress at the ceremony. Henry Cadbury was selected to receive the award on behalf of the American Friends Service Committee, and you can be sure that the Quaker candy heir didn't own a set of tails. Henry was also very certain he wasn't going to go out and buy a set, just for a single wearing.

The AFSC collects used clothing, to distribute to the poor. Henry inquired whether there might be a set of white tie and tails to be found in the used-clothing bin, and luckily there was. It had been collected on behalf of the Budapest Symphony Orchestra when that impoverished but distinguished group of musicians was invited to give a concert in London. One of the monkey suits more, or less, fit Henry.

So, after investing in dry cleaning and pressing, the Quaker Cadbury packed it up and went off to Oslo, to meet the King.

3 International Visitors Council

International Visitors Council   1515 Arch Street, 12th Floor Philadelphia, PA 39.955, -75.1658

IVC stands for International Visitors Council, now approaching its 50th anniversary. As you might suppose, it is located at 1515 Arch Street, near the old visitors center. Philadelphia has a new visitor center on 5th Street, of course, and perhaps it takes time to move, or maybe moving isn't in the cards. We had another Visitors center on 3rd Street that came and went, so proximity between Center and Council perhaps isn't as important as rental costs, or leases, or other issues.

The Council has a modest budget, but a great idea. Anyone who has traveled much knows that you tend to follow the travel agent's set agenda for a town, you see a lot of churches and museums, but you can almost never get tickets for the local entertainment events, and you almost never meet any local people except taxi drivers and bellhops. That's even more true of young travelers, who don't have either the money or the experience to anticipate the issue, or enough local friends to guide them around the obstacles (This exhibit closed on Mondays, that event is all sold out, this event was spectacular, you should have been there yesterday, sorry we didn't know you were coming we have a wedding to go to, *etc.*). On guided tours, it is remarkable how few things seem to happen after 4 PM.

So, fifty years ago, some imaginative Philadelphia leaders got the idea that a lot of Philadelphia residents would enjoy taking some foreign tourists under their wing, maybe have somebody to know when they, in turn, make a reciprocal visit, maybe boast about our town a little. Furthermore, by getting involved with the US State Department, young visitors can be identified as potential future leaders in their country. If the guess is a good one, and the experience favorable, Philadelphia might prosper from the publicity and from the later return visits, now in the triumph of success. That was the founding spirit of the Philadelphia International Visitors Council.

So that's how it came about that Margaret Thatcher, Tony Blair, the President of Poland, and the head of the Russian Space Program were once visitors in Philadelphia homes. People who like to do this sort of thing tend to like each other, so the monthly receptions are interesting Philadelphia social occasions in their own right. Success begets success, and the CCP (originally Business for Russia) has affiliated itself, along with the Philadelphia Sister Cities Program, the Consular Corps Association, The Philadelphia Trade Association, and probably others.

Look at it from the visitors' viewpoint. New York has larger colonies of foreign nationals than Philadelphia does, but New York is an expensive place to visit. Washington has dozens and dozens of embassies, but a visitor soon learns the last thing an embassy staff wants to see is a citizen from home. So those places aren't really a typically American place to visit. Indiana is plenty American, but there isn't much to see there. So Philadelphia has many attractions, lots of history, it's as thoroughly American as a city can be, and all it needs is someone to open up and show it to you. Cleverly organized, the IVC has undoubtedly put the Philadelphia stamp on many foreign visitors, without their exactly recognizing they are being told This is America. If the State Department is shrewd in its assessment process, Philadelphia will in time be held in high esteem by the leaders of a lot of foreign nations.

In the spirit of announcing that Philadelphia is where you can find America, my own little daughter astonished me at a dinner party by telling the assembly the following story:" William Penn was nice to the Indians, so it was safe to land in Philadelphia. Pretty soon, so many people landed here they had to move west to settle down. And, folks, that's why the people to the North of us talk funny, and the people to the South of us talk funny -- but everybody else in America talks like Philadelphia!"

4 Rara Avis

The Academy of Natural Sciences 1900 Benjamin Franklin Parkway   Philadelphia, PA   39.9570, -75.1712

School children grow up in Philadelphia with an image of the Academy of Natural Sciences as a place to visit dinosaurs. Indeed, it does have on display the first dinosaur skeleton ever to be discovered, as well as a number of others. However, only about a third of the building complex on Logan Square is devoted to public museum displays. The rest is devoted to specimen storage, library and scientific work of the highest scientific eminence and value. In the scientific area, the most striking thing to a visitor is to notice how few windows there are. Scientists often spend their time looking through microscopes, so they don't care about windows. In a skyscraper business office that wouldn't be acceptable at all and the staff would all get the heebie-jeebies and quit. In the business world, the number of windows your office has is important, especially if they are corner offices, the best kind.

Logan Square

In one small area of the museum is a set of ingenious metal cabinetry containing 200,000 bird specimens, including every one of the 10,000 known species of birds on earth. In fact, about a quarter of all the "type" specimens are found there with red tags on their feet. A type specimen is the first known and described specimen of

Academy of Natural Sciences

that particular bird, ever. That's a roundabout way of relating that this is where Ornithology, the study of birds, began. It also tells you that when bird skins are treated with arsenic salts, they last a very long time - a considerable number of the specimens in the cabinets were contributed by Audubon, himself. New bird skins are acquired at the rate of a thousand a year, related to the scientific studies which go on, studying bird diseases, genetic changes due to environmental changes, and pollution effects. The recent uproar about Avian Influenza revolves around the tendency for bird diseases to undergo genetic changes themselves and become human diseases. A great many such bird diseases are maintained at the laboratory in case they are needed for a crash program of vaccine development. Environmentalists will be surprised to learn that the mercury content of bird feathers has actually declined in the past century.

With a good guide you quickly grasp the attraction of this topic of birds and birding. There are huge condors, with six-foot wingspreads; and one-inch hummingbirds. Birds of every shape and coloring, reaching some sort of extreme with the Bird of Paradise from New Guinea. Owls and eagles, ducks and chickadees. Hummingbirds defy the usual sort of nets; every single little hummingbird specimen was obtained by shooting it with a special little gun. If you see a hummingbird in your garden, just imagine what skill it takes to shoot one.

The ornithology department maintains an active program of loaning bird specimens to scientists all over the world, although this activity has recently been affected by computerization of the catalog of specimens, resulting in a massive global internet conversation among ornithologists, sort of like a Facebook of a very special sort. For all this activity going on, the collection area is an eerily silent place.

And that's just birds, crammed into an organized space of, well, maybe fifty by two hundred feet, eight feet tall, fifty shelves per typical cabinet. Right next to it is the insect collection, perhaps taking twice the cabinet space. Insects are a lot smaller than birds, so each shelf has more specimens. That sounds like an awful lot of Latin names to try to remember. And a certain amount of danger, too. Several scientists died of arsenic poisoning before the full hazard was appreciated and contained.

5 The Garden Show Evolves

The Pennsylvania Horticultural Society   100 N. 20th Street   Philadelphia, PA 39.956, -75.1731

The Pennsylvania Horticultural Society was founded in 1827, and it organized the first Flower Show in 1829. For a century it was only an amateur display, very similar to the sort of local garden club display found in many towns and villages in England. The timing of such shows is dictated by the blooming season of the flowers of the region, so the display depends on the dates of the local flowers, related in turn to soil and weather conditions. In the early part of the Twentieth Century, W. Atlee Burpee became the dominant force in the Philadelphia show. The show established a long tradition of domination by seed companies and nurseries, with elaborate displays which often took a week to set up, preceded by months or years of planning. The central difference in the nature of the Philadelphia show was that plants were forced into bloom, so much of its impact depended on displays which were seemingly entirely out of season. After World War II, Ernesta Ballard became the moving and controlling force, driving The Show into enormous popularity in the new larger quarters at Convention Hall. Considerable revenue was generated and used to beautify Philadelphia. The Show became the biggest, best, most popular and best-funded flower show in America. Ernesta was a success.

Gradually, the most elaborate or dominant displays were put on by florists, using cut flowers. That was not necessarily Mrs. Ballard's original intention, although it might have been. It is the nature of plant nurseries to take away a ball of topsoil when they sell a plant, and that tends to dictate the location of the major nurseries in places

where farmers are willing to ruin the land for farming, looking to speculate on suburban development. They thus are usually rural or exurban, because prime farmland is too expensive. Obviously, nurseries are pressed outward from the rim of the expanding city, and may even be forced to locate at a considerable distance away. These realities of the business tend to diminish the local loyalties of the nurseries and the city to each other. Mainly, cut flower arrangements resisted this trend by using greenhouses, but air freight has now made it possible for exhibitors of live plants to come from the Netherlands, Peru, and even Korea. The Flower Show is still held in Philadelphia, but it is much less a product of Philadelphians, especially amateur Philadelphians. When large single exhibits now can cost $100,000 apiece to organize, it is not surprising that the Philadelphians who do exhibit, are members of the upper crust. The Flower Show cannot run without the enthusiastic help of 3500 volunteers. The judging is done by

175 volunteer judges from all over America, coming to Philadelphia at their own expense.

The Flower Show has had memorable moments. There was a time when the Shipley School consistently won most of the prizes. There was a famous episode when the Widener Estate of Linwood had a world-famous Acacia display. When it was broken up, there was an uproar when it was given to Washington DC, instead of staying right here where it belonged. The Show goes on and thrives. But just what its future is going to be is unclear. The Convention Center has doubled its space, but whether it can double its business is uncertain. And the management has recently changed from leadership which had a focus on the show and regarded city beautification as something to do with left-over profits, to leadership with a primary interest in the beautification of the city. No business will thrive if it neglects its revenue stream. So, please be careful with our nice Flower Show.

6 SCORE

Philadelphia SCORE   105 N. 22nd Street   Philadelphia, PA
39.9565, -75.1758

Frank Pace, formerly Secretary of the Army, founded SCORE, the Service Corps of

Mark Maguire

Retired Executives, in 1964. Philadelphia was one of the main founding chapters but tended to dwindle as business large and small dwindled after the bombing of West Philadelphia by the then-Mayor; former executives living in the suburbs lost interest. In December 2006, Mark Maguire took charge and gave SCORE a new direction. This former executive of Rohm and Haas is not related to the baseball home-run king, but at least his name is easy to remember.

The new sociology of center city demanded that more small businesses will be started by minority residents, some of whom may lack experience in this sort of activity, which nevertheless is recognized as the main source of job creation in any area. So, SCORE needs to dispel a number of misconceptions and unrealistic ambitions, and familiarize these budding entrepreneurs with the tax and regulatory headaches ahead of them, and teach them to be watchful of common traps and obstacles, learn to cope with fair competition, and how to recognize the signs of fraud before it happens to them.

The usual vehicle for teaching these elements of commercial life is to induce the writing of a detailed business plan, which executives can criticize for lack of realism or inadequate capitalization, suggesting ways to succeed in a field that experiences 50-60% failure in the best of circumstances. Some of these require face-to-face discussions, lectures, and required reading. But much of it can be handled with weekly email consultations, a favorite tool of Philadelphia's SCORE chapter. Much of it can be addressed by referring the client to the proper agency or service business, or bank. SCORE has a strict ethical code for its volunteers, including a prohibition of becoming a vendor or participant in the business.

In addition to the changing nature of new small business people, there is a changing demographic of the volunteer executives who do the advising. Over 80% of them describe themselves as retired, but in fact, it is rare for one to be totally retired from all business activities. These folks really like to work, and a thirty-year vacation is not their goal in life.

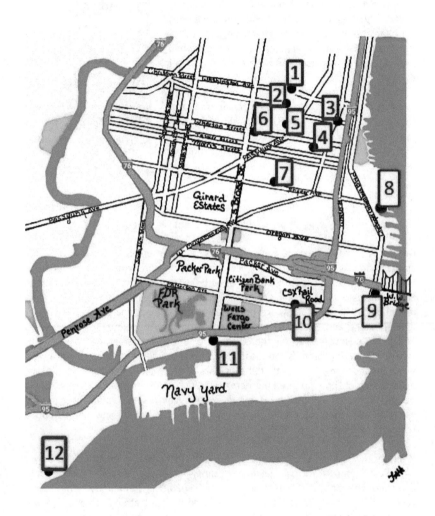

1 Blood and Honor: The Philadelphia Mafia, Lately
9th and Christian Street   Philadelphia, PA   39.9389 -75.1578

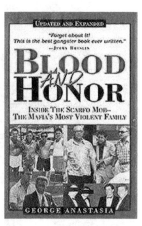

After two decades of seemingly endless dominance of Philadelphia headlines by the Mafia, the underworld has been absent from the news in the beginning of the 21st century. That's very welcome to everybody including the Mafia itself, and there are three main popular explanations. First, after 27 informal mob executions and four dozen convictions with lengthy prison terms, perhaps the mob has been eradicated. Or, possibly the immigrant population has been assimilated, now looking to quieter occupations for a source of income. And finally, maybe the mob just decided to lie low while tax-hungry politicians enact enabled legislation for legal gambling casinos for the gullible public since the main argument against casinos is they attract crime. The histories of Atlantic City and Las Vegas certainly suggest organized crime has not yet abandoned casinos.

George Anastasia's book *Blood and Honor* relates twenty years following the assassination of Angelo Bruno in 1980, averaging a murder or a prison sentence every three pages and leaving the reader with the impression of constant warfare in South Philadelphia. The book is pretty hair-raising, but after all, there is not much to talk about in a crime family except crime. To run through a brief overview of 27 assassinations and 36 major convictions is to leave a violent image of South Philadelphia. However, to say there were two to four assassinations per year plus three or four criminal trials softens that impact. The violence is appalling because it went on for so long. To note that Philadelphia, like all major American cities its size, averages about three hundred murders a year, puts mob violence in perspective. To be serious about eliminating homicide, you ought first to eliminate domestic violence. After that, you should go after street gangs and their focus on distributing recreational drugs.

Whether it was a struggle for control of Atlantic City casinos, a policy dispute over whether to get involved in illegal drugs or simply a matter of disputed succession to control of the mob, is not now clear to the law-abiding community. What seems accepted interpretation is that matters heated up a lot after Angelo Bruno was assassinated. Somebody wanted his job, and that somebody wanted to run the organization differently. It's a situation quite familiar to CEOs of corporations, Kings and Emperors, and even editors of newspapers. What distinguishes organized crime families is the violence of their methods for dealing with succession issues. What emerges in this particular little world is that Nicodemo Scarfo established himself as the new Don of the Philadelphia Mafia by 1988, and the bitterness of this succession struggle induced six or ten insider members of the mob to become police informants to get revenge. The murders and convictions which make up this twenty-year period of time can be roughly divided into the initial struggle for control, the revenge of the losers, and the subsequent assassination of traitors. Even after inactivating nearly a hundred insiders, at least twice that number of "made" members and associates were unaffected directly. It's anyone's guess whether a defeat of this magnitude is enough to eliminate the organization, or whether it merely imposed a truce, during which the mob will heal its wounds and then make a comeback.

An underground organization, whether in Philadelphia or Afghanistan, cannot hide effectively without the cooperation of honest citizens in the neighborhood. For many years, toleration was secured by keeping the streets safe from marauders belonging to other immigrant groups, and by collecting whatever debts the courts would not honor. The gray area involved such illegal activities as bootlegging in which the rest of the community participated without much sense of guilt. The Mafia was effectively a private police force for unsanctioned activity, operating within a neighborhood not fully in accord with prevailing attitudes. It seems to have been the genius of Angelo Bruno to realize that loan-sharking was the only permanently profitable component of this formula, and that loan sharking largely depended on gambling to create desperate debtors. Just about every other criminal activity attracted too much police attention to survive because the dominant society approved of suppression. Bruno's assassination seems to have been triggered by rebels who disagreed with his analysis. Perhaps they were right and the mob had been missing a big profit opportunity in the drug trade. Perhaps they were wrong and turned the legitimate community against them to the point where extermination was provoked.

Keep tuned. The outcome of this little debate could emerge suddenly and spectacularly. Or more decades of peace will pass silently, in which case Angelo will eventually be deemed correct.

2 Rail Station at Broad and Washington
Broad Street and Washington Avenue   Philadelphia, PA   **39.9365 -75.159**

Washington Avenue was named Prime Street before the Civil War and was an important transshipment center for the whole country. Rail traffic, coming down from New York and New England, came through New Jersey on the Camden and (Perth) Amboy RR, disembarked, and ferried over the Delaware to the foot of Prime Street/Washington Avenue. Passengers then took horse-drawn cabs up Prime Street to Broad, or else they walked. At that point, travelers bound for further South would enter the imposing Rail terminus of the Philadelphia, Wilmington and Baltimore RR, to re-embark. Philadelphia hotel operators hoped they would stay overnight; Philadelphia merchants hoped they would just transact their business locally, then go back home. Taking nine hours from New York, it was an inefficient transportation method by today's standards, but the Prime Street interruption served local economic purposes, which Chicago keeps in mind, even today.

The interruption also worked the other way, inducing Southerners to go no further North with their business, thus strongly contributing to pro-Southern sympathies before the Civil War. Philadelphia was indeed the most northern of the Southern cities until the 1856 Republican convention (at Musical Fund Hall) started to remind other Philadelphians that the anti-slavery Quakers perhaps had a point. Even so, pro-Southern

John Brown

feeling in Philadelphia was wide-spread, even in the early months of the war.

For example, in 1859 John Brown's body was brought forth on the PWB railroad, precipitating a pro-Southern riot at the Broad and Prime Station. There was a second riot the following year.

30th Street Station

During the Civil War itself, the PWB railroad was a major military transport, carrying military supplies and troops to the battles, and bringing the many wounded troops back home for treatment. Quite a large military hospital was built across Broad Street from the rail station. All in all, the corner of Broad and Prime was a major center of the war and may well have been one of General Lee's objectives when he launched the invasion that got stopped at Gettysburg. After the Civil War was over, attention was finally paid to the need for better North-South rail transport along the Eastern Seaboard. Up to that time, European investment had pushed American railroading in an East-West direction. The Baltimore and Ohio were aimed at the Mid-West, while the New York railroads aimed at Chicago and beyond. Local politics in the seaboard cities tended to keep the competitors from linking and thus potentially capturing trade between the manufacturing North and the agrarian South.

The Philadelphia, Wilmington, and Baltimore was the key link in the series of mergers which created the dominant Pennsylvania Railroad. Bringing northern traffic in through North Philadelphia to the new 30th Street Station, and then linking it to the stub of the PWB RR, the way was being paved for Acela Express trains to shoot from Boston to Washington, perhaps eventually to Florida. The side-track from West Philadelphia to Broad and Washington was allowed to wither, and of course, the whole Camden and Amboy RR became scarcely more than a trolley line. All that was left as a challenge to the Pennsy was to get past B and O obstructionism in Baltimore. This last step was finally accomplished with the discovery of some legal loopholes related to an existing right of way for a local commuter line in Baltimore, where permission for a branch line was broadly interpreted, and a surprise tunnel dug to link it up to the other parts of the Pennsy. Amtrak passengers nowadays usually move through the Baltimore tunnel systems without noticing them, but occasionally a train breaks down inside the tunnels. Then, they prove to be rather dark and damp as the passengers with their laptops are transferred to another train.

3 Mummer's Strut

The Mummers Museum   **1100 South 2nd Street**   **Philadelphia, PA**
39.9336 -75.1475

For over a century, and maybe for two centuries, the Mummers Parade has strutted around Philadelphia on New Year's Day. The Mummers have lots of tradition and oral history, but the authenticity of records going back to the early days of the parade do not meet very strict standards. There are those who say that the earliest mummers were "shooters" who coursed through town on the Fourth of July, shooting pistols in the air with one hand and carrying a bottle of booze in the other. Booze, by the way, was the name of a bottle manufacturer that became associated in common parlance around 1840 with the product most commonly found in the bottle. The name booze bottle was attached to a bottle in the shape of a log cabin, suggesting a possible link to the 1840

Mummers

Presidential election of William Henry Harrison, Old Tippecanoe. The other historical origin was thought to be the annual parade of the guilds: the butchers, carpenters and similar. Somehow, these two traditions came together in the annual parade on New Year's Day, with various ethnic clubs spending all year getting ready to compete with each other for attention. Many of the floats are reminiscent of the New Orleans

South Philadelphia

Mardi Gras parade, some clubs specialize as "comics" in the style of the old shooters dressed up as clowns. The increasingly dominant part of the parade is found in the ten or twelve String Bands.

The main instruments of the String band are the banjo, with the tune carried by some saxophones and a peculiar instrument that looks like a xylophone held up on a pole, emitting an octave of piercing chimes. The old favorites are "Dem Golden Slippers" "Wait 'till the Sun Shines Nellie" and similar fast marches. The costumes tend toward ostrich feathers and gaudy colors, and in recent years the string bands all put on a little show or dance in front of the judging stands. Since it takes place in January, it is usually quite cold at a Mummer's parade, and since the parade goes along streets lined with tall buildings, the wind builds up quite a "Marilyn Monroe Effect". Until recent years, the mummers have always been male.

The mandatory traditional food at a mummer's parade is a Philadelphia soft pretzel, smeared with mustard, sold by street vendors. Hot dogs, American flags, and soft drinks are for sale as well, and other beverages are provided by the onlookers themselves. The parade itself is only an annual public display for the mummer's clubs that have traditionally met weekly in the ethnic neighborhoods, arguing hotly about next year's costume (a deep secret until the day itself), drinking, dancing and sewing the costumes, rehearsing the tunes and the dance steps. There is a traditional "Mummer's Strut," in which the participants and many onlookers participate spontaneously. In its fullest expression, the mummer will hold an umbrella in one hand while holding forward the lapels of his jacket with the other hand, bending forward at the waist, throwing back the head, and more or less keeping time with the music, and shaking the umbrella at the cheering crowd. There's a museum devoted to this sport, located on Second Street, otherwise known as "Two Street". It's all lots of fun, but it is usually too blamed cold to stay there long, and most people eventually retreat to a nearby television to watch the rest of it. In the days when the parade went up Broad Street, it passed the Union League where another New Year's tradition was in progress, with the Republican members eating terrapin and drinking Fish House punch, quite comfortable in their warm quarters looking out of bay windows. Democratic Mayor Rizzo used to march in the parade, and when he passed the League, he would ostentatiously turn his head away from it. Subsequent Democratic mayors have been even more polarized; at various times the parade went up Market Street, though it came back to Broad Street, starting at City Hall and heading south.

Something to consider is suggested by the book "The Leopard," which makes the point that Garibaldi was an exterminator, not a liberator, which first drove the migrants to New Orleans before they suddenly learned about the Ku Klux Klan. Believing this version might assist moving the parade to a climate warmer than January usually provides, which is what it would take to induce me to return to future Mummers parades.

4 Meschianza

Joseph Wharton House (torn down)   5th & Wharton Street   Philadelphia, PA 39.9322 -75.15

The British under General Howe occupied Philadelphia for a little more than six months, withdrawing at the end of May 1778. Washington and his starving troops were shivering in the miserable encampment at Valley Forge that winter, and it is easy to imagine the British encircling, besieging or storming the encampment to put an end to the war then and there. Instead, Howe settled down in the enemy capital and had a merry time of it. Historians differ about the reasons for this puzzling behavior. On the one hand, Howe never did any campaigning in the winter if he could help it, somehow feeling that gentlemen soldiers had a right to revel, just as school children now feel they have a right to loaf in the summer. Perhaps there were practical military reasons to avoid winter campaigns, as well. However, it is also true that Howe had shown Whig sympathies in the past, and very likely did feel that conciliation with the colonists was not only possible but the best possible outcome of the dispute. If that was

Wharton House (since torn down)

his idea, he was listening too much to the rich Tories in Philadelphia and not enough to the scowling artisan class, or to the solemn-faced Quakers. All winter long, the British soldiers reveled in theatricals and parties, apparently oblivious to the starvation nearby, or to the appalled reactions of the sober Quakers to music, dancing, and ornamental dress. If Howe had any purpose to bedazzle the populace, he could not have put a better man in charge than his Lieutenant-General Major John Andre, whose thumb-in-your-eye attitude was defiantly underlined by his taking up Benjamin Franklin's own house as his *pied-à-terre.*

Andre certainly cut a fine figure. It would be hard to say whether John Burgoyne or John Andre was the most dashing man in England, but it was surely one or the other. They both wrote plays and poetry of professional quality, designed costumes and scenery, and organized one extravaganza after another. They were both handsome in the eyes of ladies, and fearless soldiers in the eyes of men. Anything you can do, I can do better.

About the time Howe was replaced by General Henry Clinton and recalled to England, the position in Philadelphia began to look dangerous for the British. The French signed an alliance with the American Revolutionists earlier that spring, and the concern became a real one that the French fleet might blockade the mouth of the Delaware and trap the British Army, stranded a hundred miles upriver from its own Navy. When Andre learned they were leaving, he saw they needed to have a celebration that would be remembered.

Benedict Arnold

Even today, the day-and-night revelry is indeed remembered. Andre wrote a detailed description for his local girlfriend Peggy Chew (the daughter of Pennsylvania's Chief Justice) that is really something to read. Made all the more pointed with our present hindsight that Peggy Chew was the best friend of the Peggy Shippen who married Benedict Arnold, the letter gives the celebration a made-up name, Meschianza. Sometimes spelled Mischianza, the derivation is loosely connected to the Italian word for Medley. It began with a regatta of costumed soldiers and local ladies on barges sailing slowly down the river accompanied by cannon fire, singing, and music. The main events of the week took place on the South Philadelphia plantation of Joseph Wharton, now called 5th and Wharton Streets. Horsemen of the British Army put on a medieval tournament with jousting and whatever, dressed in white and pink satin, and hats of pink silk with white feathers on the brim. There were fireworks at night and banquets. Good wine, toasts, and laughter to witty remarks. The final high point was a fancy dress ball. Wow.
And then, the British moved across the river to New Jersey and were gone.

5 Philadelphia Food: Fast Food
**Pat's King of Steaks   1237 E Passyunk Ave   Philadelphia, PA
39.9332 -75.1593**

Plenty of people in Philadelphia eat hamburgers and fried chicken at fast-food chain restaurants, so it can't be argued that Philadelphia hates manufactured food. But plenty of Philadelphians do deplore the calories, cholesterol, and grunge of these fast-food franchise stands. The amount of sugar that is poured into what we call ketchup is a disgrace, as is its advertising aimed straight at kids. At the same time, it is impossible not to admire the ingenuity inherent in engineering a frozen-food dinner. The just-in-time concept is carried to almost unimaginable extremes as the inventories of ingredients are timed to match the production of the product. Someone has to order single-use containers at just the right moment to match the hatching of an egg which will grow into a chicken, alongside peas and potatoes planted and harvested, and cooked into the orderly production of those product-filled cartons that are loaded on trucks and shipped at night to the supermarkets of the country. It's truly an amazing process of coordination of a complex perishable product, quite cheap, and reasonably edible. Add to that the rather amazing fact that in times of normal interest rates, a supermarket sells its products at zero markups. All the profit is made from the interest float generated by cash business that delays paying its bills until the end of the month, or maybe a month longer than that. Who can compete with such a relentless economic machine?

Well, it is pretty hard to compete with the juggernaut if all you have is food that tastes good, so Philadelphia fast food is struggling to survive. Those franchise restaurants on the highway are an outgrowth of the diner, and the diner was invented locally during the twenties. Just which abandoned trolley car was the first is now unclear, although diners very probably started in southern New Jersey. There are still quite a few aluminum highway restaurants that call themselves diners, although they are no longer abandoned railway cars, but prefabricated special-purpose buildings. They specialize in huge portions of quite good conventional food, quite inexpensive. Truck drivers and others who travel the roads a great deal seek them out, and keep coming back to old friends behind the counter.

At another extreme, Philadelphia soft pretzels, smeared with mustard, are sold by street vendors who buy them wholesale by the hundred and hawk them at cold-weather events like the mummers' parade, but almost any parade will do. They go well with hot coffee, bottled soda, or beer. Beer is preferred at baseball games.

As far as pizza is concerned, a disclaimer is needed to the effect that a pizza pie was invented in New Haven, Connecticut, in the Italian district there. The New Haven variety is produced in huge ovens and

Philly Soft Pretzel

ladled out with long wooden paddles, in portions for six customers singing the Whiffenpoof Song. In Philadelphia, pizza is generally prepared on metal platters, of the size of a regular pie tin. The Greek community claims this version was their idea.

South Philadelphia

Hoagies are the local term (thought to refer to Hog Island near the Navy Yard) for what is called a submarine or sub by other regions and are essentially an Italian antipasto salad rolled up in a sandwich roll. The Pennsylvania Dutch take liberties with the concept, greatly increasing its bulk with the thickness of the ham and cheese slices, big tomato slices, and comparatively little lettuce.

Philly Cheese Steak

More recently, the chicken cutlet sandwich, Italiano, is coming on strong, with provolone cheese and spinach for interest, and vegan offerings are the wave of the future. But the old standby is the Philly Cheese Steak. The meat is sliced and diced, onions added to taste, and Cheese Whiz squirted around before the whole thing is grilled and put in a sandwich roll. Bitter wars are fought by those who argue whether Pat's or Geno's is the first or the best, or some other less-known shop. Curiously, this sandwich industry began and remains near the site of the old Moyamensing prison at 10th and Passyunk Avenues. The concept has spread all over the country, but Philadelphians are certain the products produced outside of Pennsylvania are highly inferior imitations. At the risk of retaliation from outraged Italians, it really must be mentioned that southern Delaware steak sandwiches are made with real steaks, no onions, no cheese whiz. Steak has to be very tender to be eaten that way.

Gelati, or Italian Water Ice, a form of sherbet, is very popular in the summer evenings in South Philly, and it too seems to be spreading internationally.

It's truly remarkable to encounter visitors from other cities who want to visit Philadelphia, see everything there is to see, but who first plink the Liberty Bell, and second have a cheesesteak.

The nearest non-Italian competitor to these specialties is the special sandwich. Probably Eastern European in origin, the word special refers to the addition of coleslaw and mayonnaise to a thick roast beef or corned beef sandwich. It doesn't seem so distinctively Philadelphian as the other products, but that probably only reflects the present transient dominance of the Italian influence.

6 Singing Waiters

The Victor Café   1303 Dickinson St   Philadelphia, PA   39.9316 -75.1664

There was a time when the Victor Talking Machine Company in Camden had not been absorbed by RCA, and so there was a Victor Records Store in South Philadelphia, run by the Di Stefano family. In 1933 after Prohibition was repealed, the record store obtained a liquor license and became Victor's Cafe. Nobody named Victor has ever worked there, and ownership has remained in the hands of the DiStefano's. The record store used to be filled with the sound of operatic arias, and now the Cafe continues with opera-singing waiters. They are susceptible to requests for favorite arias, but they also spontaneously break into song when pauses in the demands of customers give them moments of rest. The walls of Victor's Cafe are covered with autographed photos of operatic visitors; the bartender is particularly proud that Pavarotti visited there, twice. The Italian food served is quite good, and moderately priced; the Chianti wine comes in minimum-size two-quart bottles.

This isn't an advertisement, it's a review. But there is really lots of fun in trying out what is essentially a South Philadelphia hangout at 13th and Dickinson. It's Italian, all right, but it is also a Philadelphia tradition.

7 The Godfather

**Angelo Bruno Home   934 Snyder Avenue   Philadelphia, PA
39.9232-75.1617**

There are people who deny that Philadelphia has any organized crime, and it certainly doesn't have a Mafia. That may be their view of it, but still, the rumors do persist. They say in the street that someone named Angelo was once the head of the mob, and that may not be true either. However, it is true that one day he had his head blown off sitting in his car, and it is definitely true that the sidewalks were swept and completely safe for several blocks around his South Philadelphia house. If there was an empty parking space along that block, no one took it.

One day before he met his untimely end, he was a patient on the seventh floor of the Pennsylvania Hospital, and the patient in the next room was my mother-in-law, a ninety-six-year-old starchy matron, whose faculties were a little impaired, and whose daughter was named Mary Stuart. As commonly happens with old ladies at sundown, one evening the matriarch became a little confused, and shouted out, "Mary Stuart!" After a brief pause, she repeated, "Mary Stuart, Mary Stuart!" This continued for an hour, and finally, Angelo put on his bathrobe and came around to see what was going on next door.

When he appeared at the door, the old lady sat bolt upright and said, "Young man, just who do you think you are?" Angelo smiled broadly and replied, "Why, I'm Mary Stuart."

8 Saving the United States

SS United States   Pier 82 in Philadelphia, PA   39.919 -75.1377

Anyone crossing the Walt Whitman Bridge into Philadelphia or driving along Columbus Boulevard along the port's edge can't help but see two red smokestacks rising above the pier buildings at a rakish angle. They belong to the SS United States, the fastest ocean liner ever to ply the Atlantic or any other sea. On her maiden voyage in 1952, she traveled between Ambrose Light Ship in New York harbor and Bishop Rock off Cornwall, UK, in 3 days, 11 hours and 40 minutes topping the previous record held by the Queen Mary by over 10 hours, setting a new record that still remains unbroken. They teach people at Annapolis that the top speed of a naval vessel is related to the length of the ship at the waterline. Contrary to what you might expect, the bigger the boat, the faster it is capable of going. That's just the theoretical limit, of course, and things start to shake a little when you approach that limit, which is a function of the square root of the length. Submarines generally can't outrun a liner, so in wartime, liners travel alone instead of in convoys. But now this ship unhappily is a derelict headed for the scrap yard unless efforts to raise the money necessary to bring her back to life are successful.

During WWII ocean liners were pressed into service as troop carriers; not many people were taking pleasure cruises at the time. They were fast, reliable and able to carry thousands of troops to overseas destinations and thus allow warships to be used to fight rather than as transports. The SS United States was built to Navy specs right from the start to fulfill this mission should it ever arise and yet be a premier ocean liner with all the amenities people expect from a cruise ship. The idea worked out well, and she was a spectacular success with a long list of famous people who have walked her decks. The ship was a regular player in the ocean liner trade right up until 1969, when she was decommissioned by her owners and laid up at Newport News where she had been built between 1950 and 1952. Since then she's had several owners and been idled at a number of ports. She's presently owned by a preservation group and sits at Pier 82, where she lies awaiting her fate. The SS United States Conservancy was formed to ensure that her fate is not to be converted to metal cans or whatever else thousands of tons of scrap metal might be used for. One doesn't have to be an aficionado of ocean liners to be entranced by the United States; she's not only big, beautiful and sleek but a real symbol of the power and glory that all Americans have come to associate with their country.

Several PBS documentaries have been produced to educate us Americans, frequent meetings with city planners and philanthropists take place, especially in Philadelphia and New York City where the greatest interest currently lies and where maritime museums and displays are already in place due to their own history. In the meantime, the present owners had to pay Philadelphia Regional Port Authority $2000 a day for docking fees and simple maintenance while awaiting public money to be found. Because of previous owners having stripped her in their efforts to recoup their costs, she's really just a shell at present, and whatever is finally decided to make of her (if she's saved at all) will be a project almost as big as her initial construction. Her initial cost to build in the early 1950s was $78 million. To bring her back to life, estimates at the time of this writing range from a low of approximately $200 million all the way up to $700 million. This writer fervently hopes that one day we are lucky enough to once again walk the decks of the SS United States as a museum piece and symbol of the pride of the American people.

9 Port of Philadelphia

Packer Avenue Marine Terminal Port   3301 South Christopher Columbus Blvd Philadelphia, PA   39.90535 -75.13905

When federal appropriations are doled out, it is a great advantage for the Port of Philadelphia to appeal to six U.S. Senators. However, the overlapping control of port operations can come close to paralysis. In short, we may have less chance of agreement on what we want -- but a greater chance of getting it. Right now, the ports of the world are struggling to adjust to revolutions of containerized cargo and gigantic oil tankers, plus political pressure from concern about the environment.

Port of Philadelphia

Some of the main arenas of our gladiator fights are as follows:
- DRPA: The Delaware River Port Authority operates several large bridges, the PATCO high-speed subway line, and the cruise terminal, all leading to control of potentially large sources of revenue. The 1992 Congress expanded its charter to include the economic development of the port region.

- SJPC: The South Jersey Port Corporation owns two marine terminals in Camden, and is planning a third in Paulsboro.
- DSPC: The Delaware State Port Corporation operates the Port of Wilmington, DE.
- PRPA: The Philadelphia Regional Port Authority has little to do with city politics, but is an arm of the state government of Pennsylvania, operating 7 marine cargo facilities, and planning more.

In addition, every county, city, and town along the riverbank has some degree of authority. Every business and union involved in regional or international trade is desperate to protect its interest in the politics of port regulation. Lately, the Homeland Security Agency has taken a large role. Scientists, engineers, fishermen, oil refinery operators, economists, and others abound. The news media convey their own opinions and the opinions of others. Opinions abound because most issues about ports are important.

In addition to the traditional cargoes of coal, petroleum, iron ore and forest products, which are mostly declining in importance, the rising cargoes include meat, cocoa beans, and South American fruit. General, or casual, cargo tends to be more valuable than bulk cargo but greatly complicates the Homeland Security risks. The ratio of imports to exports is important because it is expensive to have a ship return empty. Shippers will, therefore, favor a port where there are expectations of return cargo. Oil tankers are particularly likely to return empty since their ballast is mostly river water; but, who knows, perhaps global warming will make dirty river water seem valuable to some tropical oil producer. A quirky problem is that most of the crude oil entering East Coast ports is currently coming from Nigeria, a notoriously corrupt nation. This has led to a thriving business of car-jacking in the Philadelphia suburbs, with the stolen cars promptly packed in empty containers returning to Africa.

At the time of this writing, of the 360 major American ports, the Delaware River ranks second in total tonnage shipped and eighth in the dollar value of the cargo. Every year, 2600 ships call into our port, which claims to employ 75,000 people. The historical natural level of the river is 17 feet, artificially deepened to 40 feet up to the level of the Walt Whitman Bridge. It sludges up by two or three feet every few years, so dredging is a continuous issue. The enlargement of tankers and container ships leads to a need to deepen the channel to 45 feet. It is true that the Wissahickon schist pokes up at Marcus Hook and will have to be blasted out, but mainly the issue is dredging up the gunk on the river bottom, and hauling it away somewhere. In Delaware Bay below Pea Patch Island, the bottom is sandy and hence valuable. The State of Delaware has plans for riverfront development and would actually like to have the 8 million tons of sand, so no problem. The 7 million tons of clay and silt which must be dredged out of the upper Delaware River channel for a 45-foot depth is more of a problem, but users can be found for most of it. Or so the Pennsylvania representatives maintained; the New Jersey representatives said it would be an environmental disaster to dump a thimbleful on New Jersey. Feelings get pretty hot in these things. There have been, of course, a great many features of this political negotiation which are unlikely to appear in print.

The grand plan for the Philadelphia Port is to center on an intermodal complex of piers, railroads, and highways which would extend as a continuous terminal from the Walt Whitman Bridge to the old Naval Yard. No doubt this idea is linked to the round-the-world concept of Philadelphia as a way station from India to Vancouver, overcoming the empty return cargo problem by never looking back. Good luck.

10 Loaves and Fishes

**Philabundance   3616 South Galloway Street   Philadelphia, PA
39.9027 -75.157**

Philadelphia is full of people and institutions that have done wonderful things without a lot of fanfare and hype, but Philabundance surely has set some sort of record. The organization has been in existence since 1984 and is generally known as a nice charity that rescues surplus food for people in need. And how.

For a long time, they collected left-over food from restaurants and caterers and gave it directly to folks facing hunger. Nowadays, Philabundance still takes calls from restaurants and caterers but refers them to its partners to do the pickup. And what it doesn't do itself, it provides food and training to do, showing partners how to organize and run food distribution themselves.

To ensure efficiency, Philabundance often works with grocers, the Port of Philadelphia and the Philadelphia Wholesale Produce Market that can provide large quantities of food for the 90,000 people it and its partners serve each week. Much of this is perfectly good food that would otherwise go to waste because there's too much of it, because it expires soon or it has blemishes – but is still perfectly safe to eat. Along with donations and tax deductions, the savings on dumping fees make it a win-win-win,

Food stamps might be a better way to distribute food to those in need, but big cities have an acute shortage of supermarkets, as you soon learn if you live there. New York has an extensive system of neighborhood mom and pop groceries, but Philadelphia doesn't. It's hard to know whether mom and pop stores can't survive in Philadelphia for some reason, or whether New York's notoriously political-legal system is slanted in favor of them, along with rent-controlled apartments on Park Avenue. Supermarkets in the center city are hampered by the underlying supermarket the assumption that there will be ample place to park a car at both ends of the shopping trip. Since it is easy to pay $300 a month to park in center city, and even then you find the attendant may have parked someone else in the aisles, you can see that the supermarket idea, which largely developed in Philadelphia in the first place, is more popular in the suburbs.

Of course, the advantages of stores, restaurants and grocers providing leftover or surplus include getting a tax deduction, helping the environment and helping those who need it, which includes about 700,000 people in our region. Hopefully, these donors keep an upward trend in donating as poverty is not getting any better and food stamps are on the chopping block.

11 Philadelphia Navy Yard

Navy Yard   4701 Intrepid Ave   Philadelphia, PA   39.8973 -75.1756

The Philadelphia Navy Yard lies at the southernmost end of Broad Street.

Although the guard will be happy to tell you it's a dumb regulation, you aren't allowed to take pictures of the Navy Yard, or visit without a pass, in spite of the fact the area of the yard is fast being converted into business properties. A great many of the warships that won our wars were built in this yard, and many returned to a sort of floating Navy graveyard, or mothball fleet, which is best seen from the elevated highway nearby, Interstate 95. The shipyards rest on the filled-in area around Hog Island, home of the hoagie sandwich. Just north of the Navy Yard are several sports stadiums and a great deal of parking space to service them. Much muttering is heard about the tax cost of this stadium farm, whose many-million-dollar facilities are only used for between eight and eighty home games apiece each year. The stadium-sprouting process began with Municipal Stadium which was built for the Dempsey Tunney prize fight and held 110,000 spectators. In time it housed the annual Army-Navy football game, but not much else, and has since been demolished. It certainly seemed to be the windiest, coldest place on earth, but that's just a child's recollection.

At that time and for many years the area around the stadium was one huge garbage dump, and before that, it was a huge swamp, the source of mosquitoes, malaria, typhoid, and yellow fever. Fish like to eat mosquitoes, so filling in the South Philadelphia swamp badly injured the seafood industry of Delaware Bay, while admittedly ridding us of Yellow Fever epidemics. The swamp once extended as far as Gray's Ferry where the University of Pennsylvania now looms, with patches of quite rich farmland scattered in the swamp. Stephen Girard had a large farm just to the West of what is now South Broad Street where he cultivated vegetables necessary for the French cooking he favored.

As you drive north on Broad you begin to notice the quaint Philadelphia custom of parking your car in the center of the wide street. Mayor Dilworth once announced this had to stop, but the uproar from local residents forced even this ex-Marine officer to retreat. Down the side-streets a variation is seen; when the local resident drives off, he leaves trash cans in the street, indicating it is private property. Rumor has it that people who ignore the warning can get their windshields smashed with a brick. This area is as urbanized as you can get, but the spirit of the wild, wild West nevertheless prevails.

On the other side of FDR park, at 1900 Pattison Avenue, is the American Swedish Historical Museum. The Swedes were here first, and they don't let you forget it. There were a number of Swedish settlements around here, including a sizeable one in Philadelphia when William Penn arrived. Reminders of them are found in local place names (Swedesboro) and surnames (Morton, Johnson). The museum is a lovely big place and much larger than you would expect.

12 Fort Mifflin

Fort Mifflin   6400 Hog Island Road   Philadelphia, PA   39.8757-75.213

Fort Mifflin has been restored, somewhat, and gets a surprising number of visitors at Hallowe'en. The explanation offered is that it seems somewhat spooky. A far greater number of people go to Philadelphia International Airport, or the several sports stadia constructed nearby in a project whose financing is described as "borrowing to expand the tax base". In so doing, visitors travel at some height above the edge of the now-closed Philadelphia Naval Base. All visitors are naturally impressed with a view of the wide expanse of the deep and impressive Delaware River. How could such a mighty river be the site of mud islands and narrow channels so shallow that British sailboats couldn't navigate past the Friesian Horses sunk on the bottom?

Well, as water spreads out, it gets shallower. Conversely, as water is compressed into narrower channels, the channel gets deeper, eventually deep enough for nuclear aircraft carriers. So, think back to the days when the Dutch sailed around here, finding the first solid land along the Schuylkill at Gray's Landing, opposite where the University of Pennsylvania now has a row of medical skyscrapers on the West Bank. Everything south of that point was once swamp, so there were miles and miles of shallow water before you got to the Delaware; you could sort of say that the

South Philadelphia

Delaware River was five miles wide at that point. Lots of fish, and ducks, muskrats and beaver. The main highway to the South, the one that Washington and Jefferson traveled regularly, ran near Gray's Landing, along the edge of the great Philadelphia swamp. Later on, the railroads were built along the same path, and the industrial devastation of that area was accelerated immediately. It was a natural place for "landfill", which is to say it was a good place to dump garbage. By 1940, you had to drive for miles through garbage dumps to reach the Municipal Stadium, where the Army-Navy football game, attended by 105,000 spectators, was played in the freezing winds. The Naval Yard had been moved from the foot of Federal Street to a filled-in island near Fort Mifflin and provided a railroad spur on which the President of the United States regularly parked his private railroad car as he attended The Game. Some enormous liquor distilleries were built near the garbage dumps, and it was difficult to prove which was responsible for the greater odor. World War II caused a great proliferation of war industries on the banks of the river to the south, and the gasoline refineries in the area added to the aroma and river pollution.

In time, the garbage dumps were covered with dirt, and thousands of houses were built where the mosquitoes used to swarm. When the wartime river traffic declined, unemployment set in, and housing got cheaper, even abandoned. There, in a nutshell, you have South Philadelphia, waiting for an industrial revival. Meanwhile, the swamps are mostly gone, and the river is a lot deeper.

The famous Fort Mifflin, whose defeat marked the end of Philadelphia's resistance to the British invasion, shows a lot of signs of two centuries of wear and tear because for a number of decades after the Revolution it was still in use as a fortification. Built on a swamp, one most notable feature is it can be very wet, much of the time, and is subject to repeated floods that most of us on the higher ground pass off as rainstorms. But it's still there, and it must be pretty sturdy.

The general arrangement at the time of the Revolution was: Fort Mercer on the top of the New Jersey cliff called Red Bank (now National Park), overlooking the blockaded channel. On the other side of the ship channel, Fort Mifflin on an island. A second channel between Fort Mifflin's island and the Pennsylvania shore was quite shallow, allowing special American gun barges and galleys to come down and attack the larger British vessels, then to escape pursuit by fleeing upstream. The Americans had two years to perfect this defense, and it was formidable. Only one or two large sailing vessels could maneuver near it downriver, and at least the Pennsylvania side was difficult to attack across the mud flats.

British frigates were patrolling the upper Delaware well before July 4, 1776, and Benjamin Franklin was a member of the Committee on Safety. As such, he is given credit for inventing the *chevaux de frise*, which filled in the gaps in the mudflats at the turn of the river. These inventions are best imagined as the "do not reverse" treadles of modern parking lots, buried in the riverbed and quite effectively preventing the sailing ships of the day from passing upstream. Fort Mercer was placed on a small bluff protecting the New Jersey side, and Fort Mifflin held the Pennsylvania side of the river, but more notably wallowing in the mud.

The fort had been named after Thomas Mifflin, Pennsylvania's first governor. Unfortunately, Mifflin was the main conspirator in the so-called Conway Cabal which later tried to dislodge George Washington from the role of Commander while he was still at Valley Forge. Mifflin was a total drunkard, and behaved disgracefully as Governor, signing over huge plots of state land to himself, along with his subverted controller, John Nicholson.

An interesting part of the Fort Mifflin site is to discover that the powder magazines were buried underneath the foundation footings of the main brick defensive wall. The gunpowder effectively had a roof of the entire main wall. That made it particularly difficult for cannon fire to ignite the gunpowder stores and probably played a large role in the ability of the Fort to hold out against the British for considerably longer than anyone expected. Since the fort had been built while the British were still in control before the Revolution, the attackers were eventually able to consult with the architect, who advised them to bombard the Pennsylvania side of it, which was mainly made of mud rather than solid brick. It should be remembered that the British had disembarked at the head of Elk in Maryland when they launched the original attack behind Philadelphia. They thus carried minimal supplies and food on what was mainly a cavalry charge, taking a great risk they would not be able to rejoin the British fleet in time. The fleet circled back down the Chesapeake Bay and returned up to the Eastern Maryland coast to Delaware Bay. When they found their way blocked for days and weeks at Fort Mifflin, Lord Howe's troops inside Philadelphia were at great risk of starving, and/or running out of ammunition.

Four or five hundred Americans were in each of the two forts, and eventually, most of them were wiped out, at least half of them by starvation and exposure as much as cannon and musket fire. They had British on both sides of them, heavy guns bombarding them, under attack for weeks. The British kept at it because to fail meant the loss, by starvation and snipers, of almost the entire British expeditionary force in America. A contingent of Hessians under von Donop was sent to Haddonfield and down the King's Highway to attack Fort Mercer from the rear. In a moment famous in Haddonfield, a champion runner named Jonas Cattell sneaked out of the town and ran to Fort Mercer to tell the troops to turn their guns around for an attack from the rear but lie concealed behind the guns, while meanwhile the Quakers in the little town entertained the Hessians in a very friendly way. There was more to it than that, with some heavy fighting in the open, but von Donop and most of his troops were casualties. The fort had been made smaller in the past, unexpectedly presenting the attackers with a second set of fortifications after they surmounted the outer ones. Later on, a second assault by a different contingent of Hessians did level the Fort. If not, there would have been a third or a fourth assault, because a river passage simply had to be forced to relieve starving Philadelphia.

Washington seems to have recognized the advantages he had and was willing to sacrifice the fort for a prolonged defense. The British Navy on the downside of the Fort, equally aware of the need to break through quickly, pummeled the Fort with thousands of cannon shot and shell. The Americans inside the fort adopted the ingenious strategy of building the walls up at night, ready at dawn to withstand another day of bombardment. It has been reported that most of Ft. Mifflin's defenders were teen-aged boys, perhaps mostly overestimating the odds of their own survival.

It was a gallant try, but eventually the overwhelming force of the British Navy broke through. The American capital had been taken.

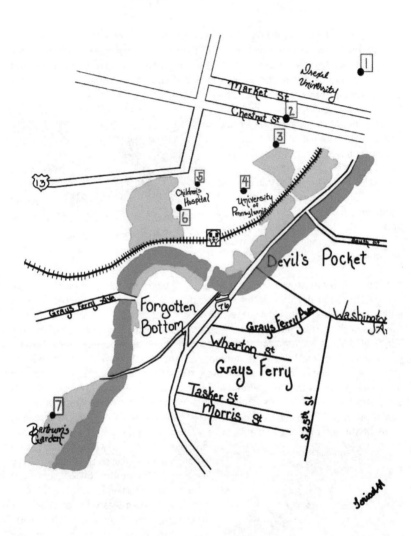

1 Market at Schuylkill

30th Street Station   2955 Market St. 30th Street Station   Philadelphia, PA
39.9575 -75.1826

Two columns of commercial high-rise office buildings are now advancing west on Market Street. The last four or five blocks before you reach the Schuylkill are in a state of decay characteristic of real estate waiting for a developer. Because the land rises to a summit around 22nd Street and then slopes off to the river, Market Street

at this point becomes the approach to a bridge, and the buildings have their front doors considerably above the ground. One apartment building and a furniture design building (there's a very good restaurant inside) take advantage of the view over the river, which can be quite spectacular at night. Outdoor lighting at sundown suddenly emphasizes the impressive classical architecture of 30th Street Station and the Art Museum on its acropolis.

Kelly Drive River Side

But down at the bottom of the buildings, well below street level on the bridge approaches, is a pretty intimidating scene right out of some novel by Charles Dickens, with cobblestones, dark alleys, deserted parking lots, and dim street lights. This is the area of the former terminal of the Baltimore and Ohio Railroad. In its time, the Terminal building was an admired product of the imagination of Frank Furness (pronounce: "furnace"). It will be remembered that the Pennsylvania RR tracks run along the West bank, converting this lovely river into a depressing sight for several miles. The B&O was the first railroad in America, and for a while, the two railroads were booming competitors. Both railroads have of course gone through bankruptcies and mergers, their names are gone. It's even hard to say for sure who owns what is left of them. Just about every railroad in America (the European ones

River View 30th Street

are government-subsidized) has been through bankruptcy, so the whole railway industry had a century of the boom but now has an uncertain future. The B & O at first only headed westward to Ohio, but then turned North to try for New York-Washington dominance by coming up the Schuylkill on its East side, going through a tunnel under the Acropolis that now holds the Art Museum, and then turned East along Race Street to join the Reading Railroad at 12th Street. The Reading had a

North-South spur called the Trenton Cut-Off which was to be the trunk line for the combined East Coast railroad. Eventually, the Pennsylvania Railroad won this battle by avoiding acquisitions and using leased rights of way. Although it eventually became the dominant railroad of the country, Pennsylvania only owned the property between Philadelphia and Pittsburgh, leasing all the rest from about 70 partner lines; it proved a better business model than purchasing the trackage.

A major economic event was the discovery of oil in upstate Pennsylvania. Almost all freight traffic on the great national railroads was going from East to West, so the trains returned East without much cargo. But the discovery of oil was soon followed by the construction of refineries in Philadelphia, creating the return traffic needed to put the Pennsylvania Railroad ahead of its competitors, especially the New York Central. Heavy rail traffic and smoking refineries create a wasteland around them, and that was the price Philadelphia paid for its boom.

2 The University City

University of Pennsylvania   3451 Walnut Street   Philadelphia Pa
39.9539895 -75.189848

The University of Pennsylvania moved from 8th and Market to West Philadelphia around 1870. (The South Street Bridge was constructed to be the entrance to art and education.) In 1920, the University of Pennsylvania graduated **34** students with B.A. degrees, and **134** with M.D. degrees. Today, the campus is a little

University of Pennsylvania

self-contained city of 50,000 inhabitants. The transformation of the campus during that period is an outward expression of revolutionary expansion of the student body, involving demolitions, restorations, new construction. And the nearly constant shortage of parking space.

The disappearance of the railroad-based industrial area of West Philadelphia has been an economic problem for the city, but of course, this abundance of vacant land has created a major opportunity for the University of Pennsylvania. One reflection of this abundance is the opportunity to become the developer for much of the whole region around the campus, working with private developers who wish to be in the University area. They are therefore willing to coordinate their plans with those of the University. It's a remarkable opportunity.

Cira Centre

As the graduation statistics illustrate, not so long ago the University was largely a medical school, with appendages. There are rumors of considerable friction from time to time, between the President of the University and the Dean of the Medical School as to who was boss; it is easy to imagine the trustees swinging from one side to the other. The most notable Provost of the University in modern times was Jonathan Rhoads, who also happened to be Professor of Surgery. If you knew Quakers, you knew that disputes were seldom rancorous. And if you know Jonathan, you know he almost always won the disputes.

While today the dominant change is caused by the Cira Centre buildings and the acquisition of the former Post Office building, it is well to keep in mind that the new Cancer Center is a billion-dollar project. A great deal of the medical school expansion is centered on burgeoning research, particularly in molecular biology, largely financed by the National Institutes of Health. While the leaders of the NIH have long struggled with Congress to keep politics out of both the administration and the substance of research, it seems to old-timers that the politicians are slowly winning. Senator Specter's seniority on the Appropriations Committee may have had as much to do with the prosperity of West Philadelphia as the quality of research, however eminent.

3 Engineering at Penn
220 South 33rd Street   Philadelphia, PA   39.9521 -75.1907

We once (1940-55) used calculating machines, which are sort of overgrown calculators. As big as baby grand pianos, bearing no resemblance at all to hand calculators which sit on top of desks, calculating machines were noisy as all get-out. A typical "calculating shop" used to contain eight or ten machines, each with a specialized function. Key-punch machines, usually several of them, put holes in cards to be fed into the machines. A couple of sorting machines, to count the holes in the cards and shuffle them into pockets for specified holes, specified by temporary wiring boards on the back of the machine. A collator, which was capable of more complicated sorting and sequencing. And the calculator itself, which was able to count various combinations of holes in cards, and even print out the calculations on very large rolls of paper tape with perforated holes along the edges. Five or six trained operators would move the piles of cards around, feeding them into the appropriate machines in a prescribed order. Sitting off in a corner was the super-operator, whose job it was to design sequences of manipulation and string wires around a wiring board at the back of the machines. His were the brains of the calculating system, and the wires were strung around in accordance with his design. My recollection is that IBM refused to sell these machines, and a typical cluster rented for $1100 a month in 1955. The Pennsylvania Hospital was considered very advanced for having this arrangement as its billing system, but its primitive quality can be seen in the system architecture. The whole system revolved around the concept of producing a bill for every patient in the hospital, every day. If the patient went home, he was given the latest bill. If he remained another day, the old bill was discarded and a new updated one made. It was simple, it was clever, and please don't tell Jefferson. (On the other hand, something appears very wrong about all this progress that fifty years later, the same hospital with hundreds of computers, today cannot produce a hospital bill within a month of patient discharge.)

Well, back to adjectives. John Mauchly the mathematician came to the fundamental recognition that just about everything in mathematics and calculating could be done by "iteration", and re-iteration. Don't be afraid of the words. They only mean you take a small piece of arithmetic, and perform it over and over, millions of times. You really don't need to redesign new machines for each new process, since anything you might want to do could be done by reducing it to the same sort of iteration. So there's the first adjective: Mauchly's iterative design concept

Electronic Numerical Integrator and Computer

amounted to a "general purpose" computer. Many different patterns, perhaps, but all performed on the same machine, just as many different pieces of music are performed on the same piano.

His graduate student, John Presper Eckert, eliminated the moving parts. Instead of metal hammers and prongs moving around, Eckert moved electrons. This step vastly increased the speed of the processing and even decreased effective maintenance. The early computers required a man to go around with a wheel-barrow, constantly replacing vacuum tubes as they burned out. But by moving electrons instead of mechanical parts, the iterative speed was so great that overall maintenance, per million calculations, was less. Eckert gave us the "electronic" computer. Together with Mauchly, the two ideas blended into the electronic, general-purpose, computer.

West Philadelphia

So then along came John von Neumann, observing this thing at work. Millions of punched cards were fed into the machine, but the holes in the cards represented data; the instructions were still wired in by physically connecting one contact to another, which had to be changed when the instructions changed. Von Neumann immediately saw how to get rid of half of this non-electronic effort. His contribution was to punch the instructions into program cards and feed them into the machine when the program instructions changed. So now, we had "stored instruction sets". As we still have today, the trio created the idea of a stored-instruction, general-purpose, electronic computer, and actually made a working model of it. That's what promoted it ahead of the Mark I and other mechanical computers that had been developed in Europe. Vastly increased speed, vastly decreased costs -- and lots of big bucks for the manufacturer.

So, off to court, to sue for patent protection. Thousands of patents have been granted for various small innovations in the system, but who was entitled to claim ownership of the basic idea? Who invented the general-purpose, electronic, stored-instruction calculator? Some puzzled judge finally worked his way out of that jig-saw puzzle by declaring that no one owned the right to have an overall patent. His reasoning was that since von Neumann had rushed to publish his work rather than rushing to the patent office first, it had become the property of the public and no longer belonged to the inventor. Compared with the contributions of a great many present computer billionaires, it really seems as though Mauchly, Eckert and von Neumann were conservatively entitled to a trillion dollars apiece. But life is not fair, and the law is an ass. Or is that so?

In later lawsuits, of which there were a great many, it came out that Mauchly and Eckert were employees of the University of Pennsylvania. They did what they were told to do and were paid for doing it. Maybe the University is entitled to trillions, thereby allowing them to pay their history professors better. But then, one final idea. The University accepted government money to do the job. Maybe all of us citizens are entitled to trillions since we collectively commissioned and paid for this work. So, to recover, we seek out a class action lawyer. Standard procedure for class action lawyers is to take most of the money for themselves, sending each member of the class a share which is less than the postage required to send it.

The final outcome in this particular case was a suit between Honeywell (in Minneapolis) and Univac in Philadelphia. Univac essentially decided to go into the patent infringement business and Honeywell refused to pay royalties. Meanwhile, IBM engineers had been called as consultants for some rush job and reported to Mr. Watson that those people in Philadelphia had something really great. So, IBM paid several million to settle the patent infringement claim and started to mass-produce these things, with economic success everybody knows about. Meanwhile, the Honeywell/Univac case droned on and was eventually won by Honeywell when they produced a professor from Iowa who claimed he had the same ideas earlier. The computer concept was thus declared to be "prior art", preventing patent enforcement. By that time, IBM had such a long lead on the litigants, that the market was theirs, and IBM competitors just sort of dwindled away. Thus Philadelphia lost its chance to be the epicenter of the computer revolution.

4 The Republican Convention (1900)

Children's Hospital of Philadelphia   **34th Street and Civic Center Boulevard**
Philadelphia, PA   39.9487 -75.1937

The Republican Presidential Convention of 1900 was held across the street from what is now Children's Hospital at 34th and Spruce Streets. Although the re-nomination of an incumbent President (McKinley) is always a boring, foregone conclusion, the Vice-Presidential nomination, in this case, was a hilarious circus. Boss

Theodore Roosevelt

Platt of New York hated Governor Teddy Roosevelt and wanted him out of Albany. So he persuaded Boss Matthew Quay of Pennsylvania to engineer Roosevelt's nomination as Vice President, which Quay did by threatening to deprive the Southern states of half their seats at the next convention, then relenting when they agreed to vote for Roosevelt. This was highly displeasing to Boss Mark Hanna of Ohio, the National Chairman, who didn't like Roosevelt and hated even worse to be beaten on any issue. It looked like Roosevelt was going to win, except for one thing. Roosevelt didn't want the job, which is a notorious political dead end. In the event, after much scheming and rumoring, Roosevelt was the unanimous choice of the convention, except for one vote. He voted against himself.

The Convention presented two other ironies. The first was that everybody had it all wrong. McKinley was assassinated, and Roosevelt became President. Everyone involved would surely have voted the other way if it had been known what would happen.

The other irony was contained in a large electric sign on Broad Street during the convention. Two thousand light bulbs, quite a novelty for the time, displayed in large letters: THE PHILADELPHIA INQUIRER. MORE REPUBLICAN READERS THAN ANY PAPER IN THE COUNTRY.

5 Old Blockley (P.G.H.)

**Philadelphia General Hospital   37th and Curie Blvd   Philadelphia, PA
39.9491 -75.1983**

For a long time, the Philadelphia General Hospital was the largest hospital in town, even growing briefly to seven thousand patients during the Civil War, but leveling off at about three thousand at the beginning of the Twentieth Century. At the end of World War II, it had shrunk to about 1500 beds, but it was Medicare and Medicaid

Old Blockley

in 1965 which finally did it in. By 1977 it was costing the City of Philadelphia about five million dollars a year beyond its revenues to run the place with only 300 patients, while the running expenses of the local private hospitals were actually less, per patient. Titles XVIII (Medicare) and XVIV (Medicaid) of the Social Security Act constituted Lyndon Johnson's Great Society, and in effect they made every patient at PGH resemble a walking government check in the mind of hospital administrators. The local hospital association made the argument to Mayor Rizzo that everybody would be better off if the hospital closed and those government checks were directed to the local voluntary institutions. After a few years, the federal government inevitably squeezed the generosity out of the bargain they would of course now like to abandon. But that's the way it goes. PGH is gone and it isn't coming back. The eighteen acres in Blockley Township, now West Philadelphia, were given to the University of Pennsylvania next door, and gigantic amounts of federal money were contributed to the building of skyscrapers replacements for the original PGH. Ironically, the two hundred children's beds now on the location are fewer in numbers than the three hundred adults once considered too uneconomically few to maintain, and the cost per day of hospitalization is roughly ten times the PGH cost which had been described as unsupportable. The rest of the real estate is built up with buildings involved in medical research, which is also an activity dedicated to working for its own extinction. Discovering a cheap cure for cancer would quickly create a need to fill the vacancies with something else. No one regrets this system of creative destruction, but everyone should regret the diminution of the spirit of local philanthropy which underlay it.

PGH was one of a dozen or so big-city charity hospitals, like Bellevue in New York, Charity in New Orleans, or Cook County Hospital in Chicago. Of these hospitals, PGH had surely been the best, and at the turn of the Twentieth Century a Mayor's commission issued a report about the place which began, "Philadelphia can surely be proud...." Having worked in Bellevue and having visited most of the rest, I can testify that was likely true. When PGH was finally torn down, the walls and floors had such substantial construction that changing the wiring and plumbing to some other purpose had become almost impossible. The PGH nurses were famous for running. Although the alcoholic and drug-addicted patients might be called the dregs of society, the alacrity of the student nurses in running them bedpans or answering other calls, was spectacular to watch. When a doctor came on the floor, they jumped to their feet and were usually ready with

Dr. William Osler

the patient's charts, unasked. Unlike Bellevue, where the floors were creaky and wooden, the open wards at PGH were spacious, clean, well maintained and equipped. At Bellevue, the forty-bed wards were crowded with sixty or seventy patients, so close together you could almost roll from one end of the room to the other without touching the floor. I can remember seeing one seventeen-year-old Bellevue student nurse tending such a ward at night alone, the intern sharpening needles, and the medical resident developing electrocardiograms in the darkroom. None of this would have seemed acceptable at PGH.

Old Blockley was the place where modern systems of medical education originated. Up until William Osler came to Philadelphia, medical education mostly consisted of attending eight hours of lectures a day. Osler had an electrifying personality and wandered among the sick at PGH with a train of students following him. He is much quoted, and once suggested his obituary ought to read, "Here lies the man who took the students into the wards." A somewhat more elegant statement of the value of the practical experience was included in his dedication speech at the Boston Library: "To treat patients without books is to sail an uncharted sea. To read books without seeing patients is never to go to sea at all." Osler was somewhat underappreciated during his time in Philadelphia and went on to found the medical school at Johns Hopkins in Baltimore. Nevertheless, the main reason he later left John Hopkins and went to Oxford was his dismay at the adoption of the "full-time" system, which is to say the faculty stopped having a private practice of their own to act as a gold standard for their research and teaching. When all is said and done, there are some areas of discomfort in the transition of students from observers to actors. The PGH system of learning surgery was commonly reduced to a slogan, "See one, do one, teach one,"; things have progressed to the point where it is probably right for the public to insist on greater supervision and control than the old almshouse provided. The disappearance of old Blockley ended a controversy, or even something of a mystery, about which was the oldest hospital in America, PGH or the Pennsylvania Hospital at 8th and Spruce. There had been an infirmary in Old Almshouse at Eleventh Street, and there is no doubt the almshouse was there first. PGH grew out of the almshouse. However, there were many comments at the time of the founding of the Pennsylvania Hospital that it was now the first; that's a strange thing to say when the almshouse was three blocks away. Social historians need to look into the mindset of colonial America, which seems to have included the distinction between the worthy poor and the unworthy poor. Somehow, the founding principal of the Pennsylvania Hospital was to get people back to work who were capable of productive work, possibly even paying for themselves in that way. In their minds, apparently just giving solace and help to those who were down and out was not quite the same thing.

6 Veterans Hospital

Philadelphia VA Medical Center Home   3900 Woodland Avenue   Philadelphia, PA 39.9481 -75.1999

The Civil War was barely over before Abraham Lincoln instituted programs designed to aid those wounded soldiers returning home from battle. Over the years such aid was expanded as both the needs and treatment expertise increased, and in 1930 the Department of Veteran Affairs was officially established. President Clinton elevated the department to cabinet-level in 1996, and today there is virtually nothing that cannot be handled.

It's not too difficult to imagine how the horrors of war can affect our soldiers in both body and mind in ways that could not be imagined back in the 1860s when Lincoln

Philadelphia VA Medical Center

first recognized our duty to those who put their lives on the line for us. Today, with such sophisticated ways of destroying life, the challenges call for specialized programs and the department seems to be doing a reasonable job at keeping up with destructive devices. Nothing bad ever seems to go away, we just find new types of injuries all the time to add to the list. For instance, we're seeing many cases of head injury caused by percussive types of weapons which cause severe brain damage while affecting only slightly the outer layers, like the skull and scalp. Special groups and operations have been formed within the department all along the way, the latest dealing with the special needs of the Iraq and Afghanistan troops.

The psychiatric clinic is especially busy as its services are recognized as being every bit as important nowadays as an actual trauma treatment. Substance abuse, post-traumatic stress disorders, suicide prevention, and severe depression are being treated aggressively by teams of doctors and social workers using both medication and therapy. If only we could treat those people who take us to the brink of war and beyond, maybe we could put the need for such departments as this out of business. Maybe someday...

The Department of Veterans Affairs is the second-largest department of the federal government, and since the only bigger department is the Department of Defense, the combination of the two shows you how far we have come from the nation's original opposition to "standing armies." The fact that these two components of our war machine are separate, on the other hand, surely symbolizes some hidden tensions between our regular armed forces and the American Legion, or the hidden frictions between two congressional committees, or else some other mystery of bureaucratic politics.

Originally, the Philadelphia VA Hospital was designated as a Deans Hospital, signifying the intention to confer prestige and lessen friction with the medical schools. Originally, Philadelphia's VA was affiliated with several medical schools, but in time its proximity to the University of Pennsylvania led to the elimination of ties with other schools. Although the bed capacity is growing in reaction to America's successive wars, its open wards converted after 1960 to more semi-private style, and its focus on medical activity shifting with changes in medical science, "The VA" remains isolated from the rest of the city and the rest of Philadelphia medicine. Part of this is physical; the hospital is confined by the University of Pennsylvania, the parking complex next to the Amtrak line, and the Woodland Cemetery, so there is little room to grow. And comparatively little commonality with the neighbors. There are 2000 employees and a $30 million budget, marooned in a sea of automobile traffic going elsewhere in a big hurry, too big to ignore but too small to influence the local culture.

The patients are distinctly different from those you find in other hospitals. There is a great deal of chronic mental disorder, a heavy influence of alcohol and substance abuse and rehabilitation, and even some residential apartments for patients. On a national level, between a third and a half of homeless people are veterans, but for some reason in Philadelphia, only a tenth of the homeless are veterans. During the Vietnam War, the system of draft avoidance through educational exemptions resulted in that generation of veterans coming from an unusual concentration of low income and low educational subgroups.

The system of government pensions and promotions tends to retain employees in the system for a lifetime. It's true that informal transfer arrangements allow a certain amount of migration to Florida (in the winter), or Maine (in the summer), or California (to see what LaLa land is all about), but those who do this stay within the VA system. Consequently, the interchange of ideas and techniques that professionals carry with them between hospitals is curtailed, confined somewhat to variations within the VA system, conforming to its social norms. But by far the greatest source of distinctiveness in the VA hospitals comes from the byzantine eligibility standards for the patients. The reimbursement systems of Medicare, private insurance -- which more or less copy each other -- changed around 1988 in a way that more or less eliminated psychiatric inpatient care in the community, especially if it lasts more than a month. The VA, on the other hand, was forced by circumstances to increase its attention to this area. Consequently, all social workers everywhere inquire immediately whether an addict or a schizophrenic might be a veteran. A differential sorting process quickly gets underway, with the VA as the preferred place to send such patients if at all possible. Non-veteran victims of the same conditions tend to have a worse time of it, because the pressure on state and local governments to make some provision has been relieved.

At the other extreme, the social elite of the armed forces is not admitted, either. President Eisenhower was unquestionably a veteran, but he had his famous hospitalizations at Walter Reed Hospital. There's an income limit for VA admission, which automatically cuts off 20-year veterans above a certain rank, possibly major. And there are overlapping disability classifications for military hospitals and veterans facilities, with considerable latitude available to uniformed boards of three serving officers, only one of whom is a physician. The result is a general perception that if you have any influence at all, you can generally avoid the VA and be treated in a military hospital, probably in a VIP unit. Good for them; I'd take advantage of it if I had a chance, too. But by siphoning off the top brass, a lot of pressure to improve quality is removed as well. If a VA hospital had eight or ten Admirals and Generals as patients, with academy classmates coming to visit, it's safe to assume that courtesy, orderliness, and cleanliness would instantly improve. And take it from me, the quality of care would improve, as well.

7 Gardening Survives
Bartram's Garden   5400 Lindbergh Blvd   Philadelphia, PA
39.9328 -75.2124

The Philadelphia region is pre-eminent in the garden world and has been so for several centuries. While it is true that Philadelphia has a mild enough climate to be suitable to two climate zones, the early settlers came from a region of middle England that has been a garden center since Roman times. And they were Quakers, uncomfortable with the outward show in buildings and furnishings, but flowers were innocent instruments of the display. Although Chanticleer was created by a Pennsylvania German family, the great centers of public gardens are mostly traceable to the influence of Quakers, and the du Pont family. Since one or two years of neglect will ruin almost any garden, the essence of great gardens lies in the ability to survive.

In fact, the Philadelphia area contains hundreds of gardens that have decayed and virtually disappeared. The Horticultural Society is at the heart of garden

Bartram's Garden

preservation, financed in large part by the annual flower show, but even that thriving organization is hard-pressed to do justice to the vast areas that need tending. Woodlands would be an example of an area needing tending, and Friends Hospital is an object lesson. When that venerable institution was sold to sharp pencil types from out of town, the Azalea gardens on the grounds were closed to visitors, except for two hours a year. It makes you tremble to imagine how long this famous azalea collection will probably survive. Meanwhile, Germantown's famous gardens are maintained in a minimal way, stretching the resources of the owners who have more urgent demands to meet in their buildings and furniture. Indeed, it is hard to name a really outstanding garden within the city limits, with the exception of the Morris Arboretum, which barely makes it within city boundaries. The area back of the Art Museum along Boathouse Row makes a brave attempt in the spring, but it's a pale reminder of the glory which used to be seen in East Fairmount Park, especially at Lemon Hill, Stenton, and Cliveden. Stotesbury is just a relic.

Many notable public gardens were not designed to be show gardens, but were originally the hobbies or passions of the original owner for private enjoyment, and later were opened to the public. These abound in Philadelphia, sometimes somewhat decayed, often truncated as the land was sold off, but constantly increasing in interest as the boxwood, trees, and shrubs continue to grow in size and rarity. Quite often, the estate houses to which they belong are better known than their gardens, and the original owners just regarded their gardens as a normal part of the house.

While there are dozens of such places, the more notable ones are Grumblethorpe in Germantown, The Grange in Delaware County, Andalusia along the Delaware, and two famous gardens in decrepit neighborhoods along the lower Schuylkill, John Bartram's Gardens and William Hamilton's ("Woodlands"). There is a record that the

West Philadelphia

Continental Congress once adjourned to visit Bartram's garden, and Hamilton's garden is mentioned by several famous Revolutionary figures since it was on what was then the main route from Philadelphia to the Southern Colonies. John Wister's 1744 garden at Grumblethorpe was 188 by 450 feet in size; some of the boxwood has had a long time to grow.

Morris Arboretum

Gardens have moved to the suburbs. Chanticleer, the Morris Arboretum, Longwood Gardens, Nemours, the Scott Arboretum at Swarthmore, West Laurel Hill, The University of Delaware in Newark, Cabrini College in Villanova, Haverford College Arboretum, Temple University's Ambler campus, and the Trenton Sculpture Gardens on the old fairgrounds -- all would demand mention in any list of outstanding gardens in America. But only a few of them aspire to the standards of an outdoor sculpture garden, where the goal was to surround each piece of sculpture with a garden in such a way that only one sculpture could be seen at a time. Now, that was gardening on the grand scale.

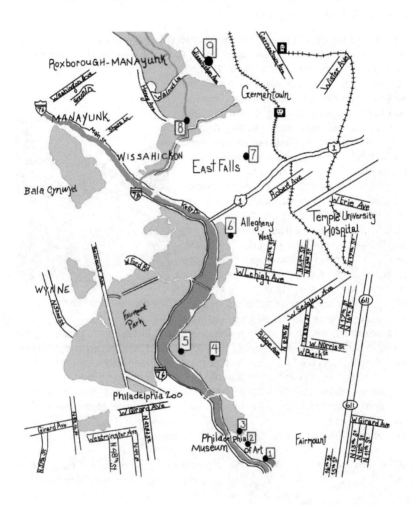

1 Benjamin Franklin Parkway

Philadelphia Museum of Art   2600 Benjamin Franklin Parkway   Philadelphia, PA
39.9642 -75.1791

Philadelphia has straight streets and square blocks in all directions, by the hundreds. Just a few streets slant off at an oblique angle, and most of those, like Germantown Avenue, are following old Indian Trails. The one, cold-blooded, deliberate slant street is the Benjamin Franklin Parkway which runs from City Hall to the acropolis holding the Art Museum aloft. Just whose idea it was is unclear, although the architect Horace Trumbauer gets the most credit. In 1915, the actual design was given to a Frenchman, Jacques Greber, presumably because it imitates the effect of the Champs d'Elysee in Paris -- a broad sweeping boulevard with lanes of trees along the side and in the medians. As things turned out, a simple idea was pretty hard to put into practice. First of all, plenty of people in Philadelphia don't like anything if it's French, and an even larger number don't like the idea of messing around with our nice traditional system of squares, and at taxpayer expense. The people who lived in the

Benjamin Franklin Parkway

area were naturally upset to see the ends of blocks chopped off, destroying the corner property entirely and exposing the backyards of the neighbors to public view. At the beginning of the Twentieth Century, the Pennsylvania Railroad's Chinese Wall cut off the center of town from "North of Market", and the Parkway thus created a triangle of desolation that could only recover when the Swann Fountain appeared, named after Dr. Wilson Cary Swann the President of the Philadelphia Fountain Society. The sculpturing was done by Alexander Stirling Calder, the son of the sculptor (Alexander Milne Calder) of William Penn atop City Hall.

The original design made the mistake of planting all the trees as red oaks, and so

Swann Fountain

most of them died of the same disease at the same time, requiring replacement with mixed varieties of trees that would not be so susceptible to epidemics. People were reluctant to live in the isolated triangle of land to the South of the Parkway, and also in the strip of land north of the Parkway up the steep hill to Eastern State Penitentiary on Fairmount Avenue. Accordingly, the land was filled with public buildings, including the semi-prison for adolescents, the Central Detective Bureau, and so on. The deep cut for the railroad spur connecting the Baltimore and Ohio (along the Schuylkill) with the Reading Railroad running out of 12th and Market, didn't help encourage people to raise their children in the area, either. And that wasn't all. The Swann Fountain was designed in such a way that you couldn't get underneath it to change a light bulb, so a set of tunnels had to be dug underneath the fountain plaza as an afterthought. Planting the plaza with Paulownia trees was a stroke of genius at the time. Although this non-native species has since turned out to be invasive and problematic, and the blue blossoms are only spectacular for one week out of fifty-two, the massive limbs are always striking, even in the dead of winter. The Rodin Museum came along, and although it is a little isolated, it is a grand display in the same spirit as the boulevard itself, including the modernist sculpture of Alexander Calder. There is talk of creating a museum on the Parkway for the three generations of Calders, and of course the Barnes Museum moved in from Merion with its massive collection of Impressionist art. With the Academy of Natural Sciences, the Franklin Institute and the Art Museum itself, the boulevard is still growing and evolving.

When traffic is heavy, people just want to get home as fast as possible, but most of the time the Parkway uplifts the soul, just as it was intended to. It's an outdoor thing, not an interior one, and there is something symbolic about the famous movie run of Rocky, pounding up the stairs to turn, holding up his victorious arms, to a breathtaking view of the city. But remember, although now closely associated with the Art Museum, he never went inside.

2 Waterworks

**The Philadelphia Water Works   640 Waterworks Drive   Philadelphia, PA
39.9669 -75.1839**

Even to those folks who've been to the Water Works in Philadelphia, it may come as a surprise to hear that, in the late 1800s, this neo-classical gem sitting on the Schuylkill River behind the Philadelphia Museum of Art was the second most-visited attraction to out-of-towners in the whole U.S., second only to Niagara Falls.

Back at the end of the 1700s, Philadelphia's source of water was primarily the Schuylkill River which was then a pristine stream whose water was clear and refreshing. In spite of this, an epidemic of yellow fever swept through the city in 1799 and wiped out a quarter of the city. It wasn't the river itself that was at fault. At the time, the water supply facility was located where City Hall presently sits. Water was pumped to a reservoir nearby, and this was the source of pollution (although Walter Reed later proved that Yellow Fever is not a water-borne illness but rather carried by mosquitoes). Not only was the reservoir unclean, but it was also tiny, having a reserve of just 25 minutes at the rate of use. This wake-up call was answered with plans for an entirely new facility right on the Schuylkill using all the latest technology of the time (did they have "technology" back then?). Besides being convenient to the source of water, a new reservoir alongside was remote from the sources of pollution of the city, which extended only to about the area of present-day 13th street.

The new facility, designed by Frederick Graff and John David, was begun in 1819 and consisted of just the building that now houses the restaurant. Originally steam engines were used to pump the water into the three million gallon reservoir, but these were eventually replaced using the water of the river itself for power. A 1204 foot dam was built across the river to direct the flow to three water wheels which ran the pumps. Along with this improvement, further construction was needed which resulted in all the buildings we have today. The dam also opened up the river to recreation and industry - it seems that we always must take the good with the bad.

Fairmount Water Works
Thomas Birch 1821

Since the post-dam river was such a great source of power, transportation, and water for industry, several firms began operation not far upstream from the Water Works. The concomitant pollution was a source of worry, and the city founded Fairmount Park to prevent the industry from operating in the area and thereby keep the river clean. So, because of Philadelphia's forward-thinking leaders of the early 1800s, we now have a lovely Greek Revival series of buildings on the river, a matching Greek Revival art museum that ranks with the best of the best, and the largest park in the world wholly contained within a city. Not only that, the Water Works has spawned many other developments such as jewelry and Chinaware with reproductions of this wonderful sight. Back in the olden days, both the Schuylkill and Delaware rivers froze solid during the winter, and with the ease of access and slower flowing water because of the dam across the Schuylkill, the business of harvesting ice also became quite profitable. This, in turn, led to something that many Phillies and Eagles fans of today can relate to. Beer. Lager style brewing needs cool temperatures. With ice being easily available, German immigrants began making lagers locally which led to a robust and diverse brewing industry, now superseded by craft breweries. All this because of the need for a better water supply.

3 Fair Mount

The Schuylkill Navy at Boathouse Row   4 Boathouse Row   Philadelphia, PA
39.9689 -75.1852

Although the Art Museum now dominates the end of the Benjamin Franklin Parkway, the earlier focus of the acropolis once called Fair Mount is just down the hill behind it, in the old Grecian complex of the Philadelphia Water Works. When the Schuylkill was dammed at that point, the effect was to calm the rapids, drown the falls at Midvale Avenue upstream, and turn this portion of the river into a placid fresh-water lake. The result was the creation of an ideal place for public boating and skating.

The transformation of this area can be seen in retrospect as an impressive civic response to economic upheaval. The War of 1812 (by cutting off ocean access to bituminous coal via the Chesapeake) had first forced Philadelphia to use anthracite hard coal, and the discovery of anthracite's superiority in making steel caused a continuing reliance on it and the canals that brought it here. By 1850, the Philadelphia and Reading Railroad made the canals obsolete and created this splendid opportunity for urban renewal. The waterfalls had created a natural boundary between industry oriented to

The Faire Mount

upstate coal and other industry oriented to oil and commerce coming up the Delaware. It is a great pity that the lower section of the Schuylkill, once so famously beautiful, has never stimulated the same vision and imagination in response to the eventual decline of the industrialization which defaced it.

Boathouse Row

To return to Boathouse Row, a large azalea garden starts the Park, and then the East River Drive winds along the attractively landscaped riverbank. Just beyond the azalea garden, the first of ten Victorian-style boathouses starts the home of the Schuylkill Navy, an association of rowing clubs which are now a century and a half in residence there. When the Schuylkill auto expressway was created on the other side of the river, someone had the bright idea of decorating the rowing houses with lights along their edges in the manner used for Christmas decorations in South Philadelphia, especially on Smedley and Colorado Streets. Ever since, the entrance to Philadelphia from the West has become one of its most arresting beauties. Add a few cherry blossom trees in the spring, and you have quite a memorable centerpiece.

Rowing - sometimes called crewing, or sculling - is a central focus of Philadelphia society and is curiously not something in which the city can claim to be first or the oldest. As you might expect, "regatta" is a word invented in Venice five hundred years ago, there are records of rowing races as far back as 400 BC, and New York -- ye Gods! -- had the first American boating club. The Philadelphia Schuylkill Navy was formed as an association of rowing clubs in 1858, and the oldest member, the Bachelor's Barge, was only formed in 1856. The development was largely spontaneous and is said to have been briskly stimulated by a beer garden nearby, run by a former Philadelphia sheriff. About the same time, the British became crazy about the sport, having the Henley Races as the most famous regatta in the world, and both the Australians and the Bostonians occasionally have the largest, most expensive, most widely advertised regattas. Foo. Philadelphia has the Schuylkill Navy, and it is central to our existence.

Edward Hanlan

There are a couple of things that are unique about rowing. In the first place, it is hard to think of a way to cheat. You can hire engineers to redesign the shape and size of your boat, but engineering really doesn't make a lot of difference once the basic development of oarlocks and movable seats was perfected. A good boat can cost as much as $30,000, but that is largely because all boats approach the limit of speed. If you have heavier or stronger oarsmen, it doesn't make that much difference. What matters is coordination, and in the longer boats, teamwork. Pull up with your shoulders, push with your legs, don't start with your buttocks, the art of rowing involves your whole body. The greatest champion of all time, Edward "Ned" Hanlan, only weighed 155 pounds. Not only was he world champion from 1876 to 1884, but he was also undefeated in any race during the last four years. True, he was born in Toronto, and eventually, he was thrown out of polite Philadelphia racing for deliberately ramming another boat, but those are private Philadelphia comments, not something you want to talk too much about.

The whole secret of rowing is to manage the fact that the boat travels farther between strokes than while the oars are in the water; if you row too fast, you actually slow the boat.

Fairmount Park to Lincoln Drive

There are two other Philadelphia names associated with the Schuylkill Navy. One is Thomas Eakins, the great American painter, one of whose most famous pictures is that of Max Schmitt in a Single Scull (on the Schuylkill). The other name is Kelly. John B. Kelly of Philadelphia won two Olympic gold medals in 1920 and did it within one hour. He won a third Olympic gold medal in 1924. But when he tried to race in the Henley Regatta, he was declared ineligible to row, because he had worked with his hands (summer work as a bricklayer), and thus could not really be called a gentleman. Anyone who has ever heard Irishmen talk about Englishmen can imagine the reaction this caused in the Kelly family. The resentment took the form of pushing his son, Jack, into racing, and in 1947 John B. Kelly, Jr. won the Diamond Sculls at Henley. Meanwhile, the father vindicated himself in other ways. The firm of Kelly for Brickwork was an enormous financial success, right up there next to Matthew H. McCloskey and John McShain, the political builders of the Pentagon and numerous other government buildings. John B. Kelly unsuccessfully ran for Mayor of Philadelphia in 1935 during the 75-year period when Philadelphia Mayors were always Republicans, but for decades was in the much more powerful position of head of the local Democratic party. The Republicans at that time would meet for lunch at the Union League, and so John Kelly reserved a lunch table at the Bellevue Hotel, next door, where he could be seen holding court every day.

The result was not entirely favorable for the Bellevue; more than one wedding reception was rescheduled to some other hotel in order to avoid the Democrat taint. But you always knew where you could find Kelly at lunch, and it was fun to watch the various minions come forward to the table, almost as if they were in chains, to pay homage which involved provoking loud laughter from the great man with a salacious joke.

John B. Kelly

The rowing clubs are mostly big barns with old boats high up on the walls, and silver cups and wooden memorial plaques lower down. They have lockers and showers, but no dining rooms, except at catered events in the evening for parties. For a century, no women came there, but now almost half of the rowers are female. Membership is not difficult to obtain - although you have to be good to get on the club teams - and the dues are not expensive. If you show promise, you are expected to spend most of your waking hours working at it. Jack Kelly was famous for rowing three hours every morning, going to lunch, and then coming back for a couple of hours of more rowing. That doesn't leave much time in your life for anything else, so the friendships developed among active club members are very strong, just like the horsemen over at the City Troop. They sort of live in the past a little, with many anecdotes about sculls that broke apart and sank in the midst of a race, or a race that was lost because of too much recreation the night before.

The lingo has to do with the fine points. A race can be between "eights" or "fours", or doubles, or singles. It can have a coxswain, or not, and be box-coxed or stern-coxed. When a pair of rowers have two oars apiece, it is the normal arrangement. A much more difficult boat to control has two rowers, with one oar apiece. Like Hercules or Achilles, stories are told of Hanlan, great Hanlan, who sometimes would win a one-mile race by eleven lengths. Or who would get so far ahead of his competitors that he would lie down in the boat and wait for another boat to catch up -- and then race ahead to beat him. This sort of person can be a little hard to take, and it is privately muttered that Hanlan was sent off to Australia, where people do that sort of thing more commonly.

4 Reservoir on Reservoir Drive

Reservoir Drive   Philadelphia, PA   39.9825 -75.1919

William Penn planned to put his mansion on top of Faire Mount, where the Art Museum now stands. By 1880, long after Penn decided to build Pennsbury Manor elsewhere, city growth outran the capacity of the new reservoir system which had then been placed on Fairmount. An additional set of storage reservoirs were placed on another hill across East River (Kelly) Drive, behind Robert Morris' showplace mansion now called Lemon Hill (Morris merely called it The Hill); the area was eventually named the East Park Reservoir. In time, trees grew up along the ridge and houses got built; the existence of these reservoirs right in the city was easily forgotten, even though the towers of center city are now plainly visible from them. These particular reservoirs were never used for water purification. That's done in four other locations around town, and the purified water is piped underground to Lemon Hill, for last-minute storage; gravity pushes it through the city pipes as needed.

Now, here's the first surprise. Water use in Philadelphia has markedly declined in the past century. That's because the major water use was by heavy industry, not individual residences, so one outward sign of the switch from a 19th Century industrial economy to a service economy is -- empty old reservoirs. Only one-quarter of the reservoir capacity is in active use, protected by a rubber covering and fed by underground pipes. The rest of the sections of the reservoir are filled by rain and snow, but gradually silting up from the bottom, marshy at the edges. Unplanted trees have grown up in a jungle of second-growth, attracting vast numbers of migratory birds traveling down the Atlantic flyway. Although there are only a hundred acres of water surface here, the dense vegetation closes in around the visitor, giving the impression of limitless wilderness, except for the center city towers peeping through gaps in the forest. It's fenced in and quiet except for the birds. For a few lucky visitors, it's easy to get a feeling for how it must have looked to William Penn, three hundred or more years ago, and Robert Morris, two hundred years ago. In another sense, it demarcates the peak of Philadelphia's industrial age, from 1880 to 1940, because that kind of industrialization uses a lot of water.

The place, in May, is alive with Baltimore Orioles. Or at least their songs fill the air and experienced bird watchers know they are there. Even a beginner can recognize the red-winged blackbirds, flickers, robins, and wrens (they like to nest in lamp posts). The hawks nesting on the windowsills of Logan Square suddenly makes a lot more sense, because that isn't very far away. In January, flocks of ducks and geese swoop in on the water surface, which by spillways is kept eight feet deep for their favorite food. Just how the fish got there is unclear, perhaps birds of some sort carried them or their eggs in. The neighborhoods nearby are teeming with little boys who would love to catch those fish, but it's fenced and guarded much more vigorously since 9-11. In fact, until recently you had to sign a formal document in order to be admitted; it said "Witnesseth" in big letters. Lawyers are well known for being timid souls, imagining hobgoblins behind every tree. However, there are some little reminders that evil isn't too far away. Just about once a week, someone shoots a gun into the air in the nearby city. It goes up and then comes down at random, with approximately the same downward velocity when it lands as when it left the muzzle upward. That is, it puts a hole in the rubber canopy over the active reservoir, which then has to be repaired. No doubt, if it hit your head it would leave the same hole. So, sign the document, and bring an umbrella if the odds worry you.

Treasures like these just aren't going to remain as they are, where they are. It's hard to know whether to be most fearful of bootleggers, apartment builders or city councilmen, but somebody is going to do something destructive to our unique treasure, possibly discovering oil shale beneath it, for example, unless imaginative civil society takes charge. This is what happened when Outward Bound and Audubon Pennsylvania came up with an ingenious plan to put up the Discovery Center, which opened in 2018, right at the fence, where the city meets the wilderness. That restricts public entrance to the nature preserve, but allows full views of its interior. Who knows, perhaps urban migration will bring about a rehabilitation of what was once a very elegant residential neighborhood. And push away some of those reckless shooters who now delight in potting at the overhead birds.

Discovery Center

This whole topic of waterworks and reservoirs brings up what seems like a Wall Street mystery. Few people seem to grasp the idea, but Philadelphia is the very center of a very large industry of waterworks companies. The tale is told that the yellow fever epidemics around 1800 were the instigation for the first and finest municipal waterworks in the world. There's a very fine exhibit of this remarkable history in the old waterworks beside the Art Museum. But that's a municipal water service; why do we have private equity firms, water conglomerates, hedge funds for water industries, and other concentrations of distinctly private enterprise in the water? One hypothesis offered by a private equity partner was that the success of the municipal waterworks of Philadelphia stimulated many surrounding suburbs to do the same thing; it was surely better than digging your own well. This concentration of small and fairly inefficient waterworks around the suburban ring of this city might well have created an opportunity for conglomerates to amalgamate them at lower consumer cost. Anyway, it seems to be true that if you want to visit the headquarters of the largest waterworks company in the world, you go about seven miles from the city hall and look around a nearby shopping center. If you were looking for the world's acknowledged expert in rivers, you used to go to the Academy of Natural Sciences of Philadelphia on Logan Square and look around for Ruth Patrick, who worked there to age 100 and died at 105. And if you have a light you are trying to hide under a bushel, come to Philadelphia.

5 The Houses in the Park

Mount Pleasant Mansion   3800 Mt Pleasant Dr   Philadelphia, PA
39.9834 -75.1996

New York's Central Park was created when it became clear there would be no park unless it was deliberately planned and its boundaries vigorously defended against real estate developers. Philadelphia's Fairmount Park, on the other hand, was to some degree a slum clearance project. The swift waters of the Wissahickon provide excellent power sources, provoking the construction of many mills. With steam power, they were abandoned, leaving desolate industrial hulks that blotted the landscape. Fairmount Park cleared out the remains of deserted mills, which had moved upriver to Manayunk, closer to a supply of coal. Fairmount Park was a creation of the Pennsylvania State Legislature, but the State never funded it. And it has thus always been somewhat larger than the City could afford.

Fairmount Park to Lincoln Drive

Fairmount Park is said to be the largest park (7000+ acres) within the limits of an American city, and in fact, maybe just a little bigger than the city can afford to

Strawberry Mansion

maintain. The Park has long constituted a symbolic interval between center city and the suburbs. Since the construction of the river drives and later the expressway, the commute along the river amidst trees and parkland has made an entrance to town a pleasant experience. If the town planners had been able to foresee automobile commuting, they might have anticipated that the sun would be in the driver's eyes coming East during morning rush hour, and in his eyes as he went home toward the West in the evening. Driving safety might perhaps have been impaired by the tendency of this glare to direct attention to the park rather than straight ahead, but nevertheless redoubles the effect of the park views as a daily aesthetic experience. Even the pollution idea had its ambiguous side since animals increase the bacterial runoff from their grazing areas, and the original houses in the park had many pastures. Strip mining, however, allows mineral contaminants to be washed by rain into the watershed. The city waterworks today extract nearly 800 tons of sludge from the water supply, daily. Whatever the effect downstream, the high ground had less malaria and less typhoid than swampy lowlands, so many of the original houses were useful summer retreats for city dwellers during the early years of the city.

The park is governed by the Park Commission and at one time had its own police force, the fourth largest police force in the state. Started in 1868, the Park Guards changed their name to the Park Police and then became part of the Philadelphia Police in 1972. The original 28 officers had grown to 525, had their own police academy and a proud tradition. It seems very likely that some deep and dirty politics were played in this shift of authority, and it might be a fair guess that some bitterness still survives in the circles who know and care about these things. In 2008 a scarcely-noticed rule change gave the Park to the City Department of Recreation, thus placing it just a little closer to ambitious real estate development. Our present concern, however, is with the houses in the park. There are seven of them, kept up and maintained by the Philadelphia Museum of Art. Guided tours are provided intermittently by the museum, but since funds are limited, only three of the houses are open year-round. The others are equally worth a visit but unfortunately are closed during the height of the spring flowering season.

Fairmount Park to Lincoln Drive

The southern end of the central north-south ridge of Philadelphia is now called Lemon Hill. It was the site of William Penn's intended manor house, until he later relocated to Pennsbury, up near Trenton. In time 300 acres of the area became -- by way of Tench Francis -- the country home of Robert Morris, probably the richest man in America and masterful financier of the Revolution. There is little question The Hill became the most glamorous social center in America, with George Washington staying overnight many times, and Martha Washington becoming a firm fast friend of Robert Morris' wife Molly White Morris, sister of William White, first Episcopal Bishop in America. It's true there were real lemon trees on The Hills, also true the estate was sold at sheriff's sale when Morris got thrown into debtor's prison for three

Forbidden Drive
Thomas Moran 1870

years. The cause of his financial collapse was not the Revolutionary War, but overzealous speculation in real estate in the District of Columbia when it was decided (against his loud objections) to move the Nation's capital to the swamps of the Potomac. Morris was a great patriot for his country and his city, but he was also a bold and reckless speculator. Eventually it caught up with him. Since the loss of the Capital was the greatest defeat Philadelphia ever experienced, it could easily be supposed the judges of his bankruptcy were unsympathetic with his attempt to profit from the deal.

Two other year-round houses represent the two extremes of Philadelphia culture, since Mount Pleasant was owned by a buccaneer ("privateer") named McPherson who lived at the height of 18th Century elegance, while Cedar Grove was originally a Quaker farmhouse of the greatest simplicity consistent with honest comfort, a style which persisted relatively unchanged until late in the 19th Century. Benedict Arnold and Peggy Shippen looked at Mount Pleasant with an eye to purchase but never lived there because they were called away by national events. With the addition of modern plumbing and air conditioning, Mount Pleasant would be an elegant place to live, even today. McPherson had to sell the place to pay his debts, whereas the Wister and Morris descendants of Cedar Grove still populate the Social Register in large numbers. The two houses completely typify the underlying philosophies of the two leading Philadelphia classes of leadership. One group measures itself by how much it spends, the other group measures success by how much it has left.

6 Laurel Hill

Laurel Hill Cemetery   3822 Ridge Avenue   Philadelphia PA   40.0041 -75.1876

There are two Laurel Hill Cemeteries in Philadelphia, sort of. Although both are described as garden cemeteries, the older part in East Fairmount Park is more of a statuary cemetery or even a mausoleum cemetery. When its 74 acres filled up, the owners bought expansion land in Bala Cynwyd, which could come closer to present ideas of a memorial garden. Particularly so, when the older cemetery area started to fill in every available

Laurel Hill Cemetery Gate 1840

corner and patch and began to look overcrowded. The name was used by the Sims family for their estate in the original area. Since June-blooming mountain laurel is the Pennsylvania state flower and a vigorous grower, it seems likely the bluff overlooking the Schuylkill was once covered with it. Somehow the May-blooming azalea has become more popular throughout the region, particularly in the gardens at the foot of the Art Museum. If extended a little, merged with laurel on the bluff, and possibly with July-blooming wild rhododendron, there might someday arise quite a notable display of acid-loving flowering bushes from the Art Museum to the Wissahickon, continuously for two or three months each spring.

There are interesting transformations in the evolving history of cemeteries, best illustrated in our city by the traditions of the early Quakers when they dominated Philadelphia.

Thomas Grey

Objecting to the ornate monuments which Popes and Emperors erected for their military glory, and probably to the aristocratic custom of burying important people inside churches where they could be worshiped along with the stained-glass saints, early Quakers were reluctant to mark their own graves with headstones, or even to have their names engraved on such "markers". By contrast with the splendor accorded aristocrats, the common people in Europe were largely dumped and forgotten, providing an unfortunate contrast. During the early part of what we call the romantic period, Thomas Gray popularized these attitudes in *Elegy in a Country Churchyard*. To be fair about it, the early Christian Church had a strong tradition of collecting the dead of all classes into catacombs. The Romans were quite reasonably upset by the potential for spreading epidemics through people living within such arrangements, although feeding the Christians to the lions seems like an overreaction.

~ 187 ~

At any rate, and to whatever degree the French Revolution was what shattered previous traditions, the Victorian or romantic period produced a new vision: garden cemeteries in Paris.

The concept soon spread to Laurel Hill, and thence to the rest of America. Acting with what probably had some commercial motivation, cemeteries then moved away from churches to suburban parks, promoted as places of great beauty in which to stroll and hold picnics, perhaps to meditate. The private expense was not spared in statues and mausoleums, which often became display competitions between dry goods merchants and locomotive builders. Revolutionary heroes were dug up from

their original graves and transported here to be more properly honored, as were some private persons whose descendants wished for more suitable recognition than conservative church rectors had offered. The Civil War created a staggering number of 632,000 war dead; based on the proportion of the population, that would be equivalent to six million in today's terms. Since they were almost all male, there must have been at least a half-million surplus women as a consequence. The nation and this almost unbelievably large cohort of single women had an impact on society for thirty or forty years after The War. Eventually, this would lead to colleges for women, suffrage and other forms of feminism, but the

George Gordon Meade

initial manifestations of what we now call Victorianism took the form of formalized grief, particularly the 75 National Cemeteries of crosses row on row. But private initiatives also took a variety of forms, including Laurel Hill's statuary to honor the valor of the fallen, ranked by the number of generals buried there and visits by sitting Presidents of the United States. Laurel Hill, East holds 42 Civil War Generals. It will be recalled that Lincoln's Gettysburg Address was delivered at a much larger final resting place for fallen soldiers, but Laurel Hill had the generals, including George Gordon Meade, himself. It is probably significant that Laurel Hill West, three times as large, was opened in 1867. At the headstone of each Civil War veteran is found a metal flag-holder, put there by the Grand Army of the Republic and marked with GAR surrounding the number 1. This is the home of Post Number One, the Meade Post, the original home of this organization responsible for many patriotic movements like the Pledge of Allegiance and commemorative reunion encampments and reenactments. A main purpose of the war was to preserve the unification of a continental nation, and the GAR sought to raise patriotic consciousness to a point where fragmentation would never again be conceivable.

Two names stand out in the history of these cemeteries, Notman and Bringhurst. John Notman was one of the early architects who fashioned the look and feel of

Philadelphia. His identifying feature is brownstone, as seen cladding the Athenaeum building on Washington Square, and St. Mark's Episcopal Church at 15th and Locust. At Laurel Hill, the main entrance confronts a brownstone sculpture by Notman of "Old Melancholy", depicting a typical Victorian romantic vision; just about all other monuments in the cemetery are either of acid rain-eroded marble or indelible granite. Brownstone from Hummelstown PA provided the characteristic look of New York residential architecture during this era. Philadelphia brownstone probably came from the same place. The other name is Bringhurst, dating back to 17th Century Germantown, long associated with the underlying sanitary purposes of the cemetery. The family finally and gladly sold the undertaking business a few decades ago.

John Notman

Somehow, the image of cemeteries has now transformed from public places of meditation and reverence to places that are "spooky". Their greatest surge of visitors, these days, occurs at Halloween.

7 Encampment at East Falls

West Queen Lane and Fox Street Philadelphia, PA 40.0186 -75.1830

The urban intersection at Queen Lane and Fox Avenue in East Falls is a busy one, and except for a few stately residences, it easily escapes notice by commuters. However, the landscape forms a bowl atop a steep hill, fairly near the Schuylkill River. George Washington had evidently picked it out as a strong military position near the Capital at Philadelphia, either to defend the city or from which to attack it, as circumstances might dictate.

Washington's plans and thought processes are not precisely recorded, but when Lord Howe had sailed south from the Staten Island- New Brunswick area, he ordered his troops to head for an East Falls encampment at the southern edge of Germantown. Crossing the Delaware River at Coryell's Ferry (New Hope), the troops marched inland a few miles and then down the Old York Road to this encampment. Their stay at the beginning of August 1777 was quite brief because Washington changed his mind. When it took Howe's fleet longer than expected to appear in the Chesapeake, Washington became uneasy that Howe might be conducting a feint designed to draw the Continental troops south, and after cruising around the coast, might still return to attack down the undefended New Jersey corridor from Perth

Amboy to Trenton. That proved wrong, but in Washington's defense, it must be said it was a plan that had actually been considered by the British. Anyway, Washington ordered his troops to pull out of the East Falls encampment and march back up Old York Road to Coryell's Crossing, which would be a more central place to keep his options open for the time when Howe's true intentions became clear. Washington and his headquarters staff went on ahead of the main body of troops, setting up headquarters at John Moland's House a little beyond

Encampment at East Falls

Hatboro and a few miles west of Newtown, Bucks County. The Hatboro area was a pocket of Scotch-Irish settlement, without any local Tory sentiment, thus preferable to the rest of largely Quaker Bucks County.

To jump ahead chronologically, the East Falls encampment site must have seemed agreeable to the Continental Army, because a few weeks later it would be sought out as the main refuge and regrouping area, following the defeat at the Battle of Brandywine. The American troops were to withdraw from the Brandywine Creek when Washington realized he had been out-flanked, and headed for Chester. Quickly recognizing that Chester was vulnerable, they then headed for East Falls. Not only was Washington preparing to defend Philadelphia at that point, but he was using the Schuylkill River as a defense barrier. As he had earlier done at the Battle of Trenton, he ordered all boats removed from the riverbanks, and artillery placed at any likely fording places, all the way up the Schuylkill to Norristown. Having accomplished that, this extraordinary guerrilla fighter then moved his troops from Germantown up the river to defend the fords. Meanwhile, Congress decided to move to the town of York on the Susquehanna, just in case.

The views along the charming, curving, leafy Kelly Drive from the Art Museum to the (former) Falls of the Schuylkill are dominated by rowing and the rowing clubs, so it isn't surprising that Philadelphia's most famous oarsman, John B. Kelly, used to live in East Falls, the residential area just at the end of the rowing area. I was once sent to see him by a mutual acquaintance when we were considering buying a house in his neighborhood. "East Falls," he said, "will remain a nice place as long as I am alive but not longer than that." He might have added the names of Connie Mack (Cornelius McGillicuddy) the fifty-year owner and manager of the Philadelphia Athletics who lived on School House Lane, and Harry Robinhood, who lived on Warden Drive and was the only real estate agent who ever seemed to have properties available in the area. But the friendly warning that Kelly was intoning seemed quite plausible, and we didn't buy the house.

There seems to be no question that Frank Sinatra and Ava Gardner were married in Philadelphia on November 1951 and that Jimmy Duffy did the catering. It's only hearsay, strongly asserted, that the wedding took place in a big white house at the corner of School House Lane and Henry Avenue. That would, I believe, be the house where Connie Mack the baseball team owner and manager, lived. Just what connection these movie stars had with Connie, is undocumented.

Kelly Drive

Decades later, however, East Falls continues to be a curious little cluster of three thousand houses, very close to the center of town but leafy and suburban, surrounded by other neighborhoods which underwent serious urban decay long ago. The Wissahickon Valley on one side, Roosevelt Expressway on a second, and the Schuylkill River on a third give it physical isolation, and the brow of the hill is held apart from West Germantown by a couple of large schools and college campuses. Even the strip of small commercial businesses along Kelly Drive serves to discourage random wanderers. But that's just as true further east along the comparable strip near the Delaware, where it doesn't have the same result.

More likely, the fact that so many judges and politicians live there (the list includes Mayor Governor Rendell and Senator Specter) guarantees police protection of a high order, and probably also makes inconvenient government construction, or regulation, highly unlikely. The local school is good, the local private schools are even better. If you are ever seeking to improve local residential amenities (and real estate values), you ought to study what it is that enhances East Falls, and quietly act on your discoveries.

8 Wizards of the Wissahickon
Kelpius Historical Marker   Hermit Lane, between Barnes Street and Henry Ave.
Philadelphia, PA   40.0249 -75.197

The Holy Roman Empire comprised about 120 little kingdoms along the Rhine River, mostly Germanic, stretching from Amsterdam to Switzerland, and loosely associated with the Papal States extending onward to Sicily. Napoleon and Bismarck unified much of this territory into what we might now recognize as a map of Western

Europe. Before that, it had been roughly the battle line between Catholic and Protestant populations, provoked by the influence of Martin Luther spreading through what had for centuries been an entirely Catholic region. After the Treaty of Westphalia in 1648, it became a rule of the Holy Roman Empire that the state religion of a country was whatever the local king said it was.

Peace Treaty of Westphalia

With this history and more, it is unsurprising that the region was filled with small stranded religious sects who were out of local secular favor. William Penn's mother was Dutch, so he could speak the local language and had lived in the region. When this immensely rich Englishman acquired the colony of Pennsylvania, it was natural for him to offer religious sanctuary to Germanic sects as well as to the dissident Quakers of England, in that free-religion colony he planned for his wilderness region, larger than the whole of England.

Johannus Kelpius

From this history it emerges that "Dominie Johann Jacob Zimmerman, a noted German mathematician, astronomer, and defrocked Lutheran minister", led a remarkably well-educated group of "Pietists, millennialists, Rosicrucians, and Separatists" to London and then to Rotterdam, picking up some Swiss, Transylvanians, Swedes and Finns. Among them was a young Transylvanian scholar originally named Kelp, which in scholarly tradition had changed to Johannus Kelpius. Responding to the astronomical calculations of Zimmerman, it was believed the millennium of peace and tranquility predicted by the Book of Revelations would begin more or less immediately. The group resolved to accept the offer of William Penn and go to Pennsylvania to enjoy that millennium. Unfortunately, Zimmerman died as the ship was departing and young Kelpius, who himself was later to die of tuberculosis at the age of 34, was appointed the new leader.

Evidently, on arrival in Philadelphia in 1694, they encountered earlier inhabitants who had a tradition of a bonfire midway between the solstice and the equinox. Their fire was on top of "Fire Mount", and was taken as a sign that the millennium was now beginning. The group moved up to the top of the Wissahickon, next to where Rittenhousetown is now to be found, and just beyond it in Roxborough was a hollowed-out formation resembling an amphitheater. It is now believed an astronomical observatory was created on the projecting rock next to the present foot of the Henry Avenue bridge; it was at that place that two celibate monasteries (for men and for women) lived together, slowly dying out as celibate communities necessarily do. Eventually, the death of Kelpius caused the final break-up of the little colony, but not before it had established itself as a center of music, poetry, and literature for the growing Germanic settlers of the surrounding states. One group of them went further west to the Cloister at Ephrata, and others scattered in different directions. It is notable that a great many names of settlers in the Kelpius colony are still to be found in Germantown, Philadelphia, and Harrisburg, although tracing the genealogy has been difficult. Some of the music has been found in scraps and reconstructed, and discovered to be quite sophisticated and beautiful, although precise authorship remains uncertain.

Kelpius Cave

9 Germantown Before 1730

Historic Rittenhouse Town   **Rittenhousetown Lane**   **Philadelphia, PA**
40.03153 -75.1886

The flood of German immigrants into Philadelphia after 1730 soon made Germantown into a German town, indeed. From 1683 to 1730, however, Germantown had been settled by Dutch and Swiss Mennonites, attracted by the many similarities between themselves and the Quakers of England. They spoke German dialects to preserve their separateness from the English-speaking majority but belonged to distinctive cultures which were, in fact, more than a little anti-German. This curiosity becomes easier to understand in the context of the mountainous Swiss burned at the stake by their Bavarian neighbors, Rhinelanders who sheltered them from various warring neighbors, and Dutchmen at the mouth of the Rhine, all adherents of Menno Simon the Dutch Anabaptist, but harboring many differences of viewpoint about the tribes which surrounded them.

Anabaptism is the doctrine that a child is too young to understand religion, and must be re-baptized later when his testimony will be more binding. In retrospect, it seems strange that such a view could provoke such antagonism. These earlier refugees were often townspeople of the artisan and business class, rapidly establishing Germantown as the intellectual capital of Germans throughout America. This eminence was promoted further through the establishment by the Rittenhouse family (Rittinghuysen, Rittenhausen) of the first paper mill in America. Rittenhousetown is a little collection of houses still readily seen on the north side of the Wissahickon Creek, with Wissahickon Avenue nestled behind it. The road which now runs along the Wissahickon is so narrow and windy, and the traffic goes at such a dangerous pace, that many people who travel it daily have never paid adequate attention to the Rittenhousetown museum area. It's well worth a visit,

Rev. Wilhelm
Rittenhausen

although the entrance is hard to find (try going west on Wissahickon Avenue then turning around, a little beyond the entrance).

Even today, printing businesses usually locate near their source of paper to reduce transportation costs. North Carolina is the present pulp paper source, several decades ago it was Michigan. In the Seventeenth and Eighteenth centuries, paper came from Germantown, so the printing and publishing industry centered here, too. When Pastorius was describing the new German settlement to prospective immigrants, he said, "Es ist nur Wald" -- it's just a forest. A forest near a source of abundant water. Some of the surly remarks of Benjamin Franklin about German immigrants may have grown out of his competition with Christopher Sower (Saur), the largest printer in America, and located of course in Germantown.

Francis Daniel Pastorius was sort of a local European flack for William Penn. He assembled in the Rhineland town of Krefeld a group of Dutch Quaker investors called the Frankford Company. When the time came for the group to emigrate, however, Pastorius alone actually crossed the ocean; so he was obliged to return the 16,000 acres of Germantown, Roxborough and Chestnut Hill he had been ceded. Another group, half Dutch and half Swiss, came from Krisheim (Cresheim) to a 6000-acre land grant in the high ground between the Schuylkill and Delaware rivers. The time was 1683. The heavily Swiss origins of these original settlers give an additional flavor to the term "Pennsylvania Dutch".

Where the Wissahickon crosses Germantown Avenue, a group of Rosicrucian hermits created a settlement, one of considerable musical and literary attainment.

The leader was John Kelpius, and upon his death the group broke up, many going further west to the cloister at Ephrata. From 1683 to 1730 Germantown was small wooden houses and muddy roads, but there was nevertheless to be found the center of Germanic intellectual and religious ferment. Several protestant denominations have their founding mother church on Germantown Avenue, Sower spread bibles and prayer books up and down the Appalachians, and even the hermits put a defining Germantown stamp on the sects which were to arrive after 1730. The hermits apparently invented the hex signs, which were carried westward by a later, more agrarian, German peasant immigration, passing through on the way to the deep topsoil of Lancaster County.

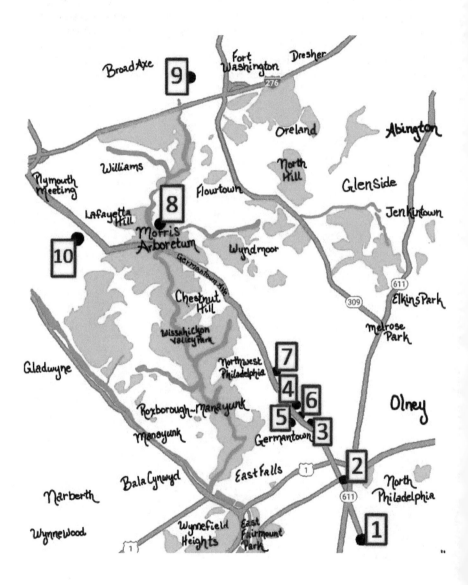

1 Germantown Avenue, One End to the Other

Fair Hill Burial Ground   **2901 Germantown Ave**   **Philadelphia, PA**
39.9968 -75.1461

Chestnut Hill really is a big hill poking up in the middle of Philadelphia, and Germantown Avenue follows an old Indian trail from the Delaware River right up to that hill. The waterfront area of the city has been built and rebuilt to the point where it's now a little hard to say just where Germantown Avenue begins. From a map viewpoint, you might look for a four-way intersection of Frankford Avenue, Delaware Avenue, and Germantown Avenue, underneath the elevated interstate highway of I-95.

Here is the first of four segments of Germantown Avenue, and it's a pretty sorry sight. Although Germantown Avenue has wandered northwestward from this uncertain beginning for over 300 years, up to the rising slope of the town toward Broad Street, it is now rather difficult to make out anything which could be called historic along its path amid the wreckage of the vast de-industrialization of the once-proud Philadelphia manufacturing might. There is hardly any structure standing which has

Fair Hill Burial Ground

a colonial shape, and no Flemish bond brickwork is seen in the tumble-down buildings.

Approaching Temple University Medical Center at Broad Street, you will pass the Fair Hill Burial Ground, burial place of Lucretia Mott and other 19th century abolitionists. Given by William Penn to George Fox in 1703 as a "Meeting House, a burial ground, and a place for the children of the town to play", the 4 acres of green space managed by a group of Quakers has been important in revitalization of the neighborhood and provides a respite for the residents of this poor neighborhood as

Chew Mansion (Cliveden)

much as any Center City upscale park-like Rittenhouse Square. Crossing Broad Street, the busy intersection suggests 19th Century prosperity in its past, and on the west side of Broad, you can start to see signs of historic houses, either in colonial brickwork or grey fieldstone. The road gets steeper as you go west towards Mt. Airy, where it almost brings tears to the eyes to see brave remnants of another time. George Washington lived here for a while, and the

Germantown Avenue

Wisters, Allens, and Chews; Grumblethorpe and Wyck.

The huge stone pile of the Chew Mansion known as Cliveden glares at the imposing Upsala mansion, where British and Americans lobbed artillery at each other during the Battle of Germantown. Benjamin Chew the Chief Justice built this house as a summer retreat, to get away from Yellow Fever and such, and started the first migration to the leafy suburbs. His main house was on 3rd Street in Society Hill, next to the Powels and where George Washington stayed. At the peak of the hill in Chestnut Hill, a suburb within the city, Germantown Avenue rather abruptly goes from the relics of Germantown mansions to the charming elegance of Chestnut Hill, known as "Philadelphia's Garden District". At the very top is the mansion of the Stroud family, now in the hands of non-profits; across the road is Chestnut Hill Hospital, once the domain of the Vaux family. Then down the hill to Whitemarsh, where the British once tried to make a surprise raid on Washington's army. As you cross the county line into Montgomery County, it's conventional to start calling the Avenue, Germantown Pike. Germantown Pike was in fact created in 1687 by the Provincial government as a cart road from Philadelphia to Plymouth Meeting. Farmers used to pay off their taxes by laboring on the dirt road, at 80 cents a day. Germantown Pike, Ridge Pike, Skippack Pike, Lancaster Pike, and others are a local reminder that Pennsylvania was always the center of turnpike popularity; that's how we thought roads should be paid for. Privatizing state infrastructure is still considered from time to time, perhaps not to raise revenue, but to provide collateral for more state borrowing.

From a modern perspective, the third segment of the Germantown road runs from Chestnut Hill to Plymouth Meeting, with lovely farmhouses getting swallowed up by intervening, possibly intrusive, exurbia. The township of Plymouth Meeting is a hundred years older than Montgomery County, having been built to be near a natural ford in the Schuylkill River. Norristown, a little upstream, is the first fordable point on the Schuylkill, with Pottstown making a third. Plymouth's colonial character survived a period of industrialization based on local iron and limestone and has established several prominent schools for the surrounding area. But the construction of a substantial highway bridge attracted a large and busy shopping center. The shopping center looks as though it will eradicate the quaint historical atmosphere more effectively than industrialization ever could.

The fourth and final segment of Germantown Pike starts at the Schuylkill and goes over rolling countryside to its final destination at Perkiomenville, where it joins Ridge Pike at the edge of the Perkiomen Creek. That's an Indian name, originally Pahkehoma. Perkiomenville Tavern claims to be the oldest inn in America, although that honor is contested by another one along the Hudson River near Hyde Park. The WPA during the Great Depression constructed a large park along the Perkiomen Creek for several thousand acres of camping and fishing, so Perkiomenville has several large roadhouse restaurants and antique auctions for bored wives of the fishermen. In the V where Ridge Pike and Germantown Pike come together, a dozen or more colonial houses are tucked away in a town called Evansburg. This formerly Mennonite terminus of Germantown Pike obviously still has a lot of charm potential, and its local inhabitants are very proud of the place. But it's easy to zip past without noticing the area, which includes an 8-arch stone bridge, said shyly to be the oldest in the country. It's hard to know whether you wish more people would visit and appreciate, or whether you are happy that obscurity might permit it to survive another century or so.

The name change of the Germantown road from Avenue to Pike is probably not precisely where the turnpike began, but it is now notable for some pretty imposing mansions, standing between the humble row houses along the Delaware, and the charmingly humble but well-preserved Mennonite villages, at the other end. It is arresting to consider the two ends, whose houses were built at the same time; only the Mennonites endure. Somewhere just beyond the Chestnut Hill mansions is an invisible line. West of that point, when you say you are going to town, you mean Pottstown. When you say you are going to the City, you mean Reading. And as for Philadelphia, well, you went there once or twice when you were young.

2 Quaker Efficiency Expert: Frederick Winslow Taylor

Midvale Steel Co   **Nicetown**   **Philadelphia, PA**   **40.01436 -75.1529**

For at least seventy-five years after Fred Taylor turned it down, any rich smart Philadelphia Quaker attending Phillips Exeter would have been automatically admitted to Harvard. We don't know why he did it, but instead, F.W. Taylor just walked a few blocks down the hill from his Germantown house and got a job at the Midvale Steel Company as an apprentice patternmaker. During the twelve years, while he rose to become chief engineer of the company, he took a correspondence course for a degree in mechanical engineering at Stevens Institute and invented a process for making tungsten steel, called high-speed steel. That made Midvale Steel rich, but Taylor was going to make Philadelphia rich, and after that, he was going to make America rich. When he died, he was widely hated.

F.W. Taylor

Evidently, his lawyer father greatly admired German efficiency, having sent little Freddy to a famous Prussian boarding school where he was in attendance at the time of the Battle of Sedan. General von Moltke had used Prussian efficiency and discipline to defeat those indolent lazy French, and Fred Taylor evidently absorbed and retained these stereotypes for the rest of his life. Whatever he was looking for at Midvale Steel, what shocked him most was to find workers "soldiering on the job". That's a Navy term, by the way, invented by sailors to describe the useless shipboard indolence of any Army they were transporting. Taylor later went to Bethlehem steel, reduced the number of yard workers from 500 to 180, and was promptly fired. It seems that most of the foremen at the plant were owners of local rental houses, which were emptied of tenants when Taylor reduced the workforce. Even management came to mistrust Taylor. When the railroads wanted a rate increase, Louis Brandeis defeated them with the argument that they wouldn't need higher rates if they adopted Taylor's system of efficiency. In his later years after he became enormously rich, he toured the country giving speeches without fees, promoting the doctrine of finding the one best way and then doing everything that way.

Louis Brandeis

Over time, Frederick Taylor had come to see that the industrial revolution had proceeded to the factory stage by merely bringing craftsmen indoors, each one treasuring his little trade secrets. Bringing the point of view of the company's owners onto the shop floor, Taylor could see how vastly more profitable the steel company would be if all those malingering tradesmen would stop soldiering on the job. No doubt the young Quaker soon learned that little was to be accomplished by remonstrating with workers, just as bellowing foremen had learned that bullying was also useless. Out of all this familiar scene emerged Taylorism, the idea of paying financial incentives to those who produced more, splitting the rewards of efficiency with the management. It sort of worked, but it didn't work enough to satisfy F.W. Taylor. When he walked around with a stopwatch, he collected the data showing how much more might be produced if the workers were perfectly efficient. Not only did that create the stereotype of the stop-watch efficiency expert, but it also provoked Congressional hearings and federal law against stopwatches which stayed on the books from 1912 to 1949. Although management responded by forming dozens of Taylor Societies to honor the approach, the unions invented the term "Taylorism" and bandied it about as the worst sort of epithet. Curiously, the Taylor approach proved to be enormously appealing both to Lenin and Stalin, who applied it as a central part of their five-year plans and general approach to industrialization. As we now all recognize, the Communist approach was a two-tier system instead of the three-tier system that was needed. It isn't enough to have a class of comrades called planners and another called workers; you need a layer of foremen, sergeants and chief petty officers in the middle. In addition to the elaborate time and motion studies leading to detailed written procedures, there needs to be an institutional memory for the required skills of the trade. In a funny sort of way, Fred Taylor the

Quaker may have organized the downfall of the communist state before it was invented.

Another peculiar outgrowth of Taylorism may be the partisan lines of our own political parties. If you trace the American ideological divide to the 1932 election of Franklin Roosevelt, you can see we are still fighting the battles of the depression. It happens that Herbert Hoover, another Quaker, was totally captivated by Taylorism. Not only that, he was adamant that to get rid of the depression all the country needed was to return to self-reliance, individual responsibility, and hard work. Those were qualities Hoover himself had in superabundance. One telling remark that he probably regretted saying but nonetheless firmly believed was, "If a man hasn't made a million dollars by the time he is forty, he can't amount to much." Franklin Roosevelt had the million all right, but his family had given it to him. The Cadburys and Clarks could have given it to Fred Taylor, too, but he chose to make it himself.

3 Germantown After 1730

Grumblethorpe   **5267 Germantown Ave**   **Philadelphia, PA**
40.0320 -75.1684

The early settlers of Germantown were Dutch or German-speaking Quakers. They were proud of the craftsman class but, unfortunately, that made them rather poor subsistence farmers. With a whole continent stretching beyond them, professional farmers would not likely choose to settle on a stony hilltop, two hours away from Philadelphia. Germantown's future lay in a religious congregation, in papermaking, textile manufacture, publishing, printing, and newspapers. Plenty of stones were lying around, so stone houses soon replaced the early wooden ones. Since Philadelphia in 1776 had fewer than 40,000 inhabitants, and only thirty wheeled vehicles other than wagons, it was not too difficult for Germantown to imagine it might eventually eclipse that nearby seaport full of Englishmen. Two wars and two epidemics brought those Germantown dreams to an end, but in a sense, those calamities were stimulants to the town, as well.

In 1730 real German peasants began to arrive in large numbers from the Palatinate section of the Rhine Valley. They arrived as survivors of a horrendous ocean sailing experience, packed in such density that it was not unusual to find dead bodies in the hold, of passengers that had only been supposed to have wandered into a different part of the ship. Quite often, they paid for their passage by selling themselves into what amounted to limited-time slavery, and a customary pattern was for parents to sell an adolescent child into slavery for eight or ten years in order to pay for the voyage of the family. They were uneducated, even ignorant, and often were proponents of small new religious sects. All of that made them seem to be a primitive tribe in the eyes of the earlier settlers. But they were professional farmers, and good at it. They knew, and a quick tour of Lancaster County today confirms their belief, that if you had a reasonable amount of very good land, you could live a life that

approached that of the craftsmen in comfort, and usually far exceeded them in personal assets. They have therefore taken a long time to rise from farm to sophistication, while the already sophisticated craftsmen in Germantown wasted no time in abandoning farming. The peasant newcomers arrived in Philadelphia, made their way to nearby Germantown, learned a little about the new country and the refinements of their Protestant culture -- and then pressed on to the great fertile valley to the West, where the way had been paved by those twenty-five German families who had landed on the Hudson River several decades earlier and come down the Susquehanna via Cooperstown. Only a minority of the after-1730 Germans stayed on permanently in that

Grumblethorpe

steadily growing little German metropolis on a hill, and none of the very earliest German pioneers further west had even landed in Philadelphia.

During this period, the Athens of German America also invented the Suburb. The pioneer of this concept was Benjamin Chew, the Chief Justice, who built a magnificent stone mansion on Germantown Avenue, which was to become the main fortress of the Battle of Germantown in the Revolutionary War. Present-day visitors are still impressed with the immensity and sturdy mass of this home. Grumblethorpe, Stenton and a score of other country homes were placed there. Germantown in 1750 still wasn't a very big town, but it was plenty comfortable, quiet, safe, intellectual and affluent. Its first disruption came from the French and Indian War.

4 The Yellow Fever 1793

Germantown White House   5442 Germantown Ave   40.0338 -75.1722

The French Revolution stretched from 1789 to 1799 and created the opportunity for a second revolution in the New World which a second overstretched European country would lose. The slaves of Haiti just about exterminated the white settlers, except for the few who escaped, taking Yellow Fever and Dengue with them. Both diseases are mosquito-borne, so they flare up in the summer and die down in the winter, although the Philadelphians who welcomed the exiles didn't know that. Yellow Fever in Philadelphia was bad in 1793, came back annually for three more years, and flared up once again in 1798. It could be easily observed to be more frequent in the lowlands, absent in the hills. Seasonal, it reached a peak in October, disappeared after the first frost. In the early fall, people died a horrible yellow death, jaundiced and bilious.

The Yellow Fever epidemic had a profound effect on many things. It was one of the major reasons the nation's capital did not remain in Philadelphia. It made the reputation of Dr. Benjamin Rush who announced a highly unfortunate treatment -- bleeding the victims -- thus provoking numerous anti-scientific medical doctrines based on the relative superiority of doing nothing at all. In Latin, Galen had capsulized the doctrine of Hippocrates in the "Epidemics" as *primum non nocere* ("At least do no harm.") It took a full century for American scientific medicine to recover from this blow to its reputation. Whatever criticism Rush may deserve for his Yellow Fever blunder, it definitely is not true that he was a scientific lemon. Medical students are regularly surprised to learn that he is the physician who first identified and described the tropical disease of Dengue, or "break-bone fever", which was a somewhat less-noticed feature among the Haiti exiles in Philadelphia. In still other scientific circles, Benjamin Rush is often referred to as the "Father of American

Psychiatry". He was one of the founders of the College of Physicians of Philadelphia, the oldest medical society in North America. Medical colleagues who today scoff at the yellow fever episode seem to forget that Rush stayed behind to tend the sick during a devastating epidemic, while many of his more cautious colleagues fled for their lives. An unhesitating signer of the Declaration of Independence, whatever Rush did, he did courageously. Non-academic physicians have sarcastically referred to this episode ever since, as proving that "some people" think it is "better to publish than to perish".

Dr. Rush

One very good non-medical thing the Yellow Fever epidemic accomplished was to put an abrupt end to the torch-light parades of window-breaking rioters agitating, with Jefferson's approval, for an American version of the guillotine and the terror. Federalists like John Adams and William Bingham never forgave Jefferson or his admirers for this, so the class warfare movement might likely have got much worse if everyone had not suddenly dropped tools, and headed for the hilly safety of Germantown.

The President of the new republic, George Washington, was in Mt. Vernon in the summer of 1793, wondering what to do about the Yellow Fever epidemic, and particularly uncertain what the Constitution empowered him to do. He finally decided to rent rooms in Germantown and called a cabinet meeting there. His first rooms were rented from Frederick Herman, a pastor of the Reformed Church and teacher at the Union School, although he later moved to 5442 Germantown Ave, the home of Col. Isaac Franks. Jefferson chose to room at the King of Prussia Tavern.

During this time, Germantown was the seat of the nation's government. As was fervently hoped for, the cases of yellow fever stopped appearing in late October, and eventually, it seemed safe to convene Congress in Philadelphia as originally scheduled, on December 2.

Although Germantown was badly shaken by the experience, it was a heady experience to be the nation's capital. Meanwhile, a great many rich, powerful and important people had come to see what a nice place it was. Germantown then entered the second period of growth and flourishing. Walking around Germantown today is like wandering through the ruins of the Roman forum, silently tolerant of visitors who would have never dared approach it in its heyday.

5 The Schools of School House Lane

The Pennsylvania School for the Deaf   100 W. School House Lane   Philadelphia, PA 40.0321 -75.1744

The region of Philadelphia defined as Germantown is recorded by the last census as having about 41,000 inhabitants today. Germantown has always had an unusual concentration of schools of the highest quality, and here on one street alone there are four. School House Lane runs off to the West of Germantown Avenue and was originally right at the center of town, the center of the action during the Revolutionary War. The most historic of the schools, the Union School founded in 1759, changed its name to Germantown Academy, and more recently picked up and moved to new quarters in Fort Washington. George Washington sent his nephew there, and its building served as a hospital for the wounded in the Battle of Germantown. When Germantown Academy moved

School for the Deaf

out of Germantown, the Pennsylvania School for the Deaf moved into the vacated quarters. This school had been originally founded in 1820, and is one of nearly a hundred special schools for the deaf in the United States, operating as a quasi-public institution for about 170 students. A remarkable thing about all schools for the deaf is the high IQ of their students. Perhaps deaf underachievers are somehow filtered out by the struggle to adapt before they apply for admission, or perhaps there is something about being deaf that makes you smart. In any event, the average SAT scores of students from PSD, like all schools for the deaf, are always in the very highest ranks among secondary schools.

Germantown Friends School

More or less next door to it, fronting on Coulter Street, is the Germantown Friends School (GFS), which enjoys and deserves the reputation of the most intellectually rigorous school in the Philadelphia region. There is little question about the Quakers of this school, founded in 1845, but relatively few of the students are now Quaker children. It's pretty expensive and quite uncompromising about its academic standards, but if you want to be accepted by a famous University, this is the place that can boast the most achievement of that variety. By no means all of its graduates become teachers, but alumni of this school do tend to gravitate to the top of academia. That could eventually put them on college admission committees, of course, and perhaps the admission process promotes itself. There can be little doubt that if most of a given college's admission committee happened to play the tuba, that university would soon fill up with tuba players.

Further West on School House Lane is the William Penn Charter School. It's also Quaker, and while it doesn't work quite so hard at it as GFS does, it has plenty of social mission, a great deal more discipline, and plenty of competitive athletics. A minority of its students, also, are Quakers; but as a guess, most of its graduates are headed for disproportionate affluence anyway. The middle school is named for and was donated by, the former chairman of Morgan Stanley back before Morgan Stanley sold itself to Dean Witter. This school was founded in 1689, and for a long time was located at 12th and Market Streets in

Penn Charter

Philadelphia, right where the famous PSFS building was built, the one that later converted to Lowe's Hotel.

Finally, near the crossing of Henry Avenue with School House Lane, is Philadelphia University. Since it was founded in 1894 it is the youngest of the schools on School House Lane, specializing in architecture and design, and seems headed for even broader curriculum. The University was formed by the merger of Ravenhill Academy for Girls, and the Philadelphia Textile School. The Textile School was itself formed during the 1876 Philadelphia Centennial, when local industrialists became concerned with how backward America seemed in its quality and design of textiles, compared with other nations which exhibited at that World's Fair. Next door was once the home of William Weightman, a chemical manufacturer who was reputed to be the richest man in Pennsylvania. After his death, the rather grand estate became the site of the Ravenhill School for Girls, which was the school that could boast Grace Kelly for an alumna. That was natural enough since she lived just around the corner on Henry Avenue and could walk to school. The contrast between the two ends of School House Lane, Henry Avenue on one end, and Germantown Avenue on the other, is just astounding.

Philadelphia University

Beyond this long list are even more schools, including Greene Street Friends School and undoubtedly others which I don't know about, for which I apologize.

So there you have School House Lane. A few short blocks with multiple distinguished preparatory schools and a university. Plus, the site of other famous schools which have either moved or merged. You might think Germantown was the home of myriads of school teachers, but that isn't exactly so. It's hard to say just what this complex anomalous situation proves, except to voice the opinion that it is somehow at the heart of what Philadelphia really is.

6 Early Germantown-Music

Germantown Historical Society   5501 Germantown Avenue   Philadelphia, PA 40.0342 -75.1712

What we now call Germany was a collection of small principalities until Bismarck unified the country in the Nineteenth Century. That probably accounts for the several different traditions of German Music, ranging from Oom-pa-pa brass bands to Wagnerian Opera. In addition, there were several waves of German immigration into Pennsylvania, each one of which had its favorite musical style of the moment, which then persisted as a tradition in some pocket of immigrant descendants. Germans in Germany would, therefore, relate a somewhat different history of musical evolution than Americans of German descent would recognize.

The intellectual German Quakers who settled into Germantown in the Seventeenth Century were highly musical, while the English Quakers down the hill in Philadelphia distinctly were not musical at all. There was a central musical feature to the Germantown hermit monks under Johannes Kelpius, their leader, who was a musician of some note. The printing and publishing houses of Germantown spread this music up and down the inland valleys of the Atlantic Coast region so that even after Germantown itself ceased to be the cultural center of things, the Ephrata Cloister carried on. The present center of 18th Century German music is now in the Lehigh Valley. Although Johann Sebastian Bach had been dead for a hundred fifty years before it was founded, the Bach Choir of Bethlehem now conducts the oldest continuous Bach Festival in existence. It's well worth the short trip to Bethlehem if you can get tickets, and more importantly if you can find a place nearby to park.

7 The Battle of Germantown: Oct. 3, 1777

Battle of Germantown   **6401 Germantown Ave**   **Philadelphia, PA**
40.0480 -75.1812

After its brief commotion from the unwelcome French and Indian War (see Stop 9), Germantown settled down to a 22-year period of colonial inter-war prosperity and quite vigorous growth. Most of the surviving hundred historical houses of the area date from this period.

Two decades passed. What we now call the American Revolution started rumbling in far-off Lexington and Concord, soon moved to New York and New Jersey. General William Howe, the illegitimate uncle of King George III, then decided to occupy the largest city in the colonies, tried to get his brother's Navy up the Delaware but hesitated to persist in a naval attack on the chain barrier blocking the river. He considered but abandoned trying to outflank the New Jersey fort at Red Bank, the land-based artillery at Fort Mifflin, and heaven knows what else along the twisting shaggy Delaware River. Giving up on that approach, Howe sent the navy down to Norfolk and back up the Chesapeake, landing the troops at the head of the Elk River. Washington was outflanked at the Battle of the Brandywine Creek trying to head him off, although he suffered far fewer casualties than the British. A rainstorm, presumably a fall hurricane, disrupted his planned counterattack near Paoli. So Howe invested Philadelphia, organizing his main defensive position in the center of Germantown. His headquarters were in Stenton and Morris House, General James Agnew was at Grumblethorpe. The Center of British defense was set up at Market Square where Germantown Avenue crosses School House Lane. With Washington retreating to Valley Forge, that should take care of that. Raggedy rebels were unlikely to attack a prepared hilltop position with a river on either side, defended by a large number of British regulars.

Washington did not look at things that way, at all. Cut off from their fleet, the British situation would be precarious until the Delaware could be re-opened. He had watched General Braddock conduct with bravado an arrogant suicide mission in the woods near Ft. Duquesne, and also knew the British always based as much strategy as possible on their navy. Washington's plan was to attack frontally down the Skippack Pike with the troops under his direct command, while Armstrong would come down Ridge Avenue and up from the side. General Greene would attack along Limekiln Road, while General Smallwood and Foreman would come down Old York Road. In the foggy morning of October 3, the main body of American troops reached Benjamin Chew's massive stone house, now occupied by determined British troops, and General Knox decided this was too strong a pocket to leave behind in his rear. Precious time was lost with an artillery bombardment, and unfortunately, the flanking troops down the lateral roads were late or did not arrive at all. The forward movement stopped, then the British counter-attacked. Washington was therefore forced to retreat, but he did so in good order. The battle was over, the British had won again.

But maybe not. Washington hadn't routed the British Army or forced them to leave Philadelphia. They did leave the following year, however, and there was meanwhile no great desertion from the Colonial cause. Washington's troops suffered terrible privation and discouragement at Valley Forge, but the crowned heads of Europe didn't know that. For reasons of their own, the French and German monarchs were pondering whether the American rebellion was worth supporting, or whether it would soon collapse in a round of public hangings. From their perspective, the Americans didn't have to win, in fact, it might be useful if they didn't. But if they were spirited and determined, led by a man who was courageous and resolute, their damage to the British interests might be worth what it would cost to support them. The Battle of Germantown can thus be reasonably argued to have been an advancement of colonial goals, even if it could not be called a victory. However, when the news of Burgoyne's defeat at Saratoga soon reached them, the European enemies of England decided the colonists would be useful allies.

In Germantown itself, the process of turning a military defeat into a strategic victory soon began, with severe alienation of the German inhabitants against the destructive experiences of British military occupation. After a winter of near starvation, Germantown would never again see itself as the capital city of a large German hinterland. It was on its way to becoming part of the city of Philadelphia.

8 Morris Arboretum

Morris Arboretum   100 E. Northwestern Avenue   Philadelphia, PA
40.0916 -75.1712

Morris is the commonest Philadelphia name in the Social Register, derived largely from two unrelated Colonial families. In addition to their city mansions, both families had country estates. The country estate once belonging to the Revolutionary banker

Germantown Avenue

Robert Morris was Lemon Hill, just next to the Art Museum, where Fairmount Park begins. But way up at the far end of the Park, beyond Chestnut Hill, was Compton, the summer house of John and his sister Lydia Morris. This Morris family had made a fortune in iron and steel manufacture and were firmly Quaker. Both John Morris and his sister were interested in botany and had evidently decided to leave Compton to the Philadelphia Museum of Art as a public arboretum. John died first, leaving final decisions to Lydia. As the story is now related, Lydia had a heated discussion with Fiske Kimball, at the end of which the Art Museum deal was off. She turned to her neighbor Thomas Sovereign Gates for advice, and the arboretum is now spoken of as the Morris Arboretum of the University of Pennsylvania. It is also the official arboretum of the State of Pennsylvania. To be precise, the Morris Arboretum is a free-standing trust administered by the University, with the effect that five trustees provide legal assurance that the property will be managed in a way the Morris's would have wished. In Quaker parlance, Lydia possessed "steely meekness."

Morris Arboretum

A public arboretum is sort of an outdoor museum of trees, bushes, and flowers, with an indirect consequence that many museum visitors take home ideas for their own gardens. Local commercial nurseries tend to learn here what is popular and what grows well in the region, so there emerges an informal collective vision of what is fashionable, scalable, and growable, with the many gardeners in the region interacting in a huge botanical conversation. The Morris Arboretum and two or three others like it go a step further. There are two regions of the world, Anatolia and China-Korea-Japan, with much the same latitude and climate as the East Coast of America. Expeditions have gone back and forth between these regions for a century, transporting novel and particularly hardy or disease-resistant specimens. An especially useful feature is that Japan and parts of Korea were never covered with glaciers, hence have many species found nowhere else in the temperate zone. Hybrids are developed among similar species found on different continents, and variants are found which particularly attract or repel the insects characteristic of each region. The Morris Arboretum is thus at the center of a worldwide mixture of horticulture and stylish outdoor fashion, affecting millions of home gardeners who may never have heard of the place.

Fernery

As explained by the curator of The Morris Arboretum, there are a few other ferneries in the world, but the Morris has the only Victorian fernery still in existence in North America. That doesn't count a few shops that sell ferns and call themselves ferneries;

we're talking about the rich man's expensive hobby of collecting rare examples of the fern family in an elaborate structure. That's called a Victorian fernery. The one we have in our neighborhood is really pretty interesting; worth a trip to Chestnut Hill to see it.

Although our fernery was first built by the siblings John and Lydia Morris, it was rebuilt at truly substantial cost by the philanthropist Dorrance Hamilton. It is partly above ground as a sort of greenhouse, and partly below ground, with goldfish and bridges over its pond. Maintaining an even temperature is accomplished by a complicated arrangement of heating pipes. The temperature the gardener chooses affects both the heating bill and the species of fern that will thrive there. You could go for 90 degrees, but practical considerations led to the choice of 58 degrees. The prevailing humidity will affect whether the fern reproduction is sexual or asexual, a source of great excitement in 1840, but survivors of Haight-Asbury are often more complacent on the humidity point.

There are little ferns, big ferns, tree ferns, green ferns, and not-so-green ferns; the known extent of ferns runs to around twenty thousand species. Not all of them can be found in Chestnut Hill, what with humidity and all, but there are enough to make a very attractive and interesting display. For botanists, this is a must-see exhibit. For the rest of us, it's probably the only one of its kind we will ever see, a jewel in Philadelphia's crown, and shame on you if you pass it by.

9 Germantown and the French and Indian War
Germantown Academy   340 Morris Rd   Fort Washington, PA
40.1364 -75.2166

From the Allegheny Mountains with which to trade and possibly convert the Indians, the French had a rather elegant strategy for controlling the center of the continent. It involved urging their Indian allies to attack and harass the English-speaking settlements along the frontier, admittedly a nasty business. The survivors of General Braddock's defeated army at what is now Pittsburgh reported hearing screams for several days as the prisoners were burned at the

The Survivors of General Braddock's Defeated Army

stake. Rape, scalping and kidnapping children were standard practice, intended to intimidate the enemy. The combative Scotch-Irish settlers beyond the Susquehanna, which was then the frontier, were never terribly congenial with the pacifism of the Eastern Quaker-dominated legislature. The plain fact is, they rather liked to fight dirty, and gouging of eyes was almost their ultimate goal in any mortal dispute. They had an unattractive habit of inflicting what they called the "fishhook", involving thrusting fingers down an enemy's throat and tearing out his tonsils. As might be imagined, the English Quakers in Philadelphia and the German Quakers in Germantown were instinctively hesitant to take the side of every such white man in every dispute with any red one. For their part, the Scotch-Irish frontiersmen were infuriated at what they believed was an unwillingness of the sappy English Quaker-dominated legislature to come to their defense. Meanwhile, the French pushed eastward across Pennsylvania, almost coming to the edge of Lancaster County before being repulsed and ultimately defeated by the British.

In December 1763, once the French and Iroquois were safely out of range, a group of settlers from Paxtang Township in Dauphin County attacked the peaceable local Conestoga Indian tribe and totally exterminated them. Fourteen Indian survivors took refuge in the Lancaster jail, but the Paxtang Boys searched them out and killed them, too. Then, they marched to Philadelphia to demand greater protection -- for the settlers. Benjamin Franklin was one of the leaders who came to meet them and promised that he would persuade the legislature to give frontiersmen greater representation, and would pay a bounty on Indian scalps.

Very little is usually mentioned about Franklin's personal role in provoking some of this warfare, especially the massacre of Braddock's troops. The Rosenbach Museum today contains an interesting record of his activities at the Conference of Albany. Isaac Norris wrote a daily diary on the unprinted side of his copy of Poor Richard's Almanack while accompanying Franklin and John Penn to the Albany meeting. He records that Franklin persuaded the Iroquois to sell all of western Pennsylvania to the Penn proprietors for a pittance. The Delaware tribe, who really owned the land, were infuriated and went on the warpath on the side of the French at Fort Duquesne. There may thus have been some justice in 1789 when the Penns were obliged to sell 21 million acres to the Commonwealth of Pennsylvania for 60 cents an acre.

Subsequently, Franklin became active in raising troops and serving as a soldier. He argued that thirteen divided colonies could not easily maintain a coordinated defense against the unified French strategy, and called upon the colonial meeting in Albany to propose a united confederation. The Albany Convention agreed with Franklin, but not a single suspicious colony ratified the plan, and Franklin was disgusted with them. Out of all this, Franklin emerged strongly anti-French, strongly pro-British, and not a little skeptical of colonial self-rule. Too little has been written about the agonizing self-doubt he must have experienced when all of these viewpoints had to be reversed in 1775, during the nine months between his public humiliation at Whitehall in London, and his sailing home to meet the Continental Congress. Furthermore, as leader of a political party in the Pennsylvania Legislature, he also became vexed by the tendency of the German Pennsylvanians to vote in harmony with the Philadelphia Quakers, and against the interest of the Scotch-Irish who were eventually the principal supporters of the Revolutionary War. It must here be noticed that Franklin's main competitor in the printing and publishing business was the Sower family in Germantown. Franklin persuaded a number of leading English non-Quakers that the Germans were a coarse and brutish lot, ignorant and illiterate. If they could be sent to English-speaking schools, perhaps they could gradually be won over to a different form of politics.

Since the Germans of Germantown was supremely proud of their intellectual attainments, they were infuriated by Franklin's school proposal. Their response was almost a classic episode of Quaker's passive-aggressive warfare. They organized the Union School, just off Market Square. It was eventually to become Germantown Academy. Its instruction and curriculum were so outstanding as to justify the claim that it was the finest school in America at the time. Later on, George Washington would send his adopted son (Parke Custis) to school there. In 1958 the Academy moved to Fort Washington, but needless to say, the offensive idea of forcing the local "ignorant" Germans to go to a proper English school was rapidly shelved.

10 Lafayette, We Are Here

Barren Hill, PA   40.0879 -75.263

It will be recalled that Lafayette was 19 years old at Valley Forge, spoke no English, had no previous military experience. He nevertheless demanded, and got, a commission as Major General on the prudent condition that he have no troops under his command, at least for a while. Washington had been strongly reminded by various people that this young Frenchman was one of the richest men in France, a personal friend of the Queen, and thus essential to the project of enlisting French assistance in the war. Under the circumstances, it was shrewd to send him on the project of enlisting Indian allies among the Iroquois, since many tribes, particularly the Oneida, spoke French and held their former allies in the French and Indian War in great esteem. The chief of the Oneida Wolf clan (Honyere Tiwahenekarogwen) was visiting General Philip Schuyler in Albany at about the time Lafayette showed up on his mission to get some help for Valley Forge. General Horatio Gates was busy at the time rallying a colonist army to defend against the British under Burgoyne, coming down from Quebec, eventually to collide at the Battle of Saratoga.

Earlier in the war, Honyere's Oneida tribe had tangled with their fellow Iroquois under the leadership of Joseph Brandt (the Dartmouth graduate who was both biblical scholar and commander of several frontier massacres); the Oneida had many new scores to settle with the English-speaking Iroquois tribes. Honyere made the not unreasonable request that before his warriors went off to war, his new American allies would please build a fortification to protect his women and children from Brandt's Mohawks. Lafayette readily put up the money for this project, quickly becoming the Great French Father of the Oneidas. After some scouting and patrolling for Gates, Honyere and about fifty of his braves followed Lafayette to Valley Forge, where they soon made a nuisance of themselves to the Great White Father George Washington. Lafayette was a hero, but not quite the man he is remembered as. Finally, word of the official French alliance with the colonists reached London, Howe was replaced by Clinton, and the British began to withdraw from their isolated position at Philadelphia.

It was thus that the jubilant rebels at Valley Forge learned that the fortunes of war had turned in their favor, and the French alliance was the source of it. With the British making preparation to abandon Philadelphia, it seemed a safe thing for Washington to give Lafayette command of two thousand troops, including the fifty Oneida Indians, and post them to Barren Hill (now Lafayette Hill), along Ridge Pike near Plymouth Meeting. Washington gave the strictest orders that they were to take no chances with anything, and particularly were to remain mobile, moving camp every day. This was not exactly what the richest man in France was anticipating, and wouldn't make a very saucy story to tell Marie Antoinette about. So, he promptly set about fortifying Barren Hill. Local Tory spies quickly spread this news to General Clinton, who promptly

**Gilbert du Motier,
Marquis de Lafayette**

led eight thousand redcoats up the Ridge Pike to capture the bloody Frog. Clinton's plan was good; a detachment went around Lafayette in the woods and came back down Ridge Pike from the other direction, driving the Americans down the Pike into the open arms of the main body of British troops, coming up Ridge Pike. From this point onward, two entirely different stories have been told.

The more widely-held account has Lafayette climbing the steeple of the local church and noticing that there was an escape path, leading down the hill to the Schuylkill River at Matson's Ford. The Indian scouts were sent forward to hold off the British while the troops made their escape. Clinton sent a cavalry charge of Dragoons forward, yelling and waving their sabers, generally making a terrifying spectacle. The Indian scouts, as was their custom, were lying in the brush shoulder to shoulder, and at command by Honyere rose from the ground to let out a resounding chorus of war whoops. The Indians had never seen a cavalry charge, the Dragoons had never heard a war-whoop, so both sides fled the battlefield without doing much damage.

Meanwhile, Lafayette and his troops escaped to safety on the far side of the Schuylkill.

Other accounts of this episode relate that when Washington heard of it he remarked sourly that either they were pretty lucky, or else the enemy was pretty sluggish. In any event, a few soldiers were killed on both sides, the Americans crossing the River were described as "kegs bobbing on the pond", and it does seem the British army mostly just watched them do it. In the confusion, of course, everyone involved was fearful of being surrounded by unseen troops, and the British may well have worried the whole thing was a trap.

The saddest postscript to the Battle of Barren Hill is the fate of the Indians. After the war was over in 1783, the colonists busied themselves with taking over Indian land. Honyere pitifully petitioned the New York legislature for some consideration of his tribe's wartime service. They ignored him.

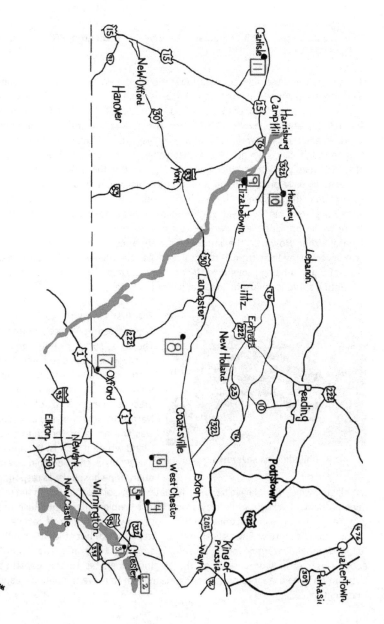

1 Lazaretto

Lazaretto Building   **93 Wanamaker Avenue**   **Essington, PA**
39.8607, -75.3001

The Lazaretto was the oldest quarantine station in the Western hemisphere, and the sixth oldest in the world. It was built in 1800 responding to the Yellow Fever epidemic of 1793, followed by those of 1797, 1798, 1799, 1820, 1853, and 1870. If an incoming ship had a case of Yellow Fever on board, the patient was institutionalized at the Lazaretto and the ship captain had to pay for his care until the patient recovered, or until he didn't. Since we now know that Yellow Fever is transmitted by mosquito bites, it probably didn't do much good, and by locating the Lazaretto in a swamp, it may actually have promoted the spread of the disease. It thus fits into the story of Dr. Benjamin Rush hastening the death of his Yellow Fever patients by bleeding them of several pints of blood, as well as the construction of the Philadelphia Water Works to purify the drinking water, which we can now see had nothing to do with the disease, either. However, the waterworks were a marvel of engineering and must have saved many lives from Typhoid Fever. As recently as 1970, I can remember cases of anthrax being brought to the port on Pakistani ships, so quarantining and quarantine stations are useful ideas, some of the time.

Philadelphia Lazaretto

The first Lazaretto was built on the Aegean Sea at Venice, around 1450. There is some dispute about the name, which is said to come from the patron saint of lepers, St. Lazarus. The followers of St. Nazareth maintain the present name is a corruption of Nazaretto however, since St. Lazarus was the name of the church on the island where it stands. It seems most likely that the original Venetian quarantine hospital was responding to the plague, which would have benefited greatly from isolation, although the rats and mice probably quickly found a way around their problem. Benjamin Rush thought that Yellow Fever was transmitted by the overpowering stench of rotting coffee beans, which is quite wrong as Walter Reed later showed, but at least it would lead to the idea that quarantine might be useful. Historically, the rumors and suppositions about this matter were useful to the Virginia delegates to the Constitutional Convention, who used it to promote their campaign to move the national capital to Washington, D.C.

The Schuylkill empties into the Delaware River at a sharp bend in the Delaware, which slows the river and causes silt to be dumped there. William Penn had earlier decided to locate his new colony at Chester, just below the bend. However, he soon saw that it was more defensible to locate Philadelphia on the upstream side of the mud flats, as it proved to be in the Revolutionary War. Fort Mifflin was located just above the mud flats and could be kept supplied by flatboats coming down the Schuylkill from Valley Forge and Reading, the arsenal city of the Revolution. On Benjamin Franklin's suggestion, the channels between the mud flats were blocked by the *chevaux de fries*, underwater spiked contraptions which were much like the blockages to the entrance of parking lots. On the Jersey side of the Delaware was Ft. Mercer at what is now called National Park. It was a formidable defense that almost ended the War by starving the British troops who had occupied Philadelphia from the rear via Germantown but were long unable to get past Fort Mifflin with their fleet, coming upriver. Most of South Philadelphia was a swamp, and there are many reports of flocks of swans paddling around the entrance of the Schuylkill. Hog Island became a shipyard, then a Naval Base. And then the airport was built on the mudflats, pretty much-obliterating everything else. There is the talk of making this area into the main intermodal transportation hub of the east coast, since ocean shipping, air transport, interstate highways, and railroad are all crowded together, quite close to the urban centers.

Benjamin Rush, a signer of the Declaration of Independence, was still active at the Pennsylvania Hospital in 1800. It was still the only general hospital in America and the model for much of subsequent American medicine. One striking memento of that connection at the Lazaretto is the cupola on the center building, which is very similar to the cupolas on the roof of the building at 8th and Spruce Streets. The brickwork is also a Flemish bond. The ten-acre site of the Lazaretto is very accessible, except perhaps for the suspicious Tinicum Township police. It was long a tradition to have a banquet and picnic at the Lazaretto at the beginning and end of the quarantine season, roughly June 1, and October 1. Yellow Fever shots not required.

2 Corinthian Epistle

The Corinthian Yacht Club   300 W 2nd Street   Essington, PA   39.8611, -75.3049

Philadelphia had ups and downs as a maritime center. Right now, it's rather down, but what's bad for commercial shipping sort of encourages recreational boating. There was once a time when almost everyone in town had some connection with the sea, and there were a hundred sailing clubs, many of them quite rowdy. Out of this environment grew the Corinthian Movement of amateur sailors, sometimes stated as requiring the owner to sail his own boat. Wanamaker, Drexel, and similar names were once associated with the formation of sailing clubs that wanted to distance themselves from the characteristic rowdy behavior of professional sailors. Yachting thus acquired a snooty flavor. It also had to contend with the plain fact that people with enough money to own a big sailboat were often not agile enough to handle them. Corinth is not terribly far from Olympia in Greece, and it seems likely that qualification for entry into the Olympics was influential in the development of sailing club rules, which tend to emphasize the manner in which the sailor learned his skills. If you learned to sail as an amateur, you qualified, even if you were crewing on someone else's boat. Learning your skills in the Navy is also sort of an ambiguous situation, so membership in a Corinthian Yacht Club cleans up your Olympic credentials.

Corinthian Yacht Club

It thus happens there are quite a number of Corinthian Yacht Clubs in America, mostly unrelated to each other except competitively. Philadelphia has a Corinthian Yacht Club founded in 1892 out of the remnants of other clubs, and located in Essington on the grounds of former Governor Printz's estate. The food there is famously good, and sunset buffets at the head of Delaware Bay are quite memorable.

3 The Corinthos Disaster

Marcus Hook   617 E. 10th   St. Marcus Hook, PA   39.8182, -75.4156

Fire, huge fire. The Corinthos disaster of January 30, 1975, was the biggest fire in Philadelphia history, and one hopes the biggest forevermore. Its immensity has possibly lessened attention for some associated issues which are nevertheless quite important, too. Like the issue of punitive damages in a lawsuit, or the need to balance environmental damage with a national need for energy independence. And the changing ways that law firms charge their clients. We hope the relatives of the victims will not be offended if the tragedy is used to illustrate these other important issues. On that cold winter day, two big tanker ships were tied up alongside the opposite banks of the Delaware River at Marcus Hook. The Corinthos was a 754-foot tanker with a capacity of 400,000 barrels of crude oil, tied up on the Pennsylvania side at the British Petroleum dock with perhaps 300,000 barrels still in its tanks at the time of the disaster. At the same time, the 660-foot tanker Edgar M. Queeny, with roughly 250,000 barrels of specialty chemicals in its hold, let go its moorings to the Monsanto Chemical dock directly across the river in New Jersey, intending to turn around and head upstream to discharge the rest of its cargo at the Mantua

Creek Terminal near Paulsboro. Curiously, a tanker is more likely to explode when it is half empty because there is more opportunity for mixing oxygen with the combustible liquid sloshing around. A tug stood by to assist the turn, but the master of the Queeny felt there was ample room to make the turn under her own power.

With no one paying particular attention to this routine maneuver, the Queeny seemed (to only casual observers) to head directly across the river, ramming straight into the side of the Corinthos. Actually, the Queeny had engaged in a number of backing and filling maneuvers, and the sailors aboard were appalled that it seemed to lack enough power to stop its headlong plunge at the Corinthos. There was an almost immediate explosion on the Corinthos, and luckily the Queeny broke free with only its bow badly damaged. Otherwise, the fire might have been twice as large as it proved to be with only the Corinthos burning. The explosion and fire killed twenty-five sailors and dockworkers, burned for days, devastated the neighborhood and occupied the efforts of three dozen fire companies. A graphic account of the fire and firefighting was written by none other than Curt Weldon who was later to become Congressman from the district but was then a volunteer fireman active in the Corinthos tragedy. There were surprising water shortages in this fire on the river because the falling tides would take the water's edge too far away from the suction devices for the fire hoses on the shore. The tide would also rise above a gash in the side of the burning ship, floating water in and then oil up to the point where it would flow out of the ship onto the surface of the river. Oil floated two miles upstream from the burning ship and ignited a U.S. Navy destroyer which was tied up at that point. Observers in airplanes estimated the oil spill was eventually fifty miles long.

All of these factors played a role in the decision whether to try to put out the fire at the dock or let it burn out; experts continue to argue which would have been better. There were always dangers the burning ship would break loose and float in unexpected directions, that the oil slick would ignite for its full length, and that storage tanks onshore would be ignited. The initial explosion had blown huge pieces of iron half a mile away, and the ground near the ship was littered with charred, dismembered pieces of flesh from the victims. Of course, there was a big lawsuit. When a ship is tied up at a dock it certainly feels aggrieved when another ship crosses a river and rams it.

The time-honored principle of admiralty law holds that the owner of an offending ship is not liable for damages greater than the salvage value of its own hulk, which in this case might have been about $3 million. The underlying assumption is that the owner has no way of knowing what is going on thousands of miles away, no control over it, no power to respond in a useful way. Enter Richard Palmer, counsel for the

Corinthos. Palmer was aware that the National Transportation Safety Board collects information about ship maintenance inspections in order to share useful information for the benefit of everyone. His inquiry revealed that the inspections of the Queeny for four years before the crash had repeatedly demonstrated that the stern engine had a damaged turbine, and was only able to drive the ship at 50% of its rated power. Why this turbine had not been repaired was now irrelevant; the owners of the

Marcus Hook

ship did have relevant information and had failed to act in a timely safe fashion. The limitation of liability to the salvage value of the hulk now no longer applied if the negligence was judged relevant. The defendants, the owners of the Queeny, decided to settle. While the size of the settlement is a secret of the court, it is fair to guess that it approached the full value of the suit, which was $11 million. Mr. Palmer, by using his experience to surmise that maintenance records might be available at the Transportation Agency, and recognizing that the awareness of the owner might switch the basis for the compensation award from hulk value (of the defendant's ship) to the extent of the damage (to the plaintiff's ship), probably tripled the damage settlement.

Reflections on the extraordinary benefit to the client from a comparatively short period of work by the lawyer leads to a discussion about the proper basis for lawyer's fees. Senior lawyers feel that the computer has revolutionized lawyer billing practices, and not for the better. Because it is now possible to produce itemized billing which summarizes conversations of less than a minute in duration, services for the settlement of estates can be many pages long, mostly for rather routine business. Matrimonial lawyers are entitled to charge for hours of listening to inconsequential recriminations; lawyers can bill for hours of time spent reading

documents into a recording machine, or sitting wordlessly at depositions. Since the time expended can now be flawlessly measured and recorded on computers, there is little room for a client to remonstrate about their fairness. Discomfort about this system underlies much sympathy for billing for contingent fees, where the lawyer is gambling all of his expenses and effort against a generous proportion of the award if he wins the case, nothing at all if he loses. This latter system, customary in slip and fall cases and justified as permitting the poor client to have proper representation, undoubtedly promotes questionable class action suits and often leads to accepting personal liability suits which should be rejected for lack of merit. The thinking underlying personal injury firms is widely said to be: most insurance companies will settle for modest awards in cases without merit because the defense costs would be no less than that amount, and occasionally a personal liability case gets lucky and extracts a huge award. Listen to one old-time lawyer describe how legal billing used to be. After the case was over, the lawyer and the client sat down to a discussion of what was involved in the legal work, and what it accomplished for the client. A winning case has more evident value than a losing one, provided the lawyer can effectively describe the professional skills that helped bring it about. The whole discussion is aimed at having both parties leave the discussion satisfied. To the extent that both parties are satisfied with the value of the services, the esteem and reputation of the legal profession are enhanced. And the lawyer is a happy and contented member of a grateful community. If he can occasionally claim a staggering fee for a brief but brilliant performance, as in the case of the explosive fire on the Corinthos -- well, more power to him.

It does not take much familiarity with oil refineries to make you realize that cargoes of crude oil are a very dangerous business. We are accustomed to hearing jeers at those who protest, "Not in my backyard", and we deplore those who would jeopardize our national security to protect a few fish and trees in the neighborhood of potential oil spills. Since we do have to import oil and we do therefore have to jeopardize a few selected neighborhoods to accomplish this vital service, the opponents are sadly destined to lose their protests. But that doesn't mean their concerns are trivial. The shipping and refining of oil are dangerous. We just have to live with it and be ready to pay for its associated costs.

4 Defeat and Disaster: Philadelphia Falls to the Enemy

Brandywine Battlefield   1491 Baltimore Pike   Chadds Ford, PA
39.8744, -75.5762

Helen of Troy had launched a thousand ships. Lord Howe only launched four hundred and thirty, but they were bigger. It is estimated a thousand oak trees were cut down to build just one man o' war. This flotilla was parked in lower New York harbor while forty thousand redcoats conquered Brooklyn Heights, Manhattan, Washington Heights, Perth Amboy, New Brunswick, Princeton, Trenton -- and then Washington promptly made fools of Howe and Cornwallis, at Trenton, Princeton, New Brunswick. Howe, and Cornwallis, in particular, were raging mad. The first year of the two-year siege of Philadelphia was over, and at half-time, the British team was popped up. The grand plan laid out in London by Lord Germain was for Howe to capture New

York, and maybe Philadelphia if it would be useful, while Gentleman Johnny Burgoyne took an army from Canada along that giant cleft in the earth which starts at the St. Lawrence River, down Lake Champlain, then down the Hudson from Albany to New York. The Hudson is very wide, and the British Navy would have no trouble sailing upriver to Albany, landing an army to meet Burgoyne coming south, with the effect of cutting New England off from the rest of the Colonies. Burgoyne got his orders in London shortly after Howe's January disaster in Trenton arrived in Quebec in May and started on his campaign June 20. Nothing dilatory about him. Howe, however, had six months to get to Albany before that, and several months more before Burgoyne would get to Saratoga, tromping through the woods and black flies. From Staten Island, it might have taken Howe ten days to sail to Albany in plenty of time.

Instead, Howe solitary and without advice, decided to take Philadelphia. Although the British never dwelt much on the fine points, the actual rebellion was only taking place in New England at the time the fleet set sail. It was the arrival of the fleet which triggered the Declaration of Independence, not the other way around. Lord Howe therefore probably felt some justification in revising the agreed plans and orders under which he set sail. As has been described already, the initial foray to Trenton ended embarrassingly. So, the capture of the enemy capital would now help people forget Princeton, and it would be sweet to whip Washington.

Unfortunately, they wasted a lot of time doing it. Finding the Delaware too well fortified, and almost as snaggy as Henry Hudson had found it more than a century earlier, he sailed all the way to Norfolk, came up the Chesapeake and landed at the head of Elk, and marched for Philadelphia. The Brandywine Valley has deep sharp cliffs off to the right, so Cornwallis was sent off to the left as a flanker past Dilworthtown while Howe attacked Washington head-on at Chadds Ford. It was to be the largest battle of the whole Revolutionary War. When Washington found himself facing encirclement, he had to order a withdrawal.

Weather satellites, television and so on have taught us much about hurricanes that was unknown in 1777. Benjamin Franklin, it should be noted, was the first to observe that Atlantic Coast "Nor'easters" actually begin in the South and North, even though the wind seems to be blowing in the opposite way; what's moving toward the northeast is a low-pressure zone. We now know that hurricanes begin in Africa, travel west and then veer north when they reach Florida. A great deal is still to be learned about hurricanes, but the most important thing about their timing is contained in a maritime jingle:

June, too soon.
July, stand by.
August, you must.
September, remember.
October, all over.

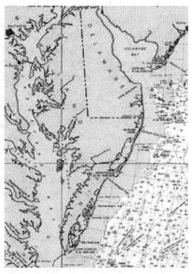

Along the Atlantic east coast, the end of August to the middle of September is hurricane season. That's when houses blow down in Florida, and heavy rains hit Pennsylvania. Admiral Howe might have had some clue to this since Franklin made his observation around 1750, and storms are important to Admirals. But very likely his brother the General just thought it was one of those things when the British landing at Elkton, Maryland in late August 1777 was greeted with an unusually severe downpour of rain. Howe had planned to surprise Philadelphia from the rear by hitting the ground running on horseback. However, he underestimated the debilitating effect on the horses of three weeks at sea on sailboats; to unload and forage horses during a hurricane was almost too much for the plan. For that purpose, he had given orders for the troops to disembark without waiting to pitch camp, or unpacking their gear. But the drenching rain gave Washington several extra days to organize a defense, although he has been given too little credit for the strenuous accomplishment of moving an army from Bucks County to the banks of the Brandywine in that weather. Howe, whose trademark was surprise, deception, outflanking, had anticipated a sudden cavalry thrust into the backyards of unprepared Philadelphia. What he got was 2000 casualties in the biggest battle of the Revolutionary War, against Washington's well-prepared defense along the steep-sided Brandywine Creek.

Howe won this battle, in the sense that Washington was forced to withdraw, because Howe employed another British military trademark, of driving his own troops beyond human limits in a huge outflanking movement. The countryside around Kennett Square is hilly and broken almost to West Chester, and the American Army felt reasonably prepared along a front of ten or twelve miles. But Howe drove the main force of his army seventeen miles to the north, to Dilworthtown, before turning the unprepared American right flank. And, in the now hot August weather in full uniform and battle pack, the drive continued for twenty-four consecutive hours until

Washington saw he had to withdraw. This was what the British meant when they boasted of seasoned regular troops; you win by enduring more than your opponent can endure.

One has to have equal admiration for Washington. Although he was dislodged from his position, losing the opportunity to catch the British in a hostile region without a reliable source of supplies once the fleet weighed anchor, he preserved his army of marksmen and deer hunters intact during the retreat. The two armies started at roughly the same size, and Washington had only about 1300 casualties; his men had more certain supply sources, and they were fighting for their homes. The British, somewhat outnumbered, had the prospect of fighting their way without resupply through an enemy's home territory, capturing the enemy's capital, but still facing the possibility that the British fleet might not get past the Delaware River defenses. If that happened, they could celebrate their victory by starving to death. Just about the only weakness of the Continental Army was its discomfort with bayonet warfare. They could hit a squirrel at a hundred yards, but those long bayonets on the end of very long muskets were designed to protect foot soldiers from cavalry charges. It takes training to put the butt of the musket against a stone on the ground, hold your ground against an oncoming gallop of horsemen, and trust that at the last moment the horses will rear back and throw the riders. But it also takes naked bravado to wave a sword and ride full tilt into a forest of pointing bayonets, trusting that at the last moment the defenders will break and run.

Washington knew what he was doing. He pulled the troops back to Chester, then over the Schuylkill to the Germantown encampment at Fox and Queen Lane, then up the Schuylkill to Norristown, the first ford in the river that Howe must use when the boats and bridges were destroyed. The river would hold the British while the Americans came at them from the rear; this was essentially the same river strategy he used at the Battle of Trenton. Washington picked his battlefield in Chester County and got ready to fight the second installment of the Battle of Brandywine. The campus of Immaculata University now occupies the site.

And then it rained again. Hard. The gunpowder on both sides was soaked, useless. In what has come to be known as the "Battle of the Clouds", the fighting was called off by mutual agreement. The second hurricane of the year had arrived, and Washington more or less helplessly had to watch Howe take over Philadelphia unopposed. General "Mad Anthony" Wayne was dispatched with fifteen hundred troops to hassle the rear of Howe's army. Wayne was confident he could hide his troops in the Radnor area where he had been brought up, but the region, in fact, had many Tories to report his movements. Howe ordered Major General Lord Charles Grey to take the flints from his troops' muskets, attack the American camp near Paoli's tavern in the night, and use only bayonets. Wayne's' troops were scattered and slaughtered, in what came to be known as the Paoli massacre.

The British set up their defenses at Germantown, seven miles from the center of town. Three weeks later, Washington attacked Germantown in a three-pronged assault that mainly failed because two of his formations attacked each other in the fog. That was October 4, 1777. The news soon reached them that Burgoyne had surrendered the other British army --starving in the woods -- at Saratoga, New York on October 17. Howe had in effect abandoned Burgoyne in order to take Philadelphia, but it was probably as much a result of getting drawn into a tangle, as a single decision to disregard the grand plan.

In retrospect, it was quite a bad choice. All the world -- and the King of France in particular -- could see that Washington had beaten Howe at Trenton and then Gates and Benedict Arnold had soon beaten Burgoyne at Saratoga. General Gates, of course, was in charge at Saratoga, but Arnold was the flamboyant hero. Adding to his earlier exploits in Quebec and later providing the captured cannon of Ticonderoga for General Knox to drag over the mountains to Boston, thereby allowing Washington to drive the British fleet to safer distances, Arnold now essentially won two more battles at Saratoga. The first was to defeat Leger, who had been sent down Lake Ontario to come back up the Mohawk Valley to Albany. Then, turning his troops through the woods, Arnold joined Gates at Saratoga and definitely led the charge that smashed the British line, when Gates would have been satisfied with containment. Arnold, like Alexander Hamilton, was a flamboyant man after Washington's heart.

Washington lost the capital, provoking dismay among the colonists, but his masterful strategy taught the British to respect him. When the British were later considering whether to hold or abandon Philadelphia, this growing respect for their adversary helped tilt their thinking toward prudence.

Meanwhile, Howe settled down to enjoy winter at Philadelphia. His court jester and chief entertainer was Major Andre, who took wicked pleasure in using Ben Franklin's Market Street home as his own. There was an additional satisfaction in knowing that Washington was freezing at Valley Forge.

5 Brandywine Museum

Brandywine River Museum   **1 Hoffman's Mill Rd.**   **Chadds Ford, PA**
39.8599, -75.5886

Artistic talent must be inherited; some of us don't have any at all, while other families seem to have unusual talent in every member. Around Philadelphia, one notable example is the Peale family, and another is the Wyeth clan. Three generations of Wyeth's show their work as a group in a former Brandywine Creek grist mill which has been elaborately restored and enlarged for the purpose. Using large glass windows, part of the display is the Brandywine Creek itself, with the high banks that once made it seem like a perfect defense line for George Washington in the biggest battle of the Revolutionary War. Outside the museum entrance are several of those inevitable Delaware tip-offs, large millstones that may in this case have ground grist, but often were used to grind gunpowder by the DuPonts.

Millstone

Andrew Wyeth spent much of his early career doing watercolors and then turned to tempera as re-popularized by N.C. Wyeth, his father. That's a fairly drastic change, since a watercolor must be completed in one sitting before it dries. Oil base paint dries slowly and allows the painter to work on a piece for a number of days. Tempera, using the protein in milk and eggs to hold the pigment, dries hard and fairly quickly. But another layer of tempera can be painted on top of the hardened base layers, making a glowing effect possible, a peculiar luminosity if the artist chooses to bring it out. Andrew Wyeth migrated to what he called dry-brush, where the paint on the brush

Brandywine Museum

is mostly squeezed out, so extremely detailed fine lines can be painted. Thus, he spent his early years with fast blurred watercolors, and the rest of his life with meticulous slow painting, where detail is everything. He chose to use this technique to produce a haunting silent scene, even if it contained people. His son, Jamie, tends to emphasize dancers, so you can see the typical family rebellions alternating between generations, at the same time that the Wyeths (and Howard Pyle, the artistic forefather) preserve strong family unity. From what the neighbors say, there were plenty of family clashes, but that's artists for you.

6 Furniture for the Horse Country

Kinloch Woodworking, LTD   **1721 West Doe Run Road**   **Unionville, Pa**
39.8951, -75.7328

Passersby can only view the low-key exterior of this business, but the drive to Unionville is a pretty one. Low-end furniture for America is now mostly made in China, and seldom made of wood. Truly American cabinet making tends to be high-end, and high priced. That tendency goes to some sort of extreme around Unionville in Chester County, where a 25-year old company named Kinloch Woodworking holds pride of place. The owner, D. Douglas Mooberry, picked the name Kinloch at random from a map of Scotland, but his selection of southern Chester County was not an accident. The influence of nearby Winterthur has infused that whole region with an interest in fine furniture craftsmanship, and museums like the Chester County Museum and others throughout the nearby Pennsylvania Dutch country provide an ample source of authentic pieces to serve as examples. There's one other factor at work. As Doug Mooberry quickly noticed, people with money usually have lots of it. There really is a market for $28,000 tall case clocks, $18,000 highboys, and $12,000 tables -- if you can convince people in Chester County you are really good.

Although this 12-person company repairs antique pieces, it does not make exact reproductions. It produces new pieces in the old style of the region, based on careful analysis and evaluation of museum pieces from earlier times. Kinloch once aspired to equal the quality of the early artisans, but now aspires to surpass them in quality of materials and workmanship. The more conventional stance of fine artists is to attempt to excel in today's current style, whatever that may be, probably "post-modern." Kinloch artists, however, choose to excel in the style of a long-past era, taking care not to claim the product is antique. Artisans grow up in cooperative clusters; there's a world-famous veneer company

Kinloch Woodworking

nearby and a pretty good hardware company, although the best craftsmen of furniture hardware are still found in England.

The characteristic style of Chester County furniture in the Eighteenth Century was a mixture of two neighboring cultures, Queen Anne, Chippendale, ball and claw Georgian style of Philadelphia; and the "line and berry" inlay style of the Pennsylvania Germans. If carefully executed, this hybrid style can be very pleasing, and you had better believe it requires painstaking craftsmanship. Others will have to explain the significance or symbolism of intersecting hemi-circles in the lines, and the inlaid wood hemispheres, the berries, at the end of the lines. But the technical difficulty of laying strips of 1/16 inch wood in curved grooves only a thousandth of an inch wider, or the matching of 3/8th-inch wood hemispheres into hemispheric holes gouged out of the main piece -- making the surfaces of the inlays perfectly smooth -- is immediately obvious to anyone who ever tried to whittle. Ultimately, however, true artistry lies in combining two unrelated styles without producing an aesthetic clash. By the way, you would be wise to wax such furniture once a year.

The factory is on Buck and Doe Run Road, and here's another culture clash. At one time, Lammot du Pont cobbled a 9000-acre estate out of several little country villages. In 1945 it was sold to the Kleberg family, the owners of the King Ranch in Texas. From 1945 to 1984, Buck and Doe was used as one of several remote feedlots for Texas Longhorns bred to Guernseys, the so-called Santa Gertrudis breed. Originally, Texas cattle were seasonally driven to Montana for fattening, then on to railheads for the stockyards. As farmers began to build fences interfering with the long drive over the prairies, it became cheaper to fatten cattle closer to the markets. So satellite feedlots like Buck and Doe Run were developed. You can pack more cattle in a rail car when they are younger and smaller, and advantage can be taken of price swings by suppliers who are close to the market. In this case, the markets were in Baltimore. Since the King Ranch is larger than the state of Rhode Island, such 9000-acre farms were pretty small operations in the view of the Texas Klebergs, an opinion they did not trouble to conceal from the irritated local gentry. The point was even driven home in high society circles by holding large parties at Buck and Doe Run, allowing guests to wander around the roads, unable to find the house of their host even though they had been on his property for most of an hour. In 1984 the Buck and Doe was sold and converted into a nature conservancy.

7 Serpentine Rock from Serpentine Barrens

Nottingham County Park   **Park Road**   **Nottingham, PA**   **39.7414, -76.0428**

Even in pre-revolutionary Colonial days, it was recognized that patchy areas of Chester and Lancaster counties were covered with twenty-foot stunted evergreens instead of two-hundred-foot oaks. They were "barrens", resembling the pine barrens of central New Jersey. In time, these barrens were particularized as Serpentine barrens, out of a recognition that this stunting of vegetation was somehow associated with greenish stone in the bedrock. So,

the serpentine barrens in time became serpentine rock quarries, but they seem somehow less barren now that surrounding deciduous forests have been cut down to make nice farmland. The greenish stone was a novelty, especially because it was usually (but not invariably) soft sandstone and easy to quarry, and the bedrock was only an inch or so under the topsoil, or even appeared on the ground surface as outcropping. These qualities made serpentine a popular building material, but in retrospect, it should have been more apparent that sandstone crumbles easily, and what can stunt tree growth probably wasn't very good for you.

Well, the green color comes from chromium salts. Sometimes the greenish color is diffused throughout the volcanic rock, but more commonly concentrated in green veins "snaking" through sandstone. Diffuse is better for building because the greenish intrusions create fracture lines in response to acid rain. In modern times, we mostly think of chromium as imparting a shiny look to plated auto bumpers.

Building constructed with serpentine rock

Some automakers was once quoted as saying he sold more cars using $10 worth of chrome than with $100 worth of engineering. That's metallic chrome because central to the definition of a metal is that it looks shiny. Even high school chemistry scholars can tell you it is a "salt" of chromium, the chromic ion, which imparts a greenish tinge when dissolved in water. So, chromic salts dissolved in the local water are what dwarf the vegetation of a serpentine barren, not chromate (which is yellow), and not metallic chromium (as in auto trim). So, although one might suppose otherwise, a few years ago when local builders started up modern quarries of serpentine rock, the environmentalists of Chester County were up in arms. Demonstrations were held, editorials written, politicians hectored. The Serpentine Barrens was a local treasure, requiring legal protection; protective ordinances were demanded.

Although building construction with the serpentine rock had a considerable flurry in the late 19th Century, the crumbly nature of sandstone caused the disappearance of all but a few examples. A building in boathouse row on the Schuylkill, a pre-revolutionary house on the Brandywine battlefield, College Hall on the campus of the University of Pennsylvania, pretty much comprise the notable surviving examples. But in a certain way, the Serpentine buildings do sort of define Victorian Philadelphia.

It probably should be mentioned that Serpentine is the official California rock, as would be natural for a substance which composes about 2000 square miles of its bedrock. It's green in color, but has high magnesium content, and seems to originate with the grinding of tectonic plates as they throw up mountain ranges, with attendant earthquakes. California also has serpentine barrens, but local geologists blame that harmful vegetation effect on magnesium competing with soil calcium (rather than the less notable chromic ions in West Coast serpentine). We're getting into some pretty fine distinctions, here. Pennsylvanians will probably be content to know we found ours first, that it had a flurry in Victorian architecture, and it's just a bit quaint. And, that it doesn't pose a significant risk for asbestos poisoning. A California geologist, in defending their state rock honor, recently proclaimed there was a greater statistical risk of dying from their state animal (the grizzly bear) than from their state rock.

8 J. Edgar Thomson, Pres. PRR 1852-1874

Railroad Museum of Pennsylvania   300 Gap Road   Ronks, PA
39.9822, -76.1606

The third president of the Pennsylvania RR converted a local Philadelphia line into a national railroad, the largest corporation in the world. Thomson, born in the Quaker country of Springfield, Delaware County, was the son of a chief engineer of the Delaware-Chesapeake Canal and had worked closely with his father. After an introduction to the rail business, he worked on four other railroads before joining the Pennsy at the age of 29. The State of Pennsylvania had by then constructed a series of unsuccessful canals along most of its important waterways during the Whig days of faith in government, but Thomson knew canals very well and recognized that their rights of way were best transformed into rail lines. By acquiring these unprofitable companies, he rapidly changed the PRR into a state-wide rail network, of which the famous Horseshoe Curve at Altoona was the most notable achievement. From there he moved to convert wood-burners into the coal-burning locomotives developed in Philadelphia and shifted from iron rails to steel ones. The probably unexpected effect was to convert all railroads in the nation into customers of steel and coal, Pennsylvania's main resources. Andrew Carnegie was so pleased he changed the name of his main steel company to the J. Edgar Thomson Works.

Thomson was quiet and conservative, never engaging in the high-jinks so characteristic of the rail barons of that day, leasing land rather than buying it whenever possible, expanding steadily but methodically, and never confusing revenue growth with profits. By 1870, Pennsylvania had expanded to a Jersey City terminus at New York harbor, and Chicago and St. Louis at the western ends. Within Pennsylvania, the line had expanded from 250 miles of track to over 6000. It was the largest corporation in the world. Underneath all this expansion was the Thomson system of decentralized management, essentially consisting of giving local control to division superintendents, but standardizing the corporation to superior approaches as they surfaced among the networked superintendents. His was a brilliant synthesis of the precision of an engineer combined with the cooperative sharing of a Quaker meeting. It was easy to describe but difficult to imitate, particularly by executives who boasted lifelong avoidance of the approaches of both the engineering profession and the cooperative diffident Quakers, in favor of

Railroad Museum of Pennsylvania

swashbuckling, over borrowing, and muscle -- so popular at the time of the Gilded Age. Thomson's fortune grew to seven or eight million dollars. While that was both comparatively modest by railroad standards and yet extremely affluent for the times, at his death, he had mostly given it to charity.

9 Three-Mile Island

Three Mile Island   3140 PA-441   Middletown, PA   40.1531008, -76.7175155

On a mudflat of the Susquehanna River called Three Mile Island, a nuclear energy plant had been built around 1970. The mud flat was in front of the entrance of the Swatara Creek, where Middletown, the first town in the County had been laid out in 1732. Later on, the town of Harrisburg became the capital city of Pennsylvania, located a few miles north of the Swatara Creek at what had been called Harris's Ferry, later Harrisburg. For quite a while, Middletown and Hummelstown, also on the Swatara Creek, were the two main towns in the area, but the location of the state capital attracted railroads and steel mills to Harrisburg. One of its main claims to fame was that Confederate General Robert E. Lee was thought to have it as his primary objective for invading the North, frustrated in this goal of course by his defeat at the battle of Gettysburg. Meanwhile, Middletown has declined to a small country town and was therefore originally glad to have the industry of electricity generation located next to it. It's true the huge cooling towers loomed ominously, and huge plumes of evaporated water rose in clouds to be seen for miles. But Middletown slowly took on the look of a refurbished 18th Century town, fancy new restaurants and all, prosperous and waiting to be discovered as a tourist attraction. Maybe in time, it would be the next Williamsburg.

On March 28, 1979, some valve got stuck within Reactor Number Two. The plant had two reactors, each with a spare cooling tower so it looked as though there were four nuclear plants instead of two. Warning lights and whistles went off, and it is easy to imagine a general panic within the operators of the plant, especially since a popular movie, The China Syndrome had just been issued two weeks earlier, depicting an imaginary implosion of a similar nuclear plant with famous movie actresses running around screaming. It took about five days for the plant operators to make a preliminary assessment of the TMI situation, which did not seem as bad as it might have been. It would take six months to reach a final evaluation of just what had gone wrong, and why. In the meantime, almost anyone could say or imagine almost anything; no one could prove they were wrong. The local citizens held a referendum; they wanted all of the facility to be closed, permanently. Secretary of Health Gordon MacLeod wanted a somewhat more reasonable thing, which was large supplies of sodium iodide pills to be distributed to the populace to prevent the radioactive iodine content of escaped gases from being attracted to the thyroid glands of the population, especially children and child-bearing mothers. Unfortunately, he took the unforgivable step of criticizing the state government for not having stock-piled the pills, and the Governor fired him, thus demonstrating strong decisive action in an emergency. The news media were equally at sea because this was big news. When all was finally said and done, there was no evidence that anyone was injured as a result of the accident. More than thirty years later, there is still no sign that anyone was ever hurt.

We might not have been so lucky, of course. When the Russian plant at Chernobyl had a worse accident in 1986, literally thousands of Ukrainians were sickened, and the death rate was appreciable. In Japan, the victims of the Hiroshima explosion were closely followed for many years, and the incidence of cancer of the thyroid among the survivors was truly frightening. However, after more decades elapsed, it was possible to determine that the overall death rate from thyroid cancer was not increased, suggesting these new thyroid cancers were not particularly

**Remaining reactors at
Three Mile Island**

malignant. But in a different set of circumstances, when the Chinese set off their tests of nuclear weapons, it became clear that these tests were followed in a few years by a world-wide epidemic of Hashimoto's Disease of the thyroid. Radioactivity in mushroom-shaped clouds is mainly radioactive iodine, with a half-life of seven days. Unfortunately, the clouds sail around the earth, eventually settling into the dirt on the ground. Grass grows there, and cows eat the grass. By this time, the radioactivity is much diminished, but the digestive systems of cows concentrate this weak radioactive iodine, which then gets into milk in a more active form. The kids drink milk and get Hashimoto's disease. So, amidst a welter of conflicting evidence, it is still possible to say almost anything about nuclear power risks without fear of provable contradiction. It is only safe to repeat that radioactive iodine exposure doesn't do anyone any good.

Thirty years after the accident, we now all understand it would be a good thing to develop energy independence from Middle East sources, but we remain unsure just how unsafe we are willing to become in order to re-adopt nuclear energy. Since the accident, our government has made it impossible for a single atomic plant to be built in America, and the remaining reactors at Three Mile Island were shut down entirely in 2019.

10 Cost of Medical Care

Penn State Hershey Medical Center   **500 University Drive**   **Hershey, PA**
40.2647, -76.6749

On several occasions, Richard A. Kern M.D. (1891-1982) told the story of his part in the founding of the Hershey School of Medicine. Dick Kern was a distinguished professor of Medicine at Temple University, well known for his contributions in the field of asthma and allergy, a past president of the College of Physicians of Philadelphia, and a former Grand Master of Pennsylvania Freemasonry. The Milton S. Hershey School was considering the creation of a medical school and needed advice.

Milton Hershey

Milton Hershey had been a strict Mennonite and had accumulated a huge fortune making chocolate candy. He left generous trusts to endow a theater and various other public services in the town of Hershey, but his ownership shares in the chocolate company had been left to the Hershey School for orphans. The value of the shares had far outgrown the ability of the school to employ them usefully, and they were considering a medical school. In 1963, as at present, everybody else was wondering how to get out from under the crushing cost of running a medical school. The sudden inquiry from a donor both willing and able to start a whole new medical school from scratch was an opportunity not likely to appear again soon. Kern carefully considered the options, including the danger of scaring off the naive potential donors with too high a price. Finally, he screwed up his courage and suggested a price to the trustees, of fifty million. The prompt answer was, done, you've got your medical school.

In due course, Kern found himself on the platform at the inaugural ceremonies of the school, sitting next to the guest of honor, that man who had made such an instant decision. Chatting amiably, Kern mentioned that he had always wondered how high the Hershey Foundation would have been willing to go. The answer was just as prompt as the original one. "Hundred-twenty."

Hershey Medical Center

11 Army War College in Carlisle

US Army Heritage and Education Center   **950 Soldiers Dr**   **Carlisle, PA**
40.2068, -77.1604

The history of the Army War College in Carlisle goes back to 1757, including Ben Franklin, and also includes some interesting anecdotes which might not have been expected of a War College.

Like all land in Pennsylvania, this plot within what is now the town of Carlisle, PA, once belonged to William Penn. Nobody else owned it until 1757 when Ben Franklin was sent to negotiate its transfer from the Indians. William Penn had been careful to buy land from the Indians, even though he also formally owned it as part of a deed from Charles II of England. Other land proprietors had not been so scrupulous, often complaining of the Indian massacres which resulted, although seldom adopting Penn's rather inexpensive method of avoidance.

During the Revolutionary War, Carlisle was a comfortable distance from the British Navy and served as a backwoods artillery arsenal along the Appalachian Mountains, much as the Ho Chi Minh Trail served our enemy in the Vietnam conflict, along with an Asian mountain range. From 1790 to 1860, Carlisle served as a cavalry post, and then General Robert E. Lee invaded Pennsylvania up one side of a mountain ridge, with General Meade bringing up the Union forces from Washington DC on the other side of the ridge. The two valleys come together at Carlisle, so that spot had long been recognized as commanding both. Lee only got as far as Gettysburg before Meade caught up with him, but General Ewell's Corps took Carlisle as an advance guard. Confederate cavalry General JEB Stuart took Carlisle without sustaining a fight. Meanwhile, General Lee was fretting that Stuart was supposed to be his eyes and ears, keeping him informed of Union opposition, and it is possible that Stuart's Carlisle diversion thus had some influence on the outcome of the Battle of Gettysburg.

Army War College

By 1879 there remained little purpose in a Carlisle military post, so it was turned into an Indian Industrial School, a couple of miles East of Dickinson College. After the Civil War, the nation lost its taste for exterminating Indians and turned to the idea of removing Indian boys from their families in order to assimilate them to white customs. Unfortunately, this did not work very well, and in fact, nothing worked very well. There are over 340 Indian languages from Eskimo to Aztec, but there is no record of any tribe allowing itself to be assimilated. The Spanish tried slavery, the French tried intermarriage, and the Americans tried forced assimilation. Eventually, we gave up and isolated them on reservations, but not before a wide-spread attempt was made to isolate Indian boys in boarding schools, hoping to remove them from tribal influences. That didn't work, either, but it was being attempted at Carlisle in the late 19th century. Interestingly, Carlisle is named after the family of the Earl of Carlisle, who was sent by Lord North after the disastrous British defeat at Saratoga, in order to see if the colonists might still be interested in Taxation with Representation. We weren't, so the Revolutionary War dragged on for another six years. Somehow, when war fever captures countries, small victories seem to close minds to what they had been originally fighting over. If the War College has time for another lesson, I suggest they add that one to their curriculum.

Earl of Carlisle

Before going back to the origins of the Army War College, we should salute the momentous football game of 1912, between the West Point cadets who included Dwight Eisenhower, and the Carlisle Indian School team which included Jim Thorpe. Thorpe was a member of an Oklahoma Indian tribe, but in many ways has been regarded as the best all-around American athlete in history. Eisenhower was pretty good, too, but Carlisle won the game. The Army War College was not started here, but at Fort McNair in Washington, DC, as a result of President McKinley's disappointment with officer performance in the Spanish American War. The school was moved to Carlisle in 1951, into what looks like a pretty little country college campus. Whether President Eisenhower had anything to do with moving it to Carlisle is unclear, but it certainly sounds plausible. The school now has 325 students, mostly from the Army, but includes about 75 officers of a Lt. Col. equivalent, drawn from the Navy, Marines, Air Force and Coast Guard. There are another 70 or so "fellows" from various foreign countries, not yet including either Russia or China. Most of these foreign fellows have their way paid for them by their countries, but about a quarter of them come from countries so small and impoverished that their way is paid by the USA. This intermingling is generally agreed to be a beneficial thing, particularly in later years when many of them reach command rank in their countries.

Meanwhile, the other American services still have their own war colleges, which include a minority of students from the Army. It's hard to know whether this overlap is a transition step in the direction of consolidating the Armed Forces entirely, or whether the present service divisions are considered to be permanent, therefore requiring permanently separate schools of command. These are vitally important issues within the armed services, even though the rest of us tend to regard talk of cutting the defense budget to the bone as mainly political theater. President Thomas Jefferson tried that once, and we nearly lost the War of 1812 because of it. Or, stated more precisely, we did lose the War of 1812, but Napoleon diverted Great Britain's

attention so much the British lost interest in the American nuisance and was glad to sign a peace treaty with us. (General Jackson won the Battle of New Orleans after the peace treaty had been signed.) Because of wariness of "standing armies" by the Founding Fathers who were shaking off European ideas of rule by the aristocracy, the Constitution speaks of "raising" an Army, but "maintaining" a Navy. So the Army tends to feel more threatened by budget cuts than the Navy does, even though it's awfully expensive to build an aircraft carrier.

XIII Main Line: Overbrook to Paoli

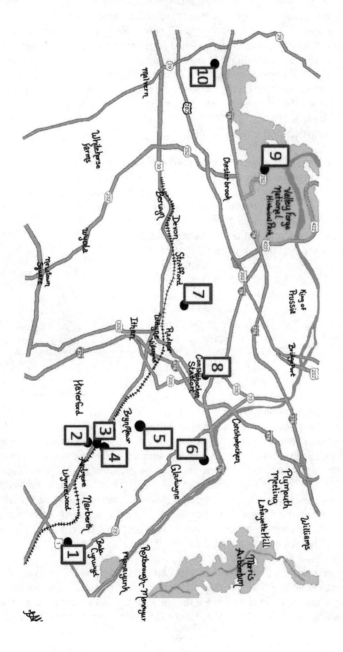

The Main Line

"In the Philadelphia suburbs, set in an autumnal landscape so ripe and misty that it might have been painted by Constable....lives an oligarchy more compact, more tightly and more complacently entrenched than any in the United States, with the possible exception of that along the North Shore of Long Island....The Main Line lives on the Main Line all year around...It is one of the few places in the country where it doesn't matter on what side of the tracks you are. These are very superior tracks.....What does the Main Line believe in most? Privilege."
John Gunther -- Inside U.S.A 1947

The Main Line is the set of commuter rail stops from Overbrook to Paoli, representing what was once the heart of the Pennsylvania RR. It changed into a spur of the line that ran from New York to Chicago, the central monument left by Alexander Cassatt, its president. Times really do change a lot. The Pennsylvania Turnpike was just too much competition, and air travel has eliminated all railroad passenger interest in further points like Pittsburgh, Chicago, and points west. The real mainline of long-distance rail on the East Coast now runs north-south, called the Northeast Corridor, essentially beginning in Boston and ending at Washington DC. Philadelphia is central to all of these versions of main lines, although a thirteen-year lawsuit was required to break combined Pennsylvania and New York Central railroads into SEPTA, Amtrak, and Conrail. At the moment, Conrail the freight line is making tons of money, Amtrak the passenger long-haul line would soon die without

Alexander Cassatt

government subsidy, and all commuter railroads are subsidized by their local communities. There is a lot of talk about billion-dollar investments in high-speed trains like they have in Japan and France, but anyone familiar with the economics of rail transportation just shudders at the thought. Railroads are profitable ways to haul long-range bulk cargo. Passenger lines, long and short, can only be justified financially if they cost less than expanding highway and airline transportation, which the public obviously prefers. Philadelphia is in the peculiar position that the real estate investment has already been made in passenger rail; is it cheaper to build on what already exists, or is that a doomed relic of the past?

But back to the revered and treasured 19th Century stations on The Main Line. They were mostly built from 1860 to 1890, along the path of what was then the mainline to Chicago, but destined to become a spur leading to the real center of east-west traffic, which went from New York to Chicago further north from Philadelphia, intersecting with what became the Philadelphia spur at Paoli. In the days when Philadelphia was one of the richest cities in the world, the spur was a glamorous

Bryn Mawr College

suburban real estate development. The stations were built, the mansions scattered along at some distance, and servant's houses clustered around the stations. The towns were renamed with Welsh names like Bryn Mawr (instead of Humphryville). A culture was built up, probably unique in the world for being centered on railroad executives, and novels like Kitty Foyle and movies like The Philadelphia Story celebrated the glamor of it all. It's probably true that you can find more fifty-room mansions there than just about anywhere else, but the automobile and good

public schools mainly drove the prosperity of the 20th Century, as the railroads dwindled away. The stops on the Main Line begin with Overbrook and continue on through Merion, Narberth, Wynnewood, Ardmore, Haverford, Bryn Mawr, Rosemont, Villanova, Radnor, St. David's, Wayne, Strafford, Devon, Berwin, Daylesford, and Paoli. The mainline starts where Philadelphia taxes end and get progressively newer in harness with the gradual construction of fashionable homes as you get further from the city. At first, Paoli was a place where the out of service trains were stored, but gradually became a fashionable area, which is beginning to leapfrog over the King of Prussia shopping center into the farmlands to the north.

The center of gravity of suburban aspirations moves steadily further into the surrounding countryside but is outgrowing the old commuter rail system, and there is something of a movement back to the city. That is to say, urban sprawl is running into the discovery that it's just too traffic-jammed to commute that far, except by train. Most folks are familiar with the jingle that "Old Maids Never Wed And Have Babies" which is supposed to help commuters remember what stop they

Centennial Exhibition in Fairmount Park

are approaching. However, the topic mentioned by the jingle and the fact that it ends with Babies (Bryn Mawr) instead of Paoli, strongly implies it was written by a student at Bryn Mawr College for Women.

The old brick stations have been adopted by affectionate commuters, turned into historical preservation societies. They have a varied history, but quite often the station master lived upstairs, and the first floor housed a branch of the post office.

When the railroad straightens out its right of way, the stations have to be moved, often at great expense. As they progressed further into the countryside, sometimes grand resort hotels were built for those who wanted to escape the summer heat in the city, or in 1876, to house attendees to the Centennial Exhibition in Fairmount Park. As these hotels lost popularity, they became excellent bargain real estate for a new college. Alexander Cassatt insisted that all transcontinental trains must make a stop in Paoli near his home, and there are even a few stations like Upton which were for the sole use of a single estate. So, at one time when ignorant non-Philadelphians on the transcontinental trains would sniff, "Why would the trains all stop out here in the country?" Philadelphians in the know would just bury themselves in their newspapers.

Narberth, formerly Libertyville, was a village long before the railroad came along, and it still holds itself a little aloof from the rest. Narberth quickly became the center of fashionable summer hotels. Bryn Mawr used to be Humphrysville, Cynwyd was once Academyville, and Marionville became Merion.

1 Albert C. Barnes, M.D.

Former Barnes Museum   **300 N. Latches Lane**   **Merion Station, PA**
39.998, -75.2405

A Bottle of Argyrol

A private investor has the general goal of accumulating enough wealth so, come what may, there will be a little left when he dies. If he has dependents or heirs, he needs somewhat more. Either way, he is not planning for perpetuity or thinking in astronomical time periods. Albert C. Barnes (1872-1951) had to switch his investment goals, in the 1920s, from investing for a comfortable retirement to investing for a perpetual art foundation. Perpetual.

Having graduated from medical school (University of Pennsylvania) in 1902, and then writing a doctoral thesis in chemistry and pharmacology at the Universities of Berlin and Heidelberg, Barnes invented a patent medicine that quickly made him rich. Argyrol was a mildly effective silver-containing antiseptic with the unfortunate tendency to turn its users permanently slate-gray. The advent of antibiotics has since made Argyrol almost sound like quackery, but it was effective enough at the time to require factories in America,

The Main Line

Europe, and Australia, and Barnes became immensely rich with it. The American Medical Association strongly disapproves of physicians who patent remedies, so Barnes was never held in high regard by his colleagues; but it could well be argued that he had as much training as a chemist as a physician, and spent his entire professional life as a chemist, manufacturer, and investor.

The Old Barnes Gallery

Barnes was eccentric, all right, but on Wall Street, the saying goes, "What everyone knows, isn't worth knowing." Guided by that principle, in 1929 he sold his company at the very peak of market euphoria, getting out of common stocks at the top of the market. It is small wonder that he soon instructed his Foundation to invest its endowment entirely in bonds. During the 1930s, commodities were extremely cheap because no one had any money. Barnes, of course, had a potful of money and bought hundreds, even thousands, of artworks very cheaply. He also bought 137 acres of Chester County, PA, real estate, and a 12-acre arboretum in Merion Township on the Main Line. Although he is famous for acquiring hundreds of French Impressionist paintings with the advice of Gertrude Stein who herself was advised by William Glackens, he also bought great quantities of Greek and Roman classical art, African art, and the art of the Pennsylvania German community. He picked up a notable collection of metallic art objects. Most of these "losers" went down in the basement because he had so many Renoirs, Matisses and Picassos (some of them may be worth $200 million apiece) that the upstairs galleries were pretty well stuffed with them. Viewed from the perspective of an investor with a goal of perpetuity, of course, the things in the basement just happen to be temporarily out of fashion, just like those bonds in the portfolio.

In 2004, when the Foundation found itself strapped for ready cash, Judge Stanley Ott of the Montgomery County Orphans Court was urged to allow the Foundation to break Barnes' will in some way or other. Move the museum to downtown Philadelphia where it can attract more paying visitors. Sell some of that land. Sell some of those paintings in the cellar. Fire some of those employees. But all of these suggestions are short-term solutions, which may injure the long term. Everybody had an idea of what Barnes the rich eccentric would have done if he were alive to do it, but I suspect he would have rejected the whole lot. Barnes the shrewd investor would have taken the most expensive painting off the wall, and sold it to the highest bidder. Buy low, sell high, and the niceties of non-profit professionals be damned.

Barnes wasn't in love with one single painting, or one particular school of painterly interpretation, he was in love with Art.

Investment theory has improved in the past fifty years; there have even been some Nobel prizes awarded for new insights. But it still isn't possible to put an investment portfolio on autopilot for perpetuity. Every museum, university, and the foundation has the same problem, with the result that the landscape is littered with the bones of perpetual organizations destroyed by following a fixed formula. With the singular success that Barnes displayed, it isn't surprising that he went a little too far with instructing his successor trustees in what to invest in. Never sell the paintings or the real estate, avoid common stock, were ideas that worked brilliantly, and may even work most of the time. But sooner or later, the institution will be endangered by following them too literally. Somebody has to have some flexibility. But there is something else that is inevitable, too. Sooner or later, whether it takes fifty years or five hundred years, sooner or later someone will be given the responsibility and the necessary flexibility -- but will try to run off with the boodle, for himself. The balance between necessary prudence and necessary flexibility is impossible to maintain forever, and the Judge must have had a hard time deciding what Barnes would have decided. In the end, flexibility won the day, and the Barnes museum was moved into town.

2 Skating and Humane
Philadelphia Skating Club and Humane Society   220 Holland Avenue
Ardmore, PA   40.008, -75.3006

There was a time when ice skaters and rowing enthusiasts were having a little war on the Schuylkill, and the rowers won. We are indebted to our dear friend the late Elmer Hendricks Funk MD, a past president of the Philadelphia Skating Club and Humane Society, for some of the histories.

Ice skating is both dangerous and seasonal. In the Eighteenth Century, ice skating was concentrated near the center of the population on the Delaware River, and that's where you found the Skaters Club. You also found the Humane Society, whose main function was to pull drowning skaters out of the water. The Humane Society got to be quite rich because people  were inclined to be sympathetic to lifesavers. In time, however, as people moved away from the Delaware, the two clubs - Skating and Humane - merged. No doubt the skaters thought they would be acquiring the substantial endowment of the life-saving club, but in fact, the Pennsylvania Hospital got most of the money in one of those genteel struggles that volunteer organizations sometimes get into. Skating moved from the Delaware to the Schuylkill, and the club built a little house on what is now boathouse row, right next to the lighthouse.

Turtle Rock

The lighthouse at Turtle Rock was useful for the southern terminus of the canal just across the river on the West Bank, and for many years there was a little canal house on the Westside, making it easier to see what this was all about. The lighthouse became incorporated into a boathouse for the first women's rowing club, but the club died out and this combined, Sedgley, became a women's luncheon club. Next door was the Skaters and Humane, fighting to survive among all the rowers. Since rowing has a much longer season than skating, the skaters feared they would be overwhelmed. They passed a club by-law that no officer of the club could be a rower.

However, the skaters had another enemy in the ice companies, who tended to chop up the first and best ice to form in the area. And the final blow came when the Arena was built at 45th and Market Street with artificial indoor ice. So, the boathouse became the home, in 1938, of the Philadelphia Girls Rowing Club, and the skaters and lifesavers moved first to the Arena, and then to Ardmore. Haverford College was glad to sell them a swamp they owned there since it wasn't much good for a college but the local springs provided needed water for the

Skating Club and Humane Society

skating rink. With a rink, skating became year-round, and there was a roof to protect against snow and rain. You can't fall through the ice in a rink.

The club had a number of lucky breaks by being first, constructing its building cheaply in the depression, being able to use ammonia as a refrigerant, and getting cheap land. There are other skating clubs, but few of them own their own rinks, and no other skating club has the national prestige of the Philadelphia Skating Club and Humane Society. It is the oldest, the first, the best, and the most famous. If you are anybody in skating, this is where you want to skate.

3 Rufus Jones, Quaker

Haverford College   370 Lancaster Avenue   Haverford, PA   40.0128, -75.2998

Rufus Jones

Rufus Jones (1863-1948) dominated the Quaker religion for two generations, causing a transformation that deserves to rank with that of George Fox, William Penn, and Elias Hicks. A few elderly Quakers still remember him in person, mostly as an old gentleman who tended to lean back while he spoke, usually hooking his thumbs in the sides of his vest. He was a prodigious writer, having once made a promise to himself that he would read a new book every week, and write a new book every year. He kept that up for thirty years.

As a matter of fact, that understates his output. His published works were collected by Clarence Tobias at Haverford College, and run to 168 volumes, plus 8 boxes of pamphlets and articles. His family also donated his personal papers to the College, and they require 75 linear feet of shelf space.

His stated occupation would have been Professor at Haverford College, where his personal influence on the undergraduates was as profound as their influence was to be on the rest of the world. He is regarded as one of the founders of the American Friends Service Committee and the single greatest influence in reuniting the two divisions of Quakerism, although some of the formalities were not completed until after his death.

Haverford College

One other index of his remarkable energy was that he crossed the oceans more than two hundred times during his lifetime.

Perhaps the arrival of mass communication has made it possible to have an equal impact with less effort. But Rufus Jones stands for the principle in life, that it never hurts to work just a little harder. If high school students are thinking of applying for admission to Haverford, they better understand what is going to be expected of them.

4 Lawn Tennis at the Cricket Club

The Merion Cricket Club   325 Montgomery Avenue   Haverford, PA
40.0161, -75.2983

Lawn tennis isn't terribly ancient, having originated in England around 1880 as a variation of badminton which was brought back from India during the days of the British Empire. As the name suggests, it was originally played exclusively on grass courts, which proved hard to maintain. It was supplanted for a while by clay courts, and more recently by hard and artificial surfaces. Lawn tennis on lawns has largely become a game for the rich because of the cost and difficulty of maintaining a playable surface in hot weather.

Merion Cricket Club

When I last wandered into the Merion Cricket Club, I found lawn tennis in the grand style, viewed from luncheon tables under a roofed porch. The long relatively narrow porch is right up against the grass courts, but it's also sort of a Peacock alley where everybody at the tables wishes to seem to know everyone else. There are times when the athletic entertainment becomes cricket out there on the field beyond the porch, but a larger proportion of the lunchers turn their backs on the field during that season than when exciting tennis championships are reaching the finals.

In addition to being more expensive to maintain the courts, tennis on the grass is a different game from tennis on a hard surface, like clay or asphalt. The ball tends to skid when it hits the grass, so it is more effective to volley it before it hits or before it takes much of a bounce. The bounce tends to be more nearly straight up, while on harder surfaces the ball bounces at a low angle. Either way, the consequence is a tendency for a faster game on grass. The players run harder to get the ball at the bounce, and the advantage goes to those who serve hard and return the ball hard -- and fast.

The rather special nature of the game adds to the upscale atmosphere. And makes it just as attractive for the Kitty Foyles at the tables, as for the Kathryn Hepburns, both of whom have their own attractions for the Cary Grants. The parking lot is also a good place to form an opinion about the latest in high-priced autos.

5 Harriton House

500 Harriton Rd   **Bryn Mawr, PA**   **40.033, -75.3104**

Three hundred years ago, in 1704, Roland Ellis acquired 700 acres of the Welsh Barony in what is commonly called Philadelphia Main Line and built a palatial house on it. He called his homestead Bryn Mawr, or great hill, after his ancestral home in Wales of the same name, thereby explaining why Bryn Mawr College and Bryn Mawr town have the name but are not notably situated on hills. The town of Bryn Mawr was once called Humphryville. But Bryn Mawr sounded nicer, even though there are plenty of Humphries still around to defend the older designation.

About fifty thousand acres were set aside by William Penn as the Welsh Barony, and there was the willingness to allow it to be self-governing, although that didn't much happen because the inhabitants saw no point in being self-governing. Nevertheless, the term isn't just an ethnic allusion but has some historical meaning.

In any event, Ellis proved to be an unsuccessful manager of his estate, which rather soon passed into the hands of the Harrison family, who lived on it for about two

Harriton House

hundred years until real estate development, and the taxes related thereunto, forced the creation of a complicated arrangement, with the township of Lower Merion owning the property and a non-profit group called the Harriton Association managing it. The neighbors in the area, all living on land that formerly belonged to the Harrisons, are said to constitute the richest neighborhood in America. By building the original farmhouse rather far from the main road (Old Gulph) and remaining surrounded by neighbors who want to have privacy, Harriton House has fewer visitors than it deserves because it is so devilish hard to find.

There was a little local skirmishing during the Revolutionary War, but the main historical significance of the House was that Charles Thomson married a Harrison and lived there all throughout the period of the Revolution and the Articles of

Confederation (1774-1789) as the Secretary of the Continental Congress. His little writing desk is, therefore, the most notable piece of furniture at Harriton House since every piece of official paper involved in the whole Revolutionary episode passed through it or over it. Modern organizations would do well to notice that Thomson was not given a vote and was expected to be totally unbiased about Congressional affairs. Even in those days, there must have been cautionary experience with secretaries who tinkered with the minutes for their own preferences. It certainly was entirely fitting that this last steward of the Articles of Confederation was designated to carry the news to George Washington at Mount Vernon, that he had been elected President of the new form of government. No doubt, Washington was pleased but unsurprised to learn of it.

While Harriton House is imposing on the exterior and was the likely prototype of many characteristic Main Line stone mansions, the inside of the house is quite primitive. In those days it was cheap to build a big house but expensive to heat it. In 1704 surrounded by a continent of a forest, firewood may not have seemed a problem, but it quickly posed a transportation problem, and later houses tended to shrink in size. In any event, the interior of the house seems strangely bleak and bare, quite in keeping with the early Quaker principle of building a structure "without paint, or other adornments". The curator spent quite a lot of time and effort to determine that the random-width flooring had never received any shellac, varnish or wax. Those are beautiful floors, but the "finish" is just three hundred years of oxidized dirt.

6 Heavenly House

Woodmont   **1622 Spring Mill Rd.**   **Gladwyne, PA**   **40.0636, -75.291**

Woodmont

While prosperous people, on deciding to enter a retirement community, are often heard to say they are tired of managing a big house, it can also be noticed that people who get the foreign travel bug usually drift around to see the palaces, castles, and estates of kings and emperors. The king's bathroom plumbing is a stop on most tours. Places like Buckingham Palace, the Vatican, the Temples of Karnak, Fortresses of Mogul Conquerors of India, or similar places in Cambodia, are all vast looming piles of stone dedicated to the memory of departed leaders who Had it All. That's probably all you need know, to understand that

The Main Line

Americans who have it all tend to build huge showplaces, too. A great many do discover the castles to become just too much bother. Safe protection and privacy are somewhat separate issues, reasons given for putting up with a big place past the time the thrill has worn off. Perhaps such jaded feelings appear at the end of the wealth cycle. Nevertheless with enough affluence, if you had unlimited money and inclination, where around Philadelphia would you put a dream palace, one built for a modern Maharajah? Answer: close to Conshohocken. The Schuylkill takes a sharp bend at Conshohocken because it flows around a big cliff on the west side of the river. It was there the White Steel Company built the first wire suspension bridge in the world, as distinguished from cable (twisted wire) suspension bridges invented by Roebling at Trenton. The bridge was swept away by a flood, the steel mill replaced by the Alan J. Wood Steel Company. Alan Wood prospered mightily, and built his mansion ("Woodmont") on 75 acres on the top of the big rock on the west side of the Schuylkill, in such a way he could watch the smoke rising from his factory down below at the foot of the cliff. The Philadelphia Country Club is across the road from Alan Wood's mansion, with fairways clinging to the cliffs, a Gun Club for trap shooters who want to aim away from houses and toward mountainsides, and a cliff-top road leading straight for Gladwyne between dozens of mansions with five-acre lots. Down the hill, however, rocky projections force the road to funnel into a winding crooked road which ends up near the filling stations of Conshohocken, passing ancient farm structures on the way. Railroads and expressways tend to fill the valley, the old White bridge is gone, and two distinct cultures are within a few hundred oblivious yards of each other. To the west stretches the Main Line, now filled with houses almost as large as the mansion, but air-conditioned and filled with other modern amenities. Seventy acres of a lawn is nice, but it's a lot of grass to cut.

Father and Mother Divine

The Alan Wood Steel Company had a hard time in 1929, recovered somewhat after World War II, and then declined to the point where Lukens and Phoenix Steel took over. And then Indians from India took over the lot, forming part of the largest steel complex in the world, now headquartered abroad. In 1952, one of Father Divine's religious followers named John Devoute gave Father the Wood mansion; which then became the new headquarters of his religious sect. He died in 1965 but Mother Divine continued to live there in stately and tasteful semi-seclusion until her death in 2017. Father's mausoleum is near the house.

The house itself is patterned after Biltmore in Asheville, NC, although perhaps only a quarter as large. Just inside its porte-cochère, the oak-paneled living room has a ceiling 45 feet high, and many oriental rugs. There is a music room, off to the side of which is Father's former office, bearing a strong resemblance to the Oval Office in the White House in Washington. As planned, the living room window looks down the valley to the site of the old steel mills, although when the trees are leafed out it may be difficult to see. The dining table probably seats forty people, although the paneled dining room was fitted with electronics and used to broadcast sermons to religious adherents across the country. In the living room are testimonies to the many who seemed to rise from the dead, or who had their blinded sight restored, or who were crippled but enabled to walk. The attendants take visitors on tours, where Mother Divine used to to meet them, coming down the sweeping staircase without noticeably showing her age. The greeting of "Peace" replaces the usual "hello" and "goodbye".

At one time, the Religion housed a large number of single women in several hotels, and the invested proceeds of their work as domestics still support the Religion. The religion frowned on gambling, drinking, smoking, and sex. However, celibacy inevitably leads to a decline in numbers, particularly evident since the death of the founder.

7 Military School

Valley Forge Military Academy   **1001 Eagle Road**   **Wayne, PA**
40.0537, -75.382

In the middle of the pacifist Quaker farm region, in fact, in the middle of William Penn's Quaker Welsh Barony, sits Valley Forge Military Academy. Co-educational since 2006, its location seems even stranger when you consider the nearest town, within easy walking distance, is Wayne, PA described by David Brooks in *Bobos in*

Paradise as the East-Coast epicenter for yuppie education-based elitism, with all its air of entitlement. In fact, Brooks does not mention the Academy once in his three hundred page book about the town. What is VFMA and why is it located where it is? Three names, Baker, Mellon, and Annenberg pretty much explain it. Lieutenant General Milton Baker, a great friend of the Eisenhower family, was passionate about Valley Forge, its history, its parks, its military hospital, its renovation, and its preservation. If Baker founded a school (in 1928), it was going to be here. The money was Mellon and Annenberg's money, but Baker was their man.

The Main Line

Military schools are now in a period of decline. A flurry of a building after the Civil War created about 600 of them, in recognition that the North nearly lost the Civil War to the Confederate States who had a much stronger military tradition, especially in Virginia. It's therefore not surprising that Valley Forge wanders from Southern traditions, and is consciously modeled after Sandhurst, the British Royal Military College. Valley Forge competes with Canada, Australia and Great Britain for foreign students, while the Southern schools are more provincial. There seem to be two main reasons to send your child to a military boarding school.

The first is the tradition of the military aristocracy, traceable in a sense to feudalism and the Knights of the Round Table. During the formative years of the American republic, the resounding emphasis was placed on having no standing army. That was a cloaked way of restraining a military aristocracy and seems to have provided the main reasoning behind the constitutional Second Amendment, which projects a  general right of all citizens to bear arms. It follows the model of Switzerland where military service is universal, as contrasted with limiting firearms to specialists, whether police or military. If that was the goal, it seems to have been effective; military elites now seem most appealing to foreign cultures, like Latin America, Korea, Saudi Arabia. Tony DeGeorge, former president of Valley Forge, told of an astounding phone call from one Saudi prince, who responded to an alumni fund-raising appeal by offering to buy the whole school. The Saudi noticed one supposes, that "Storming' Norman" Schwarzkopf, the hero of the First Gulf War, was an alumnus of Valley Forge.

The other traditional reason to send your children to a military boarding school is that they are too unruly to handle at home. Here is another seemingly delicate matter the school makes no bones about. All new entrants must spend six weeks as "plebes", enduring a ferocious hazing discipline that weeds 'em out. The solution to cell phones and Internet games is to forbid them. Valley Forge confronts the matter of recreational drugs head-on. All students are subject to random drug testing, and a positive test means get off the school grounds -- permanently -- within four hours. The exercise program is not only mandatory, but it is also rigorous beyond description. The result is that many alumni have gone on to play professional football in the NFL, the polo team is regularly the national champion. Somewhere General

Baker got the idea that playing music helps your mathematical ability, so every single 9th grader plays the violin. The marching band is internationally famous, and by gad, it better stay that way. Only about a third of the graduates go on to a lifetime military career, but another third of the alumni are CEOs of companies. Even what happens to the remaining third bears some thought. J.D. Salinger and Edward Albee were both alumni of Valley Forge Military Academy. True, General Baker told Salinger that The Catcher in The Rye was rubbish, and one need not speculate much on how he would have reviewed *Who's Afraid of Virginia Woolf?* Nevertheless, it cannot be denied that the collision between these two social misfits and the plebe hazing experience contributed significantly to the depth and power of the serious literature they produced. It is not easy to name two alumni of Andover, Exeter or Lawrenceville who have contributed as much to 20th Century American fiction. Salinger and Albee hated the place, but it made them what they became. "Whatever that was," you can almost hear the other two-thirds of the alumni mutter.

It is a little hard, and it is certainly politically incorrect, to give this devil its due. But all Armies live by the slogan, that if you must take an objective, you must take some casualties.

8 Rebel Hill

Savona Restaurant   **100 Old Gulph Rd**   **Gulph Mills, PA**   **40.0618, -75.3405**

Old Gulph Road

The Schuylkill River, hence Schuylkill Expressway and also Amtrak, all take a big bend westward about ten miles from Philadelphia. They are making a detour around a big hill or minor mountain, tending to position the sun in the eyes of many commuters at certain hours of the day. Real estate developers are apparently responsible for naming the place Rebel Hill, and it's getting pretty crowded with houses. The Rebel they had in mind was George Washington. The father of our country was in retreat from the battle of Germantown, having crossed the river at Matson's Ford, then following Matsonford Road over and beyond the big hill, and pausing for water at the spring in the gulch formed by Gulch Creek, now more decorously called Gulph Creek. The creek tumbles down the side of a long ridge forming the south side of the Great Valley; the gulch or gulf is really a crevasse in that ridge, which in a sense makes Rebel Hill just a split-off extension of that ridge. Consequently, the gulch makes a water-level route from the Schuylkill to Valley Forge, which anyone would take to get there in a hurry. Valley Forge is a misleading term; it's a hill in the middle of the Great Valley, as the center of an angel food cake tin, and was thus defensible in all directions. The cleft in the southern ridge is where you would normally travel to get to the base of the bastion of Valley Forge.

So, everyone still takes that route, following Montgomery Avenue after it turns into South Gulph Road, but before it turns into North Gulph Road. The road up along the southern ridge is called Old Gulph Road, while the newer extension from the river is called New Gulph Road. All of these winding roads are compressed within the narrow defile beside Gulph Creek, reachable by splashing through the fords in the creek, although that is discouraged after ice forms in the winter.

Savona Restaurant

And, yes, a new road has come in at a restored old farmhouse, called New Gulph Road. The restoration has created a fancy restaurant, which somehow forgets that at the time we are talking about, it was the headquarters of (Major) Aaron Burr. The giant highway cloverleaf ahead on South Gulph Road tends to obscure the fact that it was the direct road to Valley Forge, now further obscured by lots of shopping centers. If you persist and keep a lookout for the street signs, you will eventually get to the Memorial Arch, log cabins and National Park Service facilities of Valley Forge.

Back in the gulch, however, is the spring where Washington's troops refreshed their canteens. Just beyond it is a great big rock, much mentioned in memoirs of the episode. Around 1950, the highway engineers decided to blast this rock out of the way of widening a road that badly needs widening. The Daughters of the American Revolution saved the day. Creating a giant fuss, the DAR succeeded in limiting the engineers to chiseling the bottom of the rock away. A gentleman in his eighties recently remarked he had driven past that rock thousands of times, and always wondered what it was there for. Now he knows.

9 Kenneth Gordon, MD, Hero of Valley Forge
Valley Forge, PA   40.0918, -75.4622

There's no statute of Ken Gordon at Valley Forge National Park, although it would be appropriate. No building is named after him; it's probable he isn't even eligible to be buried there. But there would be no park to visit at Valley Forge without his strenuous exertions.

Valley Forge

One day, Ken's seventh-grade daughter came home from school with the news that the father of one of her classmates said that Valley Forge Park was going to be turned into a high-rise development. That's known as hearsay, and lots of things you hear in seventh grade are best ignored. But this happened to be substantially true. At that time, the Park was owned by the Commonwealth of Pennsylvania, and Governor Shapp was finding the upkeep on the Park was an expense he needed to reduce. The historic area had two components: the headquarters area, and the encampment area. One part would become high-rise development and the other would become a Veteran's Administration cemetery. Although any form of rezoning has the familiar sound of politics to it, Dr. Gordon (a child psychiatrist) had the impression that Sharp was mostly interested in reducing state expenses, and had no particular objection to some better use of the historic area. At any rate, when Gordon went to see him, he said that he would agree to a historic park if Gordon could raise the money somehow. The Federal Government seemed a likely place to start.

Well, the sympathetic civil servants at the National Park Service told him how it was going to be. You get the consent of the local Congressman (Dick Schulze) and it will happen. If you don't get his consent, it won't happen. It seemed a simple thing to visit that Congressman, persuade him of the value of the idea, and it would be all done; who could refuse? After the manner of politicians, Schulze never did refuse, but somehow never got around to agreeing, either. It takes a little time to learn the political game, but after a reasonable time, the National Park employees told Gordon he was licked. Too bad, give up.

He didn't give up, he went to see his Senators, at that time Scott and Clark. They instantly thought it was a splendid idea, and instead of going pleasantly limp, they sent Citizen Gordon over to see Senator Johnson of Louisiana, the chairman of a relevant committee. Johnson also thought it was a great idea, and called out, "Get me a bill writer!" A bill writer is usually a government lawyer, tasked with listening to some citizen's idea and translating it into that strange language of laws -- section 8(34), sub-chapter X is hereby changed to, *et cetera*. Bill writers have to be pretty good at it, or otherwise, they will misunderstand the intent of the original idea, modified by the personal spin of the committee chairman, the comments of the authorizing committee, and later bargains struck in the House-Senate conference committee. Having negotiated all those hurdles, a bill has to be written in such a prescribed manner that it won't be found to have multiple loopholes when it later reaches the courts in a dispute. A good deal of the time of our courts is taken up with making sense of some careless wording by bill writers. That's what is known as the "Intent of Congress", an ingredient that may or may not survive the whole process.

Ken Gordon had to go through this process, including testimony at hearings, for three separate congressional committees. To get everybody's attention, he organized several hundred supporters to write letters and get petitions signed by several thousand voters. These supporters, in turn, influenced the media and started a lot of what is known as buzz. All of this is an awful lot of work, but there is one thing about this case that can make us all proud. Not once did a politician suggest a campaign contribution was essential in this matter.

A Cold Winter at Valley Forge

In time, ownership of the Park did, in fact, migrate from the Commonwealth to the U.S. Department of the Interior, hence to the National Parks Service. Everyone agrees it has been well managed, and increasing droves of visitors come here every year. It is now clearly a national treasure. Unfortunately, the encampment area got away and has been commercially developed, although not nearly as high-rise as originally contemplated. Along the way, many discouraging words were spoken about the futility of fighting against such odds. The outcome, however, is the embodiment of two slogans, the first by Harry S Truman. "It's amazing what can be accomplished if you don't care who gets the credit for it." The other slogan is older, and Quaker. All you need, to accomplish anything, is leadership. And leadership -- is one person.

Mad Anthony Wayne

One day Ken Gordon, the very busy doctor, was asked how much of his time was taken by this effort. His answer was ten hours a week, every week for five years.

10 Frederick Mason Jones, Jr. 1919-2009
St. Peter's in the Great Valley   2495 Saint Peters Rd   Malvern, PA
40.0683, -75.5247

Classical music, however else it may be defined, strongly implies music played by an orchestra or at least a group of musicians. It thus should be no surprise that the members of a famous orchestra bond together for most of their lifetimes in a sense far beyond the ordinary meaning of teamwork. If you are good, really, really good, you will come to the orchestra as a child, devote every hour of every day to the orchestra, and step down only as a famous old man or woman, when you sense that reaction times have slowed. You sit together, travel together, rehearse together, and talk a language of detail that no one else can fully comprehend. Mistakes that one of you made forty years ago in performance, are still joked about because your colleagues know you still feel the pain of it, just as they share their own infrequent but no less fully remembered, moments of failure, largely unnoticed by the audience. When one of your colleagues dies, you turn out by the hundreds for the funeral. And when the hymns are sung, the organist is ignored, struggling to keep up with the people who really know music.

Mason Jones attended the Curtis Institute, itself a collection of prodigies, and was hired by Ormandy after a single audition; a year later he took the position of a first horn and kept it until he finally sensed he was passing his prime and laid it down. He was featured in the many recordings which defined the orchestra, and the Philadelphia Woodwind Quintet. He sometimes recorded as a soloist, but he thought of himself as an orchestral horn player, teaching orchestral horn at the Curtis to many generations of aspirants. He even conducted a little, usually in small groups. His comment on that was that it doesn't take much to be a conductor. "Just ask any orchestra player." At his funeral, it was related that the second horn once had two solo passages repeated within a larger piece, but when its time came there was silence. The second time around, it was played faultlessly. Afterward, Mason was asked what happened. "Fell asleep," he answered. And the second time? "I just played it for him."

Mason's funeral was held at St. Peter's in the Great Valley, illustrating that strange combination of artistic prodigies with modest beginnings, and the highest of high society, who mix together to create a great orchestra. A very well-groomed lady was heard to remark that this was where she had her coming-out party. St. Peters was founded as an Anglican mission church in 1700 in the Welsh Barony, built a log cabin church in 1728, replaced it with a little white jewel of a church in 1856, and added

Old St. Peter's in the Great Valley

new buildings more recently to accommodate the population growth in the valley. The church has abundant well-tended land, sited on a hilltop surrounded by high hills, quite suitable for a college or private school campus. The homes in the area are a step beyond splendid, hidden in the wooded countryside. Unless you know precisely where to go, the tangle of country roads will defeat you. But the arterial of U.S. 202 is only a few miles away, and Philadelphia's Silicon Valley nestles beside the highway, inevitably closing in on the countryside. There will be horses and kennels and fox hunts in the region for another decade perhaps, but the new world is moving in on the old one, from all directions.

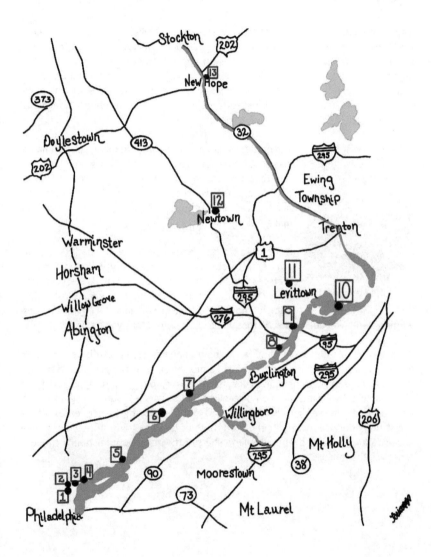

1 Stetson

Stetson Hat Factory   7th and Callowhill Streets   Philadelphia, PA
39.9584 -75.1506

John B. Stetson started a hat factory in Philadelphia in 1865, and within a few years, the Stetson was synonymous with cowboy hats. The quality was good, and the image was perfect for the migration into the West which took place after the Civil War, urged onward by that myth of the noble cowhand so enthusiastically nurtured by Philadelphia authors, books and magazines. From time to time, a Stetson hat could be seen on a Philadelphia head, but for the most part, Stetsons were synonymous with the West.

John Stetson

The matter came up recently when someone by that name was asked if he belonged to the hat family, and it turned out that was so. In one of those brief cocktail party encounters, he remarked that what ruined the Stetson hat factory was John Kennedy appearing at his presidential inaugural – hatless.

Aside from the fact that young Kennedy's hatlessness did not seem to affect the Texas factory which still makes Stetsons, there is the recollection that hatlessness was pretty stylish fifteen years before the Washington Camelot, both in men and in women. In fact, hatless young women were a Philadelphia style for quite a while before they were a national style.

It seems reminiscent of another fable about changing styles, attributed to Clark Gable. The movie star took off his shirt in a movie called "It Happened One Night," revealing bare skin. Undershirts, one is to believe, promptly disappeared from American life. There are those who recollect that undershirts suddenly got hard to find during World War II, and were replaced by T-shirts by the armed forces. There is a strong odor of Publicity Agent about both of these clothing stories, but things have got fairly advanced when even members of the manufacturing family are now repeating the folklore.

2 Edgar Allan Poe, 1809-1849

Edgar Allan Poe National Historical Site   **532 N 7th St**   **Philadelphia, PA**
39.9620 -75.1499

Between the Federalist period and the Civil War, Philadelphia quadrupled in population, mostly by Irish and black immigration responding to the urbanization induced by the Industrial Revolution. The social boundaries of this period were established by the U.S. Capital moving away to Washington, and at the other boundary, the constrained urban population was suddenly released to the suburbs by the City-County Consolidation of 1854. During that time, the Northern Liberties on the other side of Callowhill were very close by, but nearly devoid of law and order. At least along the Delaware River, the scene was like Las Vegas as imagined by Charles Dickens. Within the increasingly congested boundaries of the city itself, tuberculosis, alcoholism, riots and religious revivalism are all mentioned prominently. While it was the time of Nicholas Biddle and the Bank, and the establishment of the Drexel empire, it was a gothic period quite adequately symbolized

Edgar Allan Poe

by Edgar Allan Poe, writing for Graham's Magazine. His father abandoned the family, his mother and later his wife died of tuberculosis, he was definitely an alcoholic and probably manic-depressive. He and Charles Brockton Brown invented the gothic novel, gothic poetry, the modern murder mystery. Poe only lived in Philadelphia for six years but lived in seven different locations, the most famous of which is now part of the National Park Service, even though it is located off Spring Garden Street. Yes, he was born in Boston but lived there only briefly, and yes, he died in Baltimore, by dropping dead in the street while traveling through. He was scarcely a prototypical Philadelphian, but he was certainly a symbol of his age.

There is a big stuffed Raven named Grip in the Free Library which belonged to Charles Dickens and is claimed to be the inspiration for Poe's Raven; it certainly has an ominous look, whatever its provenance. Poe offered his famous poem to Graham, who rejected it but gave him $15 as an act of charity. Another magazine paid him $9 to publish it. This poem was widely included in elementary school anthologies by the Philadelphia book publishing industry, and its simple repetitions with a scary atmosphere continue to be popular with children. *The Murders in the Rue Morgue* were the beginning of the modern murder mystery, and seem to have started Brockton Brown off on his establishment of the Philadelphia Gothic novel, echoing the whole dark and menacing Poe tradition. From the descriptions, Poe's alcohol

Grip the Raven   problem was not so much related to the volume of consumption as to the violent manias which just a small quantity provoked in him. If your mother and your wife both died of tuberculosis, it's a fair bet you had it, too. At the age of 40, he was gone.

3 One Big Brewerytown

John Wagner Marker   905 N American St.   Philadelphia, PA
39.9646 -75.1415

It's hard to imagine that Philadelphia was once the American center of beer -brewing equipment, and horse-drawn beer delivery systems, dominating the city scene. Equally hard to imagine that the last Philadelphia brewery closed in 1987, and the biggest American brewer, Budweiser, was sold to the Belgians. What's this all about?

In the early wilderness days, water supplies were tainted and unsafe, so most prosperous Quakers had their own little brewery just to avoid typhoid fever. The first American brewery was started by Anthony Morris (the second Philadelphia mayor) in 1687, in a little brewery on Dock Creek, which became the early Brewerytown of the city, with several dozen brewpubs for sailors and the like. In 1797 there were over a hundred breweries in Philadelphia, and in 1840 there were over three hundred of them. Perot's brewery was prominent for a long time since an early Perot married a daughter of Anthony Morris. Since Philadelphia developed the first and famous city water supply in 1800, beer-drinking lost its position as a safe beverage in an unsafe city, and gradually water-drinking became the dominant beverage for the strict and upright. At one time in the early Eighteenth century, gin was cheaper than beer, so even the intemperate multitudes deserted beer for a while, although the effect of the higher alcohol content of gin was apparently fairly dramatic.

In 1840 John Wagner imported the yeast for lager beer from Bavaria, at considerable personal risk if he had been caught at it. Prior to 1840, Philadelphia beer was either stout or Porter, a very dark and bitter dose, or else ale, which had the advantage of storing fairly well and thus was popular for sailing vessels and among sailors. The yeast for ale floats to the top and ferments, whereas lager yeast sinks to the bottom of the barrel and requires some refrigeration to slow it down. In all forms of beer, the suds are created by later adding some unfermented beer to the barrel for the purpose of generating carbon dioxide. That's what

Francis Perot

is going on when you see the bartender in a British pub pulling on a lever to pump it up from the basement. Lager tastes much less beery than other beer and is by far the dominant form of beer in consumption -- a considerable improvement, in the view of most people. But it has to be cooled, and Philadelphia had a system. Brewerytown moved to Kensington, dominating the local scene. It was produced in barrels which were trucked to the east bank of the Schuylkill where ice formed on the surface of the river, stilled by impoundment above the Fairmount Dam. Caves were dug in the banks of the Schuylkill where the barrels full of fermenting beer were hauled to be cooled by the ice for the rest of the process. From there, it was trucked again to bottlers in a general ratio of one brewer for thirty bottlers. More directly, it was trucked to the beer gardens of Spring Garden to Girard Avenue, which gave that area a different sort of reputation as a brewery town.

By this time, most of the breweries had moved to the region between 30th and 33rd Streets, near Girard Avenue, and most of them still survive, made into condominiums by rehabilitation money. One by one, many sections of downtown Philadelphia acquired a beer environment. A dramatic moment in this process was the advent of

John Wagner marker

the 1876 exposition, which caused many of the Schuylkill fermenting vaults to be acquired by eminent domain. A second momentous change was introduced by the invention of refrigeration, apparently invented in Germany near Berlin, but imported and refined by York and Carrier. Philadelphia was particularly suitable for the importation of coal to fuel the heating of the brew, and the chilling of the fermentation. All of this required large numbers of brewers, bottlers, makers of bottles and inventors of brewing equipment. It took many horses to haul all this material around town, and many teamsters to drive the horses. This was a beer town, until Prohibition. During the long period of beer ascendency, the advantages of big breweries over small ones were gradually making this a major industry, rather than a local craft. Prohibition completed the destruction of the small craft brewers and brew-pubs. Only 17 of the major brewers survived Prohibition, and then even the big ones went out of business, ending with Schmidt's in 1987, almost exactly three hundred years after the first little one started by that famously convivial Anthony Morris on Dock Street.

Evidently, the same competitive disadvantages continue as even Budweiser moves to Brussels, where you would ordinarily expect the wine to be the popular drink. Changing tastes have been cited as the reason for this shift, but differential taxes seem more probable as an explanation. In most industries, you are apt to find that most of the competition takes place in Washington and Harrisburg, rather than the saloons of Main Street or the salons of Madison Avenue. But perhaps not. We hear that little Belgium is about to have a civil war because the Flemish can't get along with the Walloons. And somebody in Portland, Oregon got the idea that beer was trendy, and started up the growing phenomenon of craft brewers, usually flourishing in brewpubs. We are apparently going back to where we started in 1687.

4 The Walking Purchase

Penn Treaty Park   **1341 N Delaware Ave.**   **Philadelphia, PA**
39.9661 -75.1287

Any fair discussion of Quaker relations with the Indians must emphasize that almost all other colonists of the time coarsely regarded Indians as subhuman components of the local wilderness. Only William Penn was careful to treat the Indians as fellow human beings, entitled to fair play, dignity, and respect. Like a good politician, he entered into their games

William Penn and the Indians

with enthusiasm and definitely earned their respect by outdoing them all in the broad jump contests. Even though he had bought the land from King Charles II, he took care to buy it a second time from the Indians, and for many decades was able to enforce the wise rule of never permitting settlers on the land before the Indians agreed to its purchase. After Penn's death, however, and particularly from 1726 to 1736, a major wave of German and Scotch-Irish immigration created an overwhelming population pressure on the seaboard areas, resulting in much unauthorized pioneering and settlement. Since William Penn spent only a few years in the colonies; his agents, chiefly James Logan, had long set the tone.

Logan had been equally famous for his many efforts to treat the Indians fairly, and the grounds of Stenton, his manor house, were often filled with Indians come to pay their respects. Against all this evidence of the benign attitudes of both Penn and Logan, there stands the episode of the Walking Purchase of 1737. No doubt about it, the Indians were treated badly.

In the triangle between the Neshaminy Creek and the Delaware River, the Delaware Indians agreed to a sale with the third side of the triangle established at a distance from Wrightstown, as far as a man could walk northward toward the Wind Gap in a day and a half. That was a common form of boundary for Indian land sales, and its distance was fairly well understood. In anticipation of pacing out the distance, the colonists sent out explorers to find the easiest path, then sent out woodsmen to clear a path in the forest, and selected three of the fastest runners in the colony to do the running. The pace was so fast that two of the runners had to drop out, and the third one nearly did so. The resulting boundary was nearly twice as far into the wilderness as was commonly accepted for the measurement, taking advantage of the sharp bend in the river which widened the land in question by a great deal. The Indians were so disgusted they refused to leave the territory. Logan had already made an agreement with the Iroquois nation, to whom the Delawares were subject, and the Delawares only surrendered the land when the Iroquois began to look as though they really would act as enforcers for the bargain. Although serious Indian warfare did not break out for another twenty years, the Walking Purchase went a long way toward convincing the Delaware tribe that the Quakers were no more trustworthy than the settlers in other colonies, and is said to have been on their minds when twenty years later they helped the French decimate General Braddock's army.

There will probably never be a clear resolution of the paradox of Quakers, particularly Logan, behaving in this reprehensible manner within a very long history of the unusually honorable treatment of the Indians. With William Penn now dead and gone, no doubt Logan was caught in a squeeze between the two rather dissolute sons of William Penn, neither of them Quaker, who had over-indebted themselves with high living and were pressing their agent to make land sales to pay for it. Then there was the pressure of the new German and Scotch-Irish immigrants, brought to the New World by real estate promises, and stranded in the seaport unable to complete their land purchases. Under this pressure, Logan may have been unduly persuaded that the 1684 treaties with the Indians, along with many other treaties and understandings, were all the legal justification he needed. Whatever the specifics of the situation at the time, it is now clear the Walking Purchase was a blot on the Quaker record that can never be entirely justified within the Quakers' own standards of fairness. Within the Society of Friends, whatever other English colonists might have done in their position, let alone what French and Spanish regularly did to the Indians, doesn't matter in the slightest.

5 Look Out For That Ship!

Delair Railroad Drawbridge   Lewis Street and N. Delaware Avenue
Philadelphia, PA   39.9867 -75.0751

We are indebted to the President of the Maritime Law Association of the U.S., Richard W. Palmer, Esq. (who unfortunately died in March 2017 at the age of 97), for both a strange definition and an amusing story. An "allusion" is a collision between a ship and a stationary object, such as a bridge or a dock. As you might imagine, the ship is almost invariably at fault, mainly through errors of the pilot, although hurricanes and other severe weather conditions can make a difference. Moving ships have been running into stationary objects for many centuries, and almost every allusion contingency has been explored. Ho-hum for maritime law.

The Delair railroad drawbridge over the Delaware River at Frankford Junction is just a little different. It was built in 1896 when the Pennsylvania RR decided it needed to veer off from its Northeast Corridor to take people to Atlantic City. For reasons relating to the afterthought nature of the bridge, the tower for the drawbridge is located half a mile away, out of a direct vision of the ships going through. Also, a late development in the history of the river was the construction of U.S. Steel's Morristown plant, bringing unexpectedly huge ore boats from Labrador to the steel mill. The captains of the ships pretty much turned things over to the river pilots, for the last hundred miles of the trip.

Shortly after this iron ore service was begun, the inaugural ore boat captain had a little party with some invited guests. So it happened that the Commandant of the Port, the Admiral in Charge of the Naval Yard, and other equally high ranking worthies like the head of the Coast Guard were on the bridge of the ore boat, taking careful notes of the procedure.

The ship tooted three times, the shore answered back with three toots. In real fact, they were connected by ship-to-shore telephone for most of the real business, but this grand occasion called for an authentic nautical ceremony. Three toots, we're approaching your bridge. Three toots back, come ahead, the coast is clear. The admirals scribbled it all down.

As the ship approached the point of no return, beyond which it could no longer stop or turn in time to avoid an "allusion," the people on the bridge were appalled to see a train crossing the bridge ahead. Several toots, loud profanity on the ship to shore phone.

"No worry," answered the bridge, "we'll lift the drawbridge in plenty of time." But half a minute later the bridge controller made the anguished cry that the drawbridge was apparently rusted and wouldn't open, to which the captain shouted, "This ship is going to take away your blankety-blank bridge and sail right through it.".
At this point, the pilot took matters into his own hands, and violently threw the rudder hard left, swinging the ship sideways, soon nudging the bridge with some damage, but nothing like the damage of a head-on collision. The lawsuit, as one might imagine, was the outcome.

The attorneys for the railroad were pretty high-powered, too, and had piles of legal precedents to cite. But they were quite unprepared for Dick Palmer to put the Commandant of the Port on the witness stand, reading slowly and painfully from his very detailed notes about the conversations on the bridge, about the approaching drawbridge.

Delair Railroad Drawbridge

And so, Philadelphia can now claim to have experienced one of the very few instances where a ship ran into a bridge -- and the court found the bridge to be entirely at fault.

6 Stir

House of Corrections   8001 State Road   Philadelphia, PA   40.0333-75.0181

The Pennypack Creek empties into the Delaware River a few miles north of Center City, where spacious mansions once stood, with long sloping lawns coming down to the river's edge. The area is now a prison farm, containing thirteen City institutions, of which four are major prisons. Holmesburg closed a few years ago, joining the ranks of the other abandoned prisons strewn about Philadelphia such as the Walnut Street Prison, Moyamensing, and Eastern Penitentiary. Inside the campus along the Pennypack are several thousand inmates and employees. There are in fact eight other smaller facilities in various other locations in the City. Over ninety percent of the inmates are male, 70% are African American, and nearly half of them are there for drug offenses. The average daily population is falling, having risen to over 8,000 in 2015. This is a $250 million operation, not counting the police and courts necessary to keep the place full. Nor counting the pensions of retired employees; but only 13% of guards retire, the rest quit or transfer to some other occupation before retirement.

To an outsider, the most disconcerting statistic is that a quarter of the inmates are "detainers," which is to say they have not been convicted. The police take a detainee before a magistrate for an arraignment, they are then sent to the Detention Center for "prosing,", and after that may stay in the House of Correction for six months unless they come up for trial sooner. It seems very likely that the court system is very careful to follow designated procedures, and the vast majority of these detentions are surely guilty of something unpleasant. Still, it does not sound quite right to hear that thousands of people are forced to spend six months eating that awful food, without the formality of a conviction. Perhaps an arraignment is adequate, but the distinction is beyond ordinary citizens to understand and would sound better if modified.

Eastern State Prison

The other feature that makes us pointy-headed meddlers uneasy is the large proportion of prisoners for drug crimes. A few years ago a federal law was passed, called "The Speedy Trials for Drug Offenders Law,", which mandated that drug crimes would be processed ahead of all others on the docket. Whether this law has made the unconvicted inmate population larger or smaller is unclear, but it reawakens the proposal to decriminalize drug abuse. Now, there's a polarizing proposal if there ever was one. If we ever emulated the Netherlands in legalizing drugs, we could set several thousand Philadelphians free immediately, and probably save the taxpayers tens of millions of dollars a year in prison costs, since prison costs about a hundred dollars per day per inmate. On the other hand, recreational drug consumption would undoubtedly increase appreciably, and many more lives would be ruined.

Because Quakers have a tradition of going to jail themselves rather than obey an offensive law, they have long had an interest in prison affairs, and more sympathy than average for the plight of the inmates. The people in charge of running the prisons have mixed feelings about that, too. It's useful when the prison budget is under attack to have respected citizens in the community support the otherwise rather shame-faced prison administration, but it's uncomfortable to have impartial eyes trying to look into activities that don't always stand public exposure.

Occasionally, the seamy side does come out into the open. One prison facility is named after a warden and a deputy warden who were assassinated in a prison riot on May 31, 1973. At that time, Philadelphia General Hospital maintained a high-security prison hospital area, as well as a ward for police officers and firefighters. Some doctors and nurses remember the victims of this riot being brought in with their injuries. One guard came in with his hand cut off.

7 Glen Foerd, Torresdale, and the Feudal Industrial Style

Glen Foerd Mansion   5001 Grant Ave   Philadelphia, PA   40.0517-74.9778

Charles Macalester

The Glen Foerd Mansion sits on the small bluff where the Poquessing Creek enters the Delaware. It's on the south bank of the creek, so it is just inside the Philadelphia boundary. Charles Macalester, who built the original mansion, was a financier who sat on the board of the Second National Bank. So it is not surprising that he built a summer place just downriver from Nicholas Biddle's "Andalusia," which is on the north side of the creek. The Philadelphia consolidation of city and county government left one mansion in Philadelphia, and the other one in Bucks County. The region is perhaps better known for the little company town of Torresdale, and even better known for the Torresdale water inlet, where much of Philadelphia's water comes from the Delaware River. The Torresdale stop on SEPTA makes it an easy commute from Philadelphia, as does I-95, some of the time. The creek's inlet into the Delaware is swampy, as most such confluences are, and is a favorite place for bird watchers and nature lovers. The tidal nature of the Delaware at that point is quite apparent; at some times of the day, much of the bank of the inlet is bare ground.

Charles Macalester may well have been the right sort, but he sold the property and left his estate to Macalester College in Minnesota, so Philadelphia doesn't find much to remember him by. After all, the early Quakers wouldn't even consent to put their names on tombstones, let alone name colleges after themselves. Robert Foerderer bought the property around 1893 and embarked on an elaborate renovation project. He had made his pile of money by purchasing the French patent for making kid leather and eventually had 5000 employees in Frankford making the material for kid gloves. The mansion on the river could be said to be the apex of an industrial empire, quite typical of how Philadelphia, particularly Northeast Philadelphia, did things. He was said to have been quite a benevolent emperor of this kid-glove empire, including the little company town of Torresdale, until there was an industrial uproar of the 19th Century variety. Whereupon, he abruptly shut

Robert H. Foerderer

the whole business down, just as John Roebling did when his company town across the river wanted to run its own town. There's a sort of European flavor to this sort of story, sort of an opera about a principality on the Rhine River. This area of northeast Philadelphia and Bucks County has a number of principalities with this sort of town cohesiveness, where families who work there are clustered around their factory center, and children, and grandchildren, and great-grandchildren tend to stay in one place to live a life which ignores the rest of the world. Someone has to be the boss of such communities, tends to regard the position as hereditary, and definitely resents the idea that anyone else has much to say. Central to the concept is the Horatio Alger story of the hard-working youngster who gets to the top by merit, leading to the conviction that if someone else wants to be at the top of a heap, let him first build his own heap. Somehow, the Foerderer story seems to add realistic color to what was true about this social system.

Robert Foerderer died fairly young, having married Caroline Fischer, and producing a daughter, Florence Foerderer Tonner who married a New York hosiery tycoon named Tonner. The ornate decorations of Glen Foerd, the idiosyncratic taste in art, the parties and the ostentatious social circle, all add up to the sniffy description of "new" money, the so-called *nouveau riche*. The hundred older families of the Philadelphia establishment were very cautious about mixing socially with such newcomers and their often unexpected behavior, although there were notable exceptions. In all this uproar you can see the origins of the two present political parties, with the "old money" rich people displaying a quite surprising preference for

redistributionist economics and environmental protectionism. It's easy to exaggerate, but a good part of this enduring split is due to social resistance of the older settler families to new ways of doing things, particularly when new ways have not demonstrated unequivocal value.

Glen Foerd Mansion

But returning to Glen Foerd, the name is a composite of the original Glengarry and the newer Foerderer. Florence Tonner got one of the first television sets to be produced and put it in the middle of her gallery of fine art. She sat there watching her favorite TV shows, why not. In her will, she left the estate to the Lutheran Church, but during the Depression, the church had trouble keeping it up. Someone discovered a clause in her will which provided, that in the event the Church could not support the estate, it was to be given to the residents of Torresdale. Since Torresdale only consisted of two streets, not including East Torresdale, West Torresdale, and any other splinter communities, the ownership of the estate was pretty closely held. This small group of true believers took up the burden and tried to make the estate survive. The house was opened to visitors, and available for weddings and events. Adult education courses, small-scale Chautauquas, bird-watching and nature walks were established. Slowly, the residents have been succeeding in making a go of it, but the original residents are getting older and dying off. It's going to be a hard struggle to make the place self-sustaining on every necessary level. But we wish them well, and certainly, admire their spirit. The Union League bought the golf course and its clubhouse, but their plans for it remain uncertain.

8 Bristol, PA

Dorrance Mansion   300 Radcliffe St   Bristol, PA   40.0957 -74.8538

In 1681, Samuel Clift activated a local land conveyance, written to go into effect as soon as King Charles II signed the overall land grant to William Penn. In this way, Bristol claims to be the oldest settlement in English Pennsylvania; Clift got here before Penn did. He chose the narrowest spot in the river as an excellent place to run a ferry which was only replaced by the Burlington Bristol Bridge in 1930. A ferry landing is an excellent place for an Inn, which he also built there. The town he founded was called Buckingham, and the surrounding county became Buckinghamshire, Bucks for short. The name later changed to Bristol. The New Jersey town on the other end of the ferry ride was called Bridlington, later Burlington, NJ. North of this narrow spot in the river was a several-mile extent of marsh and swampy inlets, and then the river turns abruptly northwest at what used to be called the falls at Trenton.

William Penn had considered building his house sixty miles south of there at the Southern end of Philadelphia Bay, at Chester, then pondered building it on the Faire Mount where the Philadelphia Art Museum now overlooks the Schuylkill. In the end, he built a Philadelphia house near Dock Creek (subsequently covered over and renamed Dock Street) and a palatial manor house, Pennsbury, in the swampy marshes above Bristol, where a tourist visit is now a valuable experience.

No doubt being near the Proprietor's estate gave Bristol some class, but it was also half-way on a two-day stagecoach ride from Philadelphia to New York. A succession of inns and resorts grew up in Bristol, and it became a busy trans-shipment place, a good place to build schooners. A local Captain John Cleve Green is celebrated as the first to carry the American flag to China, although it must be admitted his cargo included opium; Green is regarded as the financial founder of the nearby Lawrenceville School, which I attended. The terminus of the Delaware canal brought coal from the anthracite region in 1827; more prosperity ensued as coal was loaded on ships in the Delaware, or utilized instead of water power for the Bristol Mills which had been founded by Samuel Carpenter in 1701. John Fitch invented the first steamboat and tried it out here; more prosperity ensued, although not for poor Fitch, who committed suicide. Little Bristol gradually filled up with imposing waterfront mansions, the declining shells of which can still be admired.

The advent of the railroad isolated Bristol when it cut off the corner of the bend in the Delaware River. Four-lane highways eventually consolidated the isolation of the little river town, but the turning point was around the time of the Civil War. For nearly a century, between the Revolution and the Civil War, Bristol was the booming little queen of northern Philadelphia Bay, and the Bay itself was an American Lake Como, lined with Federalist and Victorian mansions, their lawns sweeping down to the water's edge. Small wonder there was so much social interaction between the railroad-isolated Bristol, and planters of Chesapeake Bay. The strip of quiet charm begins at Pennsbury Manor and pretty continuously extends to Bristol, where you can go under the rail embankment and on to Philadelphia, or alternatively cross the Burlington Bristol Bridge to New Jersey. A couple of miles further

Bristol Railroad

south, the river edge is a little ragged but includes some yacht clubs and several famous mansions, notably Nicholas Biddle's Andalusia, the Foerderer family's Glen Ford, and the former mansion of Saint Katherine Drexel.

The Bristol area has had moments of fame. George Washington had originally planned to attack Trenton from both the north and the south simultaneously. He came over what is now called Washington's Crossing amid the ice floes on the north side of the Pennsbury delta, and General Cadwalader was to cross the Delaware at Bristol, on the south side of the marshes. As it turned out, the ice was worse at Bristol and the river wider, so Cadwalader was late for Trenton but caught up with Washington to help with the battle at Princeton. President Tyler's daughter married a dashing gentleman from Bristol. Republican politicians from Bristol teamed up with some others in West Chester to decide that favorite-son Seward couldn't win, so they backed Abraham Lincoln for the presidential nomination, and Pennsylvania was therefore in time richly rewarded for its political acumen. Despite the arts and crafts group that moved in around New Hope PA, Bucks County has remained a Republican stronghold ever since. The region's influence was long symbolized by Joseph P. Grundy, the gentle Quaker manufacturer from Bristol whose name struck terror in Republican politicians as well as Democrat ones, but for opposite reasons.

The Burlington Bristol Bridge is now getting a little narrow and ancient but is still serviceable. It long charged only a dime's toll because that was enough for painting and upkeep. Together with the Tacony Palmyra Bridge, which charged the same low toll, these locally owned bridges stuck a thumb in the eye of the tax-and-spend folks who owned the Philadelphia bridges and who wanted to charge three dollars toll, spending most of it on non-bridge activities. As Tacony Palmyra Bridge rests on both sides of the river, the local politics gradually shifted enough to permit a restoration of toll "equity."

9 Secret Service Visits Burlington Bristol Bridge

Burlington Bristol Bridge   **Radcliffe Street and Beech Street**   **Bristol, PA**
40.1155 -74.8344

A few years ago, the buzz around the local Secret Service headquarters was that some very good, even exceptionally good, fake hundred dollar bills were in circulation in our neighborhood. The official stance of the Service is that all counterfeits are of very poor quality, easily detected and no threat to the conduct of trade. Unfortunately, some counterfeits are of very good quality and not easily detected, and when that happens, the Service is made to feel a strong sense of urgency by its employers. These particular hundred dollar fakes were of very good quality.

One evening, a call came in: "Don't ask me who I am, don't ask me why I am calling. But I can tell you that a very large bag of hundred dollar wallpaper has just been tossed over the side of the Burlington Bristol Bridge, near the Southside on the Jersey end. Goodbye." Or words to that effect.

Very soon indeed, boats, divers, searchlights, ropes, and hooks discovered that it was true. A pillowcase stuffed with hundred- dollar wallpaper of the highest quality was pulled out of the river. By the time the swag was located and spread out for inspection, it was clear that several million dollars were represented, but they were soaked through and through. Most of the jubilant crew were sent home at midnight, and two officers were detailed to count the money and turn it in by 7 AM. The strict rule about these things is that all of the money confiscated in a "raid" was to be counted to the last penny before it could be turned over to the day shift and the last officers could go home to bed. After an hour or so, it was clear that counting millions of dollars of soggy wet sticky paper was just not possible by the deadline. So, partly exhilarated by the successful treasure hunt, and partly exhausted by lack of sleep, the counters began to struggle with their problem. One of them had an idea: there was an all-night laundromat in Pennsauken. Why not put the bills in the automatic drier, so they could be more easily handled and counted? Away we go.

At four in the morning, there aren't very many people in a public laundromat, but there was one. A little old lady was doing her wash in the first machine by the door. It was a long narrow place, and the two officers took their bag of soggy paper past the old lady, and down to the very last drying machine on the end. Stuffed the bills into the machine, slammed the door, and turned it on. Most people don't know what happens when you put counterfeit money in a drier, but what happens is they swell up and sort of explode with a terribly loud noise. The machine becomes unbalanced, and the vibration makes even more noise. The little old lady came to the back of the laundromat to see what was going on.

As soon as she got close, she could see hundred dollar bills plastered against the window, and that was all she stopped to see. She headed for the pay telephone near the front of the door. The Secret Servicemen followed quickly with waving of hands and earnest explanations, but within minutes there were sirens and flashing lights on the roof of the Pennsauken Police car. Out came wallets and badges, everyone shouting at once, and then everything calmed

Burlington Bristol Bridge

down as the bewildered local cop was made to understand the huge social distance between a municipal night patrolman and officers of the U.S. Secret Service. Now, he quickly became a participant in the great adventure and was delegated the job of finding something to do with armloads of (newly dried) counterfeit hundred dollar bills. He had an idea: the local supermarket was also open all night, and they carried plastic garbage bags for sale. Just the thing. But who was going to pay the supermarket for the bags? Immediately, everyone was thinking the same thing.

Fortunately for law and order, the one who first suggested the obvious idea of passing one the counterfeits was the little old lady. At that, everyone came to their senses. That wouldn't do at all, - quite unthinkable. The local cop was sent off for the bags, relying on his ability to persuade the supermarket clerk. And, yes, they did get the money all counted by 7 A.M.

10 Pennsbury Manor

400 Pennsbury Memorial Road   **Morrisville, PA**   **40.1353 -74.7714**

William Penn once had his pick of the best home sites in three states, because of course he more or less owned all three (states, that is). Aside from Philadelphia townhouses, he first picked Faire Mount, where the Philadelphia Art Museum now stands. For some reason, he gave up that idea and built Pennsbury, his country estate, across the river from what is now Trenton. It's in the crook of a sharp bend in the river but is rather puzzlingly surrounded by what most of us would call swamps. The estate has been elegantly restored and is visited by hosts of visitors, sometimes two thousand in a day. On other days it is deserted, so it's worth telephoning in advance to plan a trip.

After World War II, a giant steel plant was placed nearby in Morrisville, thriving on shiploads of iron ore from Labrador, but which is now closed. Morrisville had a brief flurry of prosperity, now seemingly lost forever. However, as you drive through the area you can see huge recycling and waste disposal plants, and you can tell from the verdant soil heaps that the recycled waste is filling in the swamps. It doesn't take much imagination to foresee swamps turning into lakes surrounded by lawns, on top of which will be many exurban houses. How much of this will be planned

Fairmount

communities and how much simply sold off to local developers, surely depends on the decisions of some remote corporate Board of Directors.

However, it's intriguing to imagine the dreams of best-case planners. Radiating from Pennsbury, there are two strips of charming waterfront extending for miles, north to Washington's Crossing, and west to Bristol. If you arrange for a dozen lakes in the middle of this promontory and surround them with lawns nurtured by recycled waste, you could imagine a resort community, a new city, an upscale exurban paradise, or all three combined. It's sad to think that whether this happens here or on the comparable New Jersey side of the river depends on state taxes. Inevitably, that means lobbying and corruption will rule the day and the pace of progress.

Meanwhile, take a trip from Washington's Crossing to Bristol, by way of Pennsbury. It can be done in an hour, plus an extra hour or so to tour Penn's mansion if the school kids aren't there. Add a tour of Bristol to make it a morning, and some tours of the remaining riverbank mansions, to make a day of it.

Freedom of religion includes the right to join some other religion than the one your father founded; William Penn's descendants had every right to become members of the Anglican Church. It might even have been a wise move for them, in view of their need to maintain good relations with the British Monarch. But religious conversion cost the Penn family the automatic political allegiance of the Quakers dominating their colony. Not much has come down to us showing the Pennsylvania Quakers bitterly resenting their desertion, but it would be remarkable if at least some ardent Quakers did not feel that way. It certainly confuses history students, when they read that the Quakers of Pennsylvania were often rebellious about the rule of the Penn family.

Such resentments probably accelerated but do not completely explain the growing restlessness between the tenants and the landlords. The terms of the Charter gave the Penns ownership of the land from the Delaware River to five degrees west of the river – providing they could maintain order there. King Charles was happy to be freed of the expense of policing this wilderness, and to be paid for it; to be freed of the obligation to Admiral Penn who greatly assisted his return to the throne; and to have a place to be rid of a large number of English Dissenters. The Penns were, in effect, vassal kings of a subkingdom larger than England itself. However, they behaved in what would now be considered an entirely businesslike manner. They bought their

William Penn

land, fair and square (at least from the English point of view), purchased it a second or even third time from the local Indians, and refused to permit settlement until the Indians were satisfied. They skillfully negotiated border disputes with their neighbors without resorting to armed force, while employing great skill in the English Court on behalf of the settlers on their land. They provided benign oversight of the influx of huge numbers of settlers from various regions and nations, wisely and shrewdly managing a host of petty problems with the demonstration that peace led to prosperity and that reasonableness could cope with ignorance and violence.
When revolution changed the government and all the rules, they coped with the difficulties as well as anyone in history had done, and better than most.

In retrospect, most of the violent criticism they engendered at the time, seems pretty unfair. They wanted to sell off their land as fast as they could at a fair price. They did not seek power, and in fact surrendered the right to govern the colony to the purchasers of the first five million acres, in return for being allowed to become private citizens selling off the remaining twenty-five million. Ultimately in 1789, they were forced to accept the sacrifice price of fifteen cents an acre. Aside from a few serious mistakes at the Council of Albany by a rather young John Penn, they treated the settlers honorably and did not deserve the treatment or the epithets they received in return. The main accusation made against them was that they were only interested in selling their land. Their main defense was that they were only interested in selling their land.

As time has passed, their reputation has repaired itself, and they bask in the universal gratitude which is directed to their grandfather and father, William Penn. Statues and nameplates abound. Nobody who attacked them at the time appears to have been really serious about it, except one. The exception was Benjamin Franklin, who turned from being their close friend to be their bitter enemy. Franklin tried to destroy the Penns, traveled to England to do it, and after twenty years seemed just as bitter as ever. Something really bad happened between them in 1754, and neither the Penns nor Franklin has been open about what it was. A successor volume about Franklin will explore this episode.

11 Pembertons

Bolton Mansion   85 Holly Dr   Levittown, PA   40.1604 -74.8398

Ralph Pemberton was an English Quaker well before 1650; he may have been a Quaker before William Penn was one. As an old man, he accompanied his son Phineas to Pennsylvania in 1682. They established a farm on the banks of the Delaware in Bucks County called Grove Place, and Phineas soon became one of the chief men in the colony. In the next generation, Israel Pemberton became one of the best educated, richest merchants in the colony. But it was Israel's son, also called Israel, who earned the title of King of the Quakers. He was one of the founding Managers of the Pennsylvania Hospital along with Benjamin Franklin and one of his brothers, James Pemberton, and was a generous philanthropist and leader of a number of other civic organizations. Just exactly what provoked his famous political disputes with Franklin is not clear, but he was a leading friend of the Indians, whom Franklin apparently never much liked. Israel Pemberton strongly and effectively argued William Penn's policy of friendship with the Indians, particularly insisting that sales of land to colonists should be prevented until there was a clear agreement with the Indians about the ownership. Unfortunately, pressures built up as Europeans immigrated faster than this policy could accommodate smoothly, and Franklin mostly sided with the impatient immigrants -- and squatters. This disagreement came to a head in 1756 when Pemberton negotiated a treaty of peace with the Indians at a conference at Easton. Although this treaty seemed to settle matters, it came against a background of the descendants of William Penn abandoning Quakerism. They, however, remained the proprietary owners of the Province with a more narrow focus on speeding up land sales to maximize their investment. Much of the internal dynamics of these quarrels before the Revolutionary War remain unclear and possibly somewhat misrepresented.

When the Revolution came, Pemberton viewed it with disfavor, mostly for pacifist rather than purely Tory reasons. Feelings ran high since the Pembertons were influential citizens with the potential to dissuade wavering neighbors, which made it difficult to tolerate them as invisible bystanders. However that may be, the three Pemberton brothers and twenty other wealthy and influential Quakers were arrested and, without hearing or trial, thrown in the back of an oxcart and sent into exile in Virginia for eight months. Their journey was a curious one, along a trail up the Schuylkill to the ford at Pottstown, and then down the Shenandoah Valley, an area in which they were well known and highly respected, greeted with great sympathy as they traveled. Isaac's brother John, who had spent several years as a missionary, died during this exile.

In some ways, the most curiously notable Pemberton was John Clifford Pemberton, who applied to West Point on his own initiative and was appointed by Andrew

Jackson, who had been a friend of his father. In itself, it is curious that so combative a person and so vigorous an enemy of the Indians -- as Jackson certainly was -- would have Quaker friendships. But he did not misjudge John Clifford, who became a diligent professional warrior for his country in a number of military incidents with

**John Clifford
Pemberton**

the Indians, the Mexicans, and the Canadians, rising to the rank of captain in the regular Army at the opening of the Civil War. In spite of personal efforts by General Winfield Scott to dissuade him, he resigned his commission and volunteered in the Confederate army. He was quickly promoted to major, then a brigadier general and eventually to Lieutenant General. As such, he was the commanding Confederate officer at the fifty-day siege of Vicksburg where he was finally forced to surrender to Grant's army. In a prisoner exchange, he was returned to the Confederate side, which then had no openings for Lieutenant Generals. He resigned and re-enlisted as a common soldier, but was quickly promoted to the rank of Colonel, in charge of the artillery at the final siege of Richmond. After the war, he became a farmer in Warrenton, Virginia, but was visiting at the family home in

Penllyn when he died in 1881. John Clifford Pemberton, the highest-ranking general on the grounds, lies buried in Laurel Hill cemetery right next to Israel Pemberton, who with Franklin was one of the founders of the Pennsylvania Hospital. In some sort of triumph of the South, John Clifford here out-ranks George Gordon Meade, the hero of Gettysburg. Just how his pacifist family reconciled itself to his heroism can only be imagined.

12 Edward Hicks: Peaceable Kingdoms

**Newtown Friends Meeting   219 Court Street   Newtown, PA
40.2262 -74.9364**

Edward Hicks (1780-1849), the most important folk artist of American art, was born and lived all his life in Bucks County, Pennsylvania. About a hundred of his paintings survive, 62 of which are versions of "The Peaceable Kingdom." Recently, his Peaceable Kingdoms have been selling for more than $4 million apiece, and the other works at more than a million. As is so often the case, he was born in poverty and spent his life in poverty, so the financial benefits have all gone to middle-men.

Hicks had to overcome an additional handicap. Quakers disapproved of painting things just for show, and they strongly disapproved of the vanity underlying the act of having a portrait painted of oneself. In fact, the early Quakers would not even permit their names to be placed on their tombstones.

Hicks was apprenticed into the wagon business and showed a talent for painting them. From that, entirely self-taught, he migrated into the business of painting business signs in an age of limited literacy. The Blue Anchor Tavern, the King of Prussia Inn, the Crossed Keys Tavern and the signs of various tradesmen were an essential part of conducting business. It is easy to see these tradesmen signs in the easel paintings of Hicks' later career, which reduce themselves to rearrangements of such individual sign paintings to make a coherent canvas.

Peaceable Kingdom

If you have seen one "Peaceable Kingdom" you haven't seen them all, but you only need to see one to be able to recognize the others at sight. They generally form a group of wild animals and an occasional child in the right foreground, with a grouping of Quakers and Indians in the left background, taken from Benjamin West's famous portrayal of Penn signing the treaty of peace with the Delaware Indians. The scene is taken from Chapter 11 of Isaiah, in which the lion lies down with the lamb.

Hicks was not a successful farmer, and he had to overcome Quaker resistance even to sell religious paintings with a Quaker moral. No doubt the resistance was strengthened by the fact that his cousin Elias Hicks had split the Quaker church into two (Conservatives and Hicksites) in 1827, and Edward was himself a strong itinerant preacher. Although the plain message of the Peaceable Kingdom is reconciliation between the two branches of Quakerism, he probably encountered a fair amount of coolness among the Conservative opposition.

Hicks was neither an educated nor a sophisticated man. It is forgivable that he made such a strong Old Testament statement when he and his cousin represented a dissenting sect that was gravely doubtful about the wisdom of allowing your life to be ruled by biblical verses.

13 Bi-state Fishing

Lambertville, NJ   2 Coryell Street   Lambertville, PA   40.3669 -74.9469

When George Washington was circling around Trenton to attack it on Christmas, a narrow spot up-river with a dozen houses on either side was called Coryell's Crossing or Ferry. That's now Coryell Street in Lambertville, linked to the other side of the river at New Hope, after first crossing a narrow wooden bridge to Lewis Island, the center of shad fishing, or at least shad fishing culture.

Coryell's Crossing

The Lewis family still has a house on Lewis Island, and they know a lot about shad fishing, entertaining hundreds of visitors at the shad festival in the last week of April. The river is cleaning up its pollution, the shad are coming back, but they, unfortunately, took a vacation in 2006. At the promised hour, a boatload of men with large deltoids attached one end of a dragnet to the shore, rowed to the middle of the river, floated downstream and towed the other end of the net back to the shore. The original anchor end of the net was then lifted and carried downstream to make a loop around the tip of Lewis Island, and then both ends were pulled in to capture the fish. There were fifty or so fish in the net, but only two shad of adequate size; since it was Sunday, the fish were all thrown back.

But it was a nice day, and fun, and the nice Lewis lady who explained things knew a lot. Remember, the center of the river is a border separating two states. You would have to have a fishing license in both states to cross the center of the river with your net; game wardens can come upon you quickly with a power boat. But the nature of fishing with a dragnet from the shore makes it quite practical to stop in the middle, where shotguns from the other side are unlikely to reach you. An even more persuasive force for law and order is provided by the fish. Fish like to feed when the sky is overcast, so there is a tendency on a North-South river for the fish to be on the Pennsylvania (West) side of the river in the morning, and the New Jersey (East) side in the evening. During the 19th century when shad were abundant, work schedules at the local mills and factories were arranged to give the New Jersey workers time off to fish in the afternoon, while Pennsylvania employers delayed the starting time at their factories until morning fishing was over.

Somehow, underneath this tradition one senses a local Quaker somewhere with a scheme to maintain the peace without using force. Right now, there aren't enough fish to justify either stratagem or force, but one can hope.

Delaware River North

Shad

Nowadays, we have fresh fruit and vegetables all year. When produce isn't in season locally, we get it from Florida and California. When even those places are out of season, we bring it in from Chile. But the supermarket and its attendant supply chains are recent phenomena. Before the two World Wars, our food was pretty drab and monotonous during the winter. The first sign of the culinary joys of spring was shad.

Everybody loved shad, which everybody ate in its various forms. Shad was cheap because it was abundant; indeed, it seems difficult for the modern fisherman to imagine the huge quantities of fish that came up the rivers in early March. There was even a special term for fish weighing less than three pounds; at the fish market, such fish were thrown in, free. The term "Bushwhacker" referred to the practice of beating the fish in the water to catch them. There once was a time when everybody knew how to use a shad dart, everyone could filet the bones, everyone had fried shad roe for breakfast.

Unfortunately, the diversion of fresh water from the upper Delaware to New York City, the dumping of waste from the oil refineries near Marcus Hook, and heaven knows what other pollution, wiped out the annual shad run. Once a river's shad run is depleted, the main obstacle to getting it revived is the striped bass, who feast on the fingerlings coming back downriver from the spawning areas. You can still catch a few shad at the place where Amtrak crosses the Susquehanna, and a few hardy pioneer fish are starting to make it all the way to Lambertville. But the bulk of shad in Philadelphia markets now comes from North Carolina, and you better be alert to your timing or even they will be all gone before you've had any. There once was a time when a diner could be identified as a boorish stranger picking gingerly at the strong-tasting fish, or messing around dubiously with the unfamiliar roe served on toast. Nowadays, even lifelong Philadelphians will occasionally behave like that. Lemon juice makes it delicious!

And you filet the fish. The bones of a shad are complex, going both forward and back within the flesh, so you have to be experienced to take a very sharp knife, twist, and turn, duck your shoulders and flip the fish, to produce boneless" shad." If you don't know how to do that, you may have to bake the fish for hours to melt the bones and make it edible, but tasteless. Such products can be rescued by stuffing them with bread crumbs and spices. When things reach the point where no butcher knows how to produce boneless shad, our culture is on the edge of extinction. The big center for wholesale boned shad is Dill's in Bridgeton, NJ. There is, right now, only one place where you can obtain planked shad. That's the Salem Country Club (if you look respectable they let non-members in) out at the point on the Jersey side where the Delaware takes a big bend before it flows down to the sea. A shad is planked by splitting it open and nailing it to a board, which is then placed before an open fire in the fireplace. Snap, crackle and wow.

Shad Fishing on the Delaware
Thomas Birch 1820

Maybe the conservationists can get these fish back for us. The Eagles will certainly like that; shad used to be what mainly sustained the American bird, and the depletion of the shad is part of the near-extinction of eagles. And maybe we can swallow our pride and teach the West Coast how to treat shad with respect. Shad was always an East-coast, Atlantic fish, and there is hardly a river left which has much shad. But someone transported some shad to the Sacramento, California area a century ago -- and they have flourished. Where the fish ladders of the Columbia River used to teem with salmon, nowadays they teem with shad. California likes to think it invents everything in America. Brace yourself for being told they invented shad.

Here's a tip: the only sizeable river left undammed flows through Richmond, Virginia. The boys on the banks pull in six shad at a time with a single line. The only problem is a shortage of boats to rent on the river.

XV Doylestown Area

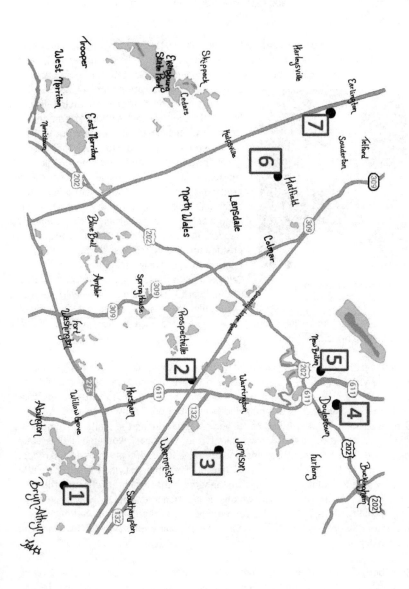

1 The Swedenborgian Church

Bryn Athyn Cathedral   **900 Cathedral Rd**   **Huntingdon Valley, PA**
40.1343 -75.0637

Among the many churches centered in Philadelphia, the Swedenborgian is probably the least typical and most difficult to understand. The church does not actively seek out a new membership, but it welcomes everyone, in the spirit of Emanuel

Emanuel Swedenborg

Swedenborg's observation that "All people who live good lives, no matter what their religion, have a place in Heaven." Without attempting to define the teachings of Swedenborg (1688-1772), who was quite able to speak for himself, it can be approximated that Heaven plays a central role in this belief system, and predestination does not. Although the ceremonial features, its main emphasis is on good works as a way of attaining the reward of Heaven. In some ways, that is an unexpected position for a noted scientist like Swedenborg to take, since generally, scientists lean toward Calvinism, with the mechanistic view that if God is all-powerful, then human free will must be impossible. There are at least four divisions of the Swedenborgian religion, but the Bryn Athyn branch is most notable in the Philadelphia region.

A very wealthy adherent of Swedenborg named John Pitcairn bought a large tract at Bryn Athyn and gathered the local church to live around a perfectly magnificent cathedral and church school. It is hard to think of any church in the Philadelphia region which approaches the magnificence of the Bryn Athyn cathedral. It has a special character in that it was conceived and built during the crafts movement of the early twentieth century, with imported European workmen deliberately organized like medieval craft guilds. The central features of this workmanship reflect and then project the belief in personal individuality within the whole religion. No two windows, or doorknobs, or carvings are the same in the cathedral, reflecting the wish for each workman to devise his own unique creation and show the way of personal responsibility to the faithful. This cathedral is one of the things in the Philadelphia region most worth visiting, but to appreciate its quality you have to know what you are looking at.

Everybody in this church is unexpectedly hard to characterize. The Pitcairn Foundation was such a successful investor that it formed a mutual fund for others to share in its good fortune. Its central philosophy is to invest only in corporations which have been dominated by a single family, preferably the founding family, for at least fifteen years. There are about six hundred eligible corporations, and recent management scandals in the newspapers illustrate the Pitcairns exactly knew the dangers of handing your assets over to a hired manager. This family-centered investing approach consistently yields better than the S & P 500, which in turn beats ninety percent of investment managers. You sort of get the idea you know where this family is coming from when you meet a courtly, meek, retiring but friendly person, who can say, "My mother is the only person I ever met who looked perfectly at home seated under a sixty-foot ceiling."

Two other famous Swedenborgians illustrate the unusual individualism of this religion. Helen Keller, the deaf-blind girl who overcame her handicap by going to Radcliffe and becoming a successful author and lecturer, for one. The other would be Johnny Appleseed (1774-1845), whose real name was John Chapman. Grammar school legends would have this bearded, barefoot vegetarian adopting a life of poverty like St. Francis, but in fact, he was an extremely shrewd businessman who died rich. He developed the business plan that American settlers would be going West into what was then the Northwest Territory, and having a tough time getting enough to eat the first year or two. So, he anticipated the paths of frontier settlement, and went ahead among the Indian tribes, planting apple trees. When the settlers arrived in the region, he sold them young apple trees and showed them what to do with them. Apples grown from seed are not the tasty morsels we know today but tend to be rather shriveled and bitter. So Johnny showed them how you make cider, and if you let it sit around a while, hard cider. The settlers would use the pulpy squeezing for compost, and he would be back to collect the seeds from them so he could continue his business plan in the next county. In short, he showed them how to drink the apples. He also let the Indians pick the apples, so they liked him and spared him the common troubles of the frontier.

If you are going to boil apples, you need a pot, and Johnny often carried his like a hat. He wasn't a nut, at all, he was a showman. In his backpack, he was also carrying a Bible. And in his head, he carried a motto, "All religion has to do with life, and the life of religion is to do good."

2 Governor Keith's House

Graeme Park   **859 County Line Rd**   **Horsham, PA**   **40.2167 -75.1494**

Route 611 begins at Philadelphia's City Hall and goes due north, headed for the Delaware Water Gap. In 1717 Lieutenant Governor Sir William Keith had decided he needed a summer residence to compliment his in-town establishment on Second Street, and acquired the 1200 acres of land from Samuel Carpenter on Easton Road, now Route 611. Sam had been entrusted with 2000 pounds against a possible French invasion, which Keith transferred to himself by taking Carpenter's land in lieu of it. The ethics of everybody in this transaction are now a little murky. The selected farm area was cool and tranquil, with creeks and level land, so a suitable three-story mansion was built of local stone, with outbuildings. A large mushroom-shaped rock was carved, polished and set on a pedestal beside the house. Tradition has it that Governor Keith asked servants and slaves to lift the stone as a test of physical strength. Keith had several Negro slaves, eight or ten indentured servants, and others who were simply hired help for a rather large farm. Criticism was heard of the elaborate luxury of a mansion fifteen miles from town which it took five or six hours to reach.

Governor Keith was an interesting person. He inherited a Scottish baronetcy from his father and is the only Governor of Pennsylvania with a claim to noble blood. His finances were meager, however, and his life was a succession of efforts to advance his own wealth and position, which he regularly consumed with high living. He involved himself in coups and rebellions in Scotland, probably out of expectation of reward from the exiled King James. Efforts at court were finally rewarded by Queen Anne making him Surveyor-General of English land from Pennsylvania to Jamaica, but only after his nearly being hanged for treason for suspected efforts on behalf of the exiled former King James. Keith lost this essentially tax-collector position which he had performed creditably when the  Hanoverian King George I took over the throne. After William Penn encountered difficulties which returned him to England, he and the Penn family were in need of an administrator in America, and Keith was at pains to ingratiate himself with Hannah Penn after William suffered several strokes from which he was to die in 1718. Most who met him felt that Keith was charming, although some regarded him as a charming rogue; he succeeded in ingratiating himself to the Penns and was appointed Lieutenant Governor of Pennsylvania in 1716, incurring substantial debts to transfer his family to America in style. After taking office, he wasted no time starting schemes and devices to enrich himself, while at the same time pursuing a populist political style which involved him in more or less constant controversy. There are many echoes in his career of that enduring subsequent conflict in America between creditors and debtors; as probably the most indebted man in Pennsylvania, his populism was highly troubling to conservative Quaker farmers. He pushed hard for paper currency, always popular among debtors, and probably sought to soften the feelings of the Quakers by pushing hard for the replacement of legally binding oaths with secular "affirmations". By doing so, however, Keith infuriated the vestry of Christ Church, representing widely held Anglican support for requiring oaths.

Keith's pandering to differing viewpoints succeeded in infuriating James Logan, the secretary of the Penn proprietorship, into setting sail for England to seek Keith's removal from office. Logan only returned with a letter of admonishment from Hannah Penn, and controversy continued to simmer. Reduced to its essentials, a case can be made that Keith behaved like an unrestrained modern machine politician exploiting every opportunity he could find.

However, certain things can be said in Keith's defense. There is no doubt the Quaker farmers were hypersensitive about the display of wealth which a Scottish baronet would find quite appropriate for a man in his station. His mansion, for example, would barely qualify today as a five-bedroom house in the suburbs, and it is a little quaint to recall that generations of Penrose's and Strawbridge's subsequently lived on the property quite proudly, or even defiantly in view of their ample means. Paper money is indeed always the favorite of debtors who seek to dishonor their debts, but the colonies in Keith's times were suffering from a severe lack of specie which can now be explained as the consequence of colonial terms of trade but which at that time was a severe economic hardship. His efforts to stop the practice of executing debtors may well have been made with his own indebtedness in the back

Horsham Friends Meeting

of his mind, but still, it seems like a step in the right direction. Even the inventory of his property probably exaggerates the ostentation of his lifestyle. True, he had 144 chairs in the house, but the shortage of currency at that time had converted chairs into a form of exchangeable value, employed by almost every shopkeeper. Land was similarly used as a form of currency, although here most people would raise their eyebrows at a governor accumulating in eight years a list of property including not only this country estate and the downtown house in Society Hill, but a dozen rather large estates in other colonies, and a particularly troublesome investment in a copper mine on the west side of the Susquehanna.

To some degree, Keith was a good Governor but was forced into a number of conflicts between the wishes of the settlers and the best interest of the Penn proprietors. Three thousand miles from the Court of St. James, he would scarcely be expected to display universal agility in shifting allegiance between the Stuart Kings, Queen Anne and the Hanoverian King George I, not to mention the Penn family and the settlers on their land. Keith did maintain reasonable stability in the colony while seeming to undermine the best interests of the Penn family. He was said to have made shrewd business decisions for the whole region converting surplus grain into malt at a time of money shortages in the colony, even though it particularly profited his own acreage. In some ways, his reputation remains chiefly tarnished by his treatment of Benjamin Franklin. Encouraging Franklin to go to England to buy some printing equipment, Keith promised letters of credit for what was presumably intended as a joint venture. The letters were never forthcoming, Franklin was stranded for months in England without means to return home. Franklin got his revenge years later in his autobiography. This was not the only example of Franklin nursing a grudge for decades. Poor Keith returned to England to defend himself against dismissal by the Penns because of all the turmoil and factionalism, but essentially never got another job and died in debtors' prison. During that time he published extensively about current affairs and economics, but the value of that writing is now difficult to judge.

After Keith returned to England in 1726, presumably to defend his interests and possibly to evade his creditors, the mansion and estate on County Line Road was sold to Keith's son in law, Dr. Thomas Graeme who was a physician at the founding of the Pennsylvania Hospital in 1751 and evidently had become quite prosperous. Graeme paneled the interior of the mansion in high Georgian style, revised the floor plan, generally making the place elegant. Records of how the region between the counties became named Graeme Park are missing but presumably Graeme would now put up no objection to it. A second house on the property was home to several generations of Penrose's and Strawbridge's; the Strawbridge family donated the estate as a park. Governor Keith having left his wife alone, forever to her distress, fathered two illegitimate children in England, making his prevailing emotions subject to uncertainty.

Around the corner, so to speak, on Route 611, the Horsham Friends Meeting is built of the same sort of stonework, with dates which suggest the meeting itself was present well before Keith appeared on the scene, and the string of similar but tavern-like buildings along 611 suggest the highway to Easton was a busy one even at an early time. Increasing traffic and construction carry an ominous prediction that growth of the area will eventually swallow both Graeme Park and Horsham Meeting in a sea of subdivisions and industrial parks. Placing a turnpike entrance nearby almost certainly hastened that fate.

3 Washington Lurks in Bucks County, Waiting for Howe to Make a Move

Moland House   1641 York Rd   Warminster, PA   40.2358 -75.0928

Although Bucks County, Pennsylvania, is staunchly Republican, it has been home to Broadway playwrights for decades; this handful of Democrats has long been referred to as lions in a den of Daniels. One of them really ought to make a comic play out of the two weeks in August 1777, when John Moland's house in Warwick Township was the headquarters of the Continental Army.

John Moland died in 1761, but his personality hovered over his house for many years. He was a lawyer, trained at the Inner Temple and thus one of the few lawyers in

Moland House

America who had gone to law school. He is best known today as the mentor for John Dickinson, the author of the Articles of Confederation. Our playwright might note that Dickinson played a strong role in the Declaration of Independence, but then refused to sign it. Moland, for his part, stipulated in his will that his wife would be the life tenant of his house, provided -- that she never speak to his eldest son.

Enter George Washington on horseback, dithering about the plans of the Howe brothers, accompanied by seven generals of fame, and twenty-six mounted bodyguards. Mrs. Moland made him sleep on the floor with the rest.

Enter a messenger; Lord Howe's fleet had been sighted off Patuxent, Maryland. Washington declared it was a feint, and Howe would soon turn around and join Burgoyne on the Hudson River. Washington had his usual bottle of Madeira with supper.

A court-martial was held for "Light-Horse Harry" Lee, for cowardice. Lee was exonerated.

Kasimir Pulaski made himself known to the General, offering a letter of introduction from Benjamin Franklin, which letters Franklin noted had been requested by Pulaski himself. As it turned out, Pulaski subsequently distinguished himself as the father of the American cavalry and was killed at the Battle of Savannah.

And then a 19-year-old French aristocrat, the Marquis de Lafayette, made an appearance. Although he spoke not a word of English, he nevertheless made it clear that he expected to be made a Major General in spite of having zero battlefield experience. He presented a letter from Silas Deane, in spite of Washington having complained he was tired of Ambassadors in Paris sending a stream of unqualified fortune hunters to pester the fighting army. Deane did, however, manage to make it clear that the Marquis had two unusually strong military credentials. He was immensely rich, and he was a dancing partner, ahem, of Marie Antoinette.

In Mrs. Moland's parlor, Washington sat down with Lafayette to tap-dance around his new diplomatic problem. It was clear America needed France as an ally, and particularly needed money to buy supplies. But it was also clearly impossible to take a regiment away from some American general, a veteran of real fighting, and give that regiment to a Frenchman who could not speak English and who admitted he had no military experience. Fumbling around, Washington offered him the title of

Major General, but without any soldiers under his command, at least until later when his English improved. To sweeten it a little, Washington seems to have said something to the effect that Lafayette should think of Washington as talking to him as if he were his father. There, that should do it.

It seems just barely possible that Lafayette misunderstood the words. At any rate, he promptly wrote everybody he knew -- and he knew lots of important people -- that he was the adopted son of George Washington.

Lafayette

Well, Broadway, you take it from there. At about that moment, another messenger arrived, announcing Lord Howe at this moment was unloading troops at Elkton, Maryland. General Howe might have been able to present his credentials to Moland House in person, except that his horses were nearly crippled from spending three weeks in the hold of a ship and needed time to recover. Heavy rains were coming.

(*Exeunt Omnes.*)

4 Doylestown
Doylestown PA   40.31 -75.13

Caught between the expansion of two metropolitan areas, Bucks County is inevitably doomed to extinction as a culture. Chester County and Bucks are in similar situations, as suburbia devours exurbia, in this case, the Quaker farm communities. So you better go have a look, while they still survive to some degree.

The political unit of the area has been the county, and the county seat is in Doylestown, a population about 8000. Within a few decades, it seems safe to predict the county population will approach a million. The town has lots of pride in itself and is just as cute as any town could possibly be. New Castle, Delaware has been preserved with the same pride but is uniform with a single period of architecture; Doylestown is a carefully preserved jumble of styles and periods, sizes and shapes. Like Princeton, NJ, and Odessa, DE, it is so attractive it brings hordes of visitors, which in turn quickly strangle it with traffic and lack of available parking space. A by-pass highway is an attempt to rescue the town, and blessings on the attempt. But the problem for these exurban jewels is not that people want to go around them, the problem is they are the main destination.

Doylestown was created in 1745 when William Doyle built a tavern at the crossroads. The county seat brings the courthouse with eleven judges and who knows how many lawyers, and the hospital. Henry Chapman Mercer brought three astonishing buildings, his 44-room mansion on 70 acres in the center of town, his famous Mercer tile factory in his back yard, and his multi-story museum of tools and crafts. All three of Mercer's buildings are made of concrete, built by

Mercer Museum

craftsmen and himself with essentially unlimited personal funds derived from fabric manufacture in New England. And then this last bastion of the crafts movement embraced the artist colony established by Redfield at New Hope, and both of them attracted all those rich Broadway stars and publishing moguls. Right in the center of town, the Mercer crafts museum sits across the street from the James A. Michener Art Museum, small but very tasteful, the museum home of the Pennsylvania Impressionist school of art. The essence of this style is a smooth careful background, overlaid with quick thick foreground brushwork, producing a strong three-dimensional effect.

Schoolchildren in buses delight in the doll's house aspects, tourists admire the very fine art, everybody likes the cute little jumble of well-preserved eclectic buildings. It's all in a setting of Quaker farmhouses for the time being, but the split-levels and the McMansions by the thousands are coming. Visitors throng to see, and the residents are proud of what they have. But, really, does everybody have to bring his car?

5 Tree Huggers: Delaware Valley College

Delaware Valley University   700 East Butler Ave   Doylestown PA
40.2987 -75.1586

At the time when Philadelphia and New York were both occupied by the British during the Revolutionary War, a backwoods highway connected the thirteen colonies. Doylestown is 35 miles due north of Philadelphia City Hall, at the point of intersection of this variant of the Ho Chi Minh Trail with the path which

Philadelphia Tories took in their flight to Kingston, Ontario. No doubt there were some interesting conversations in Mr. Doyle's tavern at the crossroads.

Doylestown is also on the invisible border between the hegemonies of Philadelphia and New York, where descendants of German and Quaker farmers make a cautious contact with the distinctly non-Quaker artists and writers fleeing south from New York. James Michener and Pearl Buck once represented Philadelphia in the cultural stew with New Yorker ex-patriots. Somehow in this interface, a place is found for the Delaware Valley College, which started life in 1896 with Jewish founders of the National Farm School. The original board of trustees included such names as Gimbel, Lit, Snellenburg, and Erlanger, but the three-year curriculum was entirely agricultural. The founder himself was Joseph Krauskopf, who got the idea after an inspiring interview with Count Leo Tolstoy.

From a single building that served as a classroom and dormitory, the college has grown into a four-year institution in numerous buildings scattered over a 570-acre plot with a second 120-acre farm in Montgomery County. The school is determinedly non-sectarian, and for fifty years has been coeducational. It has had several changes of name, from the National Farm School, eventually to its present name. The curriculum has expanded as well, with master's degree programs in business and education. Baruch Blumberg, the Nobel Prize winner in Medicine, kept an office there, and it is clear the college means to shift its emphasis toward the scientific basis of agriculture and the environment. It's also pretty clear that rising agricultural prices will soon re-establish agriculture as a dominant feature of our economy, although agriculture in the modern sense is quite a distance from farming in the old sense, and requires a different sort of educational preparation.

By the way, the tree hugger nickname comes from a campus tradition of this college, very much an active ceremony, of hugging the 400-year-old oak standing beside the president's house on the campus. The College, of course, is 250 years younger than the tree.

6 Country Auction Modernized
Alderfer Auction Company   501 Fairgrounds Road   Hatfield, PA
40.2715 -75.3169

Only a decade or two ago, the Quakertown exit of the Pennsylvania Turnpike made possible a quick trip from the city to the country, letting you off in the cornfields between Sumneytown and Lansdale. Today, the rush hour traffic is as bad as anywhere else, even on the four-lane express highway known as Forty Foot Road. A comfortable two-lane highway would be about forty feet wide, so presumably, the name denotes what was once a modern miracle of a two-lane highway, in this case until quite recently. It's all built up for miles, but almost all the commercial buildings are new. Exurban sprawl has positively lurched across the landscape, making prosperous people rich, and poor people prosperous. It won't be long before the housing subdivisions demand traffic signals to protect the school children, speed limits to reduce the collisions by teenagers, and other things destined to bring high-speed travel to a crawl, all day long. When that happens, it won't be called a farm country anymore.

On Fairground Road, where occasionally corn is still growing, a number of large new commercial enterprises have located, among them a moving and storage company with ten or so truck loading platforms in the back. Behind that is another large new building, also with a parking lot for fifty or so cars, the auction house. Different categories come up for auction on different days, so used furniture, for example,

Alderfer Auction Company

comes up every few weeks and has to be stored as things accumulate for the big day. With a moment's thought, you can easily see why the auction is affiliated with or owned by a moving and storage company. As you go through the entrance, you are invited to sign up and identify how you plan to pay, just in case you buy something; the product of this registration is a card with a number in big colored letters. That's your number, your payment arrangement, and soon you will find no one cares anything about you except that number. The auction I was interested in was for used books, one of three or four auctions conducted in different rooms.

Nearly a hundred people had numbers for used books, maybe a similar number for antique furniture and paintings. Obviously, one other purpose of the registration process is to create a mailing list of customers interested in various objects, possibly linked to a program that sends out flyers and announcements. Country auctions have always been a source of local entertainment, so non-buying spectators are able to come and watch if they wish. There seemed to be few if any casual sight-seers; just about everybody is a buyer or a potential buyer. Players, as they say.

Most of the customers probably set their alarm clocks for 5 AM or earlier; the auction is centrally located, but most everybody comes from a considerable distance. At 9 AM, very promptly, the auction began, and from his manner, you could tell the auctioneer was anxious to get started. The objects for sale had been on display for a day, but most people arrived around 7 AM to examine the goods, which are frequently sold in lots, meaning a box full of thirty or forty books more or less on the same topic. At the stroke of nine, the auctioneer chanting began, "Do I have ten dollars, yeh, ten, ten, ten, five, five, ten, fifteen, twenty, twenty, sold for fifteen. Your number, sir?" Two assistants took down the customer number, and the lot number, and the price; one of the two recorded the transaction in a computer, the other on a list by hand. One gathers the man without a computer was on the look-out for shills, people trying to bid up to the price without getting stuck for a purchase. The auctioneer repeatedly assured the audience that no one but a real bidder was allowed to bid, you owned it, and no excuses about being confused. When he reached the hundredth sale, he stopped for a drink of water, and proudly noted the first hundred sales took thirty-seven minutes. It required four other assistants to fish out the lots next in line, holding them up for confirmation only, since inspecting them at that distance was out of the question. After each sale, the assistant dumped the prize in the new owner's lap.

By one PM, seven-hundred lots had been sold, at least five thousand books. Every hundred sales, our leader took a drink of water and made a pleasantry or two, but he was otherwise all business. About two hundred of the sales were handled by a substitute auctioneer, who looked to be twenty years old but talked faster than any human being is supposed to talk, affecting a rasping quality of chant. As it came time to take over, he paced nervously near the microphone and started chanting the moment it was decent to do so. Obviously, these people loved what they were doing, and had remarkably retentive memories. On several occasions, a buyer had to fumble for his card number, and the auctioneer remembered what the number was before the card was found. New cards are issued every day. Although they were quite brusque about people who made bidding mistakes, on a couple of occasions the auctioneer had been slow in turning the lot number sign in front of him, so the bidding was repeated. The bidding stopped at the same price point, the second time around. It seems to illustrate what libertarians praise so highly about the wisdom of the marketplace; the market price is the "right" price.

And yet entitled to wonder a little. The ordinary run of books thirty or forty years old will sell for between ten and twenty dollars. Books about golf, just about any old book about golf, "go" for about forty dollars. Children's books are about sixty dollars. And, to my great surprise, boxes or albums of old photographs go for over a hundred dollars. A lady next to me excitedly brought an album of old photos back to her seat and thumbed through them. "Are you a dealer?" Yes. "Who buys this stuff?" I don't know, they come to my store and just buy it. Like the Auctioneer, she had a feeling for what the retail price would be, made a calculation, and knew what she could afford to pay wholesale. What the stuff actually represented, why people wanted it, what was a good one and what was a bad one--these people in the trade had very little idea. But they knew very precisely what was a fair price, and gradually lower it until it sells. Lots of fun. When a familiar insider makes a mistake and pays too much, the others laugh heartily at him. Why this funny system works has long been a mystery, but everyone except a socialist readily acknowledges it does work. At least it works better than any known substitute.

Although the ritual of the country auction has been essentially unchanged for centuries, it is just another transaction system. In the past fifty years, the world economy has been transformed by computerized efficiencies in transaction systems, with vast prosperity resulting from small savings endlessly repeated. Banking and Wall Street have concentrated most of the standardized transactions, in perfectly astounding volume; lots and lots of people have become immensely rich for producing small efficiencies in high volume. Those of us who have not become immensely rich can easily identify trivial innovations which resulted in wealth, and we easily sense the unfairness of old photos worth more than books of poetry. After all, the country auction is still grossly inefficient; the seller pays the auction company 20% of the price, and the buyer pays another 10%. There's 3% for the credit card company and &% for the sales tax. Forty percent of this transaction is going to the middle man, over and over and over again. The goal is to reduce transaction costs to the level of Wall Street, considerably less than one percent, which still buys lots of yachts for middlemen.

As you walk out of the country auction, it doesn't take a mathematical genius to multiply thirty percent times the number of transactions, times a guess at the average sales price. No wonder these auction people are so cheerful, so much in love with their work. But two other parties are cheerful, too. That is, the buyer and the willing seller.

7 Mennonites: The Pennsylvania Swiss

**Franconia Mennonite Meetinghouse   613 Harleysville Pike   Telford, PA
40.306 -75.3673**

Anabaptism, originally attributed to Ulrich Zwingli around 1525, centers around believing a baby is too young to understand baptism, so adults need to be re-baptized. The idea arose independently in Switzerland and Holland, and probably thousands of believers were unmercifully martyred for holding the belief. Because the worst persecutions took place during the War of Austrian Succession (1740-50), they are often attributed to the Roman Catholic Inquisition, but Magisterial Protestants, believing in the separation of church and state, were often also responsible. Many seemingly unrelated issues were introduced locally, and this period of unrest is known as the French and Indian War in America; its major battle took place in Louisburg, Nova Scotia, although George Washington's skirmish around Fort Duquesne (Pittsburgh) has acquired local fame as a major American manifestation.

Doylestown Area

The Swiss adherents moved to the Rhineland Palatinate, and from there were among the first to accept William Penn's offer of religious freedom. They were the settlers of Germantown, but have mainly moved a few miles west to southern Montgomery County, where the confusion about Pennsylvania Dutchmen is further confounded by the fact that they were Swiss. Menno the Dutchman gave his name to the order, but they themselves regard their true ethnic background as Swiss from the Zurich region. That, by the way, is not to be confused with Calvinism, which also comes from Switzerland, but by way of Geneva, not Zurich. The pacifism of the Mennonites made them mutually attractive with the English Quakers, who had made an appearance fifty or so years later in the region around Manchester, England; each group seems to have adopted some of the features of the other.

Franconia Mennonite Meetinghouse

Determined use of the German language has always held the Mennonites apart, however. From the start, it was really necessary to be somewhat bilingual in Montgomery County, using English for business conversation, and German at home and in the church. The idea of using a foreign language is based on the hope it would thus maintain a sense of distinctiveness or even remoteness from non-believers, without adopting the least hostility to them. It almost inevitably follows that the group has used its own schools, attached to their meeting houses. This sense of remoteness has persisted for almost four hundred years, surrounded by entirely different cultures. Starting only around 1960, this attitude has gradually softened, however, and it is widely assumed that in another few decades Mennonites will come to resemble the people in their environment a great deal more than they do at present. If you want to know where to find them, Harleysville is a good place to start. As the tinge of Pennsylvania Dutch accent gradually fades, and fewer of them wear the old costumes, a curious remaining hallmark of their presence can be noticed: an avoidance of foundation planting around their houses. The Mennonites themselves seem to be entirely oblivious to this unintended distinctiveness, which is however quite striking to non-Mennonite passers-by. Those who work in the fields all day have little interest in digging around their houses for decoration; those who have moved away from farming have seemingly adopted the bush-less style as a natural way of arranging things. There's no particular reason to change it, and so, there's no particular reason to notice it.

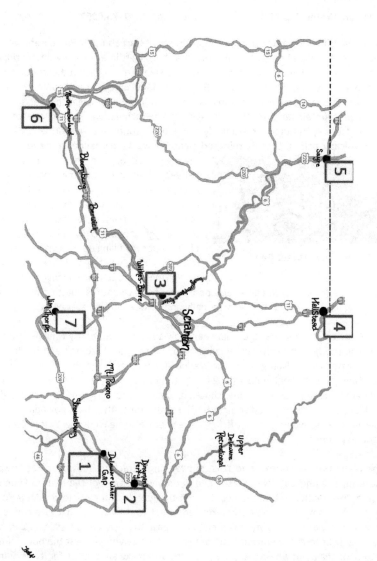

1 Delaware Water Gap

Delaware Water Gap NRA   Bushkill, PA   41.0879 -75.0067

When we think of water gaps, we tend to think of Harrisburg or Pittsburgh, with a wide river turning abruptly to run through a sharp cleft in a single mountain ridge. West Point on the Hudson might be a third well-known example. But the frontal ridge of the Alleghenies, variously called Blue Mountain, Blue Ridge Mountain, South Mountain, or Kennesaw Mountains, is several ridges wide. A gap in that sort of complex mountain range must be crooked and several miles wide to let a river of any size find its way through it. Presumably, this gap at Stroudsburg was formed by some huge volcanic action, because thick sedimentary layers are upended and exposed at

Delaware Water Gap

the river's edge, with the water winding between the towering formations. To avoid going up and over a thousand feet of the mountain, human travel must follow the same path; a railroad, a little town, and several highways are crowded into the base of the cleft now filling up with gravel eroded from the cliffs. Even the birds need to travel several miles through the winding cleft in the formidable forests, with eagles and occasional turkey vultures coasting overhead, enjoying a ride on windy updrafts, casually on the lookout for lesser prey.

The Gap is a great intersection between New Yorkers and Pennsylvanians, mostly going somewhere else. The dominant Philadelphians got there first and tended to congregate in Stroudsburg where the Waring Blender was invented, within the once-flourishing Pocono region for fishing and getting away from summer fevers. As the jolly guide at the visitor's center chuckled, the New Yorkers tend to arrive eight busloads at a time and head straight for the bathrooms. After that, nowadays most species of city dwellers buzz off for somewhere else, leaving the Water Gap to darkness, and to me.

The Water Gap has at least two other outstanding attractions, however. For fifty or more miles along both New Jersey and Pennsylvania sides of the river, a Federal Game Preservation area stretches through the forests and cliffs to the New York border. You have to be pretty determined to get to it, however, because traffic is traveling in herds at eighty miles per hour past the few entrances. You can be hopelessly beyond the entrances before you recognize you are past the point of no return, or at a point where you can if you wish only make another try for it by finding a place to turn around, pay tolls, and risk your life between the cliffs and eighteen wheelers. If you have enough courage and eye/hand coordination, however, once you do get off into the quiet woods, you pretty much have Shawnee America to yourself. The Appalachian Trail crosses at this point.

The other gem of this area is called the Shawnee, a 19th Century resort hotel of genteel note, with outstanding food and a famous golf course that you reach by footbridge to an island. PGA championships have been played here, and Fred Waring probably played some dance music once. At one time, there were a couple of dozen such mountain resort hotels scattered from Maine to Georgia, all of the American Plan, looking as though Scott Fitzgerald and Zelda would come lurching around the next corner. It's anybody's guess whether recessions and gasoline shortages will ruin these places, or whether the people who deserted this summer custom and went to Europe will remember these mountain resorts are here and save them. Right now, there are the golfers and the mountain hikers during the summer and the skiers in the winter. And then there are a few people who want to write or read novels, some conventions, a few tourists if they own a necktie.

This winding, several miles long canyon, once a forest fastness of the Shawnee, was perhaps their main bastion. That most powerful tribe of the Algonquin federation participated in a sixty-year war with the Iroquois and mostly lost. You can certainly imagine what a marvelous fortress this region was, containing protected fertile islands to grow food, interior forests which probably abounded in game, rivers full of fish, sheltering mountains with hidden entrance clefts from which to emerge and dominate the flatlanders in all directions.

2 Dingmans Ferry, Below Port Jervis
Dingmans Ferry Bridge, PA   41.2201 -74.8593

Because the area was once covered with a glacier, the northeast corner of Pennsylvania is fairly deserted. That's always been good for hunting and fishing, and more recently is good for skiing. Although the topsoil is poor, it's a beautiful area, practically guaranteed to provoke confrontation between the environmentalist movement and the Marcellus shale-gas extraction industry. The history of anthracite coal demonstrates locally that the mineral extraction industry always wins these arguments in the short run. The followers of Gifford Pinchot and Teddy Roosevelt are slowly learning to concentrate on minimizing the damage and forcing the extraction industries to pay for clean-up afterward. Right now, this semi-wilderness area is a remarkably beautiful but deserted forest within two hours drive of Philadelphia and New York City. It contains the headwaters of the three main rivers of the Northeastern United States.

Crossing those three rivers was the main geographical problem for the Connecticut invaders of Pennsylvania. Today, the landscape is not a great deal different except for the absence of Indians, and crossing the three rivers is the main event. There's a Hudson River bridge at Newburgh, and crossing the Susquehanna at Wilkes-Barre is a placid bridge within a town park. From the point of view of the Interstate highway, crossing the Delaware occurs very near the highest point in New Jersey, over a deep rocky gorge with boaters deep below. Since the traveler is at a peak point within a long wide mountain valley, the view is spectacular in several directions.

However, for centuries the builders of roads had to operate on a modest budget, and the only reasonable place to cross the Delaware in that region is a few miles south of Port Jervis, at Dingmans Ferry. The Dingman family prospered at their trade for many generations before they modernized and constructed a toll bridge, which

1903 Dingmans Ferry Bridge

is now one of the few remaining toll bridges in private hands, and possibly the oldest one. You don't have to ask the two jolly old toll collectors whether they are part of the Dingman family because they certainly act like it, adding to the wad of dollar bills in their left hand as they greet the fellas, josh the girls, and wave directions with a free hand. A quarter-mile to the south of the bridge on the Pennsylvania side is the entrance to a trail leading to a National Park Service station. The Park Guards are a friendly sort, most of them freely admitting they are members of the Dingman clan, available to help tourists interested in a trail walk, including a visit to the local waterfall. In spite of all this family connection, and Park Service training, nobody at the station had ever heard of the march of the Connecticut invaders. Or of the Proprietorships of West and East Jersey, or of the line between them which allegedly ends at Dingman's Ferry. The best they could do was to point to the local cemetery, which has a big rock at the entrance that somehow has some particular significance, or other.

As it turns out, the cemetery is quite large, with surely a thousand or more gravestones, a great many of which fly American Legion flags for veterans of one war or another, and many more are decorated with fresh flowers. Only a corner of this graveyard touches the curving road to The Bridge, and just inside the entrance is a very large, unmarked stone. Trees have been planted nearby, and their roots have half-covered the rock. But the roads and the cemetery, in general, seem designed around it. There's no marker to explain it, any more than there is a plaque at

Stonehenge. As the Park Ranger said, it has clear significance, but no one now seems to know what it signifies.

Well, if no one is likely to contradict, let's make the timid suggestion that this may be the terminus of the line dividing East from West Jersey. Yes, it's in Pennsylvania. But there is nothing more likely on the New Jersey side of the crossing, and the current Surveyor-General of West Jersey, William Taylor, is firm in the belief "the line" terminated at Dingman's Ferry. William Penn had hoped to control land on both sides of the river, and when he acquired Pennsylvania in addition to New Jersey, the issue became moot. The style of the survey had been to start at Beach Haven ("Ye inlet of ye beach of Egg Harbor") and follow the compass until it hit something large and heavy. That rock was marked, and another survey went the next step. About fifty of these markers have been discovered by later explorers, and officially represent the underlying fixed line which serves as a survey basis for every property in the state of New Jersey. Since I owned some property in New Jersey myself, it seemed important to be sure I know where it is, or else some trial lawyer may try to take it away.

3 Wilkes-Barre and the Pennamite Wars

The Battle of Wyoming Marker   **Wyoming Ave & Valley St**   **Pittston, PA**
41.3211 -75.8181

For eons of time, the site of Wilkes-Barre, PA was once a sort of finger-lake between two mountain ridges. As dammed-up rivers tend to do, this one gradually filled up with sludge until the water spilled over at Nanticoke, a few miles to the south. After the lake drained out leaving the original river in place, there was also left a flat and fertile valley on either side of it. Furthermore, the towering mountain ranges on either side protected the valley from the weather, so the Wyoming Valley became a verdant paradise in the middle of the mountains. Somehow, the Congregationalist settlers of Connecticut found out about it, dug up some old deeds from King Charles to the effect it belonged to Connecticut, and eventually set forth to resettle in this mountain valley.

Reliable records of how the Connecticut Yankees got to the Wyoming Valley are hard to find. Offhand, it is puzzling to wonder how they got past New York or crossed the Hudson River. The best way to get between the two places today is probably pretty close to the route the colonists took, however, because travel in those days was much more constrained by geography. We know they started from Litchfield, CN, and in fact, for a while, Wilkes-Barre was part of the County of Litchfield. From Litchfield, they likely crossed the Hudson near Newburgh, went to the mountain gap at Port Jervis, and either came into the Wyoming Valley over the ridges or went a little north to the Susquehanna and came down from there. On a map at least, that's a relatively straight shot.

Pennsylvania took offense at this, and the result was a series of little wars that few people have heard of, called the Pennamite Wars between the Yankee settlers on the one hand, and Pennamites (Pennsylvanians) and their British and Iroquois allies on the other. Massacres were perpetrated by both sides, though local Indians were most offended of all and did their massacring in a very thorough way, most dramatically during the 1778 Battle of Wyoming.

The six nations of Iroquois dominated Northeastern America by the same means the Incas dominated Peru -- commanding the headwaters of several rivers, the Hudson, the Delaware, and the Susquehanna, as well as the long finger lakes of New York, leading like rivers toward Lakes Ontario and Erie. They were thus able to strike quickly by canoe over a large territory. The Iroquois were quite loyal to the British because of the efforts of Sir William Johnson, who settled among them and introduced elements of European culture. Aside from Johnson, who was treated as almost a God, their leader was a Dartmouth graduate named Brant.

The Wyoming Massacre

The complicated nature of the Iroquois is illustrated by the fact, on the one hand, that Sachem Brant translated the Bible into Mohawk and traveled in England raising money for his church. On the other hand, his biographer's trouble to praise him for never killing women and children with his own hands. British loyalty to these fierce but promising pupils was one of the main reasons for the 1768 proclamation forbidding colonist settlement to the West of the Proclamation Line, which on the other hand was itself one of the main grievances of the rebellious land-speculating colonists. The Indians, for their part, saw the proclamation line as their last hope for survival.

In 1778, after Burgoyne's defeat at Saratoga, loyalist Pennamites under the instigation of British officer John Butler and their Iroquois allies set about to systematically exterminate the rather large Connecticut sub-colony and came pretty close to doing so. Children were thrown into bonfires, women were scalped and butchered. The common soldiers who survived were forced to lie on a flat rock while Queen Esther, "a squaw of political prominence, passed around the circle singing a war-song and dashing out their brains." That was for common soldiers. The officers were singled out and shot in the thigh bone so they would be available to be tortured to death after the battle. The Wyoming Massacre was a hideous event, by any standard, and it went on for days afterward, as fugitives were hunted down and outlying settlements burned to the ground.

It's pretty hard to defend a massacre of this degree of savagery, but the Indians did have a point. They quite rightly saw that white settler penetration of the Proclamation Line would inevitably lead to more penetration, and eventually to the total loss of their homeland. The defeat of a whole British Army under Burgoyne showed them that they were all alone. It was do or die, now or never. Tales of the massacre provided fuel for propaganda against the Indians. Countless other civilizations have been extinguished by provoking remorseless revenge in preference to a meek surrender.

In 1779, George Washington dispatched General Sullivan to "take care" of the Indian problem; Sullivan's methods were even more thorough than the Indians', essentially destroying the Iroquois nation by burning their houses, crops and stores, leading to starvation. The other eleven colonies were distraught to see Pennsylvania and Connecticut putting on a side-show in the middle of the War of Independence, and part of the judicial settlement was to give Connecticut the "Western Reserve" in Ohio as compensation for restoring the peace. The American Constitution of 1787 essentially made state possession of land a moot point, and the Western Reserve is just a quaint term you hear in Cleveland. Wyoming is a term that most people associate with a western state, although it is named for this valley, and Dallas is another term that has been largely transplanted from a small town near Wilkes-Barre to a big town in Texas. So, if you want to get the confusion of terms straight, about Wyoming, Dallas, Western Reserve, and Westmoreland, you will take a little time to learn about Wilkes-Barre. Westmoreland is the name of a gentleman's club in Wilkes-Barre, but it is also the name of a county near Pittsburgh where Connecticut folks thought it would be useful to flee.

The Proclamation Line of 1763

That's a lot of history for a little town, but there's more. Somehow, the joys and pleasures of living in the Wyoming Valley were carried back to people like Rousseau, who were looking for examples of the "noble savage", noble because he had not learned all of the evil things that French aristocrats invented, and therefore warranted effusive praise during the so-called Romantic Period, when France was being purified by the guillotine. The main drum-beater for this mania was a poet named Thomas Campbell, who composed a long poem in Spencerian rhyme called "Gertrude of Pennsylvania". Even those who find merit in Spencer will nowadays find it difficult to accept the notion of flamingos on Pennsylvania streams, or lying on the ocean beaches of Pennsylvania, reading

General John Sullivan

Shakespeare. Even those who have less taste for Herbert Spencer will still find a reason to distrust the judgment of those who praise the beheading of, say, Lavoisier. The noble savages in this particular case were the Iroquois.

There's a memorial in nearby Wyoming commemorating this massacre, which indeed is probably better left forgotten. There are plaques with the names of the fallen, and the names of the survivors. The idea of the Wyoming Valley as a paradise on earth was destroyed by another event. The ancient lake which once filled the Wyoming Valley was deeper and more ancient than anyone guessed. Underneath the rich topsoil was a vein of anthracite, and Wilkes-Barre became a boom town with strip mining, a fate no paradise can long withstand. A nearby coal mine that caught fire underground in 1915 has been burning ever since. Talk about pollution disasters; this one is a monster.

4 Great Bend: Joseph Smith Translates the Golden Plates
Joseph Smith Historical Marker   US 11   Hallstead, PA   41.9658 -75.7406

As the traveler up the Pennsylvania Turnpike Northeast Extension approaches the New York border, there's a chance for a fleeting glance at an exit sign pointing to Great Bend, without additional comment. The comment is definitely needed because a ten-mile detour at this point is rewarded by two interesting attractions. In the first place, the Susquehanna does indeed make a great bend there. Starting in Cooperstown, New York at a beautiful mountain lake which resembles Lake Geneva in Switzerland, the Susquehanna heads south for ninety-six miles and then turns around at Great Bend and goes back fifteen miles north to Binghamton. After that, it goes west for forty miles to Sayre and then goes south again as it picks up other branches. Greatly enlarged, it reappears to Turnpike travelers at Wilkes Barre. Thousands of travelers have sped up the wide valley without noticing that the same river which flows south from Wilkes-Barre apparently starts flowing north at Great Bend. The traveler's eye is deceived by the apparently continuous long valley which the highway follows. At Binghamton, the Susquehanna starts flowing west, but that too is overlooked in whizzing past the cloverleaves and traffic directions. The Great Bend itself is a lovely water gap with a couple of small towns on its shores but is otherwise pretty deserted.

For two and a half years, Joseph Smith the founder of the Mormon religion spent full time five miles away from the Turnpike exit, at the real bend in the river (not the town of Great Bend) writing the 275,000 words of the Book of Mormon. Although Smith was a native of Palmyra, New York, Mormonism is most easily viewed as an outgrowth of wide-spread religious uproar in upper New York State during the

1820s, it undoubtedly provoked malicious gossip from those who resist all claims of miracles, as well as staunch defense from those who believe. It's comparatively safe to say the prophet was living at the Great Bend in his wife's tiny home while she wrote down his dictated translation. The source of his vision was said to be John the Baptist, which others have since taken literally to varying degrees. Those who believe in the pregnancy of virgins and reappearances after a death must be tolerant of the sometimes overstated beliefs of others. Smith never let anyone see the golden plates from which the writings were derived, however, and ultimately it must rest that he was relating what he believed he had seen. His father-in-law described him as a charlatan, an attitude not completely rare among other fathers in law.

Joseph Smith

Smith's wife, caught between conflicting family loyalties, declined for years to join the religion that flowed from her own pen.

However, with the publication of the Book of Mormon, Smith rapidly gained adherents numbering in the thousands. He moved the center of the religion westward in several steps and was shot to death by a mob, variously styled as militia and vigilantes, in Illinois at the age of 38. Just who killed him and what the motives were are matters we normally leave to courts rather than newspaper accounts. There is little doubt that many other religions of the time were outraged by the tolerance of polygamy, and so the account that he was assassinated by offended husbands of those to whom he proposed marriage, must be somewhat discounted. All religious disputes have a tendency to get out of hand, and the frontier religions of that time were particularly feverish, flaring up in an environment of the rule of the six-gun.

The attraction of this religion seems to an outsider to have been based on its forgiveness for sinners, offering them tolerant heaven rather than the vindictive hellfire and brimstone which more puritanical protestant sects at that time envisioned for even well-behaved converts. There is a certain echo in Smith's Mormonism of the tolerant Quaker view that "There is that of God in everyone." Similarly, although it is difficult to accept his idea that the American Indian tribes

Joseph Smith House

might be descendants of a lost tribe of Israel from the 7th Century B.C., the Mormon (and Quaker) teaching of tolerance to the Indians was in keeping with changing racial views in the early 19th Century and softens somewhat the former Mormon distrust of the black race; although that, too, must be seen in the context of the then-approaching Civil War.

The Great Bend of the Susquehanna

The best-known feature of this religion used to be polygamy, however, which is difficult to defend with theological, demographic or even romantic reasonings. With a few exceptions among Mormon extremists, the religion has moved away from any defense of polygamy. As the center of Mormonism moved to Utah, Congress outlawed polygamy, and the church officially condemned the practice and gave it up. Since it is still not rare to encounter a kindly decent gentleman on the streets of Salt Lake City whose grandmother or great-grandmother had been a polygamous wife, the whole subject has come to be treated there as an ancient embarrassment, best left unmentioned, but never quite forgotten. As a matter of fact, all religions have so much to account for in their past that they are most fairly judged by the sort of behavior they seem to inspire in their followers. By that standard, the earnest, decent, hard-working Mormons of today have earned their right not to be sneered at.

As for the simple little memorial along the river, it may seem a disappointment to some. It has not been made into a tourist attraction or a place of pilgrimage. It may even be a little unprotected from vandalism. But is surely worth the small trouble to visit, adding only half an hour to anyone's trip. One does not have to accept either the history or the theology in order to wish to see the place, which is a sweet little neglected clearing with a railroad running between it and the river. As a backdrop, the great bend in the Susquehanna is a remarkable sight in itself, because the river seems to be running in the wrong direction while no one notices.

A new Mormon Temple was completed in 2016 across Vine Street and a block east of Logan Square. The interior is designed in Philadelphia Georgian style, and the spire is topped by a statue of the Angel Moroni, blowing a gleaming gold trumpet. The Mormons seem to want Philadelphia to notice them and form an opinion, which indeed we probably will.

5 Sayre / Athens

The Guthrie Clinic 1 Guthrie Square   Sayre, PA   41.9800 -76.5206

Running west from Oneonta and Binghamton, NY, the North branch of the Susquehanna runs due west for about fifty miles until it turns abruptly south at Sayre, PA. In the course of this westward run along the northernmost ridge of the Endless Mountains, it passes Apalachin NY, where the mobster chieftains got caught by the state police while holding a convention. At Sayre, named after an eastern railroad financier of the 19th Century, it joins the Chemung River at a large bowl-shaped refuge in the mountains which shelters it somewhat from the ferocious snows for which this part of Upper New York State is famous. Sayre usually gets a heavy snowfall or two in January, which lies on the ground until the spring thaw in April. But that's pretty mild for this region, and the Iroquois made it a sort of headquarters, where Queen Esther of head-smashing fame made her home just before the Wyoming massacre in which she figured so prominently. Consequently, General Sullivan made his famous march to destroy the Iroquois by going northwestward up the Susquehanna to Athens, rather than following the Northeast Extension of the Pennsylvania Turnpike, as somehow seems more probable. Sayre was more of a 19th Century town, with the original settlement concentrated a few miles south at the region of Athens. Sayre is more modern, once was the location of a huge locomotive repair center, and has the Guthrie Medical Clinic at Robert Packer Hospital. Athens is older, quieter and has more stately charm, and is actually on the Chemung River with a two hundred yard portage to the Susquehanna.

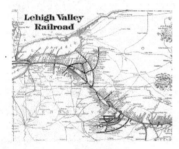

Lehigh Valley RR

Robert Packer was considered to be the ne'er do well son of Asa Packer, that go-getting industrialist of Mauch Chunk/Jim Thorpe and Lehigh Valley RR fame. The father is said to have sent his son up to Sayre to get him out of the way, but once freed of the old tyrant's grip, Robert built things up into the second-largest locomotive repair center in the world. Robert Packer never had children and eventually set about building up the Robert Packer Hospital. Much taken with the Mayo Clinic model, he called Charlie Mayo and asked if had someone to suggest for running the local institution. Indeed, Mayo had just the fellow, Guthrie, who like the Mayos was a surgeon with a specialty in removing enlarged thyroid glands. As long as the railroads flourished, the Guthrie Clinic was headed toward the status of a major medical center with private rail cars for the surgeons and the like. However, the advent of diesel locomotives put an end to the main source of local prosperity, and the Guthrie Clinic settled down to a more modest status of a regional medical center, mainly in competition with the Geisinger Clinic further south on another bend in the Susquehanna. Recent politicians have been much taken with the model of the Midwestern group practice, of which both Guthrie and Geisinger are models. Perhaps the politicians do not realize that all of these

clinics were based economically on the principle that surgeons can make enormous incomes if they are fed enough cases. Consequently, they are willing to reduce their own income in order to make group practice more attractive to the "feeders"; the department of surgery subsidizes the department of general medicine. Their competitors have long grumbled that this arrangement was an elaborate evasion of the medical ethical prohibition of fee-splitting. Most of that

Robert Packer Hospital

feeling has subsided, but a more serious present criticism is that if politicians are determined to reduce surgical fees, the whole arrangement may collapse when they do.

Curiously, prosperity may be ready to return to the Endless Mountains, in the form of the fracking method of gas extraction from the Marcellus Shale which underlies this region. Rail freight is returning to the region, and truckers by the thousand are migrating from economically depressed regions like Detroit. For reasons not immediately clear, the huge trucks which import water and chemicals for fracking are driven by non-residents. The smaller trucks which carry away (to Northern New York, they say) the brine effluent from the wells, are driven by locally recruited truck drivers. A certain number of bar room fights have been rumored to have grown out of this situation.

As the region has evolved, the third town of Waverly NY has joined the other two (Athens and Sayre) in what amounts to a seamless conurbation nestled in the cozy valley.

6 Joseph Priestley of Northumberland, PA

Joseph Priestley Home   472 Priestley Avenue   Northumberland, PA
40.8903 -76.79

There's one good thing about living near the confluence of two big rivers, and one very bad thing about it. The rivers provide transportation in three directions, but about once every twenty-five years the rivers rise astonishingly and threaten to carry everything away. That deposits rich topsoil, making it even more attractive for

Joseph Priestley

settlers to locate there. At what we now call Northumberland located on the junction of the North and West Branches of the Susquehanna, there is a monument marking off the flood levels of the past two centuries. Even the least of these floods must have covered a lot of ground, and the highest one is so far above the head of a visitor that it is hard to see how anything could have survived it. Right now, the little town of Northumberland is a burnished little jewel. One hopes the Army Corps of Engineers either has or soon will abate the potential flood danger. It would be interesting to know if flood insurance is available, just as a sign of how experts currently evaluate the risk. The Endless Mountains (that's really their name) stretching almost to Cooperstown catch a lot of rainwater and snow and occasionally funnel it all down the North Branch to Northumberland. The West Branch is even bigger. Having observed the 1936 flood in Pittsburgh, I can testify it isn't an experience soon forgotten.

It happens the most prominent resident of the area arrived there in 1794 and lived out the last ten years of his life as a widower. Joseph Priestley had stirred up enough uproar as an English dissenting minister to cause his house to be burned to the ground. No doubt, the English wanted to suppress any repetition of the French Revolution but were willing enough to be rid of a protégé of Lord Shelbourne, so the government made full restitution of the value of his property when he finally agreed to emigrate. Pennsylvania was chosen on the advice of his good friend Benjamin Franklin. He bought extensive land at the river junction and constructed what most people would describe as a beautiful mansion on reasonably high ground with a river entrance. Although it is built of wood and William Penn's Pennsbury was brick, there is a definite similarity. Priestley's house somehow seems more open and livable, although the outhouse reminds us that plumbing costs were moderate at the time. And furthermore, the original building survives as Pennsbury did not. The original plans for it were later discovered in England, and so it has been possible to make it what it used to be, outbuildings and all.

Priestley and Lavoisier did not get along even though they share the honors for discovering Oxygen. Lavoisier was a rich aristocrat, while Priestley was a prominent member of the dissenting class with advanced ideas about democracy. It is said that many of the ideas Thomas Jefferson had about the natural rights of mankind were brought into sharper focus by his association with Priestley. Priestley was primarily a political theorist, acting in the role of a minister. He regarded his chemical experiments as a hobby, motivated by the hope of discovering a bridge between religion and science. The relationship between Priestley and Lavoisier was a strange one, but it had political conjunction as well as a scientific one. Priestley was driven to America by English Tories the same year that Lavoisier was guillotined by French revolutionaries.

Although oxygen had been discovered while Joseph Priestley was still in England, he discovered carbon monoxide in Northumberland, using retorts and scientific instruments he designed and sent to his friend Wedgwood to manufacture. He also devised the idea of carbonated water while he was here. For these as well as chemical methodologies he has been described, at least by Anglo Saxons, as the Father of Chemistry. Following what he considered to be his main occupation, he meanwhile founded the Unitarian Church in America. In the little town at the Susquehanna forks, he was unable to establish a viable Unitarian congregation beyond a few followers who came to his home. So, he somehow mustered the energy to establish the First Unitarian Church in Philadelphia, at 21st and Walnut Streets. (Aside from its historic significance, the present church building is a distinguished work of architecture designed by Frank Furness). Meanwhile, he was very active in national politics; Jefferson's defeat of John Adams' reelection is often ascribed to his efforts.

His wife died of tuberculosis before they could move into the Northumberland plantation, but he lived there with his son and daughter-in-law for ten years, dying in 1804. The son was concerned with founding a utopian colony, but the wealthy daughter-in-law forced a return to England. The grandson generation returned to Northumberland, where the graveyard now has an impressive array of Priestley tombstones.

7 Mauch Chunk, Jim Thorpe, and All That

Old Mauch Chunk Train   41 Susquehanna Street   Jim Thorpe PA
40.8628 -75.738

Hundreds of millions of dollars were made in the anthracite mines during the 19th Century, and then Henry Frick invented a way to make steel with coke, a product of bituminous coal. Consequently, the steel industry moved from the Lehigh Valley to the Ohio Valley, greatly transforming the image of both the Philadelphia and Pittsburgh regions. While the town of Mauch Chunk was prospering, it was the center of activity of a financier named Asa Packer, whose mansion dominates what is left of the town in the mountains, next to a graceful church, a railroad abandoned except for scenic tourist rides, and subdued economic desperation. The mountainous valley on the north side of Blue Mountain called itself Pennsylvania's Switzerland, and it was once a scenic gem indeed, but is now choking up with traffic trying to get through the narrow passage down the hill. One of the relics of former prosperity is an Opera House, now used for rock concerts and related events in an effort to re-establish the town as an entertainment center.

John O'Hara wrote some stories using Mauch Chunk as the setting, and that author is getting to be better appreciated now that his level of bawdiness is more or less the norm. Being better appreciated is of course not the same thing as selling a lot of books, so it is now uncertain whether the transformation was mainly artistic or financial. There is no doubt that coal regions the world over tend to be pretty rough districts.

Jim Thorpe

Perhaps it was Asa Packer or some other financier who started the tradition of this town pushing the publicity button pretty hard. The town rightly promotes itself as a charming inexpensive place to spend a quiet weekend visiting the sights, including a ride on the now-abandoned rail line through the scenic mountains, the Asa Packer Mansion, antique shops and that sort of thing. The Pennsylvania Switzerland moniker suggests a touch of the P.T. Barnum approach, although a fairly innocent one. But buying Jim Thorpe's body is on quite another level. There is very little question that this offspring of an Irish father and an Oklahoma Indian mother was a natural athlete of the very highest skill; whether he was mainly an Indian or mainly an Irishman is more debatable. Thorpe played professional football and professional baseball with distinction, after winning boxes full of Olympic track medals. Dwight Eisenhower played football against him once and expressed genuine admiration for the talent he encountered. Unfortunately, he had his medals taken away because it was discovered he had played for money before he was competing for the amateur Olympic prizes. After growing too old for athletics, he turned into a chronic alcoholic with associated erratic behavior, embarrassing to his admirers. When he died, members of his family sold his body to the downtrodden town of Mauch Chunk, which renamed itself Jim Thorpe and greatly expanded its publicity efforts. His son later sued to have the body returned to Oklahoma, creating still more publicity, not all of it congratulatory.

The Town of Jim Thorpe Courthouse Square

It's sort of a sad story, but the Town of Jim Thorpe is only five miles from the Mahoning Valley exit of the Pennsylvania Turnpike extension. It's not hard to go satisfy yourself with the fairness of all this uproar.

XVII Delaware

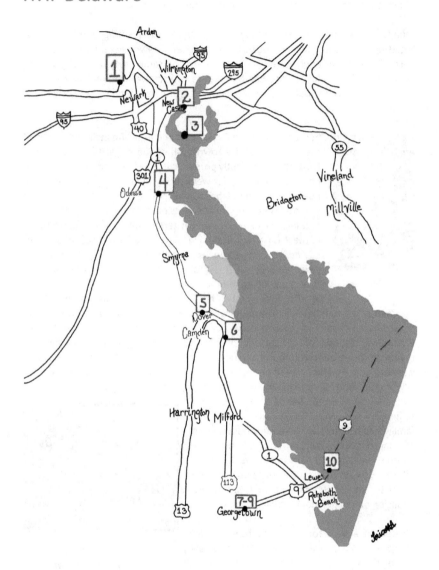

Delaware

The strip of Delaware along the south shore of the Delaware River down to Cape Henlopen and beyond provides a nice taste of the historical origins as well as the bucolic nature of the state. Like all of the colonies from the Connecticut River down to Maryland, this area was originally occupied by Dutch traders and Swedish settlers. The English king gave Delaware (then the lower three counties of Pennsylvania) to William Penn during the Glorious Revolution of 1688 without much thought for the feelings of the original settlers, who had no unusual fondness for Quakers. The confusion of the Revolutionary War provided an opportunity for this state to break away. Delaware resident and Quaker John Dickinson was governor of Pennsylvania at the time and undoubtedly had a hand in it, but full documentation of his involvement has either been lost or deliberately obscured. New Castle County in the north, industrialized and run by the DuPonts, largely went its own way. The landscape, culture and even the weather change when you get beyond the arching bridges over the Chesapeake & Delaware Canal, becoming even flatter and more similar to the Eastern Shore of Maryland. What was predominately woodland until recently is now half clear-cut to make room for the feed crops for the factory-farmed chickens.

To take the highway from Wilmington to Lewes is quicker, but history is to be found by winding along Route 9, through the moors, marshes, and farmland. You can still find an occasional old soul who remembers when "the road" was built. The road they mean is the highway that finally connected Southern Delaware to Wilmington. Before 1925, travel between the two ends of that little state was by railroad, or by boat, mostly the Wilson Line. It is natural to suspect the railroad and the boat line might have lobbied against road building, and they certainly had an economic incentive. But there were social factors, too. Although it is a tiny state, Delaware has long been a collection of independent tribes. New Castle County is of course very Ivy League; the Wilmington area claims to have more PhDs than any other American county. Southern Delaware was a slave region, forcing the state to be in favor of the Union, but also in favor of slavery -- a border state. Furthermore, pirate lairs seem to have created a mixed-race people along the shore calling themselves "Moors"; intermarriage with Indians and/or Portuguese pirates has been speculated as a source of swarthiness. Along the Atlantic coast, it is claimed that pure Elizabethan English is still spoken. Furthermore, the maritime orientation of Lewes created more social affinity to Cape May and Philadelphia than to New Castle and Wilmington. Eastern shore Maryland was even closer. Finally, in 1923, Coleman DuPont gave up on persuasion, built a 98-mile highway from one end of his state to the other at a cost of $50,000 a mile, and just gave it to the state. The legislature at first wouldn't take it, thinking it was clever to let the rich DuPont fellow pay for its upkeep. However, the sight of a DuPont cavalry of highway patrolmen raised even more discomfort, so the legislature reconsidered, accepted the gift.

You can do this tour from Philadelphia in one long day, or entertain yourself with short side trips on the way to the Delaware beaches. Alternatively, you can drive down to Lewes, take the ferry across to Cape May, and come back via New Jersey, though two days would be needed if you want to see all the sights along the way. You might want to skip the point of interest at the beginning that starts out this section, as all you will see is woods.

1 Forming the State of Delaware
The Peculiar Delaware   DE, PA, MD Circular border   39.7242 -75.7678

The northern border of Delaware is a semicircle, with a twelve-mile radius based on the cupola of the New Castle courthouse. It was originally the border of New Castle County, and it proved to be slightly imperfect. In the first place, it extended across the Delaware River into New Jersey, but it was a nuisance to go there, so that segment of land was abandoned to New Jersey. The legal border of the State of Delaware, therefore, extends to the high-water bank of the river on the New Jersey side, rather than running down the middle of the river. The significance of this curiosity appeared when the Delaware Memorial Bridges were built, and all of the tolls go to Delaware, instead of being split between the states as is more customary.

New Castle's Courthouse is the epicenter of the arc from Maryland to the Delaware River

The other problem with the semi-circular arc was that three lines meet at the northwestern corner of Delaware, and each was defined in its own way. The Mason-Dixon line goes due east-west, the border with Maryland goes north-south, and the idea was that the semicircular arc would meet the other two lines at a point. However, the instructions could be read in two different ways, leaving a little "wedge" of territory that could be reasonably said to lie in either Pennsylvania or Delaware, depending on the sequence of describing them. This was certainly a circumstance where any decision was better than no decision, but it took until 1921 for the states to harrumph their way to a final pronouncement. In the meantime, the disputed wedge of land was a good place to have duels, cockfights and other matters of questionable legality.

In the Twenty-first Century, when we know how every American creek and river run, we can see it might have been simple to establish a boundary between the new royal grant to William Penn, and an earlier grant to Lord Baltimore by the then-reigning

Delaware

king's father, Charles I. Essentially: Penn got the Delaware Bay and a lot of wilderness to the west of it. George Calvert, Lord Baltimore, had long held the top half of the Chesapeake Bay and a strip of wilderness to the west of that. Two bays, with two hazy strips of wilderness attached.

At what is now Odessa, Delaware, those two bays are only five miles apart; compromise should have settled the issue quickly. Two English gentlemen could have sat down over a pipe and a brew, working something out. However, the English nation was then changing kings, beheading them over matters of religion. A Roman Catholic, Lord Baltimore probably thought an opportunity might emerge from the turmoil if he stalled until matters went his way, since next in line of succession was James, Duke of York, who was a Catholic. But matters fell into the hands of the lawyers when principals of an argument were unable to speak. In the legal system of the day the last word from the last king was what counted in law courts, accepting any uncertainty about future latest words from future latest kings in order

David Rittenhouse

to maintain immediate peace. To lawyers of the time, all this talk about justice, fairness, and geometry was idleness when the nation needed order and stability. So the Calvert family lawyers over the course of eighty years, introduced one specious proposition after another that turned other lawyers purple with rage. Penn's lawyer, Benjamin Chew, beat them at this game, and his mansions in Delaware and Germantown attest to the value attached to this achievement. In other circumstances, posturing might have led to war, as it did in similar disputes with Connecticut. Penn probably knew better, but it takes two to compromise.

Mason Dixon Line

It must be admitted that honest confusion was possible. Sometimes, a line of latitude was a line in the sense Euclid intended: all length and no width. At other times, lawyers and kings were talking about "parallels" as if they were strips that had width. If a strip was intended, it was important for a grant to specify whether it extended to the southern edge of the strip, or to the northern edge. But in fact, the state of science in the Seventeenth Century contained uncertainty about both where the strips were, and how wide. And if the grant's language didn't even make it clear whether the parties were talking about strips or width-less lines, eighty years could be a comparatively short time for a court to decide the case. To be fair to Lord Baltimore, many people at the time didn't think these matters were capable of fair solution, so the traditional way of dealing with land disputes was either by force or by craftiness.

In William Penn the folks from Maryland were, unfortunately, dealing with a friend of the King, who had one of the most brilliant mathematicians in Western civilization as his adviser. David Rittenhouse may have been born in that little farmhouse you can still visit on the Wissahickon Creek, and made his living as a clockmaker, but his native talents in mathematics, astronomy surveying, and instrument construction were so deep and so varied that later biographers are reduced to describing him merely as a "scientist" and letting it go at that. If you want to sample his talents, spend an hour or two learning what a vernier is, and then see if you could apply that insight, as he did, to a compass. So, as it turned out, Rittenhouse was able to describe a twelve-mile circle around New Castle, Delaware, construct a tangent that divides the Delmarva's Peninsula in half, and match it up with an east-west line we now call the Mason Dixon Line. When they finally got around to laying these lines on the ground, Mason and Dixon cut a twenty-four-foot swath through the forest, using astronomical adjustments every night, and laying carved marker stones every fifth of a mile for hundreds of miles. The variation from the line devised by Rittenhouse was at most a fifth of a mile off the mark; the intersection with the north-south line between Maryland and Delaware was less successful. The survey by Mason and Dixon was not quite completed to the Ohio line because the Indians, curious at first, eventually became wild with suspicion at such behavior, particularly the part about going out and aiming cannons at the sky every night. It seems likely that George Calvert, Lord Baltimore, had no more confidence in this madness than the Indians did.

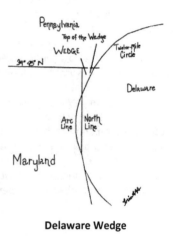

Delaware Wedge

So, the next time you take the train from Philadelphia to Washington DC, reflect that strict reading of the words in the land grants did admit the possibility that your whole trip could either have been within the State of Maryland, or else in the Commonwealth of Pennsylvania, depending on whether lawyers, or scientists, had triumphed in this dispute. Since the Mason Dixon Line later divided not merely two states, but two violently opposed cultures, Rittenhouse must stand in the history of those people who were so smart that most people couldn't understand how smart he was. Part of the eventual compromise, a semicircular northern border, didn't come out right, resulting in a wedge of no-man's land. Landowners didn't enjoy paying disputed taxes, so they held up the settlement of the wrangle into the

Delaware

Twentieth Century. Eventually, the U.S. Supreme Court cut the wedge into two pieces, giving one piece each to Pennsylvania and Delaware.

Meanwhile, disputes continued which had their basis in the way the semi-circular line was plotted out on the land. The surveyors ran 120 straight-line radii outward from the courthouse tower in New Castle, and then connected the ends. Obviously, that resulted in 120 straight chords instead of a smooth semi-circle, and a couple of bulges had to be accommodated where the circle grazed other straight borders. The semi-circle crossed the Delaware River, so New Jersey helpfully abandoned its portion, only to regret its decision later when toll bridges were constructed, and ship channels deepened.

Lord Baltimore

Two major societal changes took place between 1632 -- when Charles I granted the proprietorship of Maryland to the first Lord Baltimore -- and 1776 when all American real estate changed its rules. The first change was that the Delaware Bay morphed from a swamp into settlements of people; settlers came into possession. The second evolution was to the current view that if you sell some real estate it is no longer yours; in earlier eras, everything belonged to the king, who could take it away and give it to others as often as he pleased. In legal terms, the last king had the last word. Although acres of parchment were scribbled by lawyers pro and con, these considerations are what make clear how Lord Baltimore could hold the unchallenged legal title for fifty years to everything up to the fortieth parallel, but then have a court take away thousands of square miles. A land which was to become the three lower counties of Pennsylvania was given to William Penn by the Duke of York in 1682, using some flawed documents and only fully enjoyed by Penn's heirs for six years until they morphed into the new State of Delaware. From 1684 to 1769, legal ownership was a matter of continuing dispute. The exasperated Lord Chancellor (Hardwicke) in 1750 declared the case as one "of nature worthy of the judicature of a Roman senate rather than of a single judge".

And by the way, ocean currents moved Cape Henlopen a mile or so southward, but the real boundary problem was that common usage over the centuries confused Cape Henlopen with Fenwick's Island (to which it is usually attached by a thin barrier island), making an implicit difference in the Maryland/Delaware ownership of the corresponding strip of land at the southern border of the State of Delaware, a matter of a hundred or so square miles.

And all of this confusion was merely about the borders of one of the smallest of our fifty states. The political manner in which Delaware became a colony without a charter to the King - and became a state by gradual and mystifying degrees separate from the other counties of Pennsylvania - are other complicated stories.

Cape Henlopen

Never mind the reasons Delaware remained in the Union during the Civil War, even though it also remained a slave state.

2 New Castle, Delaware
39.6598 -75.564

New Castle is easy to get to, but hard to find. It's right on Delaware Bay, at the start of the old National Road (Route 40), next to two huge bridges, a few miles from the main north-south turnpikes, a couple of miles from an airport -- and lost in a sea of suburban housing and highway slums. It's lost, so to speak, in plain sight.

Landing place of William Penn

And yet it is a perfect jewel of early American history and architecture. It's just as attractive and historically important as Williamsburg, Virginia, except these buildings are not reproductions, but the real thing. The town says it was founded in 1651 by Peter Stuyvesant, but Peter Minuit in 1638 could make a claim to be even earlier. Located at the narrow neck of the funnel that is Delaware Bay, it was a natural place to start a colony, eventually to be the capital of the state. The Delaware River makes a rightward turn at that point, and creates a river highway all the way to Trenton. But a few miles upriver at Tinicum, now Philadelphia International Airport, the river started to fill up with islands and snags; was it better to locate upriver or downriver from the narrows? New Castle was placed downriver.

Delaware

But in 1777 the British fleet came to visit with hostile intent, and New Castle could look out the windows along the Strand right into the mouths of ships with twenty or thirty cannons pointed at them. Philadelphia, on the other hand, was protected upriver by a series of mud flats and barricades at Fort Mifflin that could quite effectively bar passage to enemy sailing ships. Delaware got the point, and shortly thereafter, the capital of Delaware was prudently moved to Dover, while even the county seat of New Castle County was moved to Wilmington. New Castle had a big

fire in 1824; rebuilding afterward accounts for much of the present uniformly Federalist architecture. The final nail in the commercial coffin of the town was driven by the Pennsylvania Railroad, which just by-passed the town. For a century, this little architectural jewel just sat there in the fields, until the narrow neck of the Delmarva Peninsula became such a transportation crossroads that the fields filled up with construction more

New Castle, Delaware

appropriate to Los Angeles. New Castle disappeared, without moving an inch.

For fifty years in Colonial days, the rector of Immanuel Episcopal Church in New Castle was one George Ross. His son, also named George Ross, became a lawyer in Lancaster and signed the Declaration of Independence. His widowed daughter Gertrude Ross Till married George Read, a lawyer in New Castle who also signed the Declaration. And, a third signer Thomas McKean, lived two houses away. George Read had studied law under John Moland, whose house served as Washington's headquarters in 1777.

3 Pea Patch Island
Fort Delaware on Pea Patch Island   Delaware City, DE   39.5894 -75.5672

There's a tradition that a boatload of peas ran aground on the mudflats of Delaware Bay near Salem in the Sixteenth Century, turning the flats into a patch of peas. In any event, the island is known to have been growing in size for centuries, and now is home to thousands of families of herons. The number of mosquito families has not been accurately counted as yet, but they are even more numerous. The island doubled in size when the Army Corps of Engineers built the present Fort Delaware on it in 1847-59.

Delaware

The War of 1812, which included the burning of Washington DC and bombardment of Baltimore, propelled America into a frenzy of coastal defense, and the first fortification of Pea Patch Island took place in 1813. A plan was adopted by Congress in 1816 to build 200 coastal forts, and about forty of them were actually completed by the time of the Civil War. These forts all had a similar appearance; the most notable example of the style was at Fort Sumter near Charleston, South Carolina, which was

Fort Delaware

nearly complete by the time of its famous bombardment. In fact, it was first hastily occupied by Northern defenders arriving just in time to be evicted. In essence, these forts were huge walls of bricks with a concrete outer shell, holding a couple dozen very large cannons and a parade ground.

The new river defenses of Philadelphia were to be provided by three forts, Fort DuPont at the mouth of the old Delaware-Chesapeake canal, Fort Delaware on the island, and Fort Mott on the New Jersey side. You can now take a ferry ride to all three, between April and September; it's a pleasant afternoon excursion. Not so many years ago, you had to go into an ominous little taproom in Delaware City and ask in a loud voice if someone wanted to take you to Pea Patch in a fishing boat. The scene was reminiscent of old movies about derelicts hanging out in Key West, complete with George Raft and Ernest Hemingway, but now the National Park Service has given it the characteristic NPS spruce-up, with pamphlets and restrooms. The place never had any serious military activity except when it was used to house Confederate prisoners after the Battle of Gettysburg. Over 12,000 prisoners were brought there, and there were about 3000 deaths among them. Historians have compared the treatment of Confederate prisoners with the treatment of Union prisoners at Andersonville, Georgia, and it would be hard to say which place was worse. There are certain diseases of poor sanitation, like typhoid, cholera, hepatitis, and amoebic and bacillary dysentery, which decimate all concentration camps at all times. And adding to them the mosquito-borne diseases of both Delaware and Georgia at the time, you don't really need to assert prisoner mistreatment to account for the morbidity and mortality. Undoubtedly there was some of that.

4 Odessa, Delaware

The Corbit-Sharp House   201 Main Street Odessa, DE   39.4551 -75.658

Delaware is a pretty small state to be divided into two civilizations, and in fact, it seems safe to predict that division will soon become meaningless. New Castle County and Wilmington are up north in DuPont country, with more Ph.D.'s than anywhere else in America, chateaux in the suburbs, plenty of Porsche's and other elements of the finer life. The other two counties, "South of the Canal," are rural, marshy, or beach front. Wal-Mart country. Aside from a distinct difference in the weather patterns, all of this is quickly changing. A limited-access toll road, probably mostly intended to carry people to the slot machines of Dover Downs, makes it breezily simple to go from one end of the state to the other in an hour. A ferry from Cape May to Cape Henlopen makes sailing across the mouth of the bay an alternative way to go from the urban areas of New York to and from Washington, Norfolk,

Corbit-Sharp House

and points South. And changes in the tax laws make Delaware a great place to avoid sales taxes, estate taxes, business taxes, usury laws and lots of other things. That brings in businesses, and they, in turn, bring in order to border, a swarm of home builders. It looks very likely Delaware will go the way of Luxembourg, urbanized from border to border.

Little Odessa (population 366) sits right at the pivotal point in this transformation. Here is the very narrowest point of the peninsula between Delaware and the Chesapeake bays. In the Seventeenth Century, there was only a five-mile portage from the head of one creek to the head of the other; the town there was called Cantwell's Bridge. Just why the two Delaware-Chesapeake canals were built a few miles further north is an engineering question, but they tended to shelter Cantwell's Bridge from Northern influences. The neck was so narrow, however, that the road couldn't avoid the town, and for a century it was a pleasure to find a little Colonial town, a little Williamsburg so to speak, popping up among the fields of clover bordering a drive to Dover. It's only a short 9-mile commute to the University of Delaware. The finest 18th Century country house, the Corbit-Sharp House sets the tone for the area, and Christmas season in Odessa is quite memorable. Rodney Sharp was the son of the local school teacher who acquired financial substance, private jet airplanes and all that, on the other side of the canal, and then restored his old home the Corbit house into the Corbit Mansion, bringing the whole farm village up to an elegant level. A visit to Odessa at Christmas, touring the open houses and visiting the festivities, is well worth the trip.

Delaware

The toll road sweeps around the edge of Odessa, and now the people going to the slot machines and the beaches can hardly see it as they race past. But that's mostly weekend traffic, and during the week all of those cornfields are quickly turning into easy commuter villages, full of McMansions. They are going to fill up the schools, demand better ones, demand traffic signals to protect the kiddies, demand retail outlets for all those upscale stores with catalogers, demand to be noticed. Eventually, all those three-car families will choke up the toll-road, and it will become a great big congested parking lot at rush hour. Sad.

One final comment about the origin of Odessa. It's named after the city in Russia because both of them were wheat exporting cities at one time, although it is doubtful if they were ever comparable in steamy nightlife. However, the one in Delaware is actually the older of the two. Cantwell's Bridge, Delaware was founded in 1731. For reasons unclear, its name was changed to Odessa in 1845, perhaps in the mistaken idea that the Russian city was where Odysseus once landed. That's what many Russians claim, but the place they have in mind was really in Bulgaria. The place the Russians call Odessa was founded by Catherine the Great in 1794, some sixty years after Cantwell began collecting toll at his bridge in Delaware. When the Bulgarian mistake was pointed out to Catherine the Great, she wouldn't change the name; she sort of liked it that way.

Odessa, Delaware

5 Delaware Declares Independence ... From Pennsylvania
Delaware Tourism Office   99 Kings Highway   Dover, DE   39.1602 -75.5239

To bewilder your friends from the State of Delaware, just ask them when and why Delaware broke off from Pennsylvania; chances are they haven't the foggiest answer. But they will recognize it is a legitimate question. Everyone does know that Delaware was once owned by William Penn and was part of Pennsylvania. It was generally referred to as the Three Lower Counties. But what happened then doesn't seem to be taught very effectively in the Delaware schools, and not much is written about it.

Delaware

Not much is written because not much happened. No revolutions, bombings, hangings or even acrimonious debate; just think how much Serbia, Russia, China, Sudan and a lot of other countries have to learn about self-determination, from Delaware.

The history of Delaware up to 1674 was of Dutch, Swedish and even some Finnish settlement and arguments. The Duke of York (later James II) owned it and seems briefly to have toyed with combining it with New York; that's how the Delaware happens once to have been called the South River, and the Hudson the North River. But William Penn acquired it in 1682, mostly with the motive of having unchallenged access to the ocean from Pennsylvania. Apparently, the people who lived away from the river felt more kinship with Maryland and expressed unwillingness to be linked with some religious experiment in Philadelphia, especially if they had to travel there to settle their affairs. There is not much Catholicism in Delaware at present, but that seems to have been part of the uneasiness in 1701. So Penn granted them quasi-autonomy and their own separate assembly, which resulted in a peaceful enough arrangement until the American Revolution. Penn got all he wanted, which was to sell off the land and

maintain a clear river passage; and by the time of the Revolution, his descendants had lost all control of things. The control of Pennsylvania over its three lower counties had never been terribly firm, and during the eight-year Revolutionary chaos, it sort of drifted away. When its votes were needed for the Declaration of Independence and later for the Constitution, it was expedient to recognize Delaware's claims.

Dover, Delaware

That's perhaps all there is to this vague story of statehood building, except for one nagging doubt. Delaware was a plantation state and a slave state. It sided with the North during the Civil War, but it remained a slave state. It voted against Lincoln's Emancipation overtures and refused to ratify the Thirteenth, Fourteenth and Fifteenth Amendments until 1901. Until the Lewes-Cape May ferries got busy with Garden State Parkway traffic, lower Delaware's population was almost exclusively either African-American or many-generation English descendants. The hospitals had

Delaware

white-only and black-only restrooms until the Second World War. Nothing better explains the claim by some that the Civil War was primarily fought to defend the Union, rather than to eliminate slavery, than the tangled local history of the border states, of which Delaware was definitely one.

And so, you have to wonder. Is it possible that the residents of the Lower Counties in 1776, especially in the southern portion where John Dickinson had a plantation, could recognize that the Quakers of Pennsylvania were relentlessly moving in a direction that surely would eventually conflict with the slave system? Maybe, looking ahead, the chaos of Revolutionary times provided a plausible moment to make a clean separation. These are awkward questions to ask, perhaps best passed by, in silence.

There has always been a rivalry between north and south Delaware, meaning below the Delaware-Chesapeake Canal. Threats from the British navy supplied the pretext if not the real reason to shift the capital from New Castle to Dover. After years as a makeshift and disorganized affair, it is now organized and permanent, and a nice little state to visit.

6 A Pennsylvania Farmer in Delaware

John Dickinson House   340 Kitts Hummock Rd   Dover, DE   39.10292 -75.44901

John Dickinson

It is difficult to have a coherent view of the mind of John Dickinson. Seriously offended by the Townshend Acts, he rightly perceived them to be the work of a few malignant personalities in British high places who would mostly soon be replaced. Later on, he refused to be troubled by the inconsequential Tea Act, which he appraised as a face-saving gesture of reconciliation, but more recent historical information demonstrates was more likely aimed at avoiding an unrelated vote of no-confidence in Parliament. Unfortunately, Dickinson was too remote from these events and additionally could not comprehend reckless hotheads among his own neighbors. Reckless hotheads in turn seldom comprehend the measured meekness of Quakers. In any event, although Dickinson played a major role in the Declaration of Independence, he refused to sign it when the time came, evidently sensing an opportunity to separate the three lower counties from Pennsylvania and its Proprietors. A few months later when the British actually invaded the new State of Delaware on the way to capturing Philadelphia by way of Chesapeake Bay, Dickinson enlisted as a common soldier and fought at the Battle of Brandywine. Obviously, he was seriously conflicted.

Dickinson had become internationally famous for twelve letters he had meant to publish anonymously. The "Letters From a Farmer in Pennsylvania" were written around 1768 out of resistance to the Townshend Acts. Because the three counties which were to become the State of Delaware were then still part of Pennsylvania, many school children have become understandably confused about the actual location of the man who became governor of both states, simultaneously.

The causes of the separation of the two colonies are still a little vague. Delaware schoolchildren are taught the two states separated, but often report they didn't retain much information about why it happened. The Dutch and Swedes who originally settled southern Delaware were not sympathetic with Quaker rule, which could be seen as a reaction to their living here for generations as Dutchmen before William Penn arrived, but then saw the colony sold out from under them. As a further conjecture, there might have been friction with the Quakers over slavery, similar to the hostility of other Dutch settlers in northern New Jersey when William Penn purchased that area. This pro-slavery attitude resurfaced in both areas during the Civil War. One alternative theory which has considerable currency in Delaware is local dissension about Quaker pacifism during the Revolutionary War. On a recent visit to Dickinson's home outside Dover, a school teacher was overheard to instruct his flock that the Dutch Delawareans wanted to fight the British King, but the Quakers wouldn't give them guns. "We value peace above our own safety," was the unsatisfying response they received from the Pennsylvania Assembly. But that line of reasoning bumps up against Dickinson's role in local affairs, his ambiguity over the Declaration, and his vacillation in warfare. One would suppose the simultaneous Governor of both states would play a major role in the separation of the two.

John Dickinson's Farmhouse

Dickinson's plantation, quite elaborately restored and displayed, is tucked behind the Dover Air Force Base. Perhaps all that aircraft noise will discourage sub-development in the area of Dickinson's plantation and the rural atmosphere may persist for years. At the time of the Cuban missile crisis, your correspondent happened to be driving past, observing the sky filled with bombers, just circling and circling until the diplomats settled matters. Since eight-engine bombers are seldom seen around Dover, it has always been my presumption that they came from elsewhere to be refueled at Dover; but that's just a presumption. One of the pilots later told me he was carrying nuclear "eggs" and was completely prepared to take a long trip to deliver them.

To get back to Dickinson's wavering about the Declaration, maybe there was a good reason to waver. Joseph J. Ellis (in *His Excellency, George Washington*) relates that after the devastating British defeat at the Battle of Saratoga, Lord North made an offer to settle the war on American terms. In a proposal patterned after the concepts of the separatists in Ireland, America could have its own parliament as long as it maintained trade relationships with England. As an opening offer, that comes pretty close to what the colonists had been demanding. Robert Morris was active in disdaining this offer, although it is unclear whether he was acting alone or as the agent of others. The offer came too late to be accepted, but it might have shortened the war by six years, and we might now have a picture of the Queen on our postage stamps.

7 Delaware's Court of Chancery

Georgetown Court of Chancery   34 The Circle   Georgetown, DE
38.69061 -75.38597

Georgetown, Delaware is a pretty small town, but it's the county seat so it has a courthouse on the town square, with little roads running off in several directions. The courthouse is surprisingly large and imposing, even more, surprising when you wander through cornfields for miles before you suddenly come upon it. The county seat of most counties has a few stores and amenities, but on one occasion I hunted for a barbershop and couldn't find one in Georgetown. (It has grown up considerably since then.) This little town square is just about the last place you would expect to run into Sidney Poitier and all the top executives of Walt Disney. But they were there, all right, because this was where the Delaware Court of Chancery meets; the high and mighty of Hollywood's most exalted firm were having a public squabble.

Original Courthouse, Georgetown

Only a few states still have a court of Chancery, but little Delaware still has a lot of features resembling the original thirteen colonies in colonial times. The state abolished the whipping post only a few decades ago, but they still have a chancellor. The Chancellor is the state's highest legal officer, and four other judges now need to share his workload, which was almost completely within his sole discretion seventy-five years ago. In fact, the Chancellor usually heard arguments in his own chambers, later writing out his decisions in longhand. The Court of Chancery does not use juries.

Going back to Roman times, the Chancellor was the highest office under the Emperor, and in England, the Lord Chancellor is still the head of the bar in a meaningful way. Sir Francis Bacon was the most distinguished British Chancellor and gave the present shape to a great deal of the present legal system. A court of Chancery is concerned with the legal concept of equity, which is a sense of fairness concerning undeniable problems which do not exactly fit any particular law. The Chancellor is the "Keeper of the King's conscience" concerning obvious wrongs that have no readily obvious remedy. You better be pretty careful who gets appointed to a position like that, with no rules to follow, no supervisor, no jury, dealing with mysterious issues that have no acknowledged solution. Delaware's Court of Chancery evolved in steps, with several changes of the state Constitution over a span of two hundred years. Under a new 1831 Delaware Constitution, the formation of corporations required individual enabling acts by the Legislature and limited their existence to twenty years. However, the 1897 Constitution relaxed those requirements and permitted entities to incorporate under a general corporation law and allowed them to be perpetual. By this time, other states were distributing equity cases to the county level, but Delaware was too small to justify more than a single state-wide Court. That court

Georgetown, Delaware

was attractive to corporations because it could become specialized in corporate matters, but retained a pleasing number of equity cases among common citizens, thus retaining a folksy point of view. In unique situations or those without a significant history of public debate, it was thought especially desirable to strive for unchallenged acceptance of the court's decision.

But other states thought they could see what Delaware was up to. In 1899 the American Law Review opined that states were having a race to the bottom, and Delaware was "a little community of truck farmers and clam-diggers . . . determined to get her little, tiny, sweet, round baby hand into the grab-bag of sweet things before it is too late." However, that may be, corporations stampeded to incorporate in the State of Delaware, and the equity of their affairs was decided by the Chancellor of that state. In one seventeen-year period of time, the U.S. Supreme Court reversed the decision of the Chancellor only once.

Delaware

Some legal scholars will have to tell us if it is so, but the direction and moral tone of America's largest industries has apparently been shaped by a small fraternity or perhaps priesthood of tightly related legal families, grimly devoted to their lonely task in rural isolation. The great mover and shaker of the Chancery was Josiah O. Wolcott (1877-1938), the son and father of three-generation family domination of the court. Most of the other members of the court have very familiar Delaware names, although that is admittedly a common situation in Delaware, especially south of the canal. This might seem reassuring when decisions are issued by a person of totally unquestioned integrity, a member of a family that has lived and died in the service of the highest principles of equity and fairness. But to recent graduates of business administration courses in far-off urban centers of greed and striving, it surely sounds quaint and sappy. And many of that sort have found themselves pleading in Georgetown. Just let one of them bribe, muscle, or sneak into the Chancellor's chair someday, and the country is in peril.

8 Georgetown Returns Day
Georgetown, DE   38.6901 -75.3858

Early in November, two days after each election, Georgetown Delaware puts on a festival called Returns Day. About two hundred years ago, there was a law that all ballots had to be cast in person at the courthouse in the county seat (Lewes, at that time), and it took two days to count the votes. Everyone, candidates included, would hang around at the courthouse to learn who had won. After a few elections, except in wartime when the ceremony was temporarily skipped, the popular tradition has continued even though of course the election results are known much earlier. Although the function of revealing election results has yielded to the news media, the ceremony has assumed importance for its own sake. Unless it rains pretty hard, the parade lasts three hours, with ten or twelve marching bands, and local amateurs struggling with bagpipes. The candidates, winner, and loser, ride gamely around the square in horse-drawn carriages. You can imagine what would happen to the political future of any candidate who declined to participate in what is now a mandatory public entertainment.

Two features of this festival are especially notable. There is a hatchet-throwing contest, trying to get the flying hatchet to catch one corner in a post. It's not an easy thing to do. And then there is hatchet-burying, which is said to date back to the Nanticoke Indians. The traditional hatchet is brought from Lewes, as is the sand. This is all said to be the origin of the folk-saying about burying the hatchet, and it's really very heart-warming to believe the election is only an election, and the competition is over. It's probably not entirely true, of course, but it symbolizes what the public wants to believe is true. And what the public is telling politicians -- had soon better become true, again.

9 Georgetown Oyster Eat: Separate But Equal

Georgetown Volunteer Fire Dept.   **100 S Bedford St**   **Georgetown, DE**
38.68876 -75.38475

It's a source of some regret never to have attended the Georgetown Oyster Eat. It occurs in the middle of February when the days are dark and short, and the weather is uncertain for driving.

Local citizens of Sussex County, Delaware, report no one alive remembers when or how the custom began. In the nature of such things, a certain amount of historical inaccuracy is thus to be expected. It certainly did start out as an all-male event, taking place in the firehouse. One inflexible requirement is that a participant must bring his own oyster knife, which is a very heavy chunk of iron with a short blade attached, sort of like a screwdriver. The ones I have seen are all one piece of iron, suggesting they have been hammered out in a blacksmith shop. The flattened-out blade serves as an eating utensil, as well as a wedge to pry open the oyster shell. The oysters are

Georgetown Firehouse

eaten raw and whole, often with some sort of condiment, like horseradish sauce. Some eaters favor a whole lot of ground pepper, and various other ancient remedies are said to make an appearance. The main beverage is beer, lots of beer.

Beyond that, not much is known or divulged to the public, although a party attended by nearly a thousand tipsy people can't keep very many secrets. Before the party, the windows of the firehouse are covered with brown wrapping paper, sealed with tape. Kegs of oysters and kegs of beer are rolled into the firehouse before other things get rolling, and a lot of loud noises and laughter emerge almost all night. The sponsors claim to bring a thousand bushels of oysters to each party, although it is hard to imagine very many people eating their quota of a bushel apiece. The per-person beer consumption is a statistic kept confidential.

There is some sort of oyster virus, and excessive fertilizer on the farm fields runs off and stimulates a bloom of algae, which depletes the oxygen of the river and kills a lot more than oysters. Anyway, the oysters are in short supply. If the local firehouse custom dies out, it won't be from lack of enthusiasm, however.

10 Delaware Bay

Ferry stop at Lewes   43 Henlopen Dr   Lewes, DE   38.7820 -75.1185

Lewes was once a little seaport, but mostly a home for river pilots. There is a canal across the base of the Cape Henlopen peninsula, and the pilots' imposing houses line the canal. But vacationers and sportsmen are now building waterfront houses as fast as they can, so old Lewes is getting lost. Just up the river, the Wesley Chapel is a place where John Wesley really preached in his tour to extend Anglicanism, and unintentionally to found the Methodist Church. Rehoboth down the road has ocean beaches and higher land, so it offers suburban living at the beach, year-round.

Henry Hudson

Captain John Smith of Virginia, sometime friend of Pocahontas, wrote a letter to Captain Henry Hudson that he understood there was a big gap in the continent to the North of the Virginia Capes, and maybe this was the Northwest Passage to China. Hudson set out to look for it. Smith's misjudgment now seems like a credible story. If you take the ferry from Lewes, Delaware to Cape May, New Jersey, you are out of sight of land for half an hour on that trip, and it's a hundred miles of blue saltwater to Philadelphia if you decided to go in that direction. In fact, the bay widens out to double the width or more, just inside the capes, and you can see how an explorer in a little sailboat might believe there was clear sailing to the Indies if you went that way. But as a matter of fact, Hudson encountered so much "shoal" that he ran aground repeatedly trying to sail into the bay, and soon gave up. He encountered a swamp, not an ocean passage. The Hudson River, and later Hudson's Bay, seemed like better bets.

What Hudson had encountered was one of the largest gaps in the chain of Atlantic barrier islands, formed by the crumbling of the Allegheny Mountains into the sea, and then washed up as beach islands by the ocean currents. At various points, the low flat sandy islands became re-attached to the mainland as the intervening bay silted up, and that's why the islands of New Jersey and Delaware seem like part of the mainland. And that's what would have happened to the whole Delaware Bay if it hadn't been ditched and dredged, and wave action diverted with jetties. The swamp was a great place to breed insects, so fish were abundant, and that brought birds in vast numbers. Two stories illustrate.

Delaware

Once a year, a zillion ugly Horseshoe Crabs crawl out of the sea onto the Lewes beaches and lay a million zillion eggs in the sand. Almost to the moment, a swarm of South American birds swoops out of the skies to eat the eggs. Those birds started flying months earlier from thousands of miles away, but their timing with regard to Delaware crab eggs is perfect, so this evolutionary semi-miracle must have been going on for many centuries.

Horseshoe Crabs

Now, coming from the other (New Jersey) direction, every hour each fall it is possible to see a hawk or two fly southward, to Cape May, then sort of disappear in the woods. And then, at some unknown signal, tens of thousands of hawks rise from the bushes and travel together on the thirty-mile passage over the bay and then go on south. Cape May has lots of migratory birds and bird watchers, and it also has Cape May "diamonds", which are funny little stones washed up at the tip of Cape May Point.

In the spring, vast schools of successive species of fish migrate up the Delaware Bay to spawn in the reeds along the shoreline, but as each school encounters the point where the saltwater turns fresh, they stop dead. They mill around at this point for several weeks adjusting to the change of water and then go on about their business. While they are there, it is possible for amateurs to catch amazing amounts of fish, if you know the best time, and if you know where the salinity changes. Since heavy or light rainfall can shift the salinity barrier fifty miles, you have to own your own boat if you want to enjoy this phenomenon, since the rental boats are all spoken for months in advance. Fishermen don't like to tell you about such things; patients of mine who literally owed me their lives have refused to say where I might find the fish this year.

Over on the New Jersey side of the bay, oysters like to grow, although they have been just about wiped out in recent decades. There is a town called Bivalve, which is worth a visit just to see the towering piles of oyster shells left over from the last century. For miles around, the roads are actually paved with ground-up oyster shells. Up north around Salem, the shad used to run by the millions until the warm water emerging from the Salem (nuclear) power plant attracted them into the intake pipes and action was taken to abate the nuisance. The Salem Country Club is one of the few places where planked shad can be obtained in season. The system is to split the fish open and nail it to a board, which is then placed in the big open fireplace to cook, and sizzle, and smell just wonderful good. On the other hand, if you want to buy shad in season (March-May) and cook it at home, the place to get it is in Bridgeton.

Delaware

At the far northern end, at Trenton, the real Delaware River flows into the bay. The area has long since been dredged, but at one time the "falls" at Trenton were notable. Even today, if you travel upriver almost to Lambertville, you will see the river drop over several small ledges. Actually, rapids would probably be a better descriptive term, since the Delaware picks up quite a strong current coming down from the Lehigh Valley. In seasons of heavy rainfall, the falls can be completely "drowned".

And down at Philadelphia where we live, the Schuylkill joined the Delaware, forming the largest swamp of all at the river junction, a place once famous for its enormous swarms of swans. The Dutch discovered a high point of land at what is now called Gray's Ferry and made it into a trading place for beaver skins from the local Indians. There seems no reason to doubt the report that they took away thirty thousand beaver skins a year from this trading post, now the University of Pennsylvania.

An English sailing vessel was once blown to what would now be Walnut Street in Philadelphia, and it was recorded in the ship's log that it was scraped by overhanging tree limbs. The high ground at that point seemed like a favorable place to situate a city because the water was deep enough for ocean vessels. They had stumbled on one of the relatively few places in the whole bay that was both defensible and navigable, where the game was abundant, and fishing was good. The rest is history.

New Jersey

New Jersey was the original Quaker state. Many of those Quakers gradually migrated across the river to form Philadelphia. Benjamin Franklin called New Jersey a keg that was plugged at both ends, with New York and Philadelphia being the plugs. The colony was in a sense split down the middle, and in many ways still is. This arrangement was formalized by the construction of the line dividing East (what we would think of as North) from West Jersey.

Once you notice the oddity of salt water in the lower reaches of the Delaware and Hudson rivers, it gets easier to understand the current theory that southern New Jersey was once an island. Like Long Island, it was separated from the mainland by a sound, but in the Jersey case the sound silted up from Trenton to New Brunswick, creating a new peninsula of "West" Jersey by uniting the island with the mainland. The colony was named after the island of Jersey off the coast of England, a gesture for Sir George Carteret, who was given the American area out of gratitude for once sheltering the exiled royal brothers Charles II and James from Cromwell, in that other Jersey. Cape May was probably a second distinct island later joined to the larger one by the transformation of the silted ocean into the bogs of the Maurice River.

Cape May started as a whaling community, populated by Quakers from New York and New England, who always maintained a social distance from the Philadelphia Yearly Meeting. The long Atlantic beaches of New Jersey now repeat the main geological process, with successive generations of barrier islands first heaved up by the ocean and then packed against the mainland, filling up the brackish bay. The cycle of forming and packing successive barrier islands takes about three hundred years before a new one starts. In a larger sense, the process consists of the former mountains of Pennsylvania crumbling into the ocean and then responding to wave action.

It's no mystery, therefore, why southern New Jersey is flat, broken up by turgid meandering streams which casually empty in either direction. The head of Timber Creek, which flows into the Delaware, is only eight miles from the head of the Mullica River, flowing toward the ocean. During the Revolutionary War, the British found it too dangerous to sail up these winding creeks, since at any moment they might make a sharp turn and be facing a battery of cannon on the shore. An arrangement quickly grew up that buccaneers would build ships in the center of heavy oak forests and sail them out to Barnegat Bay, thence out one of the inlets of the barrier islands into the blue water. The financiers of Philadelphia, many of them with names now in the Social Register, would come from the rear, sailing up the Delaware River creeks, and walking the last mile or two to privateer headquarters on the Atlantic-flowing creeks.

Auctions were conducted, in which the ships were examined, the captain interviewed, and the crew observed in target practice. If you bought a small share you would be rich when the ship returned; and if it never returned, well, you had to invest in a different one. New Jersey is indignant that these privateers may have been mainly responsible for winning the Revolution, but given little credit for it. Many more British sailors were lost to the privateers than soldiers were lost to Washington's troops, and the economic loss to Great Britain of the ships and cargoes eventually became serious. Since much of the profit from privateering was recycled into the American war effort by Robert Morris, the British found themselves facing an enemy much more formidable than just the ragged frozen troops at Valley Forge on the Schuylkill. Meanwhile, William Bingham was conducting a similar privateering operation in partnership with Morris but based on the island of Martinique, but that's another story.

In later centuries, the traditions and geography of the Jersey Pine Barrens suited themselves to smuggling and bootlegging during the era of alcohol Prohibition by the ladies, and even after Repeal, high taxes on liquor kept bootlegging profitable. As late as the 1950s, there were divisions of FBI men prowling the woods of South Jersey, on the lookout for trucks carrying bags of cane sugar, or coils of copper tubing. After housing developments started to invade the forests, the hardball politics of South Jersey reflected a Mafia culture thought more characteristic of South Philadelphia. Near Vineland and Atlantic City, it isn't just a culture, it has the accent because it also has some of the ancestries.

XVIII Cooper Creek to Rancocas River

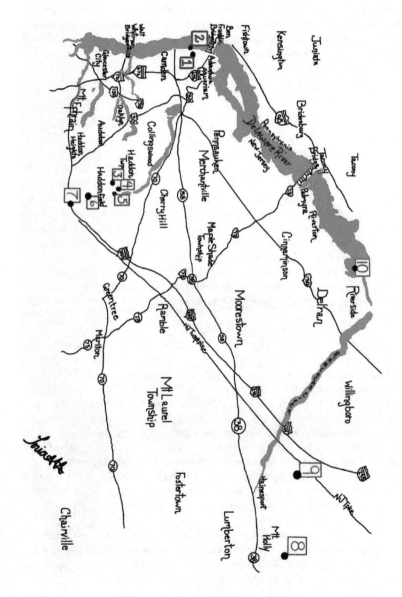

The pattern of settlement that you see now grows up at the crossing of modern roads, but originally settlement grew up along the Rancocas and Cooper Rivers, with woods and farmland in between. The rivers were navigable to somewhere around Medford and Westmont. Cherry Hill was owned by the Quaker Nicholsons with their large dairy farm which had its own pier on the Cooper River. You can easily get a feel for the area in one day. Navigate from Camden to Haddonfield; skip up to Mount Holly and head downstream to Amico State Park, then follow the Delaware River back to your starting place.

1 River Line: Camden and Amboy Revival
River Line   Camden, NJ   39.9408 -75.1284

The River Line, a sort of diesel-powered overgrown trolley car line, opened in 2004 on the Conrail tracks from Camden to Trenton. It runs every 30 minutes in both directions but unfortunately stops at night to let Conrail run freight trains at night. That's almost a perfect fit for the two operations, although it can leave some people stranded. The trains ran fairly full from the outset, partly because of their novelty, and partly because of the initial decision not to collect the $1.10 fare on Sunday, but mostly because the River Line proved to be a better idea than anyone realized it would be. It's considerably cheaper for Philadelphia commuters to Wall Street to take the River Line and transfer to New Jersey Transit at Trenton, for one thing. Even Amtrak encourages that, because high gasoline prices have filled up the Amtrak trains.

It's well worth a historical excursion on the River Line, which runs on the former right of way of the Camden and Amboy RR, the first railroad in New Jersey, chartered in 1830 by Robert L. Stevens. A genius of many talents, Stevens invented the iron rail which looks like an inverted "T," held in place by a system of plates and broad-headed spikes. The system is still in use today. Stevens also devised the use of wooden cross ties rather than granite ones, finding they resulted in a smoother ride. In 1834, he joined forces with another many-talented genius, Robert F. Stockton, who had earlier constructed a canal from New Brunswick to Trenton. Stevens then built a railroad beside the canal, subsequently extending it from Trenton to Camden. Stockton ran ferry boats from Perth Amboy to New York, and from Camden to Philadelphia. The full trip from New York to Philadelphia took nine hours, a remarkable improvement over the horse-drawn competition.

The partnership also got the New Jersey legislature not only to give the Amboy and Camden permission to use eminent domain to acquire its right of way, but also conferred a *perpetual* tax exemption, and perpetual railroad monopoly. So the arrangement was highly profitable as well as an engineering marvel.

Perpetual is a pretty unambiguous adjective, of course, and it might be an interesting topic in judicial gymnastics to observe how the state would get itself out of the impossible economic straight-jacket of conferring a perpetual monopoly on only one railroad. It proved achievable, however, when the proprietors of a new Stanhope Railroad slipped exemptions and enabling legislation for itself into one of the thousands of corporation bills which flooded through the legislature, unread by anyone except the authors. After the Governor, who also hadn't read the bill, signed this sleeper into law, the uproar was predictably loud and accusatory. In a sense, the wrangle about New Jersey railroads was not finally settled by the legislature at all but by the Pennsylvania Railroad, which preferred to bridge the Delaware River at Trenton, so the towns and track along the Jersey side of the river soon dwindled away. New Jersey had not only lost the advantage of railroad competition, but it had also essentially lost all of the main North-South railroad traffic made possible by improved bridge construction methods.

The River Line now provides a pleasant one-hour excursion along the riverbank, down the main streets of some cute little towns, past some remarkable woods and wilderness up near Trenton, and past Camden's urban revival at the other end.

2 Battleship New Jersey: Home is the Sailor
The Battleship New Jersey   62 Battleship Place   Camden, NJ
39.9397 -75.1333

Home is the sailor, wrote A. E. Housman, home from the sea. In this case, the sailor is the Battleship New Jersey. The U.S.S. New Jersey rides at permanent anchor in the Delaware River, tied to the Camden side. You can visit the ship almost any day, and with reservations can even throw a nice cocktail party on the fantail. It's an entertaining thing to do under almost any circumstances, but the trip is more enjoyable if you spend a little time learning about the ship's history. The volunteer guides, many of them still grizzled veterans of the ship's voyages, will be happy to fill in the details.

In the first place, the ship's final bloody battle was whether to moor the ship in the Philadelphia harbor, or New York harbor, when the U.S. Navy had got through using it. You can accomplish that and remain in the state of New Jersey either way, but there's a big social difference between North Jersey and South Jersey, so the negotiations did get a little ugly. Because of the way politics go in Jersey, it wouldn't be surprising if a few bridges and dams had to be built north of Trenton to reconcile the grievance, or possibly a couple of dozen patronage jobs with big salaries but no work requirement. The struggle surely isn't over. Battleships are expensive to maintain, even at parade rest; if you don't paint them, they rust. Current revenues from tourists and souvenirs do not cover the costs, so the matter keeps coming up in corridors of the capitol in Trenton.

Battleship design gradually specialized into a transport vehicle for big cannons, ones that can shoot accurately for twenty miles while the platform bounces around on the ocean surface. Situated in turrets in the center of the vessel, they can shoot to both sides. That's also true of armored tanks in the cavalry, of course, with the history in the tank's case of the big guns migrating from the artillery to the cavalry, causing no end of a jurisdictional squabble between officers trained to be aggressive for their teams. Originally, the sort of battleship which John Paul Jones sailed was expected to attack and capture other vessels, shoot rifles down from the rigging, send boarders into the enemy ships with cutlasses in their teeth, and perform numerous other tasks. In time, the battleship got bigger and bigger so in order to blow up other battleships had to sacrifice everything else to sailing speed and size of cannon. Protection of the vessel was important, of course, but in the long run, if something had to be sacrificed for speed and gunpowder, it was self-protection. There's a strange principle at work, here. The longer the ship, the faster it can go. Almost all ocean speed records have been held by the gigantic ocean liners for that reason. If you apply the same idea to a battleship, the heavy armored protection gets necessarily bigger, and heavier as the ship gets longer, and ultimately slows the ship down. As a matter of fact, bigger and bigger engines also make the ship faster, until their weight begins to slow them down. Bigger engines require more fuel and carrying too much of that slows you down, too. Out of all this comes a need for a world empire, to provide fueling stations. Since the Germans didn't have an empire, they had to sacrifice armor for more fuel space and more speed, to compensate for which they had to build bigger guns but fewer of them. Although the British had more ships sunk, they won the battle of Jutland because more German ships were incapacitated. When you are a sailor on one of these ships, it's easy to see how you get interested in design issues which may affect your own future. An underlying principle was that you had to be faster than anything more powerful, and more powerful than anything faster.

Home is the sailor, home from the sea,
Her far-borne canvas furled
The ship pours shining on the quay
The plunder of the world.

Home is the hunter from the hill:
Fast in the boundless snare
All flesh lies taken at his will
And every fowl of air.

'Tis evening on the moorland free,
The starlit wave is still:
Home is the sailor from the sea,
The hunter from the hill

A.E.Housman

Battleship New Jersey

The point here is that the New Jersey, as a member of the Iowa class of battleship, was arguably the absolutely best battleship in world history. At 33 knots, it wasn't quite the fastest, its guns weren't quite the biggest, its armor wasn't quite the thickest, but by multiplying the weight of the ship by the length of its guns and dividing by something else you get an index number for the biggest worst ship ever. The Yamamoto and the Bismarck were perhaps a little bigger, but the New Jersey was at least the fastest meanest un-sunk battleship. Air power and nuclear submarines put the battleship out of business, so the New Jersey will hold the world battleship title for all time. Strange, when you see it from the Ben Franklin Bridge, it looks comparatively small, even though it could blow up Valley Forge without moving from anchor.

One story is told by Chuck Okamoto, a member of the Green Berets who was sent with a group of eight comrades into a Vietnamese army compound to "extract" an enemy officer for interrogation. When enemy flares lit up the area, it was clear they were facing thousands of agitated enemy soldiers, and Okamoto called for air support. He was told it would take thirty minutes; he replied he only had three minutes, and to his relief was told something could be arranged. Almost immediately the whole area just blew up, turned into a desert in sixty seconds. The guns of the New Jersey, twenty miles away, had picked off the target. The story got more than average attention because Okamoto's father was Lyndon Johnson's personal photographer, and Lyndon called up to congratulate.

A number of similar stories led to the idea that naval gunfire might have destroyed some bridges in Vietnam which cost the Air Force many lost planes vainly trying to bomb, but, as the stories go, the Air Force just wouldn't permit a naval infringement of its turf. This sort of second-guessing is sometimes put down to inter-service rivalry, but it seems more likely to be just another technology story of air power gradually supplanting naval artillery. Plenty of battleships were sunk by bombs and torpedo planes before the battleship just went away. If you sail the biggest, worst battleship in world history, naturally you regret its passing.

Tourists will forever be intrigued by the "all or nothing" construction of the New Jersey. Not only are the big guns surrounded by steel armor three feet thick, but the whole turret for five stories down into the hold is also similarly encased in a steel fortress. This design traces back to the battle of Jutland, where a number of battlecruisers were blown up because the ammunition was stored in areas of the hold not nearly so protected as the gun itself. Putting it all within a steel cocoon lessened that risk, and had the side benefit that when ammunition accidentally exploded, the damage was confined within the cocoon. It must have been pretty noisy inside the turret when it was hit, sort of like being inside the Liberty Bell when it clangs. But not so; stories have been told of turrets hit by 500-pound bombs which the occupants didn't even notice. The term "all or nothing" refers to the fact that the gun turrets are sort of passengers inside relatively unprotected steering and transportation balloon. In order to save weight, most of the armor protection is for the gun. That's a 16/50, by the way. Sixteen inches in diameter, and fifty times as long. With the weight distributed in this odd manner, the Iowa class of dreadnought was more likely to capsize than to sink. Accordingly, the interior of the hull is broken up into watertight compartments, serviced by an elaborate pumping system. Water could be pumped around to re-balance a flooded hull perforation, certainly a tricky problem under battle conditions.

3 The Origins of Haddonfield
Haddonfield, NJ   39.8974 -75.0368

Haddonfield, New Jersey is named after Elizabeth Haddon, a teenaged Quaker girl who came alone to the proprietorship of West Jersey in 1701 to look after some land which her father had bought from William Penn. Geographically, the land was on what later came to be called the Cooper River, and it must have been a scary place among the woods and Indians for a single girl to set up housekeeping. It was related in the *Tales of a Wayside Inn* that Elizabeth proposed to another young Quaker named John Estaugh. Because no children resulted, she sent to her sister in Ireland to send one of her kids, a girl who proved unsatisfactory. So the kid was sent back, and Ebenezer Hopkins was sent in her place. Thus we have Hopkins pond, and

"Haddy"

lots of Hopkins in the neighborhood ever since. Eventually, the first dinosaur skeleton was discovered in the blue clay around Hopkins Pond, and now can be seen in the American Museum of Natural History, so you know for sure that Haddonfield is an old place.

Eventually, the Kings Highway was built from Philadelphia to New York (actually Salem to Burlington at first) and it crosses the Cooper Creek near the old firehouse in Haddonfield, which claims to house the oldest volunteer fire company in America, but not without some argument about what was first, what is continuous, and therefore what is oldest. Haddonfield is, in short, where the Kings Highway crosses the Cooper, about seven miles east of City Hall in Philadelphia. The presence of the Delaware River in between makes a powerful difference since at exactly the same distance to the *west* of City Hall, is the crowded shopping and transportation hub at 69th and Market Street. Fifty years ago, Haddonfield was a little country town surrounded by pastures, and seventy years ago the streets were mostly unpaved. The isolation of Haddonfield was created by the river and was ended by the building of the Benjamin Franklin Bridge in 1926. If you go way back to the Revolutionary War, the river created a military barrier, and many famous patriots like Marquis de Lafayette, Dolley Madison, Anthony Wayne and others met in comparative safety from the British in the Indian King Tavern. In a famous escapade, "Mad" Anthony Wayne drove some cattle from South Jersey around Haddonfield to the falls (rapids) at Trenton, and then over the back roads to Washington's encampment at Valley Forge. In retaliation, the British under Col John Simcoe rode into nearby Salem County and massacred the farmers at Hancock's Bridge who had provided the cattle.

At another time, the Hessians were dispatched through Haddonfield to come upon the Delaware River fortifications at Red Bluff from the rear. Unfortunately for them, they encamped in Haddonfield overnight, and a runner took off through the woods to warn the rebels at Red Bank to turn their cannons around to ambush the attackers from the rear, who were therefore repulsed with great losses. These stories are told with great relish, but my mother in law found out some background truths. Seeking to join the Daughters of the Revolution in Haddonfield, she was privately told that the really preferable ladies' club was the Colonial Dames. Quaker Haddonfield, you see, had been mostly Tory.

For a century or more, Haddonfield has had a railroad. Both the Reading and the Pennsylvania railroads ran through Haddonfield on their way from Philadelphia to Atlantic City, and later on, they were combined in the Pennsylvania-Reading Seashore Line. In 1950, the coal-fired steam locomotives still made a grade crossing on Kings Highway and tooted at the outskirts of town. A little awkward, dirty and dangerous, perhaps, but it had to be admitted that regular train service to the Shore was nice, as was regular commuting to Philadelphia. At least once a day, an elegant old train named the Nelly Bly made a round trip to New York, for those who occasionally wanted to take in a show, or do Christmas shopping in style. From the looks of some of the larger Victorian houses in town, there might even have been a few bankers going to Wall Street for important matters. Haddonfield was sleepy, but it had made things very convenient for itself.

And then, around 1970 the price of Haddonfield real estate tripled overnight. The Delaware Port Authority announced its plans for PATCO, a high-speed regular subway-surface line. Now that it is in existence, we have clean comfortable safe trains every five to fifteen minutes to the Center of Philadelphia. The express trains used to take eight minutes to Philadelphia, but now we only have locals who take seventeen minutes. The main complaint is that there is not quite enough time to read the newspaper.

There's a personal story here. In the articles about the coming high-speed line, I

PATCO High Speed Line

noticed two things: there was to be an elevated overhead track through Haddonfield, and the director of the Port Authority had been a West Point classmate of my uncle. Having spent four years in New York City, my image of an elevated train was highly unfavorable. They were noisy, and the noise created slums all along their path. Not what was wanted in tree-lined Haddonfield, at all. And the General, who among other things was a neighbor up my street a few houses, created a means to change the plans. We held a mass meeting in my house, and among those present was a former regular-Army major, who had been the track engineer for the Illinois Central. He said that he had been through

such arguments many times, had usually beaten down the opposition, but as a matter of fact, putting the rail line below grade was perfectly feasible. With that, one thing led to another, and General Casey finally one day was heard to say, "All right, I'll do it. But don't tell Collingswood." Collingswood is two stops closer to Philadelphia, and the main point was that a very popular religious radio station was located a hundred yards from the proposed line. One day, the minister of this station woke up to see an elevated -- an elevated -- being built outside his window. You can imagine all the rest, the radio broadcasts, the protests, the confrontation. But unfortunately, it was too late to make a change of plans.

As an epilogue, it can now be seen that there would have been advantages to the original design. The trains from Philadelphia to Atlantic City run immediately alongside the tracks of the high-speed line for a mile in Haddonfield. If they weren't all squeezed in a ditch, there might have been room for an interchange between the two at Haddonfield. But we don't care, we don't care. When we want to go to the shore, or to New York, we will drive.

Alfred Driscoll

A local boy named Alfred Driscoll became Governor of New Jersey, but before he did that he was mayor of Haddonfield. He had gone to Princeton and wanted to know why Haddonfield couldn't look like Princeton. All it seemed to take was a few zoning ordinances, and today it might fairly be claimed that Haddonfield is at least as charming and beautiful as Princeton, maybe nicer. At the very least, it has less auto traffic. Al Driscoll went on to be CEO of a Fortune 500 pharmaceutical corporation, and everyone agrees he was the world's nicest guy. The other necessary component of beautiful colonial Haddonfield was a fierce old lady who was married to a lawyer. Any infraction of Al's zoning ordinances was met with an instant attack, legal, verbal, and physical. A street-side hot dog vendor set up his cart on Kings Highway at one time, and the lady came out and kicked it over. If you didn't think she meant business, there was always her lawyer husband to explain things to you. She probably carried things a little too far, and one resident was driven to the point of painting his whole house a brilliant lavender, just to demonstrate the concept of freedom. Now that she and her husband are gone, the town continues to be authentic and pretty, probably because dozens of other citizens stand quietly ready to employ some of her techniques if the need arises.

4 It Ain't Necessarily So

Haddonfield Friends Meetinghouse   47 Friends Avenue and Lake Street
Haddonfield, NJ   39.9003 -75.0326

The Protestant Reformation provoked a wide variety of reasonings, and the Quaker position is at one extreme of them. One way of looking at it is to see the Reformation as largely a reaction to the invention of the printing press. At first, there was the impact of Latin versions of the Bible, or Vulgate, which could be read by priests like Martin Luther, and possibly interpreted by them to vary from established Church doctrine. Translation of the Bible into common languages subsequently permitted educated parishioners to read the Bible for themselves and draw their own conclusions. Fundamentalist branches of the church tend to place almost total reliance on what they can read for themselves, and consequently, authenticity is highly important to them. The Quakers go a step further, encouraging each member to come to his own spiritual viewpoint ("There is that of God in every man."), using the Bible as merely one important resource. Although others sometimes regard them as spiritually adrift, the Quaker idea is that if something is really true, everybody who thinks hard about it will eventually come around to much the same conclusion. (Related to this attitude is a strong belief in the ultimate triumph of democracy and the essential rightness of market-set prices.) Some people try harder than others, of course, and they come to be regarded as "weighty" Friends, likely to have reached the correct conclusion somewhat sooner than others.

One very weighty Friend was Henry Cadbury, an American relative of English candy makers. Henry decided he wanted to spend his life teaching the Bible and went to Harvard Divinity School. He became in time the leading authority in the world on the Book of Acts, editing that section of the Interpreter's Bible, and rising to be Professor of Divinity at Harvard. Henry knew his stuff, so to speak.

One fine summer day, Henry was seated in the front row of the Haddonfield Meeting. Birds twittered outside the open doors and windows, but otherwise, the gathered meeting was entirely silent. It was even beginning to look as though this meeting would be one of those occasional instances when nothing is said for an entire hour -- a "silent meeting". But, no, a visitor came through the open back door of the meetinghouse, in response to the sign found outside almost every meetinghouse, "All Are Welcome". The man was evidently a fundamentalist, and seeing a large audience all sitting silently waiting for something, he advanced boldly to the front of the meeting and began to speak.

Haddonfield Friends Meeting

The Bible was the Word of God. Every word in the Bible was true -- literally, and incontestably true. The theme was repeated several times, without an apparent response from the audience.

Finally, Henry Cadbury stirred himself. "Well, it has always struck me..." Oh, oh. Look out, here it comes.

"It has always seemed to me that the most quotable parts of the Bible are mainly based on faulty translation."

5 Ms. Mayor
Haddonfield Borough Hall   242 Kings Highway East   Haddonfield, NJ 39.8984 -75.0304

One of the great treasures of Haddonfield is a letter from Benjamin Franklin to the husband of Elizabeth Haddon, to the effect that she was the most forceful woman of the region. Indeed, it is part of the tradition of the Haddonfield Meeting of Friends that the men's meeting and the women's meeting met in separate rooms and kept separate minutes at that time. Elizabeth was the clerk of the women's meeting, and while the men's meeting would sign the minutes as "The Meeting on Stoy's Landing" or the "Meeting near Cooper's Creek" or something else topical, the minutes of the women's meeting were consistently signed in a single way. They were from the meeting in Haddonfield. Ultimately, everybody gave up and named the town Haddonfield.

Three hundred years later, the next woman mayor was Letitia "Tish" Colombi. In the tradition of forcefulness, a number of old-timers in the town remember when she first got elected by knocking on every door in the town, and then marched down the main street in the July 4th parade, wearing high-heeled red shoes. Her performance was a brilliant demonstration why politics is a full-time sport of every town in Texas. Odessa, her home town, is a few miles from Midland-where-the-oil-comes from, and she and Laura Bush probably attended the same high school. They were certainly both members of the same school.

In many ways, it was Al Driscoll who as Mayor asked why Haddonfield couldn't be like Princeton, where he once went to school. The answer he got was to change the zoning ordinances and then just wait thirty years. It worked fairly well, although Haddonfield got a parking and traffic problem along with the good features of

looking like Princeton. But it wasn't Tish's way; one might say it wasn't the Texas way. She hired some consultants at a cost of $125,000 to work out a detailed plan for changing Haddonfield for the better, and then followed the plan. It included a list of the kind of stores you do and don't want in a town of this type and the general strategy of attracting them. The zoning laws are sort of like Princeton's, but different enough to matter. Year by year, you could see the town change from a sleepy little place into a lively place to be.

Haddonfield Borough Hall

There are no empty lots in Haddonfield; to change the town, you have to remodel everything, house by house. On a summer evening, there are throngs of people on the sidewalks downtown, entertained by three or four street bands, wandering up and down at the sidewalk sales of the merchants. Haddonfield is "dry" in the sense that liquor sales are prohibited, but it hasn't kept restaurants away. The residents like BYOB a lot, and fully understand what it means.

Taxes in Haddonfield are, well, generous. But Haddonfield gets no state school aid; its schools are much like a thirty-million-dollar private school system, run by locals to local taste. And a quarter of our taxes go to Camden County. Tish boldly announced we get nothing whatever for those taxes in return. With a slogan like that, it's pretty hard to doubt she's a Republican.

6 Plays and Players, Haddonfield Version

Haddonfield Play and Players   957 East Atlantic Avenue at Crows Woods
Haddonfield, NJ   39.8837 -75.0276

First, an anecdote from my own lurid past. When I went there, Yale was an all-male institution with one exception, the Drama School. It's true that Shakspere had boys play the part of women in his plays, but Yale evidently felt that was going unnecessarily far, and had thus let the nose of the female camel get under the all-male tent. Meanwhile, I had discovered that a course in Advanced Chemical Engineering was carrying my amateur interest in chemistry sets a long way too far, and after two weeks, I wanted out of it. Out!

The Dean was sympathetic until I answered what I wanted to transfer into -- a course at the Drama School. Somehow, he felt that was immensely amusing, one he hadn't heard before. But, finding my grade average satisfactory, he gave a big wink and signed the paper. I didn't pretend to be offended, but I did pretend to be solemn. The experience subsequently served me very well, since that class of women went down to Broadway at the same time I went down to New York to medical school. Almost none of my mostly all-male class of medical students knew any women in New York, but by comparison, I knew lots. It made me very popular with both groups. It thus develops that I had the courage a number of years ago to accompany to a

Haddonfield Plays and Players

theater party in Haddonfield, a lady who had spent twenty-five years on the stage. The play was Cole Porter's Anything Goes, put on by the Haddonfield Plays and Players, which was then celebrating its 75th year of productions. You seldom see musical comedies anymore, because the large cast and orchestra requirements are pushed by Union rules to the huge expense which a professional group cannot safely risk, and amateur groups mostly cannot enlist a large enough audience to support. In addition to the orchestra, stagehands, and administration, I counted thirty members of the cast up on the stage for the big chorus numbers. There might have been a hundred in the audience to pay the bills. This wasn't the only play of the season, there were to be five I understand, so the performers had to be quick studies, which generally means considerable experience. Even with what therefore must have been a short time to rehearse, this group was good, really, really good. The lady by my side remarked these people must be semi-professionals, at least. I didn't think so, so she demanded a playbill to see. Sure enough, semi-pro.

All of which may seem a round-about way to get to an observation about the current theater revival in Philadelphia. There are at least fifty new amateur theater groups scattered throughout our region, filled with "kids" having a wonderful time playing Shakspere, Albee, Shaw and whatever. At cast parties, almost none of them expresses any interest in going to Broadway or Hollywood; they are mostly software engineers or similar. Since the Philadelphia revival of interest in performing arts is so striking, it has led to ruminations about why the theater similarly flowered in Elizabethan London, at a time when there were only two theaters in Paris, by comparison.

But maybe, I realized for the first time, there is a flight in our direction, from New York City.

7 Tavistock

Tavistock NJ   39.8738 -75.0215

Right next to Haddonfield is another town called Tavistock. It contains four houses, quite large ones, and a perfectly beautiful country club. This geo-political curiosity came about only partly because Haddonfield is dry, no liquor. The present location was created during national Prohibition (of alcohol) when it didn't matter what the

Tavistock Country Club

local option said. The really devastating local ordinance was a prohibition of playing golf on Sunday, prompting the owner of the country club to move it from its original location straddling the border or Haddonfield and Haddon Heights on North Drive. It is probably correct that abolishing liquor is a good way to keep the town looking pristine, so that Haddonfield's continuing dryness had something to do with maintaining real estate values in addition to maintaining sobriety, in the minds of local property owners. This stance was certainly vindicated when a race track was built a mile or so away, and local residents could easily imagine all sorts of high life that might grow up in the shadow of a racecourse. Haddonfield learned what it thought was the lesson in this, and continues to prohibit alcohol sales (consumption is of course quite another matter) after the repeal of the Volstead Act. So Sam Fulton and the other founding fathers of Tavistock probably knew what they were doing. The existence of Tavistock is the best evidence of the shrewd thought processes in town because in some minds you can't have a country club without liquor. You also can't have much of a golf course without some hills, and hills like Tavistock are in short supply in southern New Jersey. Sam Fulton wanted the place neat and tidy; as Mayor of the four-house town, he passed an ordinance that the birds were required to fly upside down. The legal and political defenses of this oddment seem well planned and emotionally quite prepared to dismember any politician who seeks to make trouble for something odd which isn't entirely accidental.

In 2010, trouble came to Tavistock. Then-Governor Corzine merged the school district of Tavistock with the school district of Haddonfield. The total of four houses in Tavistock collectively only had one child in school, so the burden on Haddonfield wasn't very bad, but the school taxes on Tavistock appeared to be in for a serious upgrade. Tavistock hadn't been founded as a tax haven, but over the years it became so in a minor way. The four houses in Tavistock were remarkably opulent, and of course, they were only paying school taxes to send one or two children to neighboring schools, so they were effectively taxed much less than the residents of the towns who had the schools. Using the old police maxim of cui bono (who has a motive?), one might suspect someone in Haddonfield of stirring up this little class warfare stunt. However, it turns out there are four school districts in New Jersey who are similarly affected, so it seems likely that someone did some research in Trenton. Whether the Target was someone in Tavistock, or someone in Pine Valley, or someone in the other two places, is presently unknown. Sooner or later someone will talk, of course. And since this is the Soprano State, someone else may end up with concrete overshoes.

8 Slavery: If This be done well, What is done evil?
John Woolman Memorial   **99 Branch Street**   **Mt Holly, NJ**   **39.9979 -74.7781**

The Quakers of Philadelphia Yearly Meeting can rightly claim credit for successfully starting the movement to eliminate slavery in America. John Woolman of Mount Holly, New Jersey is the member given credit for determinedly agitating to eliminate a social institution which was then thousands of years old, and still persists today to some extent in some parts of the world.

Nevertheless, even Quakers were slow to endorse emancipation when first confronting the idea. The German-speaking Quakers of Germantown were urged in 1688 to adopt the concern of four members -- Garret Henderich, Derek and Abram Op De Graeff, and Francis Daniel Pastorius -- which follows. The Germantown meeting referred it to the Quarterly Meeting, which referred it to the Yearly Meeting. All of these ultimately declined to act, stating "It being a thing of too great a weight for this meeting to determine." Nevertheless, it percolated for eighty years, until Woolman was eventually able to bring the Yearly Meeting to adopt a favorable "minute". A full century after that, the rest of the nation came around to the same position, but only after fighting the bloodiest war in our history. Things change slowly, but without someone pushing them, they may never change at all. Nothing in their history better illustrates the central Quaker approach of "steely meekness", that quiet, patient, polite -- sometimes brave -- persistence in the practical advancement of what is reasonable and just.

The Declaration of the German Friends of Germantown, Against Slavery, in 1688.

These are the reasons why we are against the traffic of men's body, as followeth: Is there any that would be done or handled in this manner? viz.: to be sold or made a slave for all the time of his life? How fearful and faint-hearted are many at sea, when they see a stranger vessel, being afraid it should be a Turk, and they should be taken, and sold for slaves in Turkey. Now, what is this better done, than Turks do? Yea, rather it is worse for them, which say they are Christians; for we hear that the most part of such negers is brought hither against their will and consent and that many of them are stolen. Now though they are black, we cannot conceive there is more liberty to have them, slaves, as [than] it is to have other white ones. There is a saying, that we shall do to all men like as we will be done [to] ourselves; making no difference of what generation, descent, or Is there any that would be done or handled in this manner? viz.: to be sold or made a slave for all the time of his life? How fearful and faint-hearted are many at sea, when they see a stranger vessel, being afraid it should be a Turk, and they should be taken, and sold for slaves in Turkey. Now, what is this better done, than Turks do? Yea, rather it is worse for them, which say they are Christians; for we hear that the most part of such negers is brought hither against their will and consent and that many of them are stolen. Now though they are black, we cannot conceive there is more liberty to have them, slaves, as [than] it is to have other white ones. There is a saying, that we shall do to all men like as we will be done [to] ourselves; making no difference of what generation, descent, or color they are. And those who steal or rob men, and those who purchase them, are they not all alike? Here is liberty of conscience, which is right and reasonable; here ought to be likewise liberty of the body, except evil-doers, which is another case. But to bring men hither, or to rob, [steal] and sell them against their will, we stand against. In Europe, there are many oppressed for conscience sake; and here there are those oppressed which are of black color. And we who know others, separating wives from their husbands, and giving them to others: and some sell the children of these poor creatures to other men. Ah! do consider well this thing, you who do it, if you would be done in this manner--and if it is done according to Christianity! You surpass Holland and Germany in this thing. This makes an ill report in all those countries of Europe when they hear of [it,] that the Quakers do here handler men as they handle there the cattle. And for that reason, some have no mind or inclination to come hither. And who shall maintain this your cause, or plead for it? Truly, we cannot do so, except you shall inform us better hereof, viz,: That Christians have liberty to practice these things, Pray, what thing in the world can be done worse, towards us, than if men should rob or steal us away, and sell us for slaves to strange countries; separating husbands from their wives and children. Being now this is not done in the manner we would be done at, [by]; therefore, we contradict [oppose], and are against this traffic of men's body. And we who profess that it is not lawful to steal, must, likewise, avoid purchasing such things as are stolen, but rather help to stop this robbing and stealing, if possible. And such men ought to be delivered out of the hands of the robbers, and set free as in Europe. Then is Pennsylvania to have a good report, instead, it hath now a bad one, for this sake, in other countries. Especially whereas the Europeans are desirous to know in what manner the Quakers do rule in their province; and most of them do look upon us with an envious eye. But if this is done well, what shall we say is done evil?

...

Garret Henderich
Derick op de Graeff
Francis Daniel Pastorius
Abram op de Graeff.

This is from our meeting at Germantown, held ye 18th of the 2nd month, 1668, to be delivered to the monthly meeting at Richard Worrell's.

9 Burlington County, NJ

Burlington County   County Clerk's Office Building   49 Rancocas Rd
Mount Holly NJ   40.0044 -74.8352

Burlington County used to be called Bridlington. It contains Burlington City, formerly the capital of West Jersey, which is how they styled the southern half of the colony, the part controlled by William Penn. In colonial times, the developed part of New Jersey was a strip along the Raritan River extending from Perth Amboy, the capital of East Jersey, to Burlington. To the north of the fertile Raritan strip, extended the hills and mountains; to the south extended the Pine Barrens loamy wilderness. The Raritan strip was predominantly Tory in sentiment, while the remaining 90% of the colony consisted of backwoods Dutch farmers to the north, and hard-scrabble "Pineys" to the south, except for the developments farmed by Quakers. The Quakers had ambiguous sentiments during the Revolution, leaving conflicts between pacifism and self-defense to individual discretion. The real fighting mostly went on between the Episcopalian Tories and the Scottish-Presbyterian rebels, both of which were sort of newcomer nuisances in the minds of the Quakers. The warfare was bitter, with the Tories determined to hang the rebels, and the rebels determined to evict or inflict genocide on the loyalists. Standing aside from such blood-letting of course inevitably led to a loss of Quaker political leadership. When East and West Jersey were consolidated by Queen Anne into New Jersey in 1702, the main reason was ungovernability, with animosities which endure to the present time in the submerged form. Benjamin Franklin's son William was appointed Governor through his father's nepotism, but when he turned into a rebel-hanging Tory, his father extended his bitterness about it into a hatred of all Tories. The later effect of this was felt at the Treaty of Paris, where Ben Franklin would not hear of leniency for loyalists, striking out any hint of reparations for their property losses. In a peculiar way, the factionalism resurfaced at the time of the Civil War, where the slave-owning Dutch in the North came into conflict with the slave-hating Quakers in the South. The problem would have been much worse if the Jersey slaveholders had been contiguous with the Confederacy, but it was still bad enough to perpetuate local sectionalism. A few decades ago, it was actually on the ballot that Southern Jersey wanted permission to secede.

Burlington is the only New Jersey county which stretches from the Delaware River to the Atlantic Ocean, including the Pine Barrens occupying 80% of the land mass in the center; fishing and resorts dominate near the ocean and former industrial areas along the river. Much of the area has been converted to agriculture for the Garden State, but about 10% is included in a National Preserve. The population has doubled in the past fifty years, so urbanization is replacing agriculture, which had earlier displaced wilderness. The county includes Fort Dix and Maguire Air Force Base, strenuously promoted for decades by now-retired Congressman James Saxton.

***

Somewhere in the past few decades, Burlington became quite activist. Although many tend to think of real estate planning as urban planning, this largely rural county went in for planning in a big way, deciding what it was and what it wanted to be. Generally speaking, its decision was to replace urban sprawl with cluster promotion. The farmers didn't like an invasion by McMansions or industries, while the towns lost their vigor through tax avoidance behavior of the commuter residents. Overall, the decision was to push urban development along the river in clusters surrounding the declining river towns, while pushing exurban development closer to logical commuting centers, leaving the open spaces to farmers. Incentives were preferred to compulsion, with a determination never to use eminent domain except for matters of public safety. To implement these goals, two referenda were passed with 70% majorities to create special taxes for a development fund, which bought the development rights from the farmers and -- with political magic -- re-clustered them around the river towns. The farmers loved it, the environmentalists loved it, and the towns began to revive. The success of this effort rested on the realization that exurbanites and farmers didn't really want to live near each other, and only did so because developers were looking for cheap land. Many other rural counties near cities -- Chester and Bucks Counties in Pennsylvania, for example -- need to learn this lesson about how to stop local political warfare. Corporation executives don't want to live next to pig farms, but pig farmers are quite right that they were living there, first. When this friction seeps into the local school system, class warfare can get pretty ugly.

In Burlington County, they thought big. The central project was to push through the legislature a billion-dollar project to restore the River Line light rail to the river towns, along the tracks of the once pre-eminent Camden and Amboy Rail Road. It was an unexpected success. During the first six months of operation, ridership achieved a level twice as large as was projected as a ten-year goal. Along this strip of the Route 206 corridor, the old Roebling Steel Works are becoming the Roebling Superfund Site, now trying to attract industrial developers. The Haines Industrial Site originally envisioned as a food distribution center was sold to private developers who have created

West Jersey Proprietors Meeting Place

5000 jobs in the area. Commerce Park beside the Burlington Bristol Bridge is coming along, as are the Shoppes of Riverton and Old York Village in Chesterfield Township. As Waste Management cleans up the site of the old Morrisville Steel plant across the Delaware River, a moderate-sized development project is becoming an interstate regional one.

No doubt there will be bumps in these roads; the decline of real estate prices nationally is a threat on the horizon, because it provokes a flight of mortgage credit. It works the other way, too, as banks decide to deleverage by reducing outstanding loans; this is the way downward spirals reinforce themselves. And anyone who knows anything about all state legislatures will be skeptical about political cooperation in a state as tumultuous as New Jersey. The Pennsylvania Railroad destroyed the promise of this state once; some other local interest could do it again. Nevertheless, right now Burlington County looks like a real winner, primarily because of effective leadership.

10 Heron Rookery on the Delaware
Amico Island Park   81 Norman Ave.   Delran, NJ   40.0342 -74.9821

When the white man came to what is now Philadelphia, he found a swampy river region teeming with wildlife. That's very favorable for new settlers, of course, because hunting and fishing keep the settlers alive while they chop down trees, dig up stumps, and ultimately plow the land for crops. As everyone can plainly see, however, the development of cities eventually covers over the land with paving materials; it becomes difficult to imagine the place with wildlife. But the rivers and topography are still there. If you trouble to look around, there remain patches of the original wilderness, with quite a bit of wildlife ignoring the human invasion.

Such a spot is just north of the Betsy Ross Bridge, where some ancient convulsion split the land into both sides of the Delaware River; the mouth of the Pennypack Creek on the Pennsylvania side faces the mouth of the Rancocas Creek on Jersey side. In New Jersey, that sort of stream is pronounced "crick" by old-timers, who are fast becoming submerged in a sea of newcomers who don't know how to pronounce things. The Rancocas was the natural transportation route for early settlers, but it now seems a little astounding that the far inland town of Mt. Holly was once a major shipbuilding center. The wide creek soon splits into a North Branch and a South Branch,

Great Blue Heron

both draining very large areas of flat southern New Jersey and making possible an extensive network of Quaker towns in the wilderness, most of whose residents could sail from their backyards and eventually get to Europe if they wanted to. In time, the banks of the Rancocas became extensive farmland, with large flocks of farm animals grazing and providing fertilizer for the fields. Today, the bacterial count of the Delaware is largely governed by the runoff from fertilized farms into the Rancocas, rising even higher as warm weather approaches. My barber tends to take a few weeks off every spring, bringing back tales of big fish around the place where the Pennypack and Rancocas creeks join the Delaware, but above the refineries at the mouth of the Schuylkill, The spinning blades of the Salem Power Plant further downstream further thin them out appreciably.

Well, birds like to eat fish, too. For reasons having to do with insects, fish like to feed at dawn and dusk, so the bottom line is you have to get up early to be a bird-watcher. Marina operators have chosen the mouth of the Rancocas as a favorite place to moor boats, so lots and lots of recreational boaters park their cars at these marinas and go boating, pretty blissfully unaware of the herons. Some of these boaters go fishing, but most of them just seem to sail around in circles.

Blue herons are big, with seven-foot wingspreads as adults. Because they want to get their nests away from raccoons and other rodents, and more recently from teen-aged boys with 22-caliber guns, herons have learned to nest on the top of tall trees, but close to water full of fish. And so it comes about that there is a group of small islands in the estuary of the Rancocas, where the mixture of three streams causes the creek mud to be deposited in mudflats and mud islands. There is one little island, perhaps two or three acres in size, sheltered between the river bank and some larger mud islands, where several dozen families of Blue Herons have built their nests. One of the larger islands is called Amico, connected to the land by a causeway. If you look closely, you notice one group of adult herons constantly ferries nest building materials from one direction, while another group ferry food for the youngsters from some different source in another direction. At times, diving ducks (not all species of ducks dive for fish) go after the fish in the channel between islands, with the effect of driving the fish into shallow water. The long-legged herons stand in the shallow water and get 'em; visitors all ask the same futile question -- what's in this for the ducks? The heron island is far enough away from places to observe it, that in mid-March its bare trees look to be covered with black blobs. Some of those blobs turn out to be herons, and some are heron nests, but you need binoculars to tell. When the silhouetted birds move around, you can see the nests are really only big enough to hold the eggs; most of the big blobs are the birds, themselves. There are four or five benches scattered on neighboring dry land in the best places to watch the birds, but you can expect to get ankle-deep in the water a few times, and need to scramble up some sharp hills covered with brambles, in order to get to the benches. In fact, you can wander around the woods for an hour or more if you don't know where to look for the heron rookery. Look for the benches, or better still, go to the posted map near the park entrance south of the end of Norman Avenue. There are a couple of kiosks at that point, otherwise known as portable privies.

Strangers who meet on the benches share the information supplied by the naturalists that herons have a social hierarchy, with the most important herons taking the highest perches in the trees.

There is quite a good bakery and coffee shop just north of St. Mihiel Street, and the new diesel River Line railroad tootles past pretty frequently. That's the modern version of the old Amboy and Camden RR, the oldest railroad in the country. It now serves a large group of Philadelphia to New York commuters, zipping past an interesting sight they probably never realized is there. However, there's one big secret.

The birds are really only visible in the spring until the trees leaf out and conceal them. Since spring floods make the mud islands impassible until about the time daylight savings time appears, there remains only about a two-week window of time to see the rookery, each year. But it is really, really worth the trouble, which includes getting up when it is still dark and lugging heavy cameras and optics. Dr. Samuel Johnson once remarked that while many things are worth seeing, very few are worth going to see. This is worth going to see.

And by the way, the promontory on the other side of the Rancocas is called Hawk Island. After a little research, that's very likely worth going to see, too.

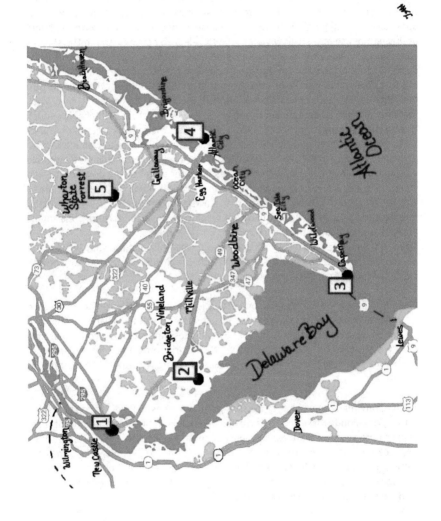

1 The Philadelphia Bay

Kelly Point   Riviera Drive   Pennsville, NJ   39.6453 -75.5419

The Capital of southern New Jersey alternated between Salem and Burlington, and the King's Highway ran between them atop a clay ridge all of fifty feet above sea level. Colonial villages are strung along Kings Highway about ten miles apart, just like villages in the Midwest and for the same reason. That's about the distance a farmer's wagon could travel to market and return in one day. Travel by boat modified that

somewhat. One unexpected feature: the marl clay ridge was eventually found to contain the first known dinosaur bones, still proudly on display at the Academy of Natural Sciences.

It's about sixty miles from Salem where the river takes an abrupt turn to the right, to Trenton, where the river takes an equally abrupt turn to the left. This is the area that could be

Joshua Fisher's 1778 Map of Delaware Bay   called the Philadelphia Bay, a protected extension of Delaware Bay. Benjamin Franklin, who sailed down this bay on his many trips to Europe, noticed that it was not exactly a river, because the saltwater seemed to invade it, whereas most big rivers have freshwater pushing out to sea. The true Delaware River comes down from the north and empties into Philadelphia Bay at Trenton. We now know that barrier islands begin out at sea every three hundred years or so, gradually move toward the shoreline, and pack themselves against the mainland about three hundred years later. Depending on circumstances, there are usually several sand reefs in various stages of development. Southern New Jersey is made up of a number of barrier islands packed together as they moved toward the mainland of Pennsylvania. The barrier islands actually have packed solid against the Pennsylvania coast, from Trenton to New Brunswick, closing off the ancient northern inlet to the bay. Barnegat Bay is a more recent variant of the same process, running parallel to the more ancient Philadelphia Bay. Since its northern inlet is almost closed at Barnegat Inlet, this seems to be a regular phenomenon of Atlantic barrier island development. Lower Delaware Bay, from Salem to Cape May, appears to have a different history, probably a volcanic split.

In the days of sail, Philadelphia Bay was the main artery of internal commerce. When the Delaware-Chesapeake canal was dug in 1829, it extended the inland waterway from Trenton to Norfolk VA. The earliest commerce took advantage of the tide and the bends in the "river" which was actually just the remnant of ocean between mainland Pennsylvania and the former barrier island of New Jersey. It had tides, but not much in the way of waves. Flatboats filled with Garden State produce would be carried up and across the river by the incoming tide, and down and across the river by the outgoing tide. When ships, particularly steamships, came along, this was the way to carry goods of all sorts up and down the Bay. At Odessa, it's only five miles between the Chesapeake and Delaware Bays, so even prior to the old Delaware-Chesapeake Canal sailing commerce was natural from Trenton to Norfolk, Virginia, and all points in between. The next step was building canals, up to the Raritan to New York Bay, and even up the "Main Line" west to Pittsburgh and beyond. The war of 1812 blocked off ocean shipping, and then another canal carried anthracite to Philadelphia, emptying at Bristol, briefly enriching Bristol, but then leaving it reduced to its present vestigial state when the tracks of the Pennsylvania Railroad cut it off. After canals came railroad tracks, usually following the path of the canals, making smoke and noise, constructing a dangerous, impenetrable barrier between the land and the water beside it. Superhighways do the same thing, replacing soot with gasoline fumes. There's a river out there somewhere, but you can't get to it. It now takes a twenty-story high rise to give you a river view; even that is best seen on Sunday when lessened traffic reduces gasoline haze.

It's really hard to imagine that the main attractions to living on the river once included not merely the view and the transportation, but also wonderful fishing and hunting among the bulrushes.

2 Greenwich, Where?

Greenwich, NJ   39.3902 -75.3392

If you sail north up the Delaware Bay, you would go past Rehoboth, Lewes, Dover, New Castle, Wilmington -- on the left, or Delaware side. On the right, or New Jersey side, it's a long way from Cape May to Salem, the first town of any consequence. That is, the Jersey side of the riverbank is still comparatively uninhabited. When the first settlers came along, with vast areas to choose among, it might have seemed attractive to settle on the Delaware side, because the peninsular nature of what is now called Delmarva (Del-Mar-Va) would provide land access to two large navigable bays, the Delaware, and the Chesapeake. To go all the way up the Delaware to what is now Pennsylvania would give trading access to a whole continent, so that eventually proved to be where immigration was headed. But as a matter of fact, the marshy Jersey shore seemed more attractive for settlement by the earlier settlers.

A settler has to think about starving the first year or two, because trees have to be cut down, and stumps pulled up before the land can even be plowed. After that, comes planting and growing, then finally harvesting. Trees, behind which Indians can

South Jersey and Shore

hide, are a bad thing all around in the eyes of a settler. The flat swampy meadows of the Jersey bank were just exactly what the Dutch knew how to manage. Dam up the creeks and drain the ground, and you will soon have lots of lands ready for the plow, without any confounded trees. By the end of the seventeenth century, the English who had made the mistake of settling in rocky Connecticut finally saw what the Dutch were able to do, and came down to take it away from them.

Greenwich NJ

That's why there is a Salem, New Jersey, and also a Greenwich, New Jersey. Greenwich (around here they pronounce it green-witch) had 804 residents at the 2010 census. It is one of the cutest little colonial villages you are likely to encounter. The local historians refer to it as an unreconstructed Williamsburg, drawing prideful attention to the fact that these houses were really built in the colonial period, and are in no way imitation reconstructions. The isolated charm of this place is in large part due to being surrounded by a maze of wandering creeks, so visitors by land travel don't get there in time for lunch unless they take great care to follow a local road map. If you arrive by water, it's no problem; just navigate up the crooked and twisting Cohansey River.

Although pioneer settlement was much earlier, the oldest house still standing in that rather damp area was built in 1730. Things are pretty much the way they were before the American Revolution because the Calvinists who settled here were not prepared for the Jersey mosquito, which obviously is abundant in such a marshy area. With the mosquito comes relapsing (Vivax) malaria, blackwater (Falciparum) malaria), and Dengue Fever (graphically known locally as break-bone fever). As a matter of fact, some causes of encephalitis are also mosquito-borne. When you don't understand the insect carrier situation, survival in such an environment depends on local fables and lore, like going to the mountains for the summer after the planting season, and only returning at harvest time. That sounds to a New Englander newcomer like a superstitious cloak for lazy living, especially since masses of fish come up the river in teeming waves, looking for mosquitoes to eat. So, Greenwich is charming, but it never was thriving.

Working hard to find something to say about the town, it would appear that Paul Revere himself came riding into Greenwich in December 1774, urging the town to join their Boston relatives in the destruction of tea belonging to the British East India Company. Greenwich accordingly had a public tea burning on December 22. Since the more notorious Boston tea party took place on December 16, 1773, and the

British Tea Act was passed in May 1773, it is not exactly accurate to say the rebellion spread like wildfire. One has to suppose that the inflammatory tale told to the local farmers by Paul Revere was likely a little enhanced, since a careful recounting of the events in Boston suggests a number of ways the uproar might have been avoided if Samuel Adams and his friends had been less provocative. Or if Massachusetts Royal Governor Thomas Hutchinson had been less flighty. Or for that matter, if Benjamin Franklin had restrained himself when he got hold of Hutchinson's letters at a critical moment when he was in London. In retrospect, the best model for behavior was provided by the Royal Navy: the whole Boston Tea Party was surrounded by armed British naval vessels, who did not lift a finger throughout the demonstration.

Anyway, little Greenwich had its minute of fame with a tea burning. Otherwise, it has had a very quiet existence for three centuries.

3 Cape May

Cape May, NJ   38.9345 -74.9594

From Greenwich, we go on to Cape May, with a brief detour to Bivalve. The point about this stop is the perfectly gigantic pile of oyster shells left over from the days as a center of oyster harvesting. Notice the roads; they're paved with oyster shells. Oysters eat algae, sewage fertilizes algae. Overfishing the oysters caused rotting algae and bacterial overgrowth in the river. The result was depletion of the dissolved oxygen, dead areas for fish, murky water instead of a clear stream. It's an opportunity for oyster farming, but the vast piles of shells at Bivalve are a warning of how far we have to go before we restore the river.

Cape May

Cape May was the first Atlantic Ocean beach resort, reached from Philadelphia and Tidewater Virginia by boat long before roads were usable. We are told Cape May was originally a separate barrier island, joined to the rest of South Jersey only later. It was once a whaling port, and the Quakers of the region were more related to Nantucket than to Philadelphia. Whale-watching is popular here, but dolphin sightings are more reliably frequent. As you would expect, this cute little place has many fine restaurants and hotels. The hotels are so authentic that strangers share common bathrooms the way they always used to do, so bed and breakfast places can be preferable for snootier tourists. Those whose great-grandparents once stayed in places like the Chalfonte, however, find it important to rough it in traditional summer places. The ocean currents "tumble" the small stones in the beach so beach-walkers can amuse themselves looking for "Cape May Diamonds". Unfortunately, even the locals often have never heard of them, so you are probably on your own.

4 There She Goes, Miss America

Atlantic City Convention Center   One Convention Boulevard   Atlantic City, NJ
39.3639 -74.4409

Atlantic City has long been a summer resort, crowded with people on the boardwalk by the sea. But families suddenly disappear at Labor Day, when the kids go back to school. So, in 1921 the merchant community hit on an idea to extend the busy season an extra week, by having a big beauty contest on the week following Labor Day. The early Miss America contest struggled for a year or two and then became an established annual national ritual. The hotels and boardwalk did indeed stay crowded for an extra week, during which a publicity campaign was conducted to build up anticipation for the big Saturday night event. The preliminaries included interviews and mini-contests, for the bathing suit division, the evening gown division, arguments about official state representation, occasional scandalous behavior, parades in open convertible cars, and whatnot and whatnot. Behind the scenes, there were little local battles, including a grim determination not to have a Negro girl represent a state from the old Confederacy. Since only one Jewish girl ever won the contest in eighty years, there were probably other issues in other states, hidden behind the curtains. Smoking and drinking were prohibited but scarcely non-existent, as was getting married or pregnant; much of the fuss about these lesser moral issues was probably intended to cloak the event with the high moral tone, counteracting some unfortunate early beginnings of the pageant, and the exciting laxity traditionally associated with summer resorts by the ocean. But they aimed at and succeeded in attracting, a certain kind of audience.

For months before the pageant by the sea, preliminary contests were held throughout various states to select the local Queen, Miss Arizona, Miss Mississippi, Miss Delaware and so on. The people involved in these local contests duly trooped to Atlantic City to see the big event and cheer their candidate. Over time, it became clear that some states worked really hard on this effort; Mississippi was a notorious big spender, and a consistent big winner, but others were almost as determined to win. The grassroots campaign was largely centered on small-town high schools, but the effort was conducted by a great many local women, mostly middle-aged, who somehow got control of local beauty politics and ran the local contests. Over the years, two of these groupies had been nurses who worked in hospitals where I was a consultant, and I got to watch their enthusiasm bubbling under the surface. One woman had worked for years as a night nurse. Perhaps as a result of sleeping all day and working all night, she was a little odd, often slightly hostile. But when I asked this ancient battle-ax every year about the contest, she immediately blossomed and went on for half an hour about the gossip surrounding this year's contestants and winner. There was something about all this which was like the fantasies of playing with dolls, fulfilling unfulfilled dreams. If you pause to think about it, that enormous convention hall in Atlantic City wasn't filled with school kids after Labor Day; the school kids were back at school. Although the publicity was all about kids and giggles, the real fans were dreaming of days long past, perhaps as former beauties, more often only wannabes, their dreaming only intensified by knowing for a certainty that this success would never be theirs.

Atlantic City Boardwalk

It was this self-delusion quality which the promoters of the contest never seemed to get through their heads; after all, the pageant was created and promoted by local merchants who mostly aimed to sell salt-water taffy to the rubes. Radio, and then television, gave the Miss America contest a big publicity push, and then eventually used up its material. When the casino crowd moved into A.C., the non-gambling ladies quickly demonstrated they didn't gamble, in fact, would sass the serious gamblers for their idiotic behavior losing money as fast as they could. TV ratings, contest attendance, and publicity began to fall off rather seriously. The idea was tried that perhaps women now wanted careers, so "points" were awarded for talent shows, musical performances, and brief contests about current events. Foo. That's not what the audiences wanted. So the contest moved to Las Vegas, and the date was shifted to January, a slow time for casinos. The awards were shifted from national tours and opportunities for screen tests to the awarding of college scholarships. Unfortunately, most of the contestants were already in college or married, and the scholarships were in fact mostly used to pay off trailing debts from colleges already attended.

South Jersey and Shore

Trapped in a Casino

Everyone who reads a detective novel or sees a James Bond movie is familiar with secret passages and hidden protection devices that suddenly trap the unwary. You aren't supposed to know about these things, but in real life, lots of people have had to know the secret, because it takes builders, architects and workmen to create it. Ancient Chinese and Egyptian emperors may have buried workmen alive to preserve the secret of secret passages, but nowadays that sort of thing is discouraged.

Since nowadays gambling casinos are bought and sold like a bottle of milk, some of the people who just have to be told the secrets of casinos are real estate appraisers; from one of them, the following tidbit derives. Casinos try not to have any windows, so the serious slot machine players won't notice the passage of time, and maybe gamble all night when so inclined. It is, therefore, no surprise the ceilings and walls are usually mirrored, to make these windowless caverns seem gay and cheerful. The casino operator doesn't want anyone to go home for any reason other than running out of money, and depends heavily on the wisdom of Adam Smith, who once said, "The more you gamble, the more certain you are to lose."

Unfortunately, these palaces of pleasure attract a fair number of cheaters, who attempt to win by memorizing the cards that have been played and changing their bets with the changing odds of what remains unplayed in the deck ("card counters"). Others are more mechanically talented and drill holes into the works of slot machines with battery-driven portable drills, for later accomplices to insert metal rods into vital wheels and whatnot on the inside. And so on. So, the mirrors on the ceiling are one-way mirrors, with people observing what goes on below, and cameras recording every action of everybody. In this modern age, some casinos can bring up videos of what happened on a particular machine at a given time, several years ago. This elaborate recorded surveillance can be used to unravel the activities of visiting crooks, who quite often do their work over a period of some time, coming back to the same machine for another step in their fiendish schemes. Now, there's another consideration at play here. The casino operator does not want a commotion on the gambling floor when some crook is accosted, because that tends to divert dozens of gambling addicts from their incessant gambling in order to watch the excitement. This would definitely be a violation of Adam Smith's law of gambling and hence would subtract from the value of stopping the crook who was caught. No good.

So, the merry men up above on the other side of the mirrored ceiling will merely watch and record the activity of the miscreant below, apparently letting him get away with it. But sooner or later the crook has stolen enough or has to go the bathroom, or for some other reason leaves the casino floor. Bang, the door behind him closes and locks, and the door on the other side of the trap is also locked. Thus, without any fuss or muss (maybe) the crook is observed by witnesses, recorded on camera, and tucked away in a security chamber until such time as the security guards can arrive to advise him of the management's disapproval of his behavior. Just exactly what does happen when one of these people is caught is not something they need to tell a real estate appraiser, so, unfortunately, I have to leave it to your imagination.

5 Goat Head Merchant

Batsto Village   31 Batsto Rd   Hammonton, NJ   39.64288 -74.64832

In 1948, one of the Intern physicians at Bellevue Hospital contracted tuberculosis. The senior medical students at Columbia were asked to volunteer to take his place, and for a month I did so. Since I knew I was soon going to Philadelphia to Intern at the Pennsylvania Hospital, my interest was particularly taken by an old Bowery bum who was talking about untaxed liquor. In New York at that time, it was common for Skid Row denizens to drink the wood alcohol in Sterno, called "squeeze" because it could be extracted from the waxy contents of a Sterno can by wrapping it in cheesecloth or a handkerchief and squeezing out the juice. Another favorite was "Smoke", which was typically a mixture of automobile radiator fluid and other sundry handy ingredients. My new best friend at Bellevue was just recovering from the effects of such recreation, and was in a mood of "never again". He observed that "When I get out of the Bell View, I'm going to get on a bus and go down to Philly. They've got a drink there called Goat Head, and, man, is it ever smooth."

The Chief Resident of the Pennsylvania Hospital was happy to tell me what Goat Head was. It was bootleg liquor, made in the Pine Barrens of New Jersey. Bags of cane sugar were fermented and distilled through coils of copper tubing, obtained from old hot-water heaters. The smooth stuff that so intrigued the bums of Bellevue was what was otherwise known as "White Lightning". It was then sold in the alleys near South Street by "Goat Head Merchants", who carried a suitcase full of small bottles, sold for about 25 cents a bottle. They say that during the Depression, Goat Head was sold out of an open bucket, at 10 cents a dipperful. One of the Goat Head Merchants used the Accident Room of the hospital as his family doctor; let us call him Walter Apple.

One day, Walter had a heart attack and was brought in on a stretcher, in considerable pain. I had just completed an electrocardiogram on him when the pain disappeared. A few weeks later, he had completely recovered and was going home. Every time I came anywhere near him, he announced to everyone in the vicinity that I was the best doctor in the world, having cured his heart attack by giving him the "wire treatment".

As he gathered up his belongings to go home, he apologized that he was not going to be able to pay his bill. He had once known Dillinger and all those other big shots wore a diamond stick-pin and drove a Duesenberg car. But now he was broke.

But grateful, too. So, if ever there came a time when I encountered someone unpleasant, who needed "pushing' around" -- just you call on Walter Apple, and Walter would be glad to pay off his debt.

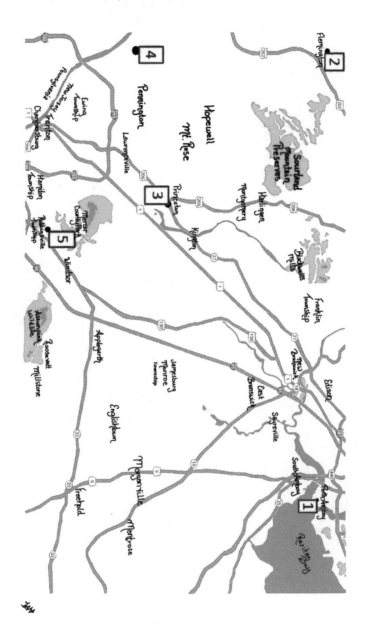

Amboy was the original capital of New Jersey, later moved to Trenton. A fertile strip connected the two and at one time was the only fertile part of New Jersey, with woodsmen to the south. Cornwallis and Washington chased each other up and down the Kings Highway in between.

1 British Headquarters: Perth Amboy in its 1776 Heyday

Proprietary House   **149 Kearny Avenue**   **Perth Amboy, NJ**
40.5033 -74.2692

Not many now think of the town of Perth Amboy as part of Philadelphia's history or culture, but it certainly was so in colonial times. The town has since become a more run-of-the-mill middle-class suburb with some decaying factories. The little house of the Proprietors on the town square and the remains of the Governor's mansion overlooking the ocean are about all that remain of the early Quaker era.

It's now moderately complicated to find Perth Amboy, even after you locate it on a map. Like New Castle, Delaware. it flourished early because it was on a narrow strip of strategic land, and like New Castle, eventually found itself cut off by a dozen lanes of highways crowded together by geography. Both towns were important destinations in the Eighteenth century, but by the Twentieth century, both were pushed aside by traffic rushing to bigger destinations. Industrialization hit the region around Perth Amboy somewhat harder than New Castle,

Proprietary House

destroying more landmarks and bringing to an end its brief flurry as a metropolitan beach resort. If you aspire to preserve your Eighteenth-century glory, it's easier if you don't have too much progress in the Nineteenth.

To understand the strategic importance of Perth Amboy to colonial America, remember that James, Duke of York (eventually to become King James the Second) thought of New Jersey as the land between the North (Hudson) River, and the South (Delaware) River. This region has a narrow pinched waist in the middle. It's easy to see why the land-speculating Seventeenth Century regarded the bridging strip across the New Jersey "narrows" as a likely future site of important political and commercial development. The two large and dissimilar land masses which adjoin this strip --

Perth Amboy to Trenton

sandy South Jersey, and mountainous North Jersey -- was sparsely inhabited and largely ignored in colonial times. The British in 1776 developed the quite sensible plan that subduing this fertile New Jersey strip would simultaneously enable the conquest of both New York and Philadelphia at the two ends of it. It was a clever plan; it might have subjugated three colonies at once.

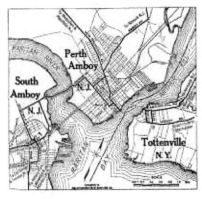

Perth Amboy Map

Perth Amboy is a composite name, adding a local Indian word to a Scottish one because East Jersey had been intended for Scottish Quakers. Like Pittsburgh at the conjunction of three rivers, Perth Amboy's geographical importance was that it dominated the mouth of Raritan Bay (Raritan River, extended) as it emptied into New York Bay just inside Sandy Hook. Two of the three "rivers" of the three-way fork are really just channels around Staten Island. Viewed from the sea, Perth Amboy sits on a bluff, commanding that junction. Amboy became the original ocean port in the area, although it was soon overtaken by New Brunswick further inland when increasing commerce required safer harbors. Perth Amboy was the capital of East Jersey, and then the first capital of all New Jersey after East and West were joined in 1704 by Queen Anne. The Royal Governor's mansion stood here - William Franklin, the illegitimate son of Benjamin, was the royal governor installed in this palace shortly before 1776 - as well as grand houses of Proprietors and Judges overlooking the banks of the bay. The main reason for the Nineteenth-century decline of the state capital region was the narrowness of the New Jersey waist at that point; its main geographical advantage became a curse. Canals, railroads and astounding highway growth simply crowded the Amboy promontory into an unsupportable state of isolation. The same thing can be said of Bristol, Pennsylvania, and New Castle, Delaware, but local civic pride has somehow not risen to the challenge to the same degree.

Howe's Choice: To Philadelphia, or Saratoga?

The Revolutionary War had been raging for a year in New England before the Declaration of Independence, a point that never ceased to bother John Adams whenever Thomas Jefferson or his devotees took credit for starting the Revolution with a piece of paper nailed to a lamppost a year after Lexington and Concord. This interval nevertheless allowed for the organization of the Continental Army, and Washington's maturing military background by the summer of '76. It also allowed the time for the surprisingly immediate landing of Sir William Howe's army on Staten

Perth Amboy to Trenton

Island at the end of June 1776. A month or so after that, his brother Admiral Howe landed more troops. By September 1776, not all of the signers had yet put their names to the Declaration of Independence, but there were about 40,000 British troops parading around the essentially uninhabited Staten Island in New York harbor, in plain sight of the inhabitants of New Jersey's capital in Perth Amboy, and scarcely a hundred miles from Philadelphia. The British shrewdly selected New York harbor as the center of their operation, since their Navy was thereby in position to shift quickly in the protected waters of Long Island Sound from New Jersey to Rhode Island, or up and down the Hudson as far as Albany, meanwhile dominating the considerable expanse of Long Island, not to mention Manhattan.

Nations at war traditionally vilify the leader of the enemy, and so Sir William Howe has usually been portrayed as a lazy, illegitimate uncle of the King, a womanizer lacking in military savvy, and a former parliamentary member of the minority party supporting peace with the colonies. But to go on this way is quite unfair to Washington, who outfoxed and out-generaled a tough and very clever soldier who was by no means a pushover, and who fought hard to win.

In retrospect, it can be seen that Howe's army was crammed into winter quarters on the Perth Amboy-New Brunswick bluff across the river from Staten Island in the winter of 1777, following the defeat at Trenton. Washington's troops were meanwhile in a fairly impregnable position around Morristown, New Jersey. If Howe went back along the Raritan toward Trenton and Philadelphia, he could expect to be butchered by snipers behind trees. If he embarked on his ships, he would be vulnerable during the two days of so required to break camp and load the ships. Washington's problem was actually just as bad. He had no way of knowing whether he had to defend against an encircling movement at Morristown against a renewed invasion toward Trenton and Philadelphia, or against a quick movement at sea by the battleships. If Howe embarked he might be going to Albany to rescue Burgoyne; or to Fort Lee to encircle Morristown; or to Philadelphia; or even to Charlestown. Any one of these choices would mean that Washington would have to hurry overland to catch him.

It now seems clear that Howe had decided it was safe to abandon Burgoyne. He might have tried to capture Philadelphia and get back to Albany by September, but evidently, this seemed too ambitious and fraught with unexpected accidents, as events later proved to be true. Clear and unambiguous orders by Lord Germain in London were mislaid and never reached him. By implication, he was being told to use his best judgment. So he decided on a double option. He would send sorties out in all directions to keep Washington guessing and to entice him to come down from his mountain fastness into a pitched battle with British regulars. Failing that, he would get on his ships and take Philadelphia. Furthermore, Howe never told another soul what his plans were except by sending a spy with misleading plans sewed into his coat, intending for him to be captured by the rebels. Washington, however, essentially refused to budge.

Finally, Howe ordered embarkation onto his ships, and actually loaded a contingent of Hessians on board. Although Washington was mistrustful of a trick, his officers persuaded him to attack the "vulnerable" British while they were loading onto the transports. As soon as Howe heard of Washington's movement he immediately issued orders to turn the whole army around and trap Washington. He thought he now had his chance to catch and destroy the Continental army.

As things turned out, it didn't work and Washington escaped with most of his troops. Fearful of another such trap, he then held back perhaps too long and helplessly watched the ships load, weigh anchor, and sail out to sea. Where were they going? Not another person on the British (or Loyalist) side knew the answer, and the ships were far out to sea, invisible before they turned in whatever direction they were going. Was it north, or south?

A week later, word came to Washington that the fleet had been sighted off the mouth of the Delaware. It was time to move south, in a big hurry, on foot. Howe was going to go to Norfolk, but it wasn't even certain whether he was coming back up the Chesapeake, or going still further South to Charleston. It remained conceivable that he would wait for Washington to move his troops south, then double back to New York and Albany to join Burgoyne.

As we now know, Howe did turn up the Chesapeake to land in the rear of Philadelphia. And then Washington also guessed right and lined up his troops at Chadds Ford of the Brandywine Creek. Both of them were shrewd and very quick. Howe had won a major victory with superior resources. But as we shall see, Washington wasn't through with him.

2 Lindbergh Baby Kidnapping Trial
Hunterdon County Courthouse   **65 Park Ave**   **Flemington, NJ**
40.5125 -74.8606

In 1935, Bruno Hauptmann was executed for kidnapping the baby of America's "Lone Eagle." Swarms of competing police and reporters made chaos of the scene, and Charles Lindbergh made it all worse by dealing directly with the criminal underworld. Even today, some question the guilt of Hauptmann, and even whether the baby is really dead.

Perth Amboy to Trenton

We are indebted to George Hawke, who went to prep school near the scene of the crime, for becoming an expert, perhaps the *preeminent* expert, on the Lindbergh Baby Kidnapping Trial. Charles Lindbergh, the son of a Midwest pro-German congressman, flew an airplane alone across the Atlantic in 1927. He became instantly famous, wrote a best-seller called *Alone*, became Colonel Lindbergh, and married Anne Morrow, the daughter of Senator Morrow of New Jersey. That's how in short order they came to settle in Englewood, New Jersey, and also could afford an elaborate country place in Hopewell, Hunterdon County. That put them physically at the northern edge of the Philadelphia region at least on weekends, although psychologically they remained part of the New York scene, where many people attracted to publicity seem to gravitate. In 1932 they had a 20-month old son, John, who one evening disappeared from Hopewell, apparently kidnapped. What followed was a Keystone Kops Komedy in the midst of a publicity storm. The local, county, and state police, plus the FBI struggled with each other for the fame of solving the case. Newspaper reporters from all over the country swarmed down the little country road to set up shop. To illustrate the consequences, a home-made ladder was found sixty feet from the house,

Charles Lindbergh

but no fingerprints were found by the first investigators. By the time the last investigators were done, the ladder had 150 sets of fingerprints on it. Police involvement on all levels can be summarized as a frenzy to be first to solve the case, followed in time by a frenzy to avoid being known for failing to solve it.

Although most of us eagerly following the case were unaware of it, the Colonel decided to take matters into his own hands. As a new celebrity, he was surrounded by many new best friends, and it was suggested to him that he should put out feelers into the Underground, the Mafia Mob. He would pay a ransom, and no questions would be asked. Somehow, a Bronx school principal, Dr. John Condon, was designated to respond to feelers, among them a particularly likely one, from a man who demanded to be met in a cemetery at night. As proof that the baby was still alive, the cemetery lurker sent Dr. Condon the baby's sleeping suit. Ransom was then paid in cash, unmarked, but entirely in gold certificates which had stopped being issued after President Roosevelt took us off the gold standard, the serial numbers carefully recorded. The extortionist then disappeared from sight, and the baby was never heard from again.

As time passed, two things happened. A partially decomposed baby's body was found buried a couple of miles from Hopewell, although it must be admitted it was only a quarter of a mile from an orphanage. The baby's pediatrician could not identify the body, although at the trial others claimed to make such identification. The baby's skull had been fractured, but several detectives had been seen turning it with sticks. The other development was that gold certificates bearing the recorded serial numbers began turning up in the Bronx. Bruno Richard Hauptmann was apprehended at a filling station after passing a ten-dollar bill of the ransom money, and when his house was searched, $14,000 more was found hidden. The police had their man. To say that the house had been searched thoroughly was quite an understatement, but a number of detectives said there was no visible disturbance in the attic. Later on, a rung of the homemade ladder found at Hopewell was found to have exactly the same grain pattern as a piece of attic floorboard, now found to be missing in the Bronx house. Although there was a testimony that Hauptmann had been beaten with a hammer, he was deemed a highly suspicious character. He had a criminal record in Germany and was in this country illegally after jumping ship.

The trial of Bruno Hauptmann in the Hunterdon County Courthouse at Flemington was a tumultuous circus. The state of New Jersey spent well over a million dollars on the prosecution, while Hauptmann spent $2,900 on his defense, most of it provided by a newspaper, and most of it spent on a defense lawyer who appeared before a jury of farmers dressed in a cutaway, wearing a Carnation and Spats, and who told people in a bar that Hauptmann was anyway guilty. That lawyer seemed visibly inebriated much of the time and often walked down the main street with a girl on both arms. Miles of new telephone wire was strung into the courthouse area for the reporters, and two switchboards were provided.

There were legal difficulties. At that time in New Jersey, kidnapping was only a misdemeanor, so accidental death in the course of kidnapping was not a capital offense. The Lindbergh Kidnapping Law was hastily enacted to make kidnapping a federal felony, but for the purposes of this trial, it was necessary to prosecute Hauptmann for the crime of burglary of the sleepsuit, with accidental death in the course of that burglary. Hauptmann steadfastly, and to some convincingly, denied everything. He was keeping the gold certificates for a friend.

The jury was understandably confused by all this, but it looked to them as though Hauptmann was surely guilty of something, perhaps extortion, and for all the jury knew Congress would now pass a special law about that, too. The defense did not make enough of the sleepsuit, but all the jurors surely knew that such garments could be bought in any department store. There was even some question whether the Lindbergh baby might not be dead at all, but the fact remained that Hauptmann was definitely guilty of something. He was electrocuted, and the newspapers made a great fuss about that, too.

3 The Scotch-Irish in the Revolution

Witherspoon Hall, Princeton University   Princeton, NJ   40.3474 -74.6601

The most eminent Scotsman in Colonial America was the Reverend Dr. John Witherspoon, an eminent Presbyterian minister and president of the College of New Jersey, later Princeton University. Already at the top of the academic heap in Scotland, he was recruited for Princeton on the advice of Benjamin Franklin, who knew his political sentiments well. From England, Witherspoon made the following exhortation to his future compatriots at the critical moment of the Declaration of Independence:

"To hesitate at this moment is to consent to our own slavery. The noble instrument on your table, which insures immortality to its author, should be subscribed this very morning by every pen in this house. He who will not respond to its accents and strain every nerve to carry into effect its provisions is unworthy the name of freeman. Whatever I may have of property or reputation is staked on the issue of this contest; and although these gray hairs must descend into the sepulcher, I would infinitely rather that they descend hither by the hand of the executioner than desert at this crisis the sacred cause of my country."

On the humbler level of popular doggerel, was the following:

"And when the days of trial came,
Of which we know the story,
No Erin son of Scotia's blood
Was ever found a Tory. "

It may not be quite true that the Scotch-Irish immigrants started the Revolution, or led it, or did most of the serious fighting. But in Pennsylvania their role was decisive. New England started most of the trouble, the aristocrats of Virginia quickly rose to the challenges of chivalry, but Pennsylvania was not so darned sure about this

business. The back-country Germans were perfectly content to farm the richest topsoil they ever heard of, the Quakers were peaceful and prosperous just as they were. It was the Scotch-Irish of the frontier, needing no pretext of Tea Taxes or Stamp Acts to hate the English King, who were ready to take the musket off the wall at the slightest provocation.

It is indeed puzzling in retrospect to wonder what the English Kings were trying to achieve. Having driven the Scots out of their Scottish homeland into Ireland where they would be less bother, they subsequently drove them out of Ireland as well. The short explanation has been offered that James

Dr. Witherspoon

II who was to be driven off the throne for his Catholic leanings, had seen Ireland as a fallback refuge in case of trouble and wanted it safely Catholic. So in anticipation of what did indeed happen under William and Mary, he wanted the Presbyterians out of there.

There is perhaps some logic to this, but try telling it to a Scot.

4 Trenton's Tomato Pie Cult

De Lorenzo's Tomato Pies   **2350 NJ-33**   **Robbinsville Twp, NJ**
40.2183 -74.6273

The ingredients of a pizza pie are so simple it comes as a shock to learn the Italian community of Trenton, New Jersey, is fanatic about putting the cheese on the dough first, and then tomatoes on top. That's the way an authentic Trenton pizza is supposed to be made, rather than the conventional method of tomatoes first, cheese on top. To emphasize the point, these pizzas are determinedly referred to as tomato pies. And to tell the truth, there is a minor difference in the taste of the product made that way. As this more or less trivial issue is dissected and debated in great detail, an important fact about ethnic food emerges. Be patient while each ingredient is examined. The crust will rise more in the warm summer than the winter, so it's thicker after it's baked. There is a faint fermentation taste which is more pronounced with a thick crust, but everyone in Trenton agrees this is a minor point. Everyone is also in agreement that most brands of Mozzarella cheese taste about the same. Tomatoes with seeds or without, or homogenized or chunky, make a minor difference. What is ultimately the essence of a Trenton tomato pie is that the cheese is put on top of the dough first, the tomatoes next spread on top, and the pie is then baked in the oven. Not everyone would notice the difference in taste, but it's definite, and in Trenton it's important. However, the locally acknowledged historian states his opinion that the thing that makes Trenton pies distinctive is not the ingredients, but the customers.

Trenton's Tomato Pie

The employees of the shop know and respect the regulars, who tend to come to the same shop at least once a week, and call out the bakers by name as they enter. When they order a tomato pie, they give the name meaningfully, almost threateningly.

According to the local historian, when the sons and grandsons of the shop owners move out to the suburbs and start a pizza shop in the strip mall, it isn't long before the tomatoes go on first, cheese on top. That's the way teenagers in the burbs are used to pizzas, and that's the way they expect to get them. As John Wanamaker used to say, the customer is always right, so the social rule which emerges is that ethnic food is not shaped by ethnic cooks, but by ethnic customers. To carry the idea a step farther, ethnic food isn't food, it's the old school tie.

5 Disorderly Retreat: From Trenton Back to Perth Amboy

Washington Crossing State Park   355 Washington Crossing   Pennington Rd.
Titusville, NJ   40.3137 -74.8629

At the Battle of Trenton, Washington was 44 years old, six feet two inches tall or more, a horseman and athlete of outstanding skill, and as the husband of the richest woman in Virginia accustomed to housing, feeding, transporting and getting submission from two hundred slaves. All of those qualities may have been of some use in the battle. But after the Battle of Trenton, Washington also emerged as a remarkably bold and creative General. In the Battle of Trenton can be seen the elements of audacity, timing, and courage that were notable in Stonewall Jackson, George Patton -- Virginians, both -- the Normandy Invasion, and the Inchon Landing. He forged, if he did not create, the American military tradition of inspired risk-taking. And he did it with a collection of starving amateurs, up against the best army in the world at the time. Probably without realizing it, his coming victory at Trenton also gave Benjamin Franklin in Paris a major enticement for the French king to support the American cause.

Cornwallis and the British regulars came thundering down the narrow waist of New Jersey from New Brunswick to Trenton, just before Christmas, 1776. Washington's troops retreated before them, fleeing to the Pennsylvania side of the Delaware River. The British then fortified the Hessians in Trenton and went back into their own winter quarters nearer New York. Plenty of time seemed available to finish off Washington in the spring, and then leisurely conquer the enemy's capital in Philadelphia. The Continental Congress thought so, too, and moved its capital to Baltimore. Only three members of the Congress, Robert Morris, George Clymer, and George Walton (of Georgia), remained in Philadelphia to run the government; Morris was essentially in charge, in the role of financier, whatever

Charles Cornwallis

that meant. With Congress seeking refuge, Morris was for practical purposes, acting President of the United States. Washington swept up all of the boats on the Delaware, set up camp on the Pennsylvania side, and begged Morris to get him some money to reward re-enlistments by January 1. Others saw the end of the year as Christmas time; Washington saw it as the end of the year when enlistments expired. He quite plainly stated that it was all over for the Continental Army unless he could get some hard currency, silver preferred, to show the troops that the rebellion could survive another year. About ten dollars per soldier would probably do it, but then there was also a need for hard money to buy food and supplies for the starving troops. Just how Morris managed to find the money is unclear, or how much of it was his own. But he did manage, with the lucky arrival of a gunpowder smuggling ship from France, and eighteen cannon somehow supplied by General Knox.

On December 21, Washington thought Howe was immediately going to sweep on through Trenton to Philadelphia. In a day or two, he saw that wasn't the plan, organized the famous re-crossing of the Delaware in bad weather, and caught and captured a thousand Hessians with a three-pronged attack which cut off their retreat and made resistance useless. The main military feature of this attack was not

Washington Crossing the Delaware

Christmas drunkenness among the Hessians, but the fact that General Knox had somehow transported eighteen cannon to the occasion. Nowadays, the event is marked by a reenactment on Christmas morning, although it took place on December 26, 1776. The timing did not have to do with religious observance, it had to do with hangovers. To the great disappointment of his troops, he made them abandon the great stores of booze in Trenton because a second detachment of Hessians was in nearby Bordentown, and meanwhile, he retreated back to the Pennsylvania side of the river. As might be imagined, Howe's Cornwallis promptly came charging down from New Brunswick to exact bitter vengeance. Instead of trying to rescue their comrades in Princeton, the Bordentown Hessians took off for New Brunswick. Defiantly, Washington taunted his enemies by again re-crossing the Delaware to the New Jersey side, put up fortifications, and just waited for them to make something of it.

Well, that's the way it was meant to seem. On the night of January 2, the two armies were facing each other with about five thousand men on both sides but with the British much better trained and equipped. The Americans had the advantage of not being exhausted by a fifty mile forced march, except for about a thousand who had been deployed forward to skirmish and delay the British advance with sniping from the bushes. The Americans made a great deal of noise and lit many bonfires behind their fortifications. But when they advanced the next morning, the British found out where the Americans really were -- by hearing distant cannon fire coming from Princeton, ten miles back to the north.

Washington had slipped five thousand men wide around the enemy flank during the night and had taken a parallel country road to Princeton where he defeated a rear guard of British at the Battle of Princeton. An infuriated Cornwallis wheeled his army around in pursuit, and the race was on for the supplies left undefended in New Brunswick. Washington might have been able to get there first, except his men were too exhausted, and he was afraid to risk his long-run strategy, which was to avoid head-on collisions with the main British Army.

So Washington went into winter quarters in Morristown still further to the north, and thousands of British soldiers were thus bottled up in winter quarters in Perth Amboy and New Brunswick, where scurvy, lack of firewood and smallpox gave them a few months to consider their miscalculations. But the most important action of all was getting the news to Benjamin Franklin in Paris, to tell the French king of the victory. A few days before that fateful Christmas, Ben Franklin had arrived in Paris to

take over our diplomatic mission with the French. When the news of Washington's victory reached him, the new American arrival was being acclaimed as the world-famous scientist and witty author and was thus in a position to make the most of it with the French court. He may be forgiven for exaggerating Washington's exploits a little. The Trenton victory was rough and ragged, but it would serve. Washington, Franklin, and Morris - the three Americans who mainly won the Revolutionary War for us - now took the stage, front, and center.

George Washington Rallying his Troops at Princeton

Meanwhile, with Congress taking refuge in Baltimore, Philadelphia was nearly deserted except for some Quakers who felt they had no quarrel with the British. And Robert Morris, who continued to run his smuggling operation with the famous playwright Beaumarchais on the French end of it. Tradition has it that some Quaker gardens were dug up to find enough silver to reward reenlistments, and if so it is unclear how much was freely contributed and how much was just plain stolen; and, indeed, how much of it might have been Morris' own money. By the next fall, Washington was able to fight the largest battle of the war at the Brandywine Creek, so Morris must have been very active smuggling guns and gunpowder to resupply the Colonials during that intervening winter and spring.

During periods of the lull in infantry warfare, other warfare, including privateering at sea, blockades, and the diplomatic intrigue in Paris were unmerciful. If Washington's army had been wiped out, the Revolution would have ended. But other misadventures might have ended it as well. The colonists were demoralized, and their dismay was summarized by a letter from Morris to Silas Deane, a line of which was the bitter observation that "Sorry I am to say it, many of those who were foremost in noise, shrink coward-like from the danger."

Index

Kelpius, Johannes, 206
Kelpius, John, 195
Kelpius Cave, 193
Kelpius Historical Marker, 191
Kemble, Fanny, 69–70, 94
Kennedy, John, 258
Kern, Dick, 233
Kimmel Center, 96, 120
Kincaid, William, 120
King Charles II, 81, 262, 269
King George III, 23, 34, 207
King's Highway, 159, 355
Kinloch Woodworking, 227
Knights Templar, 98
Kramer, Henry, 100
Krauskopf, Joseph, 290
Ku Klux Klan, 147

L
Lafayette, 17, 49, 212–14, 287–88,
   339
Lafayette Hill, 213
Lake Geneva, 302
Lakes Ontario, 300
Lambertville, 277–79, 330
Lancaster Avenue, 244
Lancaster County, 195, 202, 211
Laurel Hill Cemeteries, 187
Laurens, Henry, 13
Lavoisier, 125, 302, 307–8
Lazaretto, 216–17
Ledger Building, 66
Lee, General Robert E., 234
Legionnaire's Disease, 101–2
Lehigh Valley, 207, 308, 330
Lehigh Valley RR, 305
Leiper, Thomas, 123
Leipzig, 32
Lemon Hill, 13, 173, 182, 186, 209
Levittown, 275
Lewes, 311–12, 326, 328, 356
Lewis, Judge Edwin O., 36, 45
Liberty Bell, 64, 150, 338
Library Company, 91–92
Limekiln Road, 208

Lincoln, Abraham, 79, 170
Lincoln Drive, 175–78, 183, 190, 194
Lindbergh, Charles, 368–69
Logan, James, 91–92, 262
Logan Square, 128–29, 131–32,
   134–36, 139, 184, 304
London Coffee House, 51
London Yearly Meeting, 12
Longwood Gardens, 174
Lord Baltimore, 312–15
Lord Byron, 38, 69
Lord Germain, 221, 367
Lord North, 235, 324
Lord Shelbourne, 307
Lorenzo's Tomato Pies, 372
Lowe's Hotel, 205
Luther, Martin, 192, 341

M
Macalester, Charles, 267
Macalester College, 267
Mack, Connie, 190–91
Mad Anthony Wayne, 224, 254
Madeira, Louis, 79
Madison, James, 9, 14, 26–30, 35,
   46, 58, 64
Madison Square Garden, 116–17
Mafia culture, 332
Maguire Air Force Base, 350
Mahoning Valley, 309
Main Line, 71–72, 237–39, 241–43,
   245–46, 248–49, 251, 253–55,
   356
Manayunk, 184
Manchester, 294
Manhattan, 221, 367
Mantua Creek Terminal, 218
Maritime Law Association, 263
Market Street, 36, 41, 53–59, 73,
   107, 118, 146, 162, 243, 339
Maryland, 10, 26, 159, 223, 287–88,
   311–12, 314–15, 321
Mason, George, 29
Mason-Dixon line, 312-314
Masonic Temple, 98

Massachusetts, 24, 29, 49
Massacre, 211, 300–302
Matlack, Timothy, 12, 48
Matson's Ford, 213, 251
Mauch Chunk, 308–9
Mauchly, 165–66
  John, 165
Mayo, Charlie, 305
Mayo Clinic, 305
Mayor Governor Rendell, 191
Mayor Richardson Dilworth, 61, 157
Mayor Rizzo, 168
McCloskey, Matthew H., 181
McGillicuddy, Cornelius, 190
McKean, Thomas, 48
McShain, John, 181
Meade, George Gordon, 115 188
Medford, 334
Mendelssohn, Felix, 94
Mennonites, 132, 199, 293–94
Mercer Museum, 289
Merion, 177, 239–40
Merion Cricket Club, 245
Meschianza, 147–48
Mesmer, 37
Methodist Church, 42, 328
Michener, James, 290
Middletown, 231
Midvale Avenue, 179
Midvale Steel Company, 199-200
Mifflin, Thomas, 159
Minuit, Peter, 316
Miss America, 359–60
Mohawk Valley, 225
Moland, John, 286–87, 317
Moland House, 286–88
Monongahela River, 25
Monsanto Chemical, 218
Montgomery Avenue, 245
Montgomery County, 198, 290, 294
Montgomery County Orphans
  Court, 241
Mooberry, Douglas, 227
Mormon, 302–4
Morris, Anthony, 260

Morris, George, 78
Morris, John, 209
Morris, Lydia, 210
Morris, Robert, 12–13, 23–24, 59,
  67, 114, 182–83, 186, 332,
  373, 375
Morris House Hotel, 78
Morristown, 367, 375
Mother Divine, 248–49
Mount Holly, 334, 346, 349
Mount Pleasant, 184, 186
Mount Pleasant Mansion, 184
Mulberry Street, 51
Mummers Museum, 145
Mummers Parade, 145, 147
Municipal Services Building, 131
Museum of Chemical Heritage, 18
Musical Fund Hall, 58, 79–80, 144

N
Nanticoke, 299
Nanticoke Indians, 326
Narberth, 239–40
National Farm School, 290
National Musical Association, 80
National Park Service, 59, 252–54,
  259, 318
Natural Sciences, 31–33, 104, 106,
  136–37, 177, 184, 355
Naval Base, 217
Nesbit, Evelyn, 116–17
Neshaminy Creek, 262
Newark, 174
New Brunswick, 221, 331, 334, 355,
  366, 373–75
Newburgh, 298–99
New Castle, 288, 312, 314–17, 322,
  356, 365–66
New Hope, 189, 270, 278, 289
New Jersey Transit, 334
New Jerusalem, 119
Newmarket, 56
Newton, John, 43
Newton's Principia, 92
Newtown Friends Meeting, 276

New York, 4, 14–15, 64, 117, 135,
155, 167–68, 221–22, 238,
289–90, 299–300, 302, 334,
338–40, 344
New York Central, 163, 238
Nicetown, 199
Nicholson, John, 159
Norfolk, 207, 222, 319, 355–56, 368
Norris, Isaac, 211
Norristown, 190, 198, 224
Northeast Pennsylvania, 295, 297,
299, 302–7, 309
Northeast Philadelphia, 267–68
North of Market, 41–43, 45–52, 176
North Philadelphia, 145
Northumberland, 125, 306–8
Notman, John, 188–89
Nottingham, 228

O
Odessa, 288, 313, 319–20, 343, 356
O'Hara, John, 309
Ohio Valley, 308
Okamoto, Chuck, 337
Old Blockley, 168–69
Old Girard Trust Building, 104
Old Gulph Road, 251–52
Old York Road, 189–90
Oneidas, 212–13
Oneonta, 305
Opera House, 309
Orpheus Club, 120
Osler, William, 169
Outward Bound, 183

P
Pace, Frank, 139
Packer, Asa, 305, 308–9
Packer, Robert, 305
Packer Avenue Marine Terminal
Port, 153
Pahkehoma, 198
Palmer, Richard W., 219, 263, 265
Paoli, 207, 237–40
Paoli massacre, 224

Passyunk Avenues, 150
Pattison Avenue, 157
Patton, George, 373
Patuxent, 287
Paulsboro, 154, 219
Paxtang Boys, 211
Peaceable Kingdoms, 276–77
Pea Patch Island, 154, 317–18
Pemberton, Israel, 275–76
Pemberton, James, 275
Pemberton, Ralph, 275
Penn, Hannah, 284–85
Penn, John, 211
Penn, William, 106–7, 182–83, 186,
192, 194, 234, 244, 246, 262–
63, 269, 272–75, 311–12,
314–16, 320–21, 323
Pennamite Wars, 299–300
Penn Central, 4
Penn Charter, 205
Pennsauken, 271
Pennsbury Manor, 182, 186, 269-
270, 272–73, 307
Penn State Hershey Medical Center,
233
Pennsylvania Academy-Fine Arts,
129
Pennsylvania Assembly, 38, 48, 323
Pennsylvania Dutch, 57, 150, 194,
294
Pennsylvania Horticultural Society,
125, 138
Pennsylvania Hospital, 3, 8, 15, 75,
80–82, 84–86, 90, 151, 165,
169–70, 362
Pennsylvania National Guard, 122
Pennsylvania Railroad, 42, 51, 56,
72, 91, 98, 123, 163, 317, 351,
356
Penn Treaty Park, 262
Pennypack Creek, 265, 352
Perkiomen Creek, 198
Perkiomenville, 198
Perot, Francis, 260

Notes

Notes

Notes

Notes

Notes

Notes

CPSIA information can be obtained
at www.ICGtesting.com
Printed in the USA
BVHW011538190721
612146BV00013B/15